Building
OHIO

Building

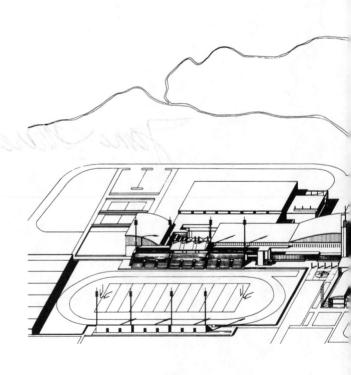

O H I O

*A Traveler's Guide to Ohio's
Rural Architecture*

by Jane Ware

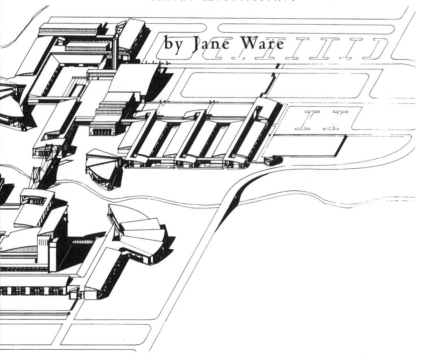

Orange Frazer Press
Wilmington, Ohio

ISBN 1-882203-74-7
Copyright 2002 by Jane Ware

Additional copies of *Building Ohio: A Traveler's Guide To Ohio's Rural Architecture,* the first volume of *Building Ohio,* which was a traveler's guide to Ohio's urban architecture, or any other Orange Frazer Press books may be ordered directly from:

Orange Frazer Press, Inc.
Box 214
37 ½ West Main Street
Wilmington, Ohio 45177

Telephone 1.800.852.9332 for price and shipping information
Web Site: www.orangefrazer.com

Library of Congress Cataloging-in-Publication Data

Ware, Jane.
    Building Ohio: a traveler's guide to Ohio's rural architecture / by Jane Ware.
        p. cm.
    Includes bibliographical references and index.
    ISBN 1-882203-82-8 (alk. paper)
    1. Architecture--Ohio--Guidebooks. 2. Ohio--Guidebooks. I. Title.

NA730.03 W369 2002
720'.9771--dc21

                                        2002075412

Acknowledgments

This is a book I could never have done without help; it's depended on the generosity of hundreds of people. My thanks to Frank Elmer, architect and friend, the first person I talked to and the one who, in the end, pulled extra talent out of his sleeve and did many drawings. My thanks to Douglas Graf, who gave me the courage to proceed, as well as help evident throughout these pages; and finally, he read the whole manuscript. My thanks to Walter Leedy and to Jeanne Reed, whose advice on formatting I followed. Some people suggested buildings, indulged me with tours and/or multiple interviews, and provided help for more than one locality for years: my special thanks to Craig Bobby, Jeff Brown, Robert C. Gaede, Glenn A. Harper, Ted J. Ligibel, Mary Ann Olding, James A. Pahlau, Mary Anne Reeves, and Rebecca Rogers. And my thanks to others, not all of them architectural specialists, who first told me about buildings included in this volume: Laura and John Bradford, Eleanor Mooney Forrer, Rebecca Rogers, Robert Schmitz, and Wanda Wilson.

My thanks to all those in these pages and to many others, who for this volume included:

Central Ohio: Circleville, Wallace W. Higgins, George Lowery, Mary Tolbert; Delaware, Kay Schlichting, Maryanne Stewart; Gambier, Jamie Pealy, Tom Lepley, Tom Stamp; Granville, Maggie Brooks, Bob Seith, Dr. Sandy Yorka, Licking County Historical Society; Lafayette, Gene Freet, Neval Pennell; Lancaster, David Benson, Pat Cope, Ruth and Pauline Farrow, Phyllis Kuhn, Mary Lou McCandlish, Stef Stahl, Whit Tussing, Josephine Voss; London, Jane Russell; Marion, Duane Behne, Phillip Payne, David Schoonover; Marysville, Dorothy Liggett-Pelanda; Mount Vernon, Mary Dvorak, Debra Fowler, Judith Kitchen, Dr. Erwin Weber; Newark, Karen Dickman, David Fetter, Bruce Goetzman, Ellie Hare and the Licking County Historical Society, Bob and Judy Vela, Samantha Williams;

Northeast Ohio: Alliance, James A. Pahlau; Atwater, Joseph A. Peters, Deloris Whittlesey; Barberton, Christine Kelleher, Steve Kelleher; Bellville, Charles Pfoutz; East Liverpool, Timothy Brookes, Mary Kay Campbell, Nancy Recchie, Phil Rickerd; Gustavus, Mike Ciba; Hanoverton, Sam Miller, Jane E. Wilson; Hiram, Father Alexander; Hudson, Priscilla Graham, Tom Vince; Jefferson, Laurelee Hinger, David Lephart, Robert Wynn; Kinsman, Alice Logan Blaemire, Richard Webb; Mansfield, Chris Buchanan, Bill Collins, Pat Horchler, Richard Hull, Tom Neel, Stephen Patrick, Robert W. Soulen; Mantua, Gail Shuss; Massillon, Richard Gerckin, Virginia Ott, James A. Pahlau; Medina, Gary Fernwood, Janet Senkar; Mineral Ridge, Alexander T. Bobersky, David Tabak; Niles, Alexander T. Bobersky, Rebecca Rogers, Ann Yancura; North Bloomfield, Judith M. and Terrence E. Sheridan; Oberlin, Geoffrey Blodgett, Mark Graham; Painesville, Jack Daniels, Ed Dunlap, Margaret Gross, Joe Hahl, Mardy McNamara, Jeff Staats, Mark Welch; Peninsula, Randy Bergdorf; Perry, Robert Geisler, Ruth Gless,

Dr. Ed Goodwin, Dr. Scott Howard, Melissa Johnson; Southington, Shari Gilanyi; Tallmadge, Dana Gibson; Twinsburg, Chris Mihalec; Warren, Henry J. Angelo, Alexander T. Bobersky; Wellington, Charles Oney, Diane Stanley; Western Reserve, Lois R. Cunniff; Wooster, Denise Monbarren;

Northwest Ohio: Bowling Green, Lyle Fletcher, Paul W. Jones, Virginia Nader, Pat Smith, Judge Gale Williamson; Carthagena, Brother Jerry Hall, Mary Ann Olding; Celina, Joyce L. Alig, Chuck Stammen, Thomas Wehrhahn; Defiance, Ted J. Ligibel; Findlay, Cindy Leister, Linda Paul, Jan Sartore; Galion, Dave Dayne, Bob Meek, Kenneth Petri, Miriam Sayre; Glandorf, Michael Leach; Gomer, Mary Ann Olding; Grand Rapids, Bob Bettinger, Sue Dennis, Ted J. Ligibel; Lima, John Carnes, John Hribar, Harry Shutt, Tonya S. Sroufe, Nancy Strouss; Maria Stein, Sister Barbara Ann Hoying, Thomas J. Wehrhahn; Milan, Ava Gardner; Napoleon, Glenn A. Harper, C. Robert Jansen; New Bremen, Angela Bezouska, Mary Ann Olding, Reuben Thiesing; New Hampshire, Tim Manchester; New London, Geoffrey Blodgett, Mark Crumrine, Jeannette Dempsey, Philip Johnson, Thom Mezick, Mary Lou Rapp, Martha Sturges, John and Dorothy Thompson; Norwalk, Joseph Casey, Marilou Creary, Richard Parsons, Henry Timman; Ottawa, Judge Randall L. Basinger, Roselia Verhoff, Carol Wise; Perrysburg, Amina Ahmad; Sandusky, Ellie Damm; Van Wert, Dr. John and Sheila Eversman, Elizabeth France Lewis, James Price; Venedocia, Wendy Pratt; Wapakoneta, Sarah Goss Norman, Franco Ruffino; Waterville, Tom and Peggy Parker;

Southeast Ohio: Archers Fork, Sarah and Steve Tokar; Athens, Tod Anderson, Bob Borchard, Sonya Coble, Alan Geiger, René Glidden, John Kotowski, Mary Anne Reeves, John Spofforth, Harriet Tong; Barnesville, Joe Bradfield, Mary Anne Reeves, Bruce Yarnall; Bethesda, Bruce Yarnall; Cadiz, Tilly Heavilin, Beverly Mason, Golda McMullen; Chillicothe, Robert B. Althoff, Deborah Barrington, Mary Anne Brown, Pat Medert, Evelyn Walker; Gallipolis, Kim Schuette; Haydenville, Jim Grover, Nyla Vollmer; Ironton, Virginia Bryant, Judy Cloran, Irene Lane, Jean McMahon, Phyllis Walton; Jackson, Gerald Rhea, Marjorie Sellers, Barbara Summers; Marietta, Michael Brown, Wes Clarke, Nancy Hoy, Marilyn Ortt, Judy Pannier; McConnelsville, Jane Christie, Galen Finley, Amy Grove, Mona Newton; Morristown, Margaret Dankworth, Simon Herbert, David Mertz; New Lexington, Jerry Smith; Pleasant City, Bernie Turanchik; Shawnee, Bob Hannah, John Winnenberg; Somerset, Beverly Henery, Deb Hutmire, Wanda Wilson; Warsaw, Bill Bucklew, Phil Day, Gary Douglas, Henry Fowler, Kristine Gross, Richard Henthorne; Waverly, Sharon Clary, Clare Fleser; Wellston, Mary Anne Reeves, Barbara Summers; West Union, Stephen Kelley, Hazel Roush; Woodsfield, Van and Marilyn Morris; Zanesville, Bernadine and Stephen Brown, Rev. Craig Eilerman, Kathryn Kehlmeier; Zoar, Kathleen Fernandez;

Southwest Ohio: Bellefontaine, Chuck Croutwater, Lois Scott; Brookville, Wayne Watkins; Greenville, Jennifer Hart, Mary Frances Shultz; Hamilton, Melissa Chaney, Mark Goodman, Mary Clark

Harlan, Thomas Rentschler, Phyllis Snyder; Lebanon, Mary Ann
Olding; Loveland, Joe Carey; Piqua, James C. Oda; St. Paris, John Bry,
Emma Lou Rust; Sidney, Mike Behr, Bob Bertsch, Sherrie Casad-
Lodge, Jim Sayre, Rich Wallace, Tony Zircher; Springfield, Floyd
Barman, Joyce Cave, Gloria Daniels, Wayne Davis, Anita Deaver,
Richard Dunbar, Mary Kestner, Cherie Lamborn, Don Scott, Tim
Strawn, Joy Suttles, Virginia Weygandt, Sara Winwood; Troy, Steve
Brown, Richard Wagar, James J. Wagner, William Hobart; Urbana,
Laura Bedford, John Bry, Jan Ebert, Pearl Sue Moyer; West Liberty,
Angie Warye; Xenia, Eric Fogarty.

Thanks to Nathalie Wright and the Ohio Historical Society
Preservation Office, which keeps the state's National Register files; to
Sam Roshon, who developed the superb Ohio local history collection at
the Columbus Metropolitan Library; to Ohio State University's Science
& Engineering Library, which includes architecture; to Ohioana
Library; and particularly to local public libraries in Coshocton,
Greenville, Hudson, Massillon, New Bremen, New London, and Niles.

Thanks for special help with illustrations: Jennifer Bachtel, Floyd
Barman, Randy Bergdorf, Robin Blair, Craig Bobby, Dick Brown,
Virginia Bryant, Mary Kay Campbell, Helen Campen, Ellie Damm,
Wayne Davis, Dave Dayne, Mary Dillon, Rick Fatica, Paul Gerard,
Jennifer Hart, Dr. Scott Howard, J. Hylton, Nancy Bushnell Johnston,
Sue Judith, Steve Kelleher, Stephen Kelley, Virginia King, Kathryn
Lehotsky, Lynn Lubin, Marjorie T.J. Mack, Leslie Miller, Rosalinda Paul,
Sam Roshon and the Columbus Metropolitan Library, Pamela L.
Pletcher, John E. Rees, Anna Selfridge, Melissa Smith, Suzanne Stewart,
Athena Tacha, Mary Beth Takacs, Steve Turckes, Anka Vaneff, Nyla
Vollmer, Jennifer Warner, Jennifer Wertz, Virginia Weygandt, Karen
Whalen, Samantha Williams, Lois Wolf, and Mindi Woolman.

Thanks to those who not only helped prepare this volume, but then
read parts of it: Robert B. Althoff, Geoffrey Blodgett, Craig Bobby,
Alexander T. Bobersky, Mary Anne Brown, John Bry, Ellie Damm,
Kathleen Fernandez, Priscilla Graham, W.W. Higgins, Nancy Hoy, Stephen
Kelleher, Ted J. Ligibel, Michael Lynch, James C. Oda, James A. Pahlau,
Linda Paul, Mary Anne Reeves, Thomas Rentschler, Judith Sheridan,
Mary Tolbert, Richard Webb, Judge Gale Williamson, John Winnenberg,
and Bruce Yarnall.

Special thanks to John Baskin of Orange Frazer Press. This book
was his idea; he particularly wanted accessible language and opinion-
ated content. He asked for the commitment that's kept me at this
project for years. And in the end, by putting these pages together with
elegant pictures, he was the one who, I think, made Ohio look good.
And finally, thanks to my husband, Brendan, who's learned way more
about architecture than he ever expected. And liked it.

illustration: Frank Elmer

photography: Ian Adams, Bill and Tom Patterson, Fred Sawall

cover: Milan, the Kelley Block, by Ian Adams

The editors received yeoman service from some of the very best documentary photographers in Ohio, notably Tom and Bill Patterson, whose book, *County Courthouses of Ohio*, was published in 2000 by Indiana University Press and Ian Adams whose photographs—nature and architecture—are found each year in his Ohio calendars from Brown-Trout. Special thanks to architect Frank Elmer, who drew so many of the buildings; to Fred Sawall, the Delaware photographer who has documented an astounding quantity of Ohio places; to Helen Campen, who permitted us to draw upon the landmark work of Richard N. Campen, *Ohio, An Architectural Portrait*, Chagrin Falls, 1973; and to the Historic Landmarks Foundation of Indiana for John Wells's illustrations of architectural styles and elements.

x

Contents

NORTHWEST 146

SOUTHWEST   232

Author's Note: On Choosing Buildings

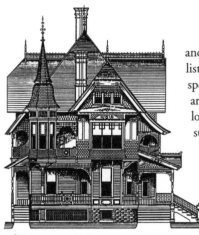

▶ Spitler House, Brookville

Early in 1996, I sat down and picked most of the buildings listed in this guide. By then I'd spent a year and a half asking architects, preservationists, and local historical societies for suggestions, vetting the literature, and driving around taking pictures—ultimately, I would have thousands of pictures from all 88 Ohio counties.

Douglas Graf, associate professor of architecture at Ohio State University, has seen almost all my pictures; he became, in effect, a co-selector of these buildings, especially for modern ones. That is not to say he would endorse every last one of these choices; I'm sure he would not; but he would agree with almost all. I am convinced that his input enhanced the overall level of selection.

What I was looking for, was varied examples of good and interesting architecture for a guide (this is *not* an architectural history). I started with architects and architectural features—styles and sites, for instance—but I've also included buildings designed by non-architects. A distinctive building had an edge.

I set up categories, mostly building types of the nineteenth or the twentieth century, and chose up to 15 good examples for each. Types included houses, hotels, churches and cemeteries, courthouses, small (Main Street) and large commercial buildings, schools and colleges, skyscrapers, recreation (park pavilions, restaurants, theaters), stores. Some categories were themes: rural Ohio or innovative reuses or small or unusual buildings, such as a one-room school in Harrison County, a little restaurant in a Columbus alley, and lighthouses. Other categories were ways of enhancing the look of places and buildings: town planning, site, ensembles.

A problem with categories is that some types are underrepresented, especially courthouses. So are houses, even though this guide has more houses than any other building type. But then too, so does Ohio.

Another factor in selecting was the availability of information. Almost always, I relied on research by local individuals and historical societies.

Some choices—often those written about briefly—were included to augment tours, especially in cities. But by and large, selections were made in a statewide context, so that although this work can claim to be a guide to Ohio architecture, it can't pretend to be definitive for any one place, especially cities.

Possibilities of place

In about 1994, I began working on an architectural guide to
Ohio. The plan was to finish it at the end of 1997. The miracle is that
now, in 2002, it may really be finished.

For eight years, I have spent most of my time on this project; and it
has been an amazing adventure. In the beginning I expected to learn
about Greek columns and High Victorian Gothic, little known Ohio
architects and Frank Lloyd Wright's Ohio houses, and how to find a

place called Gomer,
and I did. Not too
surprisingly, I also
learned about
roofing materials and
barn siding, mail-
order floorplans and
town plats, syna-
gogue interiors and
Orthodox altars.
And architecture is
emeshed with life,
present and historic,
so I also found
myself researching subjects like how apples are stored, or the world's
only female ironmaster, or the difference between current and historic
Masonic symbols.

And in the beginning, as I started looking for buildings that would
take my breath away, I knew I would find courthouses and houses, but
I didn't anticipate so many wonderful, relatively little known houses of
worship, so many fabulous schools, cemeteries, barns, and factories. I
never imagined I'd see a small abandoned Neoclassical gas station with
two columns on each of its eight sides (Delaware), or a theater auditorium with windmill blades that turn (Bellefontaine), or a dog house
built of stone (West Liberty), or Louis Sullivan stencilings biding their
time amid the ducts above a dropped ceiling (Newark).

This is the second volume of *Building Ohio*. The first volume
covered the state's eight largest cities, while this one focuses on towns
and rural areas in five regions, including about three quarters of the
state's 88 counties and 125 localities. Though cities had concentrations
of money, architects, and culture, they had no monopoly, as this book
shows; much of what's interesting in Ohio architecture—and most of
what's little known—is in towns and rural areas.

At at least some moment in the past, virtually every place in Ohio
had money, and some of it ended up in buildings. Rural areas and
towns have been more likely to keep their old buildings; if prosperity
came and then left, they kept even more. A rural site in itself may
enhance architecture, perhaps by hills, or by a flat terrain with long
vistas, or even by a desolate setting in which suddenly a wonderful

building appears. Many of the state's colleges built well historically in towns that their presence keeps vibrant today. Clever eccentrics were more likely to build in remote places. And finally, Ohio towns mostly were laid out when it was commonplace to give the courthouse a prominent site in or facing into a square, or to center the school at the end of an important road. Such design devices to enhance places and buildings, were widely familiar.

In preparing this book I needed many guides myself, and principal among them was Douglas Graf, associate professor of architecture at Ohio State University, who knows much about the architecture of Europe and the rest of the United States, as well as Ohio. By looking at all my pictures, he helped select the buildings in this guide. Most of them date from the late nineteenth- and early twentieth-century, before the Depression, an era when, Graf says, Ohio was more in the national loop than it is now; its buildings and its architects were more likely to appear in the architectural press.

Graf finds a lot to admire in this state's architecture. "How much great stuff there is in Ohio," he says. "There's so much and it's so inspired. When Ohio towns were built, people were optimistic from the get-go—'This will be the new Rome!' They bothered to plan the town, a little bit anyway, and stick in a central square. They embellished it with buildings that augmented the town." Public money meant a lot of money—deep pockets built waterworks, courthouses, schools, town halls, county homes. Buildings were better built and more carefully detailed—a function not of the style but of the culture.

But times have changed. "Now," says Graf, "society doesn't require buildings to be good and it does require them to be cheap. Low density development, requiring a huge infrastructure in a sparsely occupied area, impoverishes the public purse. We have a fabulous rural landscape that's disappearing, replaced by exurban ranch-burgers, strip malls, and self-storage units. If I want to walk in the country, where do I go? The bike trails are definitely a plus, but metro parks are too often a fake suburban reverie. There's a complete abrogation of public responsibility—we've replaced civic life with shopping. There are no stores, only chains. No builders, only developers. No neighborhoods, only developments. There's no possibility of place. All you have to do in America is not get any worse, or get worse more slowly to improve your relative advantage."

In Ohio, says Graf, "There's been this rush to the bottom." The state never recovered its pre-Depression wealth and importance; Ohio's rank in per capita income was 11th of 48 states in 1929, 25th of 50 in 1999. (In the 1990s alone, it slipped from 20th to 25th.) In Ohio the loss of home-town companies (such as International Harvester, Diamond Match Company, Quaker Oats, and Piqua's underwear manufacturers), which have a stake in the town, has been especially acute. The state's political leaders haven't had making Ohio better on their agenda. And Ohioans so rarely consult an architect when they're building a house that when they do, they are apt to find contractors have forgotten how to deal with unique projects.

Not everyone in Ohio is unaware of the problems affecting the look of the place. One person who's analyzed them and come up with a positive response for his community—including downtown building preservation and renovation—is Warren city planner Alexander T. Bobersky. (See Warren in Northeast Ohio.)

Four buildings that I intended to include in this guide have been demolished in the last several years—four so far as I know. All were unique or rare. Two were farm buildings in Northwest Ohio; they were no longer needed and represented economic deficits to their owners. In Columbus, the OHIO gate at the fairgrounds was razed. Money wasn't the problem there, for the fair had $700,000 for a replacement gate conceived originally as a metal arch, but later redesigned to incorporate 30-foot O-H-I-O letters. The greatest loss was the Polynesian-style Kahiki restaurant in Columbus, which was in fact a characteristically American work of art both inside and out. In Europe, says Doug Graf, the Kahiki probably would have been protected from razing by landmark status, while the barns, seen there as part of the landscape whole, might have received local government grants for repairs.

Perhaps this guide will help make us more aware of this place and its architecture, and will help us value what's good in the built Ohio—will even help more people see what's wonderful in a structure like the old OHIO gate.

Just as it was eight years ago, that is my hope.

▶ SOUTH MAIN STREET, CELINA

Jane Ware
Columbus, Ohio
June 2002

Key

Building Ohio is an architectural guide to Ohio, in two volumes. Volume I includes the state's eight largest cities; Volume II, the one in hand, includes towns and rural areas, which have been separated into five geographic regions and then listed alphabetically by town. A possible companion tour—another site or sites also in this guide— follows the place name; and several thematic tour itineraries are included; one, in Northeast Ohio, is listed alphabetically under Western Reserve.

All buildings in this guide are visible from street, though some are partly obscured by summer vegetation. Private houses, and their yards, are private and not accessible to the public. A few owners are willing to show their houses to visitors at least occasionally; in those cases, a phone number is included.

 How Buildings are Listed:

1) U.S. Post Office, now Museum of Ceramics, 1909

2) James Knox Taylor, supervising architect, Treasury Department, Washington

3) 400 East Fifth Street, East Liverpool, NRHP

4) Ohio Historical Society museum; open March-November Wednesday-Sunday; fee; 330/386-6001

1) Building's historic name; present name; year construction was completed

2) Architect, builder, or other designer who planned building and locality where they worked, if known; "attributed to" means there's no proof

3) Street address (sometimes *not* where the door is) and National Register listing, if any (see below); for groups, Register listing is often mentioned in preceding text

4) Present use; if interior is accessible to the public, days (but not times) when open; phone number for museums and public buildings

"Access" is how to find a site or sites. "To see more" is briefly listed additional sites or nearby places. "See also" is used for cross-references. Because this complete guide is in two volumes, a "see also" followed by a volume reference means the volume not in hand.

National Register of Historic Places

Maintained by the U.S. Department of the Interior, the National Register of Historic Places recognizes the architectural worth of many historic buildings. Abbreviations are:

NHL = National Historic Landmark

NRHP = National Register of Historic Places

HD = Building is listed as part of a Historic District

CD = Building is listed as part of a Commercial District

PD = Building is listed as part of a Preservation District

MRA = Building is on Register through a Multiple Resource Area, a type of group listing no longer used

TR = Building is on Register through a Thematic Resource, a group listing no longer used

Building
OHIO

23

Delaware ⊙

Marysville ⊙

33

COLUMBUS

70

⊙ Lafayette

⊙ London

71

23

⊙ C

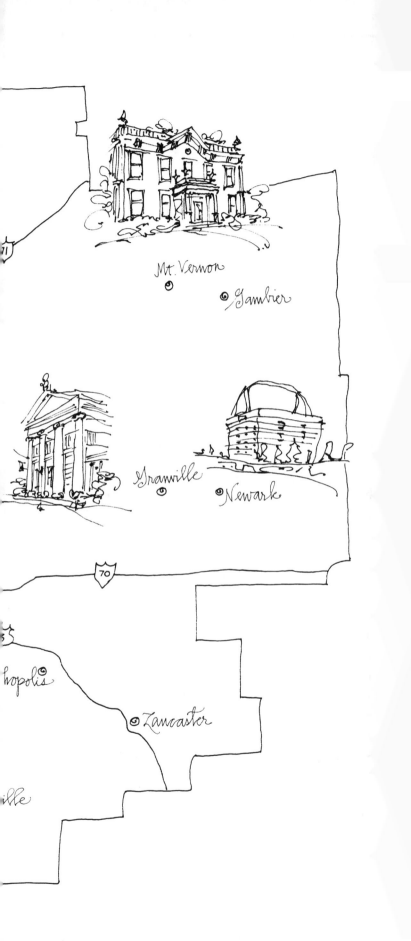

Mt. Vernon

Gambier

Granville

Newark

70

hopolis

Lancaster

ille

Central Ohio

If there is a typical Ohio, Central Ohio is it.
For one thing, says Douglas Graf, associate
professor of architecture at Ohio State University, it's a
geographical amalgam of the state, with both flat terrain
and some scrappy, unglaciated Southeast Ohio hills. To
see both at once, climb to the top of Mount Pleasant in
Lancaster's Rising Park. While the horizon to the north is
flat, you'll see that you're on one in a row of 200-foot
rocks—rocks left standing when the glaciers stopped.
¶ All his life Doug Graf has been a voracious traveler. He
has devoured towns, their hills and rivers, their plats, their
buildings, until now he has thousands of towns, mostly in
the United States and Europe, and certainly in Ohio,
stashed in his head. When he calls Central Ohio an
architectural amalgam, he illustrates with plats—how
towns are laid out, the first manmade architecture of a
place. So to Graf, Lancaster's plat looks like Virginia, and
Granville's, with the square surrounded by churches, like
New England. With its flat terrain, wide streets, and
emphatic grid, Newark, he says, is typical of the American
Midwest; Newark could be Iowa. ¶ Some of Central
Ohio's plats are not typical of anywhere, but are inventive
and distinctive. Mount Vernon's is one. It has a central
green that Graf calls a neutral midpoint between the

commercial street to the south and the uphill High Street to the east, where the county courthouse is: The Acropolis. Of Mount Vernon he sums up, "It has a sense of place. It is—or was—a perfect Ohio town, which means it's actually quite unusual." So is Delaware, even though, he says, the town founders were "too cheap to have a square. But Delaware has a wonderful grid, with ridiculously big blocks that allow little green forests in the middle of the blocks, or a villa." And there's Gambier, which he sees as "incredibly different." It's a hilltop town built along a mile-long Middle Path, with the tiny village and its shops facing two parallel streets at the halfway point. It's like nowhere else. ¶ Then, too, there was Circleville, where in 1810 the founders followed Indian mounds already in the place and laid out a circular plat with the courthouse in the middle and streets radiating out from it. "The city," says Graf, "was an event and not just a mechanism to sell land." Since it was the first of only a few round towns ever laid out in America, after a while the residents found the circular plat too unconventional, and it didn't maximize profits. By 1856 Circleville had been squared. ¶ Amalgam though it may be,

▶ PICKAWAY COUNTY COURTHOUSE

Central Ohio includes relatively few counties in this guide. That is enough for a Circleville house with an apparent Thomas Jefferson floorplan; America's first Gothic Revival building on a campus, at Kenyon College, Gambier; and one of the only two genuine Alexander Jackson Davis houses west of the Alleghenies, in Newark.

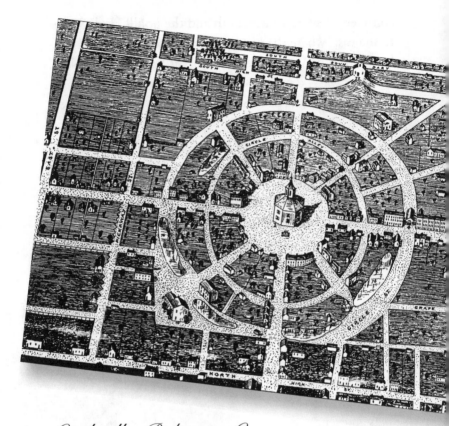

Circleville, Pickaway County

(Companion tour: Lancaster, east on U.S. 22.)

❡ "In the annals of American city planning there is no more curious episode than the planning and subsequent redevelopment of Circleville, Ohio." So pronounced John W. Reps in his 1965 book, *The Making of Urban America: A History of City Planning in the United States.* This curious episode began after Pickaway County was formed in 1810. Daniel Dresbach, the city director, set out a county seat on the lines of a preexisting circular Indian mound. After reserving a 400-foot circle in the middle for the courthouse, he laid out eight radial streets leading to Circle Street, where the mounds were. Circle Street was enclosed in a 1500-foot square surrounded by streets in a regular grid pattern. The courthouse in the hub was octagonal, with one side facing each of the streets. According to Reps, Circleville was unique in conforming to prehistoric earthworks. Its circular plan was the first of only a few ever laid out in North America; and the community's decision to go square 28 years later, became a very early example of urban redevelopment. ¶

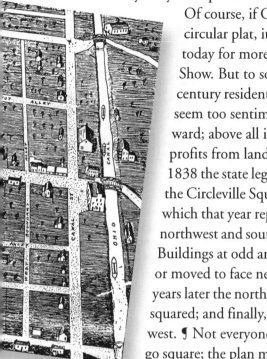

Of course, if Circleville had kept its circular plat, it would be famous today for more than the Pumpkin Show. But to some nineteenth-century residents, the circle came to seem too sentimental, or too awkward; above all it failed to maximize profits from land development. So in 1838 the state legislature authorized the Circleville Squaring Committee, which that year replatted the circle's northwest and southeast quadrants. Buildings at odd angles were torn down or moved to face new streets. Eleven years later the northeast quarter was squared; and finally, in 1856, the southwest. ¶ Not everyone in town wanted to go square; the plan met such strong opposition that, according to town historian W.W. Higgins, it qualifies as one of the two great controversies in Circleville history. The other was the loss of the 1845-47 Greek Revival courthouse, built to replace the octagonal building that lost its site in the squaring. Designed by Nathan B. Kelly, a Columbus architect who worked on the Statehouse (see also, Vol. I), the 1847 courthouse had a pedimented, six-column porch, plus a cupola. ¶ Ultimately, in 1889, Akron's Weary and Kramer remodeled Kelly's courthouse out of Greek Revival and into Romanesque. The tower is off center, Higgins says, because engineers feared it couldn't be supported in the middle, where it belonged. Lovers of the old courthouse carted off the stone columns. One is still intact, serving as a Civil War Memorial at Forest Cemetery on North Court Street.

▶ PICKAWAY COUNTY COURTHOUSE

Access: Circleville is just east of U.S. 23. Drive east into town on U.S. 22/Main Street. City Hall and the courthouse are one block to the right/ south on South Court Street. Memorial Hall is one block farther east on East Main, at Pickaway Street.

COURTHOUSE BOILER HOUSE, 1888

▶ BOILER HOUSE

Attributed to Weary and Kramer
207 South Court Street, Circleville
Courthouse heating plant

The Pickaway County Courthouse, as mentioned, has an off-center tower. Or, as Cleveland architect Robert Gaede puts it, "The tower crashes down through the nice gable end." In Gaede's view, that gives this courthouse "the ugliest facade" of any in Ohio. But the building does have some virtues. For one, the height of the tower makes it visible from a distance. For another, the interior hall, with its stained glass and marble wainscoting, is attractive. The courthouse is part of the National Register's Circleville Historic District. Behind the courthouse is its Boiler House, a small building that I am partial to. It is a gable-front red-brick house, a story-and-a-half high, set next to its towering stack, which is still in use. The house's round-arched windows and door have heavy stone hood moldings, darkened with time, so that they look like bushy eyebrows. To Ohio State's Douglas Graf, the Boiler House appears to have been architect-designed—presumably by Akron's Weary and Kramer, who did the courthouse and sheriff's residence. The boiler attendant used to live in the house, but when George Lowery took the job in 1978 he preferred to live at home and run around checking county boilers in the middle of the night. Since then the equipment has been improved, so that now Lowery checks the courthouse boiler only a couple times a day, albeit seven days a week. For vacation, he waits until summer.

CITY HALL, 1861

William Doane, Circleville
127 South Court Street, NRHP/Circleville HD
City hall

Circleville's City Hall is a three-story red-brick building with a colonnaded cupola and a notably perky overall appearance. Though threatened with demolition in the 1970s, City Hall was saved and in 1991 a renovation was dedicated. William Doane, who designed the building, served on city council for 27 years and on the school board for 28. A carriage builder by profession, he developed an interest in architecture and, says W.W. Higgins, began practicing design with this building. Originally the fire department kept its engines on the first floor. Council chambers have always been on the second floor.

MEMORIAL HALL, 1891

H.C. Lindsay, Zanesville
165 East Main Street, Circleville, NRHP
Library, community theater, Soldiers Monumental Association quarters

Circleville's Memorial Hall is a grand Victorian building, an asset to downtown, where it makes the most of its corner location with its massive size and round tower. Three-and-a-half stories in Richardsonian Romanesque, it is red brick with stone trim and has three arched entrances. The inside is less striking than the outside. The Pickaway County District Public Library has been in Memorial Hall since 1893, and expanded into space once occupied by an armory. In recent years its quarters have become so cramped that the library plans to move to a building in a mall on the outskirts. The community theater group, Roundtown Players, uses an auditorium that once doubled as a gym. Best interior spaces are the high-ceilinged rooms that the Soldiers Monumental Association uses; they've taken out the dropped ceilings. Higgins reports that if a levy to expand the courthouse (and *raze* the Boiler House) ever passes, it should also provide for the renovation of Memorial Hall. The good news is that new windows have replaced white siding that had filled in some of the larger openings for years. Zanesville architect Henry C. Lindsay also designed McConnelsville's Opera House.

▶ MEMORIAL HALL

Access: West Union Street intersects South Court Street.

DR. HARTLEY CLARK HOUSE, C. 1888
George O. Garnsey, Chicago
138 West Union Street, Circleville
Private house

Circleville has its share of fine old houses; some, including a bed and
breakfast called Castle Inn, are on South Court Street. And some are on West
Union Street, where the Dr. Hartley Clark House is a conspicuous example.
It is a grand frame Victorian, with curling trim in the gables, a corner tower
on the diagonal and, on the other side, a round oriel, or bay window. The
name of the architect came from Craig Bobby of Lakewood, who recognized
the house as the same as Buffalo Bill Cody's town residence in North Platte,
Nebraska. Cody's house was razed in the 1930s.

**Access: Mount Oval is five miles south of Circleville, on the east side
of U.S. 23, just south of Emerson Road.**

MOUNT OVAL, 1832
3601 Emerson Road, facing U.S. 23,
Circleville, NRHP
Private house

Mount Oval has an especially
interesting floor plan, focused on a
splendid central room that's 25 feet
square and 12 feet high. At three of
its corners this room has 10-foot
cubical bedrooms with porches
between on two sides, including the
front. That this was an
unusual arrangement has
always been recognized.
But imagine the owner's
astonishment when, in the
1940s, she was in
Washington, looking at a
gallery display of Thomas
Jefferson plans; and she
came upon her house. ¶
Designated as a "temple
for a garden", the plan she
saw had the same large
central room and square
corner rooms with porches

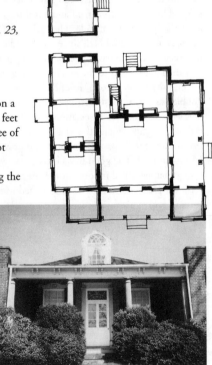

▶ MOUNT OVAL AND ORIGINAL FLOOR PLAN

between; it too had Doric columns. Jefferson adapted his garden temple from
a 1728 plan book, *Book of Architecture*, by British architect James Gibbs.
(William Howard Adams includes both the Gibbs drawing and Jefferson's in
his 1983 book, *Jefferson's Monticello*.) ¶ Even though Mount Oval isn't

identical to Jefferson's garden temple, for it has three corner rooms instead of four, and two porches instead of four, it is definitely Jeffersonian. As to how it arrived in Circleville, no one knows for sure. Perhaps a master builder who had worked for Jefferson joined other Virginians moving here. In any case, the result, as Doug Graf says, is one of amazing sophistication for its time and place. ¶ Mount Oval takes its name from the oval knoll on which it sits, overlooking U.S. 23. Set behind a white fence, it has a lawnful of shade trees, which make the house hard to see in summer. From the road it's deceptively modest in appearance; in fact, 14 rooms sprawl behind. It's red brick with stone trim—the front-porch columns are stone. Upstairs, fronting an attic room, an elegant round-arched dormer window appears to rise as high as the hip roof. ¶ One of the cubical bedrooms—front right, as seen from the road—has only one door, and that leads not into the house but onto a porch. The man who built the house, William Renick, was part of a family who took herds of shorthorn beef cattle over the Alleghenies to Baltimore and Philadelphia, and this corner room was reserved for the drover, whose separate door showed he was a business associate and not a family guest. ¶ For 33 years in the late nineteenth and early twentieth century, tenants occupied Mount Oval. Then in 1915 Elizabeth Ludwig, whose family owned the property, restored the place and moved in. Still in the same family today, the house has been beautifully kept.

Delaware, Delaware County

(Companion tour: Marion, north on U.S. 23.)
¶ In the 1990s Delaware County was Ohio's fastest growing, with much of its southern half turning into Columbus suburbs. Delaware city retains its charms, for downtown is situated happily between the Ohio Wesleyan University campus and attractive older residential areas. **To see more in Delaware:** The Delaware County Historical Society has brochures, "A Walk Down Sandusky Street" and "A Walk on Winter Street" available at the CVB, 44 East Winter Street, 740/368-4748 or 888/335-6446.

Access: From U.S. 23 north of Columbus, exit at Sandusky Street and drive north into downtown Delaware. Courthouse and former sheriff's house and jail are at North Sandusky and Central Avenue. For Asbury Church go left/west one block from Sandusky to Franklin Street; turn right/north to Lincoln. For Ohio Wesleyan go a couple blocks south from the Courthouse on Sandusky. Distances are an easy walk.

DELAWARE COUNTY COURTHOUSE, 1870

Nathan R. Jones, Delaware
91 North Sandusky Street, Delaware, NRHP
Courthouse; 740/368-1850

The Delaware County Courthouse is a red brick Italianate building with
stone trim. On top it has a two-layer wooden cupola whose lower section is
rectangular with a lacy black iron railing edging its roof, enclosing the smaller
upper cupola. On top of its roof, Justice is waving her scales. The Courthouse
interior, never ambitious, became even less so with an altered courtroom.

DELAWARE COUNTY JAIL AND SHERIFF'S RESIDENCE, 1878

David W. Gibbs, Toledo
20 West Central Avenue, Delaware, NRHP
Law library; house interior (not jail) open weekday mornings; 740/368-1775

Between the late 1860s and 1920, many Ohio counties built a substantial
house for the sheriff with a jail attached at the back; over two dozen are still
standing, though Delaware's is the only one in this guide. Designed by
Toledo architect David W. Gibbs (1836-c. 1917), this house-and-jail
complex is still handsome, though it shows that maintenance, here as

▶ DELAWARE SHERIFF'S RESIDENCE

elsewhere, was not an especially
high priority. After the sheriff
and jail moved out in 1988, the
house became the county law
library; librarian Maryanne
Stewart has taken over a desk in
what was the sheriff's office. A
metal door separates the library
from the jail wing, which has
rows of cells on two levels and
lots of bars to hold prisoners in.
Even though the cells now store
such things as county ash trays,
it's still not a place you'd want to
linger. The house that architect
Gibbs gave the sheriff is a fine
one, set facing Central Avenue
in back of the courthouse. Red
brick with stone trim, Italianate,
it has a three-and-a-half story
tower with a steep pyramidal
roof. You can spot the jail at the
back by the bars in the slender
round-arched windows.
Crenellations edge the jail's roof
line, and a small pointed
ventilation cupola ornaments
the roof. Gibbs did four Ohio
jails, all similar; the one most like Delaware's was Marion's, razed in 1969.
The architect is better remembered outside his home city of Toledo than in
it, for none of his important work there survives. In 1887, he did the
Wyoming capitol at Cheyenne.

ASBURY METHODIST EPISCOPAL CHURCH, NOW ASBURY UNITED METHODIST CHURCH, 1890

J.W. Yost, Columbus
55 West Lincoln Avenue at North Franklin Street, Delaware
Church

Asbury Methodist Church draws this response from Ohio State's Douglas Graf: "Isn't it a knockout?" It's a Richardsonian Romanesque in blue limestone with a sand-colored sandstone: a quiet and beautiful combination that's a variation from the sharp color contrasts often used in this style. The interior has fine dark wood ceilings.

DELAWARE GARMENT COMPANY, NOW OHIO WESLEYAN UNIVERSITY EDGAR HALL, 1908

W.E. Rubs, Akron
35 South Sandusky Street, Delaware
University building, classrooms and offices

This was another building that caught Doug Graf's eye. He admired the "Arts and Crafts brackets, the Chicago windows, the brick with pellets of iron." The Delaware Garment Company built this as their factory; after the 1913 flood, they spread nightgowns out all over campus to dry. In 1927 Elizabeth and Edwin Edgar bought the building to donate to the university. The interior has been altered. Akron architectural historian James A. Pahlau finds no record of W.E. Rubs there; closest name was Willard P. Rush.

UNIVERSITY HALL AND GRAY CHAPEL, 1893

J.W. Yost, Columbus
61 South Sandusky Street, Delaware,
NRHP
University classrooms, offices, and chapel/
auditorium

All in all, Delaware did very well by architect J.W. Yost. He gave the Methodists a knockout church and University Hall, a landmark building with a can't-miss tall square tower next to a round-arched, characteristically Richardsonian Romanesque entry. The interior is both good (terrazzo floors, a classroom with three tall arched windows) and less good (dropped ceilings). At the south end, the 1,100-seat Gray Chapel is the campus's principal assembly room, both a chapel

▶ UNIVERSITY HALL

(Ohio Wesleyan is affiliated with the Methodist Church) and auditorium for Delaware's Central Ohio Symphony Orchestra. Outside, looking back at the south wall, Doug Graf likes a pair of doors, one higher and round-arched, the other, adjacent but lower, straight at the top. "It couldn't be better," he says. The old building behind University Hall is Merrick Hall, 1873, NRHP, attributed to William Tinsley and presently unused.

MANSION HOUSE, NOW ELLIOTT HALL, 1833
61 South Sandusky, Delaware, NRHP
University offices and classrooms

When University Hall was built, the site was prepared by moving Ohio Wesleyan's first building, Elliott Hall, a little southeast, to where it is now. At least, Elliott was recognized as well worth keeping. It is an elegant three-and-a-half-story building in a mix of Greek Revival and Federal styles. The center is recessed for porches with Doric columns on the top two floors, and a door under an elliptical arch on the first.

¶ Though the building looks like stone, it is all pine siding over black walnut. The deception is especially impressive around the entrance, where grooves simulate rusticated stonework. Built in 1833, the building was originally a hotel, Mansion House, which closed after four years. Ohio Wesleyan, founded in 1842, purchased it in 1844 and converted one-time parlors into classrooms and faculty offices. Elliott was the only building on campus until its now adjacent clone, Sturges Library, NRHP, was built in 1856. Morris Cadwallader, the architect who designed Sturges, "had the uncommon good sense to pay Elliott Hall the compliment of copying it—in brick." So wrote

▶ ELLIOTT HALL

Eric Johannesen in his book on early Ohio colleges. Johannesen described Elliott itself as "one of the most sophisticated designs to be found in early Ohio." How and why is hard to answer. ¶ Kay Schlichting, curator of the university's Historical Collection, says a couple of investors built the hotel. Thirty-six years later, one of them, Judge Thomas Watkins Powell, recalled that an immigrant architect from England had helped them. Previously this anonymous Englishman had spent three years in an architectural capacity at Windsor Castle; so he might well be the how and why of Elliott Hall. Powell did go on to say that he himself had drawn up plans, though of course he could have been setting down the Englishman's ideas. ¶ Could that Englishman have been Benjamin Morgan, a Welshman who turned up just five years later in Granville? There Morgan designed St. Luke's Episcopal Church (see also) and, a few years later, the Avery-Downer House (see also). Morgan's credentials—he had helped remodel Buckingham Palace—were eerily similar to those of the Englishman whom Powell remembered. Elliott Hall's interior has been modernized.

Access: Between the campus and the courthouse, Winter Street intersects Sandusky Street; the Arts Castle is several blocks west.

GEORGE W. CAMPBELL HOUSE, NOW ARTS CASTLE, 1854

190 West Winter Street at Elizabeth Street, Delaware, Delaware County Cultural Arts Center, with studios, gallery, and shop; open weekdays; self-guided tour flyer in office; 740/369-2787

Set on a steep hill above the street, the Arts Castle is a romantic blue limestone house with round-arched windows and a round tower with a flared conical roof. It has been well adapted as an arts facility. Doug Graf, who liked the house,

▶ ARTS CASTLE

observed that it's stylistically naive. See, for instance, the upside-down crenellation in the hall woodwork.

Access: To see former gas station drive east on Central Avenue/State Route 37 to the intersection of Lake Street/U.S. 42.

GAS STATION, 1920s

Northwest corner, Lake Street and Central Avenue intersection, Delaware
Now storage sheds

This derelict property caught Doug Graf's eye. It's two small buildings on a corner lot. One was once a gas station—it even has a door at the back with a sign for a ladies room. It's octagonal; a pair of fluted Doric columns frame each side, with a window or door between. The whole thing was done in metal sheeting stamped into shape—now there's some rust at the column bases. The roof, in eight segments, is a metal simulation of Spanish tile, complete to the high-bump terminal in the middle. That bump is the signature of Ohio-made Ludowici Celadon tiles. (See New Lexington.) Graf also likes the structure next door, which he estimates to have been slightly later, perhaps in the early 1930s. Apparently it was a shop in which a single car could be worked on. It has a formal cornice and walls that are mostly panes of glass. Both buildings serve as storage sheds now.

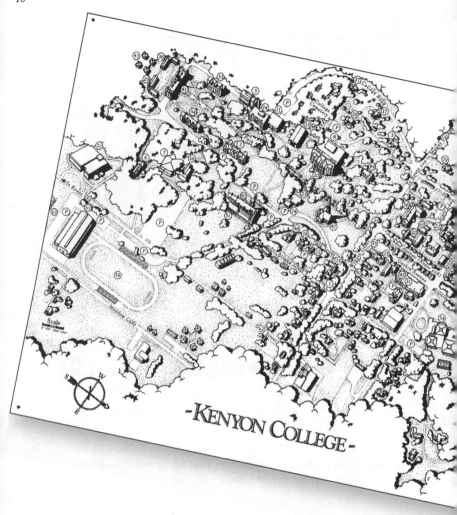

- KENYON COLLEGE -

Gambier, Knox County

(Also in Knox County: Mount Vernon.)

¶ The Kenyon College campus is straight out of a fairy-tale: a mountaintop full of castles. Out of the way, never a place people stumble on, Gambier has to be a destination. That was just how founder Philander Chase, Episcopal bishop of Ohio, wanted it to be; he thought an isolated rural setting would protect student clergymen from the temptations of urban life. Whether or not it succeeded in that (for a while in the nineteenth century Gambier had its own hotel of dubious reputation), the isolation surely has helped preserve the campus and its older buildings.

Middle Path, 1842, 1860—Gambier's layout is what Ohio State's Douglas Graf calls a hybridization—a mixture of design elements resulting in something unique. The key is the Middle Path,

campus area with newer buildings, including a nine-story dormitory. All the path above Wiggin is set in a green that's flanked on both sides by two-way roads. Once someone proposed paving the Middle Path in concrete, an idea that foundered in the ensuing uproar. The gravel stays.

Bishop Chase's original campus plan called for a broad boulevard and academic squares. The next president, David Bates Douglass, had been trained in engineering at West Point. He dropped Chase's plan, built roads around south campus, and constructed the path through the middle in 1842. To keep the path straight, he sank iron rods that grounds crews still use. Students helped install the base of coarse stone topped with finer stone and finally gravel. The northern section wasn't built until 1860, when Bishop Gregory Bedell was running the college. Bedell wanted that stretch called "Bishop's Walk", but it never was.

Unique to Kenyon, Middle Path has become the symbol of the college. Like the best symbols, it has more than one meaning. Doug Graf points out that from the far end, Old Kenyon's steeple almost looks like a continuation of the path into the sky.

a straight, gravel pedestrian walk, 15 feet wide, one mile long, lined much of the way with trees. At the north end is Bexley Hall, begun in 1839; at the south, Old Kenyon, begun in 1827. The southern third of the path's length traverses the old-campus lawn, where buildings, mostly Gothic Revival, are off to the side. The path's northern end, across Wiggin Street, passes first through the village of Gambier and then through a

▶ OLD KENYON

¶ Founded as an Episcopal seminary, Kenyon early expanded its curriculum, and gradually its graduates—including members of Lincoln's cabinet and President Rutherford B. Hayes—made it famous. The seminary, named for its building, Bexley Hall, moved away in 1968, just before Kenyon began enrolling women. ¶ The Public Affairs Department will arrange tours for groups (740/427-5000). A Kenyon College Campus Guide is available on the internet at *http://circle.kenyon.edu/visitors/tour/onlinetour/*

Access: From South Main Street/State Route 13 in downtown Mount Vernon, turn east onto Gambier Street, which becomes State Route 229. Drive east; at State Route 308 turn uphill to the left/north; road becomes Wiggin Street. Park in downtown Gambier, on Chase or Gaskin Avenue to the left, and take a walking tour of the south campus. All buildings here are open when school is in session and many (not Ascension) are open in summer too. Buildings are listed in order from Wiggin Street. Kenyon College, specifically including the Church of the Holy Spirit, Old Kenyon, and Rosse, Ascension, and Bexley Halls, is on the National Register.

▶ CHURCH OF THE HOLY SPIRIT

CHURCH OF THE HOLY SPIRIT, 1871
Gordon W. Lloyd, Detroit

New York City's Church of the Ascension gave two buildings to Kenyon College: first Ascension Hall and then this chapel. More than money linked the college and the church, for Bishop Bedell had been rector there. The architect, English-born, Detroit-based Gordon Lloyd, specialized in churches. This one has an altar with a segmented vault overhead. The pews, three rows on each side, face the aisle. For a non-spiritual view of the Church of the Holy Spirit, I talked to Tom Lepley, who sees campus buildings mostly in terms of heating and redoing brick mortar. Now head of buildings and grounds, Lepley started at Kenyon in 1970 as an apprentice electrician. He especially admires the inside of the church's tower—he's even taken his friends up there to show it off. It has four levels, the amenities diminishing with height. At the first level, reached by what Lepley calls as a "wonderful old wooden staircase," there's a 12-foot-square room where a student works the bells for special occasions, like commencement, by pushing down wooden levers controlling the bell ropes. Observes Lepley, "It's very athletic, ringing those things." A ladder reaches the next level up, where the clock mechanism is and where, Lepley says, "You've left the heated portion of the building." The third level, attained by a rickety ladder, is the belfry, where brackets support the eight bells, graduated in size from 12 inches to 4 feet in diameter. Because of louvers at this level, fresh air flows in; in winter it's not merely unheated but very cold. The very highest level has only beams for climbing and standing on—which someone has to do whenever the time changes: the clock hands have to be advanced manually.

RANSOM HALL, 1910
Charles F. Schweinfurth, Cleveland

During the first two decades of the twentieth century, Cleveland architect Charles F. Schweinfurth was Kenyon's supervising architect. Partly, that job meant managing renovations; but it also gave Kenyon several Schweinfurth structures, including Ransom Hall. Built as a library adjunct, Ransom contains Norton Hall, a one-time reading room that is such a fine

▶ NORTON HALL IN RANSOM HALL

space that it's used as a lure—a waiting room for Admissions. With its beamed ceiling and windows with stone dividers, Norton Hall shows what hallowed halls are all about. The building was given John Crowe Ransom's name in 1958 when that nationally known poet and critic retired from the faculty. Ransom made the *Kenyon Review* the country's leading literary journal and attracted young writers to campus—that's why poets Robert Lowell and James Wright and novelist E.L. Doctorow all graduated from Kenyon.

ROSSE HALL, 1845
Charles Romanoff Prczriminsky, Gambier

Rosse Hall is easy to spot because its Greek Revival style is distinctive amid all the Gothic Revival; it's dubbed "Stranger on Campus". Some Kenyonites would have preferred the Gothic church (big enough for 940 people) that Philander Chase intended to build. Before the board of trustees charged him with arrogance and ignoring money problems and sent him packing in 1831, Chase even chose a site and prepared the foundations. His successor modified them for this chapel, designed by a faculty member. He was Charles Romanoff Prczriminsky, a Pole who taught modern languages, who had previously done Columbus's Trinity Church (no longer standing), and could recycle those plans. Named for an English benefactor, the Countess Dowager of Rosse, the building is an auditorium today. First the Church of the Holy Spirit replaced it as chapel and then, in 1897, Rosse burned and had to be rebuilt. During the fire a column toppled and its capital broke off. The capital is still on the lawn where it landed, offering a look at Ionic, close up.

PEIRCE HALL, 1929
Alfred H. Granger, Chicago

This building has two special features: a tower and the Great Hall, a college diningroom. The room is about 60 feet long, with a large stone fireplace at one end and paneled wainscoting on the walls. The ceiling beams start at a height of about 20 feet, above which the ceiling rises another 15 feet. So says Tom Lepley, who knows the height because building and grounds has a telescoping 35-foot lift for changing light bulbs and cleaning woodwork. Lepley admires how the ceiling beams were installed. Holes were made in the stone and filled with wood, which jammed into place forever when a nail was driven in. Today, a builder would use a diamond drill or a gunpowder cartridge, Lepley says. The old way was slow. Peirce is Lepley's favorite building on campus. Kenyon alumnus—class of 1887—Alfred H. Granger, trained as an architect at Massachusetts Institute of Technology and Paris's École des Beaux-Arts, mixed Gothic with Arts and Crafts features in the design. Though working in the era of steel framing, he specified some two-foot-thick load-bearing stone walls. He built a strikingly tall (106 feet) tower, whose higher floors are 15-foot-square rooms. The college paper uses one; the radio transmitter is in another. At lower levels a stairway fills the tower; two landings have Tiffany stained glass windows, for which artist Charles Connick did scenes from Philander Chase's life.

ASCENSION HALL, 1860
William Tinsley, Cincinnati

Ascension Hall's most remarkable feature is two rooms that originally were the lavish halls of rival literary societies. Though nineteenth-century college societies often had ornate rooms, Kenyon's are now the only ones surviving in Ohio. A 1987 restoration removed hanging fluorescents and partitions, again revealing stained glass and carved red oak woodwork in patterns architect William Tinsley probably designed. Pre-Civil War Kenyon enrolled as many Southerners as Northerners, and the two societies split according to sectional sympathies. The Philomathesians on the second floor were northern; the Nu Pi Kappas on the third floor, southern. The Philomathesians' erstwhile

▶ ASCENSION HALL

quarters are now a classroom; student council meets in Nu Pi Kappa's; and both are used for studying (classrooms in Ascension are open all night). When I was there, during an exam period, a table in Philomathesian Hall was strewn with open, at least temporarily abandoned calculus books, and someone had written AAAAARRRGGHH on the blackboard. ¶ In Ascension Hall, Tinsley designed a Gothic Revival building of rough-cut olive shale with dressed stone trim. Altogether 171 feet long, mostly three stories, the hall has a taller, four-story central section, where the literary society rooms are. ¶ William Tinsley (1804-1885) began his architectural career in County Tipperary, Ireland. At the age of 47, he packed up his wife and nine unmarried children (aged from less than 1 to 19) and moved to Cincinnati. He was disappointed on arrival. "The American style of false and flimsy construction," as he described it, was completely different from what he was used to; he insisted on holding out for quality. So for the first year especially, he had a rough time. What is surprising, is that within just a few years, his career took off; professionally, he never looked back. ¶ Born in Clonmel, Ireland, Tinsley became a fourth-generation builder. He apprenticed with an older brother, who died; so at 21 Tinsley was independent, building cottages and churches designed by his friend James Pain, Jr., who had studied with the famed English architect John Nash.. Tinsley traveled, sketching old buildings. Later the gentry hired him to build mansions that he described as "castellated and Italian." He became diocesan architect; he contracted to rebuild part of the town of Cahir; he did a model farm for the Marquess of Waterford. So why leave? Tinsley himself wrote that economic stagnation in Ireland led to a drop-off in construction. Biographer J.D. Forbes suggests two more reasons: unfair treatment and better opportunities for his sons in America. ¶ Improbable as Tinsley's move still seems, Ohio is a beneficiary. Besides Ascension, his surviving work here includes Cincinnati's Probasco

House and Calvary Episcopal Church (both see also, Vol. I). In Indiana he designed university buildings in Bloomington. Tinsley was popular in Gambier, where in 1858 the Nu Pi Kappa literary society made him an honorary member "as an indication of our high appreciation of your worth as a Gentleman, Scholar and Artist."

OLD KENYON, 1829, REBUILT AFTER FIRE, 1950
Norman Nash, Philadelphia; Philander Chase, Gambier; Charles Bulfinch, Washington, D.C.

Old Kenyon is an Ohio rarity, a national first, at least in architectural history annals. It's the first Gothic Revival building on any campus—the first of many, nationally, which accounts for its importance. Founder Philander Chase chose the style, which dazzled him when he was in England in 1823-24 raising money for the college. When he returned home he brought both the style and the wherewithal: $30,000 from donors whose names— Gambier, Kenyon, Rosse, Bexley—endure on campus. ¶ Norman Nash was an Episcopal clergyman whom Chase met in Philadelphia. In 1823 Nash had built a small Gothic Revival church in Pennsylvania; and in November, 1826, he drew Old Kenyon for Chase. "Neither Chase nor Nash was a trained architect," Richard Salomon, a seminary faculty member, wrote in 1944, after researching Old Kenyon's origins. "They started with the facade, without giving much thought to what was to be behind it." ¶ What about Old Kenyon's traditional attribution to the renowned American architect, Charles Bulfinch? Salomon traced that to a mistake. Chase sent a letter to Lord Gambier in England, discussing Old Kenyon. He wrote, "The steeple is in good proportion, high and beautiful. The draft of it was made for me by our national architect, Mr. Bulfinch of the City of Washington." But when the letter was copied before publication, two words, *of it*, were omitted, leading to decades of confusion. When Salomon found letters proving that Chase and Bulfinch met in Washington in 1828, he accepted Chase's claim that Bulfinch had indeed drawn the steeple. Salomon was triumphant: "Old Kenyon, though in all essentials the work of amateur architects has the distinction of being connected with the great American tradition by the touch of the hand of one of its masters." ¶ But Salomon wrote before the terrible fire of February, 1949, which killed nine students and ruined the building. Afterward stones whose original location was known were marked so they could be exactly restored. A steel and concrete box was built, and the old 14-inch stones were split to use as facing. The steeple had to be rebuilt. Old Kenyon, as it stands, is only a replica.

Access: The Peter Neff house is on Wiggin Street; from Wiggin turn north onto Chase Avenue/State Route 308 to see Bexley Hall and Beta Temple.

PETER NEFF COTTAGE, 1850
Wiggin Street

This is a Gothic Revival cottage with ornate, well-kept exterior woodwork that's said to have been influenced by William Tinsley's designs for Ascension Hall's literary society rooms; it's well kept because the college workshop makes custom replacement wood finials. Almost all the interior has been modernized.

▶ Peter Neff Cottage

BEXLEY HALL, 1839-58
Henry Roberts, England

Bexley Hall is one of Kenyon's best—Ohio architectural historian Eric Johannesen called it "the most convincing Gothic Revival building on the campus", while Richard Salomon described it as "artistically, the most successful." Even so, between the trees in front of it and its relatively remote location, Bexley Hall might be easy to miss. It was set apart to house the seminary; perhaps Bishop Chase himself picked the site. After the seminary left in the late 1960s, Bexley Hall was gutted and turned into art facilities. The chapel was saved, sort of; it was dismantled and put into storage, where it remains. "Kenyon," says spokesman Tom Stamp, "has always been good about storing interesting detail." While Kenyon's other old buildings are stone, Bexley Hall is red brick with tan sandstone trim. It was named for Lord Bexley, who was generous for a second time when Charles Pettit McIlvaine, Kenyon's second president, made his own English fund-raising foray in the mid 1830s. Besides the money, McIlvaine brought Bexley Hall's design from England, where it was drawn and donated by Henry Roberts, a London architect remembered for early working-class housing. The trip didn't fully resolve chronic money woes. Bexley Hall, begun in 1839 and first occupied in 1843, wasn't finished until 1858. At the back it has a 1904 addition, Colburn Hall, built as a library.

▶ Bexley Hall

▶ BETA TEMPLE

Access: Behind Bexley Hall there's a water tower on the right; and just opposite it, a gravel drive leads into the woods to Beta Temple.

BETA TEMPLE, 1929

Imagine taking a gravel road into the woods and coming upon a little Greek temple. It happens here. The temple makes an impressive fraternity house for the Beta Alpha Chapter of Beta Theta Pi; their building was dedicated February 9, 1929. It's stone, with two fluted Doric columns in a recessed porch. The Beta Temple is not the only Kenyon fraternity house of interest here. Delta Kappa Epsilon has a small frame Gothic Revival cottage, also in the woods. Built in 1855, it's the oldest fraternity building in the United States. It's on the south side of Kokosing Drive, which turns off Chase opposite Bexley Hall, and just past Rand Drive.

Access: To reach the Quarry Chapel, from downtown Gambier drive east on Wiggin Street, then left/north on Quarry Chapel Road. Continue about a mile; the chapel will be on your right, just before Monroe Mills. The drive will show you how rural this area is.

QUARRY CHAPEL, 1864
Attributed to William Tinsley, Cincinnati
Quarry Chapel Road, near Gambier, NRHP

Officially Christ Church at the Quarry, this chapel was built for English
stone workers who settled in the area after Bishop Chase brought them over
to work on college buildings; they wanted a less high-church worship style
than that practiced at the college. With its open belfry, sloping roof and
sloping buttresses, it's a striking building. The roof fell in after the chapel was
abandoned in 1937; the exterior was rebuilt in the early 1970s. One of
William Tinsley's early churches in Ireland, at Clogheen, County Tipperary,
was probably the model for the Quarry Chapel.

Granville, Licking County

(Also in Licking County: Newark; together, one of Ohio's
best architectural tours.)
¶ In 1805 150 settlers from Granville, Massachusetts,
founded Granville, Ohio, where they lived in the village
and farmed lots on the outskirts. Until recently, the little
New England town and its college, Denison, founded in
the late 1850s, were what Granville amounted to. But by
the 1990s, Columbus commuters were moving in and
suburbia was blooming all around. In older neighborhoods, the little New England town survives, its charm
intact. ¶ Granville has a total of 120 buildings, including
all those mentioned here, in the National Register's
Granville Multiple Resource Area; and some structures,
noted below, are listed individually as well. For a map and
list of Register sites, write the Granville Historical Society,
P.O. Box 129, Granville 43023-0129.

Access: From I-70 take State Route 37 north; road passes Bryn Mawr.

BRYN MAWR, 1854
3758 Lancaster Road SW/State Route 37, near Granville, NRHP
Private house

On the west side of the country road, a big Italian Villa appears on a rise. It's
a proud house in painted brick, with high round-arched windows crowned by
hood moldings. A cupola has been removed, but in the 1920s a becolumned
two-story porch was added. In the 1980s, the Bryn Mawr was a restaurant.

Access: Continue north on State Route 37; north of State Route 16 continue straight; road becomes State Route 661, Main Street in Granville. Broadway, which intersects Main, is the principal commercial street. This downtown tour can be done on foot. The intersection of Main and Broadway has four churches on the corners. Architecturally one is of especial interest.

ST. LUKE'S EPISCOPAL CHURCH, 1838

Benjamin Morgan, Columbus, and Minard Lafever, New York
107 East Broadway, Granville, NRHP
Church; open daily; 740/587-0167

Benjamin Morgan, a native of Wales who once helped remodel Buckingham Palace, was a 28-year-old craftsman armed with builders' guides by Asher Benjamin of Boston and by Minard Lafever of New York. With help from the guides, Morgan designed St. Luke's Greek Revival exterior. For the interior, he asked Minard Lafever for drawings; Lafever's contributions included the molded plaster ceiling. The building is a 43-by-65-foot rectangle, frame, with exterior boards rounded at the edges so as to look like stone. Belfry and portico doors are from Asher Benjamin. Morgan was so pleased with St. Luke's that in his will he asked that his funeral be held there. It was, after he'd been killed in an accident during Statehouse construction in 1851.

▶ AVERY-DOWNER HOUSE

AVERY-DOWNER HOUSE, 1842

Benjamin Morgan,
Columbus
221 East Broadway,
Granville, NRHP
Licking County
Historical Society's
Robbins Hunter
Museum; open summer
and fall; check hours;
740/587-0430

A parishioner who oversaw the construction of St. Luke's, Alfred Avery, so admired the work of Benjamin Morgan that a few years later, he asked Morgan to do his house. Taking his chief inspiration from Minard Lafever's *The Modern Builder's Guide*, Morgan gave Avery a boxy two-story house with a pedimented porch and single-story wings that end in porches. Morgan found a way to use all three Greek orders: Doric on the side porches; Ionic on

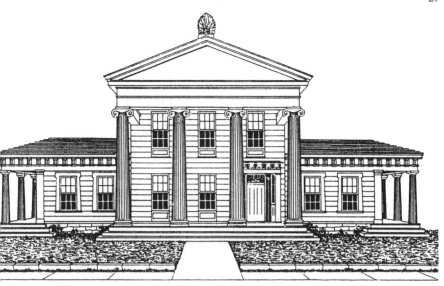

▶ AVERY-DOWNER HOUSE

the house; and Corinthian on the two columns next to the front door. Even though Morgan provided the Averys with three front parlors and six bedrooms upstairs, in 1846 they upped and moved off to New York. In the 1870s the Edward Downers added the Victorian house at the back, partly by raising a one-and-a-half-story rear wing to a full two stories. After that the place was both big and grand enough to become a Denison University fraternity house, as it did from 1902-1956. Afterwards Robbins Hunter, Jr., an antiques dealer, bought the house, furnished it, and then left it to the Licking County Historical Society to use as a museum. The society restored the house—for instance, it took off a second-floor porch added on the front—and opened the museum in 1982. The Avery-Downer House is elegant, but it was also intended to be practical. For instance, the frieze hid gutters that collected rainwater and carried it to the front columns, hollowed out to function as downspouts. However this system worked, the columns in place now are the third set. Replacements were installed first in the early 1900s, and then during the museum restoration.

ASHLEY GRAVES HOUSE, 1845

Ashley Graves, Granville
238 East Broadway, Granville
Private house

A year after he arrived from Massachusetts, builder Ashley Graves put up his own house right across the street from Alfred Avery's. It's also a Greek Revival, two stories, with a pediment and Doric pilasters at the corners. The side wing has been altered somewhat.

GRANVILLE INN, 1924

Frank L. Packard,
Columbus
314 East Broadway,
Granville
Hotel and restaurant;
740/587-3333

Two inns face each other across Broadway. One is the Buxton Inn, a frame structure built in 1812 and later expanded at the back; it has a downstairs restaurant in a series of antiquated and charming rooms. The Granville Inn was built by John Sutphin Jones, a local resident who made his money as president of the Sunday Creek Coal Company.

▶ GRANVILLE INN

Jones hired a Columbus architect, Frank L. Packard, who produced a sprawling, two-and-a-half-story Jacobean Revival manor house. Set at the back of its well-treed lawn, it looks inviting. The paneled lobby and diningroom live up to the promise. Packard also did the earlier Jacobean Revival Jeffrey Mansion in Bexley (see also, Vol. I).

Access: To reach the Denison University campus, from Broadway drive north on Main Street; at street's end, almost immediate, turn left uphill and then right at the top. Continue under the underpass and then right behind the chapel. A parking lot is between the chapel and the observatory. The road uphill is called the "Front Drag".

SWASEY OBSERVATORY, 1909

J. Milton Dyer, Cleveland
Ridge Road, Granville
University observatory

Benefactor Ambrose Swasey is best remembered at Denison because his name is on Swasey Chapel, 1924, designed by New York architect Arnold W. Brunner. Brick and stone, Georgian Revival, the Chapel has a landmark tower visible from out of town. But Ambrose Swasey's name is also on this remarkable observatory, which is near the Chapel but not nearly so obvious. This observatory must have been close to the donor's heart, for he was with the Cleveland company that produced the Werner & Swasey telescope inside. The building was designed by Cleveland architect J. Milton Dyer—what a treat to find his work so far afield. He was one of that city's best, always quirky and interesting; and this Observatory at the edge of Denison's hill is

▶ Swasey Observatory

very much in character. It's a round tower flared outward toward the base. Perhaps 30 feet high, at the top it has an observatory's customary segmented metal dome; at a level just below the dome it has a balcony that encircles the tower; at the sides it has small boxy wings, one for a library and the other for a classroom. The balcony has a ring of austere vertical metal balusters that reappear atop the wing at the right. Wonderfully, the whole thing is in white marble, which to Sandy Yorka, associate professor and resident astronomer, makes it look like a lighthouse. I asked Yorka if she could confirm my estimate of the building's height and she demurred. She measures only in light years.

▶ RED BRICK TAVERN

Lafayette, Madison County

(Also in Madison County: London. Other National Road
sites in this guide are the Headley Inn at Zanesville and
Morristown, both Southeast Ohio.)

**Access: U.S. 42, an exit from I-70, leads south to Lafayette, which is
just to the right/west on U.S. 40.**

RED BRICK TAVERN, 1837

1700 Cumberland Road/U.S. 40, Lafayette, NRHP
Restaurant and bar; open daily except Monday;
740/852-1474; 800/343-6118

When the National Road arrived in Lafayette, the Red Brick Tavern rose to
meet it. It's a fine red-brick Federal-style inn, originally built in an L shape,
with a wing at the back. The facade abuts the sidewalk, just as if this were
Philadelphia and not a place where even today three-block streets end at
fields. I.T. Frary wrote that the tavern was built as an investment by a
Connecticut man, Stanley Watson, on land that his father-in-law had
received for Revolutionary War service. His wife, who'd just been reading a
book about the French general, named the place, which was sited
conveniently, halfway between Columbus and Springfield. The inn prospered
until railroads put it out of business in 1859. Then the building became a
private residence until 1925, when, in response to automobile traffic, it once
again opened as a hotel and restaurant. After 1935 the diningroom kept on
going, but rooms were no longer available. The owner-manager lived in a
second-floor apartment while the waitresses occupied the third floor. That

was the practice when Neval Pennell, a 15-year-old Kentucky girl, began working as a waitress in 1947. Pennell met her husband here—he was a waiter—and during the years she's had two sons, three grandchildren, and four great-grandchildren, all while continuing to wait tables at the Red Brick Tavern. She was still on duty in fall, 2001. Like some buildings, some people are good for the long haul.

Lancaster, Fairfield County

(Companion tour: Circleville, west on U.S. 22.)
¶ Around Lancaster's Square 13, early residents built such a fine array of ambitious houses that visitors are often astounded. It's amazing too that Lancaster has three museums in houses on this block. Two, The Georgian and the Decorative Arts Center of Ohio, are described below. The third is the Sherman House at 137 East Main Street, the boyhood home of General William Tecumseh Sherman and his brother, U.S. Senator John Sherman.

Access: Older sections of Lancaster are just east of U.S. 33. Exit at Main Street/U.S. 22; drive east to Broad Street; Square 13 is at intersection's northeast corner. Wheeling Street borders the square's north side; High Street, the east. This tour goes around clockwise; walking is a good option. See also the marvelous alley between Wheeling and Main (and beyond), which snakes up and down rises as it passes between buildings. Gold sandstone structure at southeast corner of Main and High is Fairfield County Courthouse, 1872, by builder Jacob B. Orman. A "Square 13" brochure is available at The Georgian gift shop. So is a book on local architecture, *Heritage of Architecture and Arts: Fairfield County, Ohio*, by the late Ruth Wolfley Drinkle, revised in 1994 with Josephine Voss as editor. All houses mentioned here are part of the National Register's Square 13 Historic District.

SAMUEL MACCRACKEN HOUSE, NOW THE GEORGIAN, 1833
Daniel Sifford, builder, Lancaster
105 East Wheeling Street, Lancaster
Fairfield Heritage Association house museum; open afternoons daily except Monday; closed January-March; fee; 740/654-9923

Lancaster builder Daniel Sifford built this house for Samuel Maccracken, who had a marvelous rags-to-riches career, starting out as a humble tanner's helper and ending up a financier, Ohio University trustee, and the owner of this house. A native of Pennsylvania, Maccracken moved to Lancaster in 1810 and opened a tannery and then a general store. Ultimately he was sent to England to raise money for an Ohio Canal spur for Lancaster. While there,

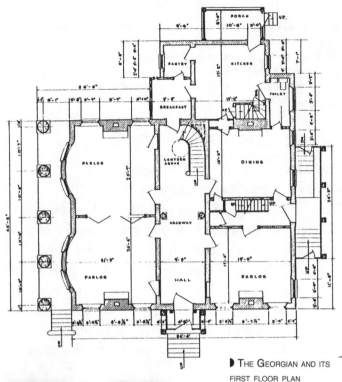

▶ THE GEORGIAN AND ITS
FIRST FLOOR PLAN

he became so entranced by English country houses that when he came home, he set about building one for himself. The result was this grand manse, which in the English manner had the kitchen and servants' quarters in the raised basement. ¶ In the 1880s a Maccracken grandson bought the house from an interim owner and Victorianized it, moving the kitchen upstairs into a rear addition. The name, The Georgian, came from a twentieth-century tearoom. When in 1972 a church thought The Georgian's site would make a nice parking lot, Ruth Drinkle and six other Lancaster women formed the Fairfield Heritage Association to buy the house and assure its future. After a restoration (the kitchen went back to the basement), the house opened as a museum in 1976. ¶ Overlooking Broad Street, The Georgian has a two-story side porch with two-story columns, in front of two two-story round bays in the wall. That's not what you'd call understated. The front has small porches, one over the other, both with doors and columns. The stairway inside, built by William Cassel, curves upward under a round skylight; and carved elliptical arches span both first- and second-floor halls. Red brick with stone trim, the house is Federal style with Regency features. ¶ Builder Sifford did other Square 13 structures. In this immediate neighborhood he built, besides The Georgian, St. John's Episcopal Church,

1848, 134 North Broad; and 118, 128, and 141 East Wheeling. (See especially 118, the lovely DeVol House, which has a beautiful door with an elliptical fanlight.) Sifford came to Lancaster as a young carpenter from Frederick, Maryland, in 1827. Broke, he left in 1852, abandoning the Main Street house he was building for himself, and spent two years looking for California gold before returning, broke, and settling in his unfinished house. He died in 1886. His own house, much altered, is now the American Legion.

JOHN HUNTER HOUSE, 1840
125 East Wheeling Street, Lancaster
Private house

What a wonderful house this is, both stately and quirky, looking down from its hillside perch. It's a mix of styles built around an 1803 log cabin. What we see are the improvements made in 1840 by a new owner, John Hunter, who wanted the house to resemble his bride's family home in Newark. He installed a Greek Revival porch and flush-matched siding on the front wall; the round-arched windows are Italianate.

REESE-PETERS HOUSE, BEGUN IN 1834
145 East Main Street, Lancaster
Decorative Arts Center of Ohio/Reese-Peters House, museum and education center, open daily except Mondays;
740/681-1423

No ordinary house could aspire to become the Decorative Arts Center of Ohio; this is one that meets all expectations. It has an exceptional

▶ REESE-PETERS HOUSE

interior, with parlor woodwork brought, almost incredibly, by covered wagon from Philadelphia. Like The Georgian, it has a curving stairway under a round skylight, built by William Cassel—little wonder his name survives. Also like The Georgian, this house has a raised basement, where the kitchen was originally. It has two floors, an unfinished attic and an impressive 8,750 square feet. It's brick, in a mix of Greek Revival and Federal styles. The front porch has composite Corinthian columns and, according to Ruth Drinkle, 80 hand-carved acanthus leaves. She must have counted them herself. One of the Reese-Peters House's admirers is Whit Tussing. "Stepping into that entry in the 1830s must have been magical, at a time when everyone else was living in log cabins," Tussing says. An architect who teaches at Central Ohio Technical College in Newark, Tussing wrote his master's thesis on Lancaster houses. In log-cabin-era towns, it was builders' pattern books that permitted elegant design and detailing. While the Reese-Peters House's portico is from Asher Benjamin, Tussing says, the door and the honeysuckle motif in the entry hall and parlor are from Minard Lafever. The man who built the house was William Reese, an attorney who in 1827 moved to Lancaster from Philadelphia. He married Mary Elizabeth Sherman, a sister of future General William Tecumseh Sherman, whose family home was one door west. Construction began in 1834, but eight years later business failures sent the Reeses back to Philadelphia. Jo Voss, who was board president during the

▶ FAIRFIELD COUNTY FAIRGROUNDS ROUND BARN

conversion into a museum, has speculated that they may never have lived here at all. In 1872 new owner Carrie Rising, a bank president's wife, lavished money on the interior, which emerged Victorian. Her descendants, the Peters family, kept the house until one set up a trust that after his death gave the property to Fairfield County as a public arts and education center. Most of the money—$1.2 million—for the $1.7 million restoration came from the State of Ohio. The Center opened in fall 2000.

Access: From Square 13 drive north on Broad Street to fairgrounds. Alternatively, take Fair Street exit from U.S. 33 and drive east two blocks. The fair program includes a map and some information on buildings.

FAIRFIELD COUNTY FAIRGROUNDS ROUND BARN, 1906
J.W. Hedges
157 East Fair Avenue, Lancaster
Fairgrounds for seven-day county fair, beginning the Sunday before the second Tuesday in October; fee; 740/653-3041. In winter buildings are rented for boat and RV storage.

Ohio State's Douglas Graf is an enthusiastic admirer of the Fairfield County Fairgrounds, which he describes as "a spectacular spot. It might be the best in the country." He's not the first to think so. In 1947 the producers of the movie *Green Grass of Wyoming* picked this as the prettiest fairgrounds and came to town for three months' shooting. Perhaps because they also corralled most of Lancaster to serve as extras watching harness races from the grandstand, people have been talking about that movie ever since—even though meanwhile a real star brought cameras to the fairgrounds: in 1978, Robert Redford filmed some *Brubaker* scenes here. *Green Grass*, third in the *My Friend Flicka* movie trilogy, also had its world premier in Lancaster in 1948. At least it had one of its world premiers. The next day it had another in Columbus. The fairgrounds has an ensemble of white frame agricultural and exhibition buildings, mostly built early in the twentieth century. The setting, just west of Rising Park and the rock called Mount Pleasant, is very nice indeed; on a bright October day Mount Pleasant provides a display of red leaves. Of the buildings the most impressive is this round barn, whose sloping red roof is topped with a windowed cupola under a conical red roof.

On fair days you'll find a round show ring inside, with seats above and straw underneath, where cattle lie. As in many of these fair buildings, the ceiling and walls display the carpenter's work.

To see more at the Fairgrounds: The white octagonal building with the pointed green roof was built before 1860 as Floral Hall; now during fairs the Lancaster band boosters run a food stand there. The curved wooden grandstand from 1909 was moved to the far side of the track to make way for a bigger steel and concrete grandstand in 1927. Barn Number One, 1920, has a raised central section with clerestory windows and, during fairs, horses in the stalls. Since the 1950s various nineteenth-century structures, including a school, a church, and a covered bridge, have been moved to the Fairgrounds from other parts of the county. In 2001 the Art Hall complex at the east end of the fairgrounds lost some of its allure when siding was installed, covering up the dormer windows.

▶ WAGNALLS MEMORIAL

To see more in Fairfield County: Lithopolis is famous because of its benefactress, Mabel Wagnalls, who was a concert pianist, novelist, and the daughter of two Lithopolis natives, Anna and Adam Wagnalls of the Funk and Wagnalls Publishing Company. Not only did Mabel Wagnalls endow a college scholarship fund for Lithopolis residents, she also provided them a library and community hall.

Access: From Lancaster best way for not getting lost is not most direct. Drive north on U.S. 33; exit at Gender Road/State Route 674 and drive south to a T junction with Lithopolis Road; turn left/southeast. The road becomes Columbus Street in the village.

WAGNALLS MEMORIAL AND COMMUNITY CENTER, 1925
Ray Sims of Cornelius & Schooley, Columbus
150 East Columbus Street, Lithopolis
Library and community center; 740/837-4765

Though large additions have sprawled out on both sides, the original Tudor
Revival Wagnalls Memorial is easy enough to identify—look for the stone
tower next to a large gable with half-timbering and an enormous window.
This original section holds an auditorium, a diningroom and kitchen, and
part of the library; features include stained glass and carved wood.

London, Madison County
(Also in Madison County: Nearby Lafayette.
Marysville, north on State Route 38, is also a
companion tour.)

**Access: From I-70, U.S. 42 leads south first to Lafayette (see also), and
then a few miles farther on, to London.**

MADISON COUNTY COURTHOUSE, 1892
George H. Maetzel, Columbus
1 North Main Street/State Route 56 at High Street/State Route 42, NRHP
County courthouse, 740/852-2972

Some ten years ago I wrote about courthouses for *Ohio Magazine*. At that
time I toured about a dozen, and then concluded that of those I'd seen,
Madison County's was my favorite. It has a good site, in a square in the
middle of downtown. It was (and is) well tended. With a dual stairway under
a ceiling vault of colored glass, it has an impressive interior. But what I liked
most was that the building was a community focal point, used for all kinds of
meetings. On election nights, people watch returns posted at the foot of the
great stairway. By now, I've spent over five years focused on architectural
Ohio. I've joined that small, manic circle of people who have laid eyes on all
88 courthouses. So how did Madison County look this time? It's still a
favorite. It was never gutted or altered in a weird way—nor was it restored
with wall panels. I did see dropped ceilings in the offices alongside the
corridors, but the woodwork was all unpainted. The exterior looked good,
and the important spaces inside, the hall and the courtroom, looked
marvelous. The colored glass in the barrel-vault ceiling includes a lot of gold,
which seemed to make the whole interior sunny. The courtroom is two
stories high, with an ornamented ceiling that has deep coves around the sides;
they carried the Second Empire look of the exterior into the courtroom.
Behind the judge's carved bench is a freestanding wooden screen, and in back
of the screen, a row of coat hooks. Sure enough, a black robe hangs on one.
When I was at the Madison County Courthouse in the late 1980s, I met a
prisoner who was restoring woodwork in the Auditor's Office. When we
started to talk I didn't know he was a prisoner, and he had to explain that

▶ MADISON COUNTY COURTHOUSE

that was why he was wearing an orange jumpsuit. He was working off some of his sentence for drunk driving by helping refurbish the courthouse. He told me a courthouse legend. "This land was donated by a family," he said. "And if [the court] ever gives anybody the death penalty, the land reverts. I've just heard that now, so don't mark my word."

J.R. ATCHISON HOUSE, 1891
Elah Terrell, Columbus
165 North Main Street/State Route 56, London
Private house

London has some good houses, one of which is the Atchison House, a wonderful Queen Anne with a tower, an open second-floor porch, variations in the siding and in the windows—rows of square windows appear in the tower's third floor and in the south gable. As a matter of form but without much hope, I asked the owner if she knew who the architect was. And lo, she pulled out the original drawings, on linen, and read off Elah Terrell of Columbus.

Marion, Marion County
(Companion tour: Delaware, south on U.S. 23.)
¶ Marion was the home of President Warren G. Harding, whose front porch was the focus of his successful national campaign in 1920. After Harding died only two-and-a-half years into his term, a memorial was built for him in Marion—a memorial that has fulfilled its planners' hopes by becoming the city's principal architectural landmark.

Access: Marion is west of U.S. 23 and north of Delaware. Exit from 23 at State Route 95; drive west; in town follow signs to the Harding Home, 1891, NHL, NRHP, an Ohio Historical Society museum at 380 Mount Vernon Avenue; 740/387-9630. Continue west on Mount Vernon to Vine; go right/north to Center Street and then left/west to Harding Centre. You'll pass the Marion County Courthouse, 1884, by Toledo's David W. Gibbs; interior was gutted about 20 years ago.

HARDING HOTEL, NOW HARDING CENTRE, 1924
C. William Earle, Indianapolis; 1997, Burris & Behne, Marion
267 West Center Street at Orchard Street, Marion, NRHP
Low-income senior housing

Because it was the president's home town, Marion has the Harding Hotel. Though Harding died before it opened, the eight-story hotel was properly elegant, with stone facing at the base, walls in brown brick, a decorated cornice. It stayed in business for 50 years and then stayed empty for another 23. It reopened in 1997, after rehabbing to provide low-income housing for the elderly. How did this come about? It seems that ten years earlier, Marion City Council had decided to raze the building. When the lowest bid for demolition was $1.2 million, they changed their minds. David A. Schoonover, city service director at the time and now the Harding Centre's assistant manager, says the bid was so high that "even the city government got involved in finding a new use." He describes the $9 million financing package ultimately assembled as the country's largest tax credit project for

▶ HARDING HOTEL

low-income elderly. According to renovation architect Duane Behne, all the upper floors were gutted and rebuilt, though on the original patterns of doors and halls. Most impressive space on the first and second floors is the two-story lobby. Most impressive restoration was the building's windows, which are all separated into small panes by wooden dividers. First the wood was repaired off-site by state prisoners. Then much of the reglazing was done on-site by Marion Correctional inmates. It had to be on-site, Behne says, because glass isn't allowed in the prison.

Access: From Harding Centre go south on Orchard to Church; then turn left/east and in a few blocks turn right/south on State Route 423, which goes to Harding Memorial.

▶ HARDING MEMORIAL

HARDING MEMORIAL, 1927

Henry Hornbostel and Eric Fisher Wood, Pittsburgh; Edward P. Mellon,
architectural consultant, New York
Vernon Heights Boulevard at Delaware Avenue/State Route 423, Marion, NRHP
Presidential tomb; with Harding House, an Ohio Historical Society site

When President Warren Harding died suddenly in late 1923, he was the
most popular president since Lincoln; donations for his memorial flooded in.
So says Robert Rupp, a historian formerly at Ohio State University, Marion.
But then the scandals broke—Teapot Dome and the other bribes, kickbacks,
and dirty dealings by Harding appointees and cronies while he was in office.
A sex scandal came as the final blow. In 1927 Nan Britton published a book
saying she'd had Harding's out-of-wedlock child in 1919. Meanwhile, even as
the late president's reputation spiraled downward, the Harding Memorial
Association managed to put up a Neoclassical Revival memorial worthy of
the most popular president since Lincoln. It's a round colonnade with a fine
ten-acre site, spacious enough for the walkway and grassy mall that provide a
striking diagonal approach from the corner. The Harding Memorial
Association solicited designs from four leading architects—including John
Russell Pope and Paul Philippe Cret—and chose the plan submitted by
Henry Hornbostel and Eric Fisher Wood because it best satisfied Harding's
wishes about his burial. "He wanted a simple grave under an open sky, like a
church yard, with plants," says Phillip Payne, Harding Home and Memorial
site manager in 1997-98. So the round colonnade in white Georgia marble is
open in the center, where the sarcophagi of Warren and Florence Harding
(she died only 15 months after he did) rest amid myrtle and under a tree.
Inside the outer colonnade is another one, C-shaped, with the opening at the
front to give a view of the graves. The inner colonnade is walled on its outer
perimeter, roofed so as to hold plants, and fronted by fluted Ionic columns.
In contrast to the massive, unfluted Doric columns outside, these inner ones

seem diminutive and delicate. Set on stairs, the structure is 103 feet in diameter, 52 feet high. A fence inside the outer colonnade keeps out prospective vandals. Metal used for the fence and plant troughs was aluminum, which wouldn't stain the marble. Though contributions poured in right after Harding's death—school children all over America donated coins—within two years contributions stopped. So the 48-column monument that Hornbostel and Wood originally designed, with one column for every state, went back to the drawing board for a budget-mandated reduction in size. As built, the two colonnades have only 46 columns.

▶ Harding Memorial

Marysville, Union County

(London, south on State Route 38, is a companion tour.)
¶ Between Honda cars and Scott lawn products, Marysville is one Ohio town whose fortunes have been in the ascent. This doesn't mean downtown looks all that fabulous, though the Courthouse, 1883, by David W. Gibbs of Toledo, probably has the best lawn of any in the state. Focus of the commercial downtown is a square at Main and Fifth Streets, between the Courthouse a block to the west and the Liggett Building a block to the east.

Access: U.S. 33 and U.S. 36 run together through the north side of Marysville; for downtown exit at State Route 31 and drive south; road becomes Main Street. From the south State Route 38 leads into downtown and also becomes Main Street.

▶ Liggett Building

LIGGETT BUILDING, 1897
Yost & Packard, Columbus
120-122 East Fifth Street, Marysville, NRHP/Marysville HD
Offices and apartments

Newton Liggett called in central Ohio's best architectural team, Columbus's Yost & Packard, to give him an ambitious building in downtown Marysville, and they delivered. Once construction was finished, Liggett, who owned the local phone company, installed the switchboard and operators on the third floor here, company offices on the second, and his drugstore in one of the two ground-floor stores, while a bank occupied the other. Today Liggett's great-granddaughter, Dorothy Liggett-Pelanda, has her office on the first floor. An attorney, she occupies the law offices her father installed in the late 1960s. She's also the granddaughter of a one-time head operator for the phone company: Tessie Liggett, who married her boss. In the late 1990s Liggett-Pelanda and her co-owner husband, Kevin Pelanda, who's also municipal judge, wanted to restore the building, starting with pulling out her father's 1960s improvements like carpeting over ceramic tile floors and wall paneling. She consulted two architects from Columbus who might shake our faith in all architects, for they didn't like her building; one called it a "sinkhole". Liggett-Pelanda found a local contractor—"someone born and raised here who cares for the building," she says—and work began in fall, 1998, on the first stage: her lobby, office, and conference room. "It just looks beautiful," she said, after the contractor had finished. Her handsome three-story building has a steep roof with stepped gables at the sides and a distinctive third-floor dormer in the middle. Second-floor windows are round-arched; first floor has, under an arched doorway in the middle, a stairway to the upstairs apartments. Materials are terra cotta and light brown brick below a red tile roof; trim is dark red. Why would two architects disparage a Yost & Packard building? Perhaps partly because they didn't know who the architect was, though that shouldn't have mattered because the good design is evident (or should be). Another Columbus architect, Frank Elmer, suggests the reason lies in a longstanding, habitual rejection of old structures by people in his profession. "Since the 1950s," he says, "architects have been saying, 'We all know it costs more to fix an old building than to build a new one.'" And *that* is not normally true.

Mount Vernon, Knox County
(Also in Knox County: Gambier.)
❡ Mount Vernon has two invaluable assets: a central green and a large collection of fine old houses, to which the Knox County CVB, 7 East Ohio Avenue off South Main, 800/837-5282 or 740/392-6102, sells a guide. ❡ In the late 1990s preservation buzz focused on the Woodward Opera House, 1851, the country's oldest theater with an intact (or, partly intact) interior. Backers set out to raise some $4 million for restoring the third-floor theater, and by early 2002 they had about half of what they needed. Goal is reopening in October 2003. Building is at South Main and West Vine, and, as befits an up-to-date old theater, it's on the web: *www.thewoodward.org.*

Access: From Columbus, U.S. 36/State Route 3 goes northeast through Bangs (where the gas company has a facility); about two-and-a-half miles after Bangs take the right fork onto State Route 80/Columbus Road, which connects to South Main Street in Mount Vernon. Drive north on Main past the square to East Lamartine Street. Turn right; Round Hill is at foot of Lamartine facing McKenzie Street.

ROUND HILL, 1859
North McKenzie, Mount
Vernon, NRHP
Private house

▶ ROUND HILL

Approaching Round Hill by
East Lamartine Street, you'll
see the house centered at the
end of the street, set back in a yard that's fronted by two brick pillars. Round
Hill is one of the landmarks of Mount Vernon. Its particular virtue is that
from 1859 to 1996, it hardly changed at all—even the furniture sat around
for decades, passed from one generation of Curtises to the next. The house
was built by Henry B. Curtis's daughter and her husband, who had been
living in New York and brought plans from an architect there. When they
lost their fortune while the house was still under construction, Henry B.
bankrolled completion; from 1871 until his death in 1885, he lived there
himself. An Italian Villa in style, Round Hill has a fourth-floor cupola, a
servants' wing to the north, 12 fireplaces, plaster fretwork, and an
extraordinary 50-foot parlor that runs the full length of the house's south
side. The 1996 purchaser, who got both house and furniture, was a
restoration-minded doctor from Newark.

**Access: Return to Main Street and the Square, and then take East High
Street east. It's a great street for houses.**

G.W. ARMSTRONG HOUSE, 1889

George Franklin Barber, Knoxville
601 East High Street, Mount Vernon, NRHP, East High Street District
Private house

Architect George Franklin Barber published magazines and sold mail-order plans; Queen Anne houses were his specialty. With a corner location, this one is easy to see. It has porches upstairs and down, bays on the side, and a can't-quit exuberance that the paint scheme, in different colors to highlight details, only enhances.

Access: Drive back toward the square and at McKenzie Street, turn left/south to East Gambier Street, then right for Russell-Cooper House.

RUSSELL-COOPER HOUSE, 1830, 1888

115 East Gambier Street, Mount Vernon, NRHP/East Gambier Street District
Bed and breakfast; to see interior spend the night (the B&B is 740/397-8638)
or bring a group for a catered lunch, by reservation only, tour included.

The Russell-Cooper House's facade is full of oversized, unexpected details, such as the etched columns at the corners and on the porch and the enormous, jug-like finials atop the porch. Except for the Federal-style arch over the door, it's all a Victorian creation ordered by Colonel William Cooper, a congressman who returned home to Mount Vernon in 1888. In fact, Colonel Cooper kept making changes until he died in 1902. So says Mary Dvorak, a descendant, who returned in 1995 to run a bed and breakfast. This was her girlhood home. At that time, she says, "It was just a house to me." That was before she'd seen any others.

▶ RUSSELL-COOPER HOUSE

Longaberger

Newark, Licking County

(Also in Licking County: Granville;
together, one of Ohio's best architectural tours.)
¶ Newark—perhaps even to the surprise of most residents—is wonderful for architectural touring; it is one of Ohio's most interesting tours, and combined with nearby Granville it gets even better. Standing on the square in front of the courthouse, you probably won't expect much, but what Newark does have, in a relatively compact area, are lots of very remarkable things: great names (Louis Sullivan and Alexander Jackson Davis: what a bonanza), variety, surprises, and a terrific courthouse.

Access: This tour starts on the east side of Newark, then visits downtown and lastly, the west side. To reach State Route 16 take State Route 161 east from Columbus or State Route 79 north from I-70. On 16 drive to Newark's east side and take Dayton Street exit; Longaberger will be visible.

THE LONGABERGER COMPANY HOME OFFICE, 1997

NBBJ, Columbus, and Korda/Nemeth Engineering, Columbus
1500 East Main Street, Newark
Corporate headquarters; lobby accessible daily for short tours; 740/754-6330

If in 25 years a company can raise sales from six handmade baskets to 7.7 million, it can jolly well have a headquarters building that looks exactly like the product. Or so the late founder Dave Longaberger reasoned; this was his idea. Design professionals equivocated, suggesting an ordinary building with, say, basket pictures or basket skin. But Longaberger wanted the real thing, the exact Medium Market Basket only bigger and weatherproof. He gave sample baskets to the NBBJ architects and the Korda/Nemeth engineers, and dispatched them to their drawing boards. ¶ So now there's a giant basket on Newark's eastern edge, between the company's home town of Dresden to the east and the Columbus airport to the west. It's a seven-story basket, with emulated weaving of basket crosswires—on a basket, supple strips of maple; on the building, stucco—around upright splints. The finished building was painted the color of a finished, varnished basket. It does have some features baskets don't have, like doors and windows. ¶ It was a tricky assignment, in part because the top of a Medium Market Basket is bigger than the bottom. Thus at each floor this structure is 14 inches bigger; dimensions increase from 192 by 126 feet at ground level, to 208 by 142 feet at the roof. Increases are absorbed in the rounded corners; steel rods in the walls provide support.

▶ LONGABERGER

¶ Architecturally, the building's most impressive feature is the 70-ton steel handles, seen from a distance as they soar over the trees. Just like real basket handles, they rest on pins, though here the pins have 8-inch diameters. So that they won't drop ice on the glass atrium skylight underneath, these handles are heated to keep water from freezing. According to Korda/Nemeth's Peter Korda and Nick Constantine, writing in *Structure* magazine, the handles, 331 feet long, are really galvanized steel boxes, 9.5 feet wide and 2.5 feet deep in cross section, with intermittent cross-bracing installed during assembly. Shipped as 13 sections each, the handles were assembled on site, then lifted one at a time by two cranes, and finally welded at the top where they rest against each other. They accounted for $1 million of the $30 million total cost, and bring the building's height to 196 feet. ¶ The interior features a large atrium under an elliptical glass vault. Windows face the atrium, to enhance office lighting; the handles are visible overhead, through the glass. The lobby has groups of livingroom-style furniture, meant to seem homey like Longaberger products. ¶ Did any Ohio building ever generate as much ink as this one has? Within a year the press packet had clips from 19 different publications; besides the likes of *Structure*, they included *People*, *The Wall Street Journal*, and *Architecture*. For a building as sign, the basket succeeded as only Dave Longaberger knew it would.

Access: From Longaberger drive over a mile west on Main Street; at Penney Avenue turn north; at next corner jog right and continue on Penney to house, on right. It's visible also from the adjacent alley.

OAKWOOD, GEORGE W. PENNEY HOUSE, 1851
Alexander Jackson Davis, New York
64-70 Penney Avenue, Newark, NRHP
Private apartments

This Gothic Revival house is a treat especially for architectural historians, for it is Ohio's only work by the renowned Alexander Jackson Davis (1803-1892), and one of only two by him west of the Alleghenies. By the mid-nineteenth century, "Davis was the outstanding American architect of romantic country houses, unsurpassed in his mastery of asymmetrical massing, control of scale and delicacy of detailing." So pronounced Jane B. Davies, the leading Davis authority, in *Master Builders*. ¶ Records from Davis's firm show that the architect corresponded with Newark client

George Washington Penney and then sent plans by mail. Though Davis did not visit Newark, Penney's builder, William A. Boss, called at the architect's New York office in winter, 1851. ¶ Starting in 1839, Davis collaborated with a horticulturist and landscape designer named Andrew Jackson

▶ GEORGE PENNEY HOUSE

Downing (1815-1852). Downing was a great promoter, the publisher of two books of plans for romantic houses that had an enormous influence on American architecture. Most of those houses were designed by Davis, some by Davis and Downing together, and a few by other architects. The Upham-Wright House, also in Newark and described below, is from one of these plan books. ¶ Both Davis and Downing designed the Penney House, though the plans were prepared initially in 1847 for a Massachusetts man who never built it. So Jane Davies wrote in 1979. When George Penney came along, Davis pulled out that unbuilt plan and dispatched it with few alterations. The result, declared historian Davies, is "of national significance." Not only it is a particularly good example of Davis and Downing's collaboration, but also it's the only built example of this particular design. As most joint Davis and Downing designs were in plan books, they were built again and again; being unique is a real distinction. ¶ When Penney built his house, of stucco over brick, it was set on 200 acres. It is known locally for having central Ohio's first bathtub, shipped from Cincinnati. The large property has long since been subdivided into smaller lots, and the house, into apartments. Though the house fell into hard times not long ago—as a drug haven, it was the scourge of the neighborhood—it now appears well kept. Much of the trim on the gables has been lost, as have turrets and tall chimney pots. Diamond-shaped windows appear to be intact.

A 4502 County Court House, Newark, O.

Access: Return to Main Street and continue west to Courthouse Square. Tour the next four downtown sites on foot, starting at the Courthouse; Tiffany's, in a former Louis Sullivan bank, is directly across Third Street from the Courthouse.

LICKING COUNTY COURTHOUSE, 1878

Henry E. Myer, Cleveland
Courthouse Square, at Third and Main Streets, Newark, NRHP
Courthouse; 740/349-6171

Licking County Courthouse is in the middle of Courthouse Square and easy to find because of its high clock tower; it's a Second Empire building that's looking very good indeed. The mix of delicate stone colors is wonderful: reddish-brown sandstone in the raised basement; rough-cut gray limestone on the walls; smooth buff sandstone for the trim. The interior is less ambitious, except for the glorious West Courtroom, which is surely one of my favorites.

It has a domed ceiling, good wooden rails and bench, and a marvelous atmosphere. I know of few other rooms where late nineteenth-century America seems so palpable. Cleveland architect Henry E. Myer (1837-1881) also did the courthouses in Athens, Columbiana, and Muskingum counties, but Robert Keiser of the Cleveland Landmarks Commission knows of no Myer work remaining in his home city.

HOME BUILDING ASSOCIATION BANK, NOW TIFFANY'S ICE CREAM PARLOUR, 1915

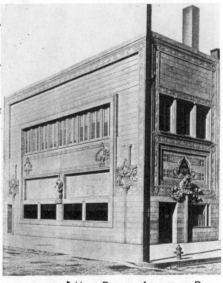

▶ HOME BUILDING ASSOCIATION BANK

Louis Sullivan, Chicago
1 North Third Street at Main,
Newark, NRHP
Former bank, now ice cream
and sandwich parlor; summer
only; 740/349-7566

Toward the end of his career architect Louis Sullivan did eight banks in small Midwestern towns, including two in Ohio: Peoples Savings in Sidney (see also) and Home Building Association Bank in Newark. Peoples, always a bank and always under the same owner, is very well preserved. But the Newark building has changed hands often; now it's an ice cream parlor. Previous owners altered windows, enlarged the door, installed a dropped ceiling in the lobby, drywall over marble walls, and signs over the mosaics outside. Though the signs have been removed, the other changes remain. ¶ Among the Sullivan banks, this one is distinctive in two ways. One is that, because Home Bank had a small lot but wanted lots of space, this structure has two stories and a finished basement and, unlike any of the other banks, second-story windows on the front facade. (The footprint is 60 by a slim 22 feet.) Another distinction is that this bank has gray-green terra cotta siding rather than brick. Sullivan biographer Hugh Morrison complained that the exterior was "cheap", but in her study of the banks, Lauren Weingarden reached a different conclusion. ¶ She pointed out that Sullivan customarily heeded neighboring buildings; in scale and materials his work fits in. In Newark, though Courthouse Square's buildings were mostly red brick Italianates, the courthouse, directly opposite the bank, is gray limestone. Rather than "the subtle integration" with neighboring structures that Sullivan realized elsewhere, here, Weingarden wrote, he chose "a more direct dialogue with the monumental civic centerpiece." Moreover, along with its mahogany benches, ceiling beams, and door, its marble floor and countertop, the Newark bank had brightly colored frescos on the ceiling and upper walls. Weingarden describes them as "patterns of intertwining shields, triangles, spirals, and botanical motifs" that are predominantly brick red, with blue, green, and gold. Whereas most of the banks were red brick outside and green inside, this one used the red inside and a gray-green outside.

▶ HOME BUILDING ASSOCIATION BANK FACADE

Amazingly, those frescos are still there, and still stunning, but hidden by the dropped ceiling. ¶ But the building's exterior is easily seen. Both outside walls have fine mosaic panels; the one on the front includes the architect's name. Both walls also have Sullivanesque terra cotta ornament in swaying stalks and curly leaves, and all the tiles have ornamental edging. ¶ Building owner David Fetter has four ice cream shops in Newark, though this is the only one that's entertained film crews and art students from Cincinnati. In 1996 Fetter spent $14,000 on ten, custom-cast terra cotta blocks to fill in a gap outside; he hoped also to restore mosaics marred by sign supports. He says that items like blueprints, bank benches, and terra cotta blocks removed when the door was widened are in hand. So too are stencils for the ceiling and wall paintings. This building could emerge again, as the work of art it is.

Access: Facing the Sullivan bank front, walk to the right/north half a block to the Arcade. Walk through the Arcade to Fourth Street; then walk half a block right/north to Church Street to see Union Square.

ARCADE, 1908
Arcade Place, Newark
Shops and offices

Between Main and Church Streets, the Arcade runs from Third Street to Fourth. It's a corridor of shops under a glazed roof shaped like an inverted V; metal framing for the glass forms a long series of inverted Vs. Both Third and Fourth Street entrances are labeled "Arcade". The one on Third is stucco; the one on Fourth is red brick with white terra cotta. Shops are mostly rented but the place could be livelier.

UNION BLOCK, NOW UNION SQUARE, 1903, 1904
21-31 West Church Street at Fourth Street, Newark
Ground-floor stores; offices

Actually three buildings that appear to be one, Union Square used to be a
three-story department store. Though brickwork is decorative and the
cornice, elaborate, the architectural highlight is a recessed balcony with
columns, balustrade and ogee arches—the sort of exotica later popular for
movie houses. Co-owner Bob Vela says that African-Americans, barred from
other places, often rented the ballroom where the balcony is. As of late 2001,
he hoped to redo the balcony, which needed redoing. Interior has been
altered. Structure connects to the Arcade.

**Access: From Courthouse Square, drive west on Main Street to Sixth
Street; turn right/north; park in front of historic buildings immediately
on left.**

▶ Union Block

SHERWOOD-DAVIDSON HOUSE, C. 1815

North Sixth Street at West Main, Newark, NRHP
Licking County Historical Society house museum; year-round except January and February; fee; 740/345-4898

This Federal style frame house is nice enough from the front but most interesting around the corner, where the side wall has a recessed two-story porch, with a balcony above and an elliptical arch over all. The side walls in the recess are angled, heightening apparent depth, an example of forced perspective: an illusion. In 1947 the house, threatened with demolition, was moved here from its original site.

▶ SHERWOOD-DAVIDSON HOUSE

Access: Continue north on Sixth Street for several blocks; at Granville Street, turn left/west to see the Upham-Wright House, just after Eleventh Street.

UPHAM-WRIGHT HOUSE, 1851

342 Granville Street, Newark, NRHP
Private house

Exactly contemporary with the Penney House on Newark's east side (above), the Upham-Wright House appeared in one of Andrew Jackson Downing's plan books, *Cottage Residences*. This was Design II, "A Cottage in the English or Rural Gothic Style" and has the book's floorplan too. With every turret and chimney pot intact, this red-brick house looks exactly like the picture in the book. Obviously it's been well tended. Set back on a wooded hill, it's seen more easily in winter. Architectural attributions for the Upham-Wright and Penney houses seem like mirror games. While the Penney House, by architect Alexander Jackson Davis, was based on a plan that Davis and Downing had done together earlier, this one is the opposite, sort of. Downing gets the attribution because it was his book, but in *Master Builders* Jane B. Davies says this design was mostly Davis's. While the Penney House has the virtue of being a unique built example, the Upham-Wright's design has the virtue of being one of the most copied. (See also the Gwynne House in Urbana.)

▶ UPHAM-WRIGHT HOUSE, AS IN PLAN BOOK

CLEVE

90

Oberlin

71

Wellington

Pen

77

Medina

76

Barberton

71

Marshallv

30

Wooster

M

Mansfield

Lucas

Bellville

Perry

Painesville

Jefferson

90

534

West
Andover

Kirtland

Chardon

Hartsgrove

11

North
Bloomfield

Gustavus
Center

Mesopotamia

422

Kinsman

Twinsburg

Hiram

Southington

80

Mantua

Warren

Hudson

Niles

80

Tallmadge

Mineral
Ridge

76

76

Atwater

Alliance

62

30

Hanoverton

30

East Liverpool

Northeast Ohio

At the end of the 1700s, Northeast Ohio was a Connecticut colony, the Western Reserve. In 1796, at the behest of the speculators who had bought the land, General Moses Cleaveland arrived with a team of surveyors. From the Pennsylvania line west to the Cuyahoga River, Cleaveland and his crew laid out five-mile-square townships—not the six miles common elsewhere. Then, after founding Cleveland, the General went back home to the East. He had laid the basic framework for Northeast Ohio as we know it. ¶ It is an Ohio region with a distinctive landscape: a Lake Erie coast of steep bluffs and relatively short, north-flowing rivers. The landscape, points out Ohio State's Douglas Graf, has hills separated by great swales, so that again and again roads offer incredibly long views—vistas that are uncommon elsewhere in the state. ¶ Northeast Ohio also has a distinctive architecture—no other part of Ohio has so much the look of another place. It's seen in the dozens and dozens of towns built by New Englanders who wanted the look of home, towns that together become an architectural ensemble. ¶ Western Reserve towns, Graf says, look like New England except for a difference that 200 years made: streets were not crooked and Medieval, but laid out on rectilinear grids.

But towns had amenities—central greens, with public buildings around, and some of those buildings are very good indeed. They were designed by New England-trained carpenters who used patterns from builder's manuals so extensively that, suggests the University of Notre Dame's Thomas Gordon Smith, the Western Reserve has the country's greatest concentration of designs by New England architect and handbook author Asher Benjamin. The handbooks, Smith says, helped some gifted builders design frontier buildings whose harmony and elegance surpassed the attainments of Benjamin himself. (For more on touring the Western Reserve, see special section beginning on page 143.) ¶ Though Western Reserve towns are the core—and crown—of Northeast Ohio architecture, they are not all there is; for by the late

▶ KINSMAN PRESBYTERIANCHURCH

nineteenth century, Northeast Ohio was industrializing. It became rich, populous, and diverse; today, for better and worse, it is ever more Cleveland's suburban hinterland. But it's a place where people have built octagons and great Victorian houses; where they developed model farms and model schools, built colleges, railway stations, town halls, and cemeteries. And not far from where a splendid classical monument honors the birthplace of a native son President, William McKinley, a water plant proves the consummate skill of an all-but-forgotten native son architect, Charles F. Owsley.

Alliance, Stark County
(Also in Stark County: Canton [Vol. I] and Massillon;
U.S. 62 and U.S. 30 link the three cities.)

**Access: U.S. 62 has a city route into downtown Alliance, where it
becomes State Street. Mount Union College is at Clark Avenue and
West State; Chapman Hall is on campus at the foot of Clark. At the
next corner east, State intersects Union Avenue/State Route 183. Turn
left/north on Union to Glamorgan Castle, on the left/west side in three
quarters of a mile at Glamorgan Street. Take Glamorgan Street to first
right, Haines Avenue, which in about half a mile intersects Market
Street; Haines House is on southeast corner.**

CHAPMAN HALL, MOUNT UNION COLLEGE, 1864
Simeon Porter of Heard & Porter, Cleveland
1972 Clark Avenue, Alliance, NRHP/Mount Union College District
College classroom and office building, usually accessible; 330/821-5320

At least in architectural history circles, Alliance is famous for Eric
Johannesen, who, while based in Cleveland with the Western Reserve
Historical Society in the 1970s and 1980s, became Ohio's preeminent
architectural historian. But before that, starting in the mid-1950s,
Johannesen spent 18 years teaching art at Mount Union College. That gave
him plenty of time to contemplate Chapman Hall, the college's main
building. He concluded that it's "a stylistic summary" of the nineteenth

century's first seven
decades. With its
round-arched
windows, the main
block, he said, is
Romanesque; he
likened it to
Cleveland high
schools Heard &
Porter had done
earlier. But the
turrets are Gothic,
the cupola Colonial
or Greek Revival,
and the cornice
brackets Italianate.
"Oddly enough,"
Johannesen wrote,
"the mixture works,
and has produced
an unusually
impressive building
with a great deal of
dignity." Chapman
has a particularly

▶ CHAPMAN HALL

fine campus setting, at the end of a tree-lined path. Three stories plus a raised basement, it has an octagonal cupola with a round copper-covered dome originally used as an astronomical observatory. It's the old main for this private liberal-arts college, which has 1,700 men and women students. Old main or no, in the mid-1960s Chapman Hall was gutted and modern fireproof construction installed. Johannesen thought the dormers added then were acceptable, but he was unhappy about "massive stone terraces at the entrances to the building, which destroy its nineteenth-century scale." Today, we might lament that interior too. Architect Porter's partner, Charles W. Heard, designed Lake Erie College Hall (see also) in Painesville. The son of Lemuel Porter and the one-time apprentice and son-in-law of Jonathan Goldsmith, Porter and Heard were the scions of Western Reserve architectural tradition.

GLAMORGAN CASTLE, NOW ALLIANCE CITY SCHOOLS, 1908

Willard Hirsch, Searles & Hirsch, Cleveland
200 Glamorgan Street, Alliance,
NRHP
School administration building
open weekdays; brochure for self-guided tour on sale; 330/821-2100

▶ GLAMORGAN CASTLE

Set back 800 feet from Union Avenue, built on raised terraces, Glamorgan Castle is a Jacobean Revival house built of money ($400,000) and Vermont marble by an industrialist, Colonel (honorary) William Morgan. He named it for Glamorganshire, Wales, the birthplace of his father, who came to Alliance and invented the overhead traveling crane. It took 65 railroad cars to bring all Glamorgan's marble from Vermont, where it was cut to specifications. The odd thing is, on the house this marble doesn't look like marble because it has a rough rock-faced finish. It could be any stone. Administrative offices make excellent use of the building, many of whose original features—for instance, the leaded glass in the rotunda dome—are intact.

HAINES HOUSE, 1834, 1842

186 West Market Street, Alliance, NRHP
Private house

This was Eric Johannesen's house, and not surprisingly he picked something interesting for himself. It's a late Federal brick structure that he bought in 1966. The best feature, the original two-story porch, with two pairs of columns at each level, had burned in 1915; Johannesen restored it in 1969. As a young man, Eric Johannesen left Detroit and came to Ohio, where in the 1970s and 1980s he became the state's preeminent architectural historian. He wrote lucidly, prolifically, and insightfully about architecture in all of northern Ohio, from Toledo to Ashtabula County; he wrote about pre-1870 college architecture all over the state. He helped and encouraged others who became preservationists and are still active today. And before he died in 1990 at 63, he prepared the only study ever of an Ohio architectural firm, Cleveland's Walker & Weeks; published posthumously in 1999, this book gave the firm the scholarly recognition it deserved.

Atwater, Portage County

(On Western Reserve church itinerary; for routing,
see Twinsburg, the starting point.)

Access: From I-76 east of Ravenna, exit at State Route 14 and take it a
short distance southeast to State Route 183; turn right/south; for a
very short distance U.S. 224 joins 183; Atwater is just after it turns off.

ATWATER CONGREGATIONAL CHURCH, NOW UNITED CHURCH OF CHRIST, 1841

John Bosworth, Rootstown
1237 State Route 183 at U.S. 224, Atwater, NRHP
Church

Atwater is an out-of-the-way hamlet that's worth the trip because of a church—one of the best in Ohio's Western Reserve. White frame, it's set back on its lawn, the second highest spot in the township, and rises an impressive 112 feet. The best feature is the three-stage tower. The style is a mix: Greek Revival with Gothic Revival windows.
¶ Builder John Bosworth did an apprenticeship in his native New England and then came to Ohio, where he married a Hale, which ultimately rescued him for posterity. His

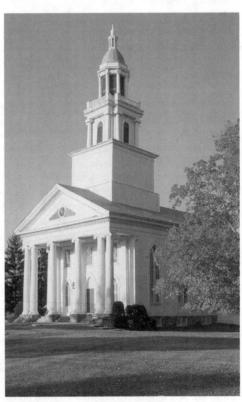

▶ ATWATER CONGREGATIONAL CHURCH

marriage brought him to the twentieth-century attention of John Horton, who did a book on the Jonathan Hale farm, a Western Reserve Historical Society museum in Bath. Horton asserts that Bosworth designed the Atwater church, though it was completed after his death in 1840. Horton also speculates that as a young man, Bosworth worked for Lemuel Porter on Tallmadge church (see also), which would have been good training, indeed. Though Horton and others have suggested that Atwater's tower was added later, that now seems unlikely to Priscilla Graham of Hudson, an authority on Western Reserve architecture. She thinks it was part of the original building. ¶ Bosworth's name is not part of the church's own official history. What the church does have a record of, is, for example, the source of the original lumber and stone: they came from Charleston, east of Ravenna. This history documents some alterations, like replacing the box pews and the original multi-pane windows. It records installing metal sheeting over the shallow, round sanctuary dome in 1899, and removing the metal sheeting for the church centennial. ¶ With the former pastor, Joseph Peters, I went up into the tower. We admired rafters doweled into posts; we passed the bell Peters rang after weddings; at the top we heard birds nearby but unseen. The heavy metal cylinders of a 1930s carillon hung overhead. No longer used, the carillon is left in place because its weight helps stabilize the tower in a strong wind. ¶ Today's congregation is small, with only 40 to 45 people, but they have had a real boost lately in taking care of the church: a large bequest from a former minister. So when I stopped by for a look in fall 2001 I found crews surveying the structure—at that moment men were drilling to check the porch floor's soundness. Board president Jasper Wilhelm, who'd stopped by for a look himself, said the hope was not only to maintain the church's looks but also to draw more people; they were starting with air conditioning. Work was expected to take five to ten years.

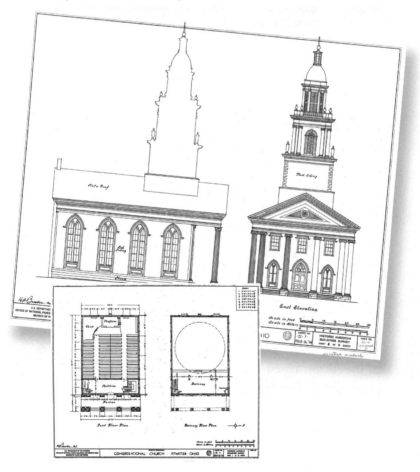

Barberton, Summit County

(Akron [Vol. I] is nearby. Or, see an experimental farm
of later vintage: Malabar Farm, at Lucas in Richland
County.)

¶ Built around Lake Anna and its park, Barberton was a
town planned for both factories and workers' homes. It
had those, but later it also had a model farm developed by
the town founder and Match King Ohio Columbus
Barber. Some of the farm's brick barns still loom in east
Barberton—thanks mostly to Steve Kelleher, who made
saving them a priority when he was too young to know
better. Over a quarter century later, he's still at it.

**Access: To reach Lake Anna, exit from I-76/U.S. 224 at Barber Road
east of Akron; take the road, which in town becomes 4th Street, N.W.,
south to the lake. Brochures, "Historic Downtown Walking Tour" and
"Anna Dean Farm Hike and Bike Tour" are available from City Planning, Municipal Building, on the south side of Lake Anna; 330/848-
6729.**

Barberton Plat

On a fine May day in Barberton, I stood at the edge of
Lake Anna and took a picture. It shows the lake, shimmering, blue and serene, with three swans, speck-like, in
the middle. Taken from under a tree whose leaves arch
overhead, the picture shows the lake entirely embraced by
greenery. It is an exquisite scene, a jewel in the center of a
small industrial city. ¶ Barberton was a town planned for
factories and workers' houses. Unlike its famous contemporary, Pullman, Illinois, Barberton was never a one-
company town, though it was dominated by one man,
Ohio Columbus Barber. He was the Match King, founder
of the Akron-based Diamond Match Company, which
produced 85 percent of America's matches and gave him
the wherewithal to dabble in a planned town. Barber
owned Barberton's site, 550 acres served by four railroads
and a canal. He gave the town his name and then, by
endowing it with the factories of companies he con-

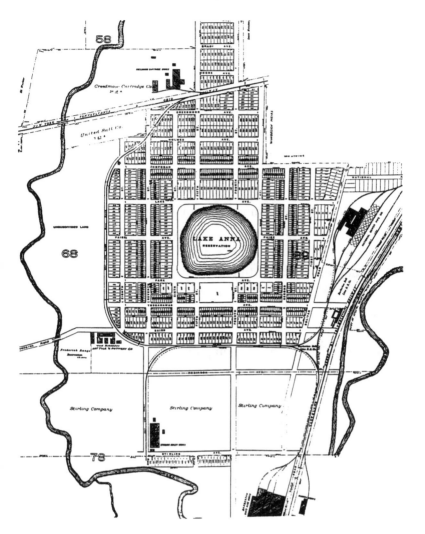

trolled, he gave it a future. In the spirit of the 1890s, when "town booming" was popular, Barberton was founded to make money. It did, at least after 1900, when it grew so fast it was called Magic City. ¶ The man who laid out the town was a civil engineer for the Pennsylvania Railroad, W.A. Johnston. He arrived in late 1890 and remained until his death in 1946; after the town was established he went into real estate. In 1925 Johnston recalled his first sight of the place: "After breakfast, I walked over the land which was to be surveyed for the new town of Barberton. I was agreeably surprised and encouraged to find such a fine layout. A beautiful ten-acre lake with sloping, grassy banks and fine big maple and oak trees was located approximately in the center of the large tract of level land." ¶ The lake was natural, an Ohio rarity: a kettle lake left by the glaciers and renewed by springs. Named Lake Anna for Barber's daughter, it is roughly circular. Johnston set it in a 22-acre square that is as fine a central ornament as a city could wish for. Two walks encircle it, one a sidewalk, the other a path along the lake's edge. At one corner a bathhouse serves a beach. In winter the pond freezes for ice skating. ¶ Houses and churches line three sides of the square; the fourth, on the south, has a funeral home, fraternal lodges, the Municipal Building, and the library. The commercial street, Tuscarawas Avenue, is a block south. Johnston assigned factories to an area starting about a quarter mile from the park. Where the Municipal Building is now, he originally put the Barberton Inn, a classy hotel that opened in 1895 and closed 20 years later. ¶ When the Panic of 1893 hit Pullman, Illinois, the founding proprietor, George Pullman, lowered wages and kept rents high; the ensuing riots gave all company towns a bad name. Compared to Pullman, Ohio Columbus Barber was a softie. When the Panic of 1893 hit Barberton, purchasers kept their homes without payments, and rents weren't collected. Then Barber shored up the eroding industrial base by moving in the Diamond Match works. Production stayed until 1958, when it left for another Diamond plant in California.

Barberton Barns Tour

When Diamond Match King Ohio Columbus Barber planned his model farm in 1909, he was not about to settle for conventional barns. He wanted something really special—buildings that, as he wrote, "from standpoints of both efficiency and architectural beauty, are unsurpassed by those on any farm in the world."

Though these barns were built to last, Anna Dean Farm endured only until Barber's death in 1920. Its legacy was not in agricultural breakthroughs, as Barber expected, but in buildings that aimed to be globally unsurpassed. Half a dozen of the farm's large, elaborate brick and concrete structures, most originally barns, survive in east Barberton. They are listed on the National Register of Historic Places and are attributed to Akron architects Harpster & Bliss.

Every year at 1:30 on the Sunday after Mother's Day, the Barberton Historical Society offers a free three-hour tour of the barns.

▶ PIGGERY

**Access: To reach the barns from Lake Anna in downtown Barberton, go
one block south to Tuscarawas Avenue; take it left/east across the
Tuscarawas River. Right away turn south/right on Van Buren Avenue to
Robinson; Piggery is visible at corner. Turn left/east on Robinson;
Heating House is opposite 4th Street.**

1) Piggery, 1912: With its central pavilion and long wings, this is one of the most
splendid surviving barns. It housed pigs only until 1915, when a cholera epidemic
wiped out the herd. Since 1965 it's been owned by a Barberton lawyer, Alex
Naumoff. After his retirement in 1996, Naumoff began renovations for a
restaurant.

2) Heating House, 1910: The boiler here heated the world's largest greenhouse
complex, which had 12 acres under glass. The Barberton Historical Society owns
the building, but its reuse is up in the air.

**Access: To see Brooder Barn, drive south from Robinson on 1st Street
to Quincy Avenue. To reach others, drive south from Robinson on 5th
Street. First turn right on Portsmouth for Barn No. 1/Yoder Brothers
and adjacent Creamery, 1909, which is now apartments. Continue south
on 5th to Austin Drive and turn left/east; drive half a mile to Colt Barn.**

3) Brooder Barn, 1910: The Historical Society hopes someday to see an employer
move into the Brooder Barn, which once housed 50,000 hens. The society, which
owns this building too, hoped to finish a full renovation in 2002.

4) Barn No. 1, now Yoder Brothers, 1909: This barn, which now houses private
corporate offices, has been the Barberton Historical Society's biggest success
story, for its renovation not only saved the building, but kept 90 jobs in town. The
only surviving Anna Dean Farm building with towers, Barn No. 1 has three of
them: two 40-foot silos on the west side and a 60-foot silo with an arcaded
observation platform on the east. The building looks so good because, while
transforming it into their headquarters, Yoder Brothers lavished $1.9 million on it.

5) Colt Barn, 1910: This is the only Anna Dean Farm building that retains its
original interior. Another Historical Society property, it's used for storage.

▶ COLT BARN

BARN CITY—Among historical societies, Barberton's is an original. For one thing, it was founded by youths. They were a group of University of Akron students, all Barbertonians, eager to block the demolition of a Barber Farm barn. Ultimately, they succeeded, and extended their interest to other Barber barns as well. Of the six large barns that were standing in 1974, the historical society saved four, and only one was demolished, in 1979. The Historical Society knew what it was doing. These farm structures are both fabulous and unique.

Town founder Ohio Columbus Barber—his real name; his friends called him "Hi" or "O.C."—who made his fortune in matches, developed the farm in the dozen years before his death in 1920. Meant to promote scientific agriculture, it was his retirement project; he poured money into his 3,500 acres, and they blossomed forth with fig trees, golden pheasants, and buildings.

Between 1909 and 1912, he built 34 large farm buildings and an even more splendid mansion. "Experts," says Steve Kelleher, president of the Barberton Historical Society, "go crazy when they see these barns. It's as if they came across some Aztec ruins." The experts are impressed by the barns' size, their 17-inch concrete block walls faced with brick, concrete quoins, towers, dormers, red tile roofs. They are like nothing else on earth.

Just east of the city he founded and gave his name to, Barber's Anna Dean Farm was named for his daughter and son-in-law, who lived in Chicago and chafed while the old man squandered much of their inheritance on soil enrichment and pedigreed cattle. On Sundays as many as 2,000 people came to marvel at the farm, which included what was at the time the world's largest cattle barn—just shy of 800 feet long with two 100-foot silos. (It burned down in the 1950s.) The mansion had a mile-long drive through its 35-acre front yard, a path to a lake, wild roses and honeysuckle, and pergolas with hanging grapes.

Just before the mansion was razed in 1965, Stephen Kelleher, a boy who lived nearby, was among the 50,000 people who lined up to see the inside. He remembers most the tufted velvet elevator. But to Kelleher, the loss of the mansion made the barns all the more important. In high school, he took his future wife to the barns to board up windows. At 21 he enlisted the help of the Ohio Historical Society to put five barns on the National Register of Historic Places.

In 1974, Barn No. 1's site was proposed for a nursing home. The fledgling society collected 3,000 protest signatures, which the city administration ignored. So Kelleher and society vice-president Bob Snyder met with the Akron Metropolitan Housing Authority, which planned to spend Federal money on the nursing home. Kelleher asked the functionary if he was aware of a law barring the use of federal funds to demolish a historical building. Then, he recalls, "The fellow looked at me and said, 'Who'd throw old ladies out of a nursing home?' I looked him in the eye and said, 'I would.'"

It didn't come to that, for the nursing home was built on an adjacent site. Then the historical society optioned the barn for $90,000, a nervy move because it had only $150 for the first month's option payment. For a year it made the payments, until the barn was out of danger. In spite of prodigious attempts, the society couldn't raise the $90,000. But the $11,500 they did raise bought another farm building, the Colt Barn. With help from the Ohio Historical Society and the city, they refurbished it.

When Ramsey Yoder saw the spruced-up Colt Barn, it looked so good that he began to think his company might move to a Barber farm building. As head of Yoder Brothers, the world's leading chrysanthemum propagator, Ramsey Yoder knew a Barber barn would be especially appropriate for his company. It was founded by two brothers—one Ramsey's grandfather—who worked on Barber's farm and went into business by buying the greenhouses from the estate. Though by now all Yoder Brothers' greenhouses have relocated to warmer places, the headquarters remain in Barberton.

In 1981, when Yoder became interested in Barn No. 1, Kelleher stepped in as volunteer mediator during a year of secret negotiations between the Cleveland owner and the Barberton mum growers. He was a volunteer not only because he wasn't paid, but also because no one ever asked him to take part. When Yoder Brothers moved into the completely renovated Barn No. 1 in 1985, Kelleher felt his finest moment had come: he had realized the one accomplishment his obituary would surely mention. He was 32 at the time.

After that, the Barberton Historical Society's radical days were over; the society had gained credibility and respect. So had the barns. A bank and a new McDonald's appeared with brick siding and concrete quoins. City hall had new blood—a government Kelleher called a "hip young administration, sympathetic to historic preservation." In the late 1990s a new high school was built in what Kelleher calls the "Barber style"—more authentic than McDonald's because the society had some design input.

But after 1985, in spite of Kelleher's ongoing activism, real progress on reusing Barber barns stopped. By early 2002, the society owned, besides the Colt Barn, two vacant barns. Even though no tenants were in sight, one was almost completely renovated.

"We've fallen back a few furlongs," Kelleher said. "But I've always viewed this as a very long-term situation."

▶ BELLVILLE BANDSTAND

Bellville, Richland County

(Also in Richland County: Malabar Farm at Lucas, Bellville, and Mansfield make a loop tour. See routing at Lucas.)

Access: The bandstand is in a park at the junction of Main Street/State Route 13 and Church Street/State Route 97.

BANDSTAND, 1879

William Lash, Bellville and Cleveland
Bellville Park, Bellville, NRHP
Bandstand

Not only did G.E. Kidder Smith include the Bellville bandstand in his two-volume 1981 survey of American architecture, but he pronounced that "it may well be the best bandstand in the country. Pure delight." The bandstand is octagonal, with eight posts, a hip roof in eight segments, and an octagonal cupola on top. The detailing is fancy, an exuberant carpenter Gothic with swirls, curls, and latticework; here no bracket is a mere support. The diameter is about 12 feet; the height, 20 feet. The structure is painted white, though it's said to have been in contrasting colors initially. Today it is used on holidays, but not for its original purpose. Says village administrator Charles Pfoutz, "We don't have the bands that we used to have." When Medina wanted a bandstand for its square in the 1970s, it copied Bellville's exactly.

East Liverpool, Columbiana County

(Also in Columbiana County: Hanoverton, northwest
via U.S. 30.)

¶ East Liverpool is an Ohio River town once famous for
pottery; some is still made here. Downtown, still blessed
with some life, has three worthy buildings within a few
minutes' walk of each other. Also in the neighborhood,
the East Liverpool Historical Society runs a house museum in a handsome Italian Villa. It's the C.C. Thompson
House, 1876, at 305 Walnut Street near East Fourth;
open by appointment; 330/385-2550.

**Access: East Liverpool is on State Route 7, which connects with I-80
to the north and I-70 to the south. From either direction follow signs
for downtown; tour sites are all east of Market Street a few blocks in
from the river. Start this walking tour at the bank, on the southeast
corner of East Fifth and Washington. The old Post office is a block and
a half east on Fifth at Broadway; and the library, on East Fourth at
Broadway.**

POTTERS BANK & TRUST CO.,
NOW NATIONAL CITY BANK, 1925

Weary and Alford Co., Chicago
200 East Fifth Street, East Liverpool, NRHP/East Fifth Street HD
Private bank; open during
business hours; 330/385-0450

The National Register lists
three bank buildings in East
Liverpool with Potters in their
name—a clue to where the
money was. This Potters
National Bank must have
attracted potters who
particularly appreciated
elegance. Stone and terra
cotta, Beaux Arts Classical, it
has high round-arched
openings on both street
facades. Although the exterior

▶ POTTERS BANK

is lovely, that the interior is largely intact comes as a delightful surprise. This
two-story banking room has a coffered ceiling, fluted pillars, and a profusion
of decorative swags, eggs and darts, and stylized flowers. Potters National
Bank was founded in 1881. It became Potters Bank & Trust after a merger in
the 1930s and now is part of National City Bank.

Post Office, East Liverpool, Ohio.

U.S. POST OFFICE, NOW MUSEUM OF CERAMICS, 1909
James Knox Taylor, supervising architect, Treasury Department, Washington
400 East Fifth Street, East Liverpool, NRHP
Ohio Historical Society museum; open March-November Wednesday-Sunday; fee;
330/386-6001

One thing about post offices, Ohio State's Douglas Graf points out, is that they're not unique. It hardly matters, for in the late nineteenth and early twentieth century, the government embellished the downtowns of places large and small with exceptionally handsome post offices. After World War II, many were abandoned for new, architecturally indifferent facilities on the community's outskirts. Attempts at reuse have had mixed results; East Liverpool is lucky that the state bought this one for an Ohio Historical Society museum. Opened in 1980, the Museum of Ceramics celebrates the city's historic pottery industry. The entry, in a projecting circular corner of the building, faces down Fifth Street. The two adjacent walls have high round-arched windows, like the bank's above; a low balustrade tops the cornice. All this is in white granite and limestone; style is Beaux Arts. Inside, under its round-vaulted ceilings, the

▶ Museum of Ceramics

old post office lobby now accommodates museum exhibits. Downstairs there's a small library that has 1887-1903 bound volumes of an East Liverpool newspaper with a wonderful name: *The Daily Crisis.*

CARNEGIE PUBLIC LIBRARY, 1902

A.W. Scott, East Liverpool
219 East Fourth Street, East Liverpool, NRHP
Public library; open daily (closed Sunday in summer); 330/385-2048

For a city of 13,600 people, East Liverpool has a surprisingly large and monumental library; it almost has courthouse pretensions. The explanation is that benefactor Andrew Carnegie had happy memories of youthful days in East Liverpool. Born in Scotland, young Carnegie lived with his parents near Pittsburgh. But for several years he came to East Liverpool for his two-week summer holiday at the home of his uncle, "Squire" Morris. With his cousins and friends, Carnegie would row across the Ohio River to raid West Virginia melon patches—a memory the philanthropist still savored when he was doling out his fortune. Thus in 1899 East Liverpool received one of the very first Ohio library grants, and, given the size of the place, an exceptionally generous one of $50,000. The city was able to build something spacious enough that, unlike the typical Ohio library, it hasn't been encumbered with additions. Nor has it been altered much. The city seems to value what it has.
¶ The two-story Italian Renaissance Revival building is in brown brick with cream-colored terra cotta trim. The most spectacular feature is the large central dome covered in red tiles and topped with a small white cupola.

▶ CARNEGIE LIBRARY

Inside, though the ceiling isn't open to the dome, the center hall has a lovely tile mosaic floor, overlooked by a circular balcony on the second floor.
¶ Youngstown architect Charles H. Owsley, who was trained in England, is usually credited with this library. But Chleo Deshler Goodman's 1962 history of the library describes the design competition in detail. She says that though Owsley was expected to win because he had a friend on the board, in a blind judging he lost out to a local architect, A.W. Scott. Doug Graf sees the library's facade as "awkward and naive", adjectives not likely to apply to Owsley's work. ¶ Communities receiving Carnegie library grants had to provide a site, as East Liverpool did. Recipients also had to promise annual tax revenues equal to 10 percent of the grant for maintenance, but only $3,000, or 6 percent, was required of East Liverpool. Even so, some East Liverpudlians were not content. Before construction, a group wrote to Carnegie asking for more money so as to include a ceramic art school. The request was denied.

Hanoverton, Columbiana County
(Also in Columbiana County: East Liverpool, east on
U.S. 30.)

**Access: Hanoverton is at the junction of U.S. 30 and State Route 9; a
block east of the intersection, Plymouth Street extends north from U.S.
30. A walking tour brochure is available from Jane Wilson of the
Hanover Township Historical Society, 330/223-1101; Spread Eagle
Tavern is open to the public, 330/223-1583**

PLYMOUTH STREET, 1817-1900,
HANOVERTON CANAL TOWN DISTRICT

Plymouth Street has a narrow roadway under the arching branches of maple
trees, with rows of brick houses alongside, abutting the brick sidewalks. The
two-story Federal houses, red brick with white trim, date from 1817-1840;
they are a type uncommon in Ohio. Here they become an architectural
ensemble, in which individual buildings that by themselves are nice but
unremarkable, enhance one another to become something special. Named
originally for Hanover, Pennsylvania, this village was founded by people who
also brought the early nineteenth-century mid-Atlantic look. Except for the
Queen Anne Presbyterian Church built in 1900, Federal style buildings
dominate Plymouth Street. The best house, with stepped gables and some
fancy windows, is the 1837 Spread Eagle Tavern; it's been altered somewhat.
The oldest brick house, 1817, is at the northwest corner of the Howard
Street intersection. An underground railway tunnel is said to connect that
house and the row houses (in spite of the four doors, just two families live
there) across the street.

▶ HANOVERTON

How a Waterless Canal Led to a Republican Mecca—

Hanoverton seems like a real-life American dream. The first time I was there was a summer afternoon when children seemed to be everywhere, even in a pick-up baseball game in a field, and Main Street was draped in red, white and blue bunting. At least a dozen people ambled up the middle of the street, where I began talking to one, a bespectacled man wearing a striped business shirt, a tie, and a name tag that read Sam Miller. He explained that Pat Buchanan had just made a speech—it was August, 1995, and Buchanan was running for President—and everyone was coming back from the rally.

Hanoverton also had campaign appearances by Jack Kemp, Dan Quayle, and, several times, then Governor George Voinovich. Having architectural tunnel vision, I assumed the Republicans were attracted by the conservative, old-style buildings. Not necessarily, said Miller. In 1990 Peter and Jean Johnson of Salem bought Plymouth Street's best house, built in 1837 and the only one with three stories. The Johnsons turned it into an inn and restaurant, the Spread Eagle Tavern. As their son David Johnson is the Columbiana County Republican chairman, he's the one who puts Hanoverton on the campaign circuit. The visitors, says Johnson, are always astounded. "They can't believe this place is nestled into the middle of nowhere."

Sam Miller, born in 1920, has spent all his life in this village; since he was three he's lived in the same 1860 frame house, across the street from the Spread Eagle. Until 1970 Miller and his wife Millie ran a grocery store; then retired to see the world. When not abroad in summer, they sit on their front porch and keep an eye on

▶ HANOVERTON

Plymouth Street, which is a quarter mile long—both ends, Miller points out, are dead ends.

Hanoverton did have a heyday, albeit in the 1830s, when in 1834 construction began on the Sandy and Beaver Canal. George Sloan, the Irish-born developer who built Plymouth Street's brick row house with four doors, also laid out the nearby community of Dungannon for the Irish laborers who spent three years carving a 2700-foot tunnel out of rock east of Hanoverton. Between the tunnel and the 1837 panic, which halted construction for a while, it was 1848 before the canal opened south of town, where U.S. 30 is today. But this was the high point on the canal route, and water reserves never were adequate. After a few years, the Sandy and Beaver closed for want of water.

Once the canal failed and the railroad bypassed Hanoverton, the village languished, saving its houses for the new heyday of Republican rallies. Unlike most voters, Hanovertonians have hobnobbed with headliners. The day after Pat Buchanan's visit, a picture of Sam, Millie, and Buchanan made the front page of Lisbon's *Morning Journal*. Right in front of the Millers' house, candidates are forever pausing to give a speech, which Sam views as a momentous announcement of what they'll do in the future. Perhaps one of these days, they'll propose making more Hanovertons.

Hiram, Portage County

(Also in Portage County: Mantua, which is closest, and Atwater, which is on the Western Reserve Church tour; routing at Twinsburg.)

Access: From State Route 82 between Hiram and State Route 44, turn north on Sheldon Road; take first right onto Allyn Road and drive about a mile and a quarter to monastery, on right and marked by sign. Phone before visiting. St. John's has two driveways. To see St. Lazarus Chapel, park at first and walk in on path beyond gate.

ST.LAZARUSCHAPEL, ST. JOHN'S ORTHODOX MONASTERY, 1988

5862 Allyn Road, near Hiram
Private Orthodox chapel; call ahead so monks will
expect visitors on the property. Chapel is locked
but interior may be seen by prearrangement;
330/274-2052

▶ St. Lazarus chapel

Two Portage County churches are in this guide. One, at Atwater, dates from 1841; the other, this chapel, was built almost 150 years later. Both churches are in rural locations, but while the large one at Atwater dominates the center of a town that never amounted to much, this tiny monastery chapel was deliberately isolated in a clearing in the woods.
¶ The abbot of St. John's Monastery, Father Alexander, a tall, imposing figure with all-black garments and a contrasting white beard, talks like Chicago, where he grew up. As we walked through the woods to the chapel, he told me its octagonal layout is an early Christian tradition, while the pointed roof is tent-like, in a Russian tradition. Originally an architect drew the plans, but the Amish carpenter and the monks agreed to eliminate the architect's flying buttresses on the roof and to incorporate gables on four of the eight sides—the four gables and the eight sides all have religious significance. ¶ With each side only about 8 to 9 feet, the chapel is diminutive; so is the copper-clad onion dome atop the roof. Walls and roof are cedar shingles; the interior is pine with beechnut wall paneling. Underneath, 13 cement pillars provide support and leave the wooden floor free to vibrate like a sounding board when people sing. Acoustics, says Father Alexander, are very fine. ¶ This small monastery moved into a one-time farm and former old folks' home in 1981. Part of the Orthodox Church in America, once the Russian Orthodox Church, the monks support themselves by making candles and selling incense. Their main chapel is in a wing of the house; St. Lazarus is secondary, used for evening prayers in summer. It has no plumbing or electricity; but it has so many angles that the Amish carpenter could dream of little else when he was working on it.

Hudson, Summit County

(On Western Reserve church tour; for routing, see Twinsburg.)

¶ With its traditional interest in its historic buildings, Hudson is as much the capital of Ohio's Western Reserve as any one place. And the town's highlight is the Western Reserve Academy campus and its fine Brick Row of buildings dating as far back as 1830.

¶ There's no doubt that the Academy values what it has, for in May 2000 trustees turned down a $6 million gift for a new administration build-ing—because it would block the view of Brick Row from Main Street. The prospective benefactor, the Burton D. Morgan Foundation, wouldn't consider an alternative site, so the school, responding to protests from 120 residents and alumni, passed up what would have been the area's largest single donation ever. For *aesthetics*.

▶ ACADEMY CHAPEL

Access: Hudson's green is between Main (the name downtown for State Route 91) and East Main Streets, just north of the intersection of 91/Darrow Road and U.S. 303/Streetsboro Road. A few blocks farther north, Western Reserve Academy is one block east of 91, at the foot of Chapel Street on College Street.

WESTERN RESERVE COLLEGE CHAPEL, NOW WESTERN RESERVE ACADEMY CHAPEL, 1836

Attributed to Isaac Damon, Northampton, Massachusetts
135 College Street at the foot of Chapel Street, Hudson, NRHP
Chapel, assembly hall, offices for private secondary school; 330/650-4400

Approach Western Reserve Academy on Chapel Street, and you'll see the Chapel straight ahead in the distance. Central in the Brick Row of buildings, framed by trees, facing across a green, the Chapel has a site that displays it for the fine building that it is. Built in a transitional Federal and Greek Revival style, it's red brick, three stories, with a three-part white tower above. The chapel occupies the two upper floors, while the ground level, formerly classrooms and library, is now offices. ¶ Priscilla Graham, a local architectural historian, has figured out—at least to her satisfaction—that Captain Isaac Damon, a Massachusetts architect, designed the Chapel. It's the tower that decided her, for it has three boxy sections, with a clock in the middle and the belfry in the lowest, which is uncommon. (Graham is sure where the bell is, because she herself climbed up to look.) In the mid-1830s, Damon was the best known church architect in Connecticut and western Massachusetts, and he did many plans by mail. Detective Graham has junketed around New England looking at Damon churches. She found that all have towers of boxes

rather than steeples, and all have the belfry in the lowest section, which she says is a Damon trademark. "Stylistically," she says, "I'm on firm ground." ¶ Architect Simeon Porter, son of the renowned Western Reserve architect Lemuel Porter, usually gets credit for the Chapel.

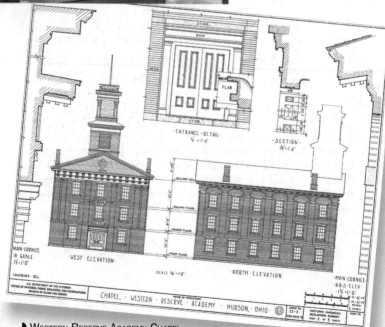

▶ WESTERN RESERVE ACADEMY CHAPEL,
PLANS AND INTERIOR

Graham disputes that. Simeon, still in his 20s, was too young, too provincial, and working only in wood when the Chapel was built. What Graham doesn't have is proof that Damon did the job, but she's confident that someday she'll find it ("I feel like Woodward and Bernstein.") For sure, it hasn't turned up in school records. "The architect wasn't what was important," she explains. "It was the trustees or who was on the building committee." ¶ Part of the dream of town founder David Hudson, Western Reserve College opened in 1826, offering classes for 11 college-level and eight preparatory students. It was modeled on Yale, and many faculty were Yale graduates. Before the end of the century the college moved to Cleveland, and its campus became the Western Reserve Academy, with some 360 boarding and day students today. ¶ To see more at Western Reserve Academy: The Brick Row. The Academy office has a campus "Walking Guide" brochure; 330/650-4400.
¶ According to Priscilla Graham, the Brick Row is one of the two oldest planned brick collegiate rows in the country. "It's pretty exciting," she says, "that this sits out here at this little prep school." ¶ The Brick Row starts at the north, just below Hudson Street, with the President's House, 1830, by Lemuel Porter (1775-1829), who learned his craft in his native Connecticut. The next building is North Hall, 1837, built from a mail-order plan from New England. Next is the Chapel, above. After that comes Seymour Hall, built in 1913 to replace two early buildings. The last building is a new (2000) library whose chief architectural virtues are its conforming scale and red brick. Finally, at 94 College Street near the south edge of the green, there's a cunning little structure with a green dome: Loomis Observatory, 1838, by Simeon Porter (1807-1871) and Professor Elias Loomis. It's the second oldest observatory in the country. Hudson Street, just north of the green, has a row of restored nineteenth-century houses reserved for faculty.

▶ CHAPEL INTERIOR

Access: The Seymour House is half a block north of campus, between College and Main Street on Prospect Street. Aurora Street is at the downtown green's north end. Tour brochures are available at the Hudson Library and Historical Society, 22 Aurora Street, 330/653-6658.

NATHAN SEYMOUR HOUSE, 1843
Simeon Porter and Archibald Elijah Rice, Hudson
15 Prospect Street, Hudson, NRHP/Hudson HD
Academy guest house

The Nathan Seymour House is a brick Greek Revival and, Priscilla Graham says, the best work in Hudson by Simeon Porter. Rice was an established architect from Waterbury, Connecticut, who helped the young Porter work in brick; after a few years, Rice returned to New England. Years later, in 1853, when he was practicing in Cleveland, Porter also did the Anson A. Brewster Mansion at 9 Aurora Street at the north end of the green. It's a stone Gothic Revival house that looks like a small castle.

WHEDON-FARWELL HOUSE, 1826, 1870s

Lemuel Porter, Tallmadge
30 Aurora Street, Hudson, NRHP/Hudson HD
Private apartments

Benjamin Whedon's house began as an exceptionally good Federal house by Lemuel Porter; flush-matched siding on all sides was a rarity. Cupola, brackets, and porch were added to modernize the place in the 1870s. Priscilla Graham reports that the interior has an original barrel ceiling, two decorative plaster ceilings, elaborate moldings and mantels, but is not accessible to the public.

Jefferson, Ashtabula County

(Jefferson is on the Western Reserve rural loop tour; for routing see Western Reserve, pages 143-145.)
¶ Though it's the seat of Ashtabula County, Ohio's biggest in area, Jefferson is a small place, with 3,572 people in 2000. The original owner of the township, Gideon Granger, postmaster general of the United States during Thomas Jefferson's administration, laid out Jefferson in 1805, when only a single cabin occupied the site. Granger ambitiously gave his community eight squares at intersections—the largest, at Market and Jefferson Streets, measured 363 by 627 feet. But, says County Engineer John Smolen, when it came time to build a courthouse the highest place in town seemed like a better site, and that was at Jefferson and Chestnut, a block west of the biggest square. Today two of Granger's eight squares survive: the biggest one, and the one where the courthouse is.

Access: To reach Jefferson, drive south from I-90 on State Route 46.

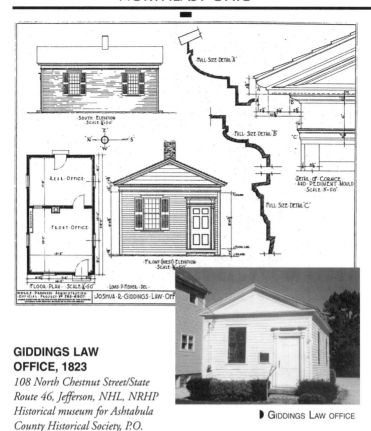

South Elevation · Scale ¼" = 1'-0"

Full-Size Detail 'A'

Full-Size Detail 'B'

Full-Size Detail 'C'

Detail of Cornice and Pediment Mould · Scale 3" = 1'-0"

Floor Plan · Scale ¼" = 1'-0"

Front (West) Elevation · Scale ¼" = 1'-0"

Works Progress Administration · Official Project № 765-6907 · Lows P. Fisher · Del. · JOSHUA R. GIDDINGS LAW OFFICE

▶ GIDDINGS LAW OFFICE

GIDDINGS LAW OFFICE, 1823

108 North Chestnut Street/State Route 46, Jefferson, NHL, NRHP Historical museum for Ashtabula County Historical Society, P.O. Box 36, Jefferson 44047; or 440/466-7337 from June–August

With its good proportions and molding on the doorway, this small building has a dignity that belies its size. Early nineteenth-century doctors and lawyers often built themselves little office buildings like this one. Here the 16-by-28-foot structure has two rooms: an office in front and a consulting room in back. Lawyer Joshua Giddings and his family lived next door, in a house that burned down in the 1870s. ¶ Joshua Giddings was an outspoken abolitionist congressman, serving in the U.S. House of Representatives for two decades before the Civil War, from 1838 to 1859. The son of an improvident farmer, he taught himself to read and write, solicited lessons in Latin from a minister, and then traveled to Canfield to study law with Elisha Whittlesey. ¶ When this office was built in 1823, Giddings was 28 and had been practicing in Jefferson for a year. In this building he wrote the Republican Party's first national platform, adopted in Philadelphia in June, 1856. His law office, a National Historic Landmark, is also a museum run by the Ashtabula County Historical Society, which bought it in 1956. ¶ The building has never been moved, but as of 2001 the foundation needed major repairs. The society planned to make them and to repaint before the 2003 bicentennial. Through the mid-1990s the museum curator was Judge Robert S. Wynn, who described being curator as largely a matter of having a key. A lawyer and part-time county-court judge, Wynn would occupy the museum for a couple hours some summer Sundays. If no one stopped in, he kept busy reading a biography of Giddings. Wynn confessed he started this book several times and finished it only once. "It bogs down at the end," he explained.
¶ Museum contents include Giddings's safe and his high desk—high because he used it while standing and he stood over 6 feet 2.

Kinsman, Trumbull County

(See Western Reserve for rural loop tour including Kinsman, pages 143-145.)

¶ John Kinsman, a former Connecticut legislator, owned Kinsman Township, where he settled in 1798, his family following in 1804. Richard Webb, an antiques dealer who lives in Kinsman, says John Kinsman made many trips back to New England, taking money from land sales to his creditors and returning with stock for a small store. He died, at 60, in 1813. His widow, Rebecca, 20 years younger, turned out to be a savvy lady, respectfully called Madame by all. She managed her money well, gave Western Reserve College a contribution that saved the institution, and in the 1830s funded a big chunk of Kinsman's new church.

Access: Kinsman, just below State Route 87, is on State Route 7, which intersects I-80 to the south and I-90 to the north. West of State Route 7, State Street also runs north-south; the Allen House is on State just north of 87. The church is on Church Street between State and State Route 7.

DR. PETER ALLEN HOUSE, 1821

Willis Smith, builder, Kinsman
8581 State Street just north of State Route 87, Kinsman, NRHP
Private house, though dinner-tours or tours for a fee may be arranged; 330/876-2931

The Dr. Peter Allen House is one of Ohio's great early houses. Federal style with Greek Revival proportions, it's renowned especially for its carving, including some readily visible on the facade. The wood siding was laid flush on the front, simulating stone. There are also Ionic pilasters, a frieze with carved swags, a pedimented gable. In his book, *Architecture of the Western Reserve, 1800-1900*, Richard Campen called this house "the masterpiece of the early architecture in Trumbull County" and claimed that its refinement of detail was not surpassed anywhere in the Western Reserve.

The Traveling Woodwork— Alice Logan Blaemire's first memory of the Allen House, is tourists asking how to find it in the late 1940s. Clutching I.T. Frary's book, *Early Homes of Ohio*, they would troop into her Times Square Restaurant in Kinsman, seeking directions.

Her second memory of the Allen House, is buying it. She submitted a bid in 1953 and got the house for $6,300. The next day, the sale made the front page of the Warren *Tribune*. "Then my phone jumped off the hook," Blaemire recalls. "Everyone wanted to buy it— 'We had no idea it would go that cheap.'" She turned her back on a quick thousand-dollar profit, and drove off to Cleveland, to see her house's parlor woodwork.

The week I met Alice Logan Blaemire, the Times Square Restaurant was celebrating its fiftieth anniversary. On April 1, 1946, Blaemire, then four years out of Ohio State and not happy with teaching, took over the restaurant. At least until the interstates were built, the high-traffic location, at the junction of State Routes 5 and 7 just south of Kinsman, gave the Times Square lots of truck drivers as regular customers. During the anniversary week, the restaurant seemed still to be a busy place with tables occupied all afternoon while Blaemire and I sat at the counter. With her white hair in a French roll, she wore a tie-dye purple T shirt and a black skirt. The Times Square is famous for her pies; the Sunday before, she'd had 24 different kinds on sale. She jokes, "I tell people I'd rather play bridge than eat, and they can tell by looking at me I don't have much time for bridge."

Her house was built in 1821 for Dr. Peter Allen, a Connecticut native who finished medical school in the East before coming to Kinsman in 1808; his office was in a wing of the house. Allen's son, Dudley, was also a physician, and so was his grandson, Dudley Peter. After Dr. Peter Allen's death in 1864, the house was sold to the Reverend James Plant, whose descendants lived there until Alice Blaemire bought it. But in 1903, Dr. Peter's grandson, Dudley Peter, by then a prominent Cleveland surgeon married to Elisabeth Severance of the Standard Oil Severances, came back and for $50 bought his grandfather's woodwork: the ornately carved parlor trim he remembered from his childhood. ("Wait'll you see it," Blaemire says. "You can't blame him.")

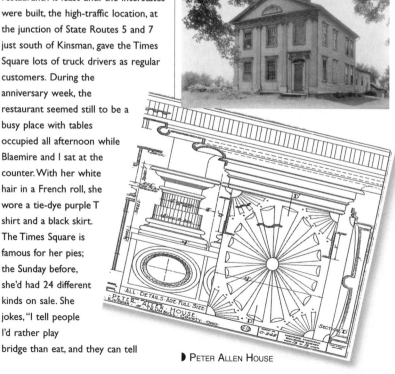

▶ PETER ALLEN HOUSE

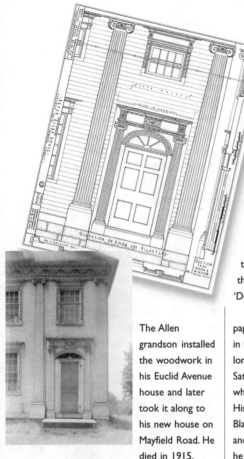

The Allen grandson installed the woodwork in his Euclid Avenue house and later took it along to his new house on Mayfield Road. He died in 1915.

The woodwork was still on Mayfield Road when, about 1945, that house was slated to be torn down. I.T. Frary, architectural historian and Cleveland Museum of Art scholar, tried to persuade the property owners to save the woodwork, but they scoffed that they were tired of it. So Frary enlisted the help of Laurence Norton, president of the Western Reserve Historical Society. Norton went to the site and paid the wrecking crews $250 for the woodwork, and the society put it in storage. That's where Blaemire saw it when she went up to Cleveland, hoping to buy it back: it was on a garage floor, behind some buggies. "Everyone at the Historical Society knew the Allen House," Blaemire says. "It was one of their favorites. They were pleased I'd bought it and would

have a tearoom. Everything was lovely. But they were reluctant to let the woodwork go."

It was October when she bought the house, and spring before she could hire a bulldozer to clear away the briars and brush and start to work on it. The house had minimal wiring, no plumbing, no heating, and hadn't been painted since 1918, so she had a lot to accomplish that spring and summer. But every other week, she'd go up to the Historical Society to look at the woodwork: "I'd pat it and say, 'Don't worry. I'll get you home.'"

By Labor Day weekend, 1954, the paper hanger had just started working in the parlor. He'd gone home for the long weekend, and suddenly on Saturday morning, Laurence Norton, who was still president of the Historical Society, arrived. Recalls Blaemire, "He came in the north door, and everything was looking lovely. Then he got to the parlor, and he said, 'Oh my, that woodwork must come back.'" On Tuesday he called a Historical Society board meeting, and on Wednesday he phoned Blaemire and told her to come pick up the woodwork. She was there the next morning, with her father, her brother, and a truck. She took her checkbook, prepared to pay whatever the charge was. Instead, the society gave it to her, on indefinite loan.

As it turned out, except for two of the four windows, the woodwork was intact. Blaemire put the original trim on the two windows opposite the room door; they're seen on entering the room, while the other two, unrestored, are curtained.

But if Blaemire wins the lottery, she'll have woodwork made for them, too.

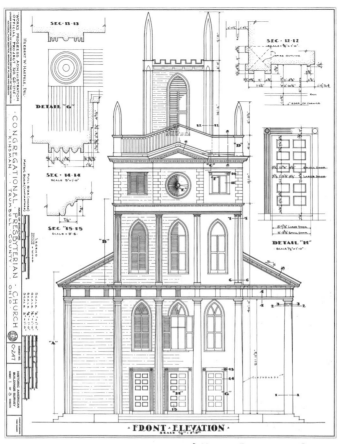

SEC·13·13

DETAIL "G"

SEC·12·12
SCALE ½"=1'-0"

SEC·14·14
SCALE 3"=1'-0"

DETAIL "H"
SCALE ½"=1'-0"

SEC·15·15
SCALE 3"=1'-0"

·FRONT·ELEVATION·

HERBERT W. HAFFELE, DEL.

WORKS PROGRESS ADMINISTRATION
OFFICIAL PROJECT NO. 65-1716

CONGREGATIONAL·PRESBYTERIAN·CHURCH
KINSMAN · TRUMBULL COUNTY · OHIO

▶ KINSMAN PRESBYTERIAN CHURCH

CONGREGATIONAL-PRESBYTERIAN CHURCH, NOW KINSMAN PRESBYTERIAN CHURCH, 1833

Willis Smith, Kinsman
6383 Church Street, Kinsman, NRHP
Church; 330/876-4485

"Exotic" and "wonderful" are the words Cleveland architect Bob Gaede chooses for Kinsman Church. On a street named Church, it sits flanked by cemeteries and in front of a cornfield. White frame, a mix of Greek and Gothic Revival styles, it has three doors and, above, three sets of three windows, rising into the tower. It looks like nothing else. ¶For a bucolic vista, look back at the church from State Street just to the west and north. ¶As for builder Willis Smith (1799-?), Richard Webb has been trying to find out about him ever since he bought a Smith house in 1973. Though altered in 1905 by a large front porch, Webb's 1828 house (at 8426 State Street) has some

unusually attractive features that provoked his interest. ¶What he's learned, is that Willis Smith came from New England in 1820, and during the next 20 years made a major contribution to early Kinsman. Besides the church, Webb lists a dozen Smith houses in town, some very much altered, but in a place the size of Kinsman—the township had 2,100 people in 1990—12 houses and a church are a substantial legacy. Webb traced them partly through records left by two carpenters who worked with Smith. These also helped identify a Smith house in Gustavus Center and four in Hartstown, Pennsylvania, about 15 miles east. Another clue to a Smith house is the mantle. A fine one will have a horizontal oval rosette in the center and smaller, vertical oval rosettes at the sides, over paired columns. (The same pattern of oval rosettes is visible over the Dr. Peter Allen House's front door. Webb points out also that a Smith mantle is on display at the Kinsman Public Library, across from the church.) ¶In spite of considerable effort, Webb hasn't learned much about Willis Smith. Webb and his wife, Susan, went to New England, but they found no record of Smith in Lisbon, Connecticut, where the Kinsmans came from, though they did see a house that reminded them of his work. Providence has large frame churches with some similarities to Kinsman's, but the use of builders' handbooks may account for that. ¶At the Trumbull County Courthouse, Webb found deeds showing that Smith sold off his Kinsman land holdings in the late 1830s. During the 1840s he bought a store in Bristolville but that failed, as a subsequent sheriff's sale showed. Census records from 1840 and 1850 showed Smith living in Mesopotamia; but Webb didn't have access to the 1860 census and doesn't know when Smith died. He is left to wonder why, before he was 40, such a remarkable builder abandoned both his profession and the town he'd helped build.

OCTAGON HOUSE, 1853

8405 Main Street, State Routes 5 and 7, which run together in town, Kinsman, NRHP
Private house

If Willis Smith has not yet brought fame to Kinsman, at least the place can lay claim to native son Clarence Darrow, the renowned late nineteenth- and early twentieth-century defense attorney. He grew up in this Octagon House. It belongs to Eleanor Brown, whose sister owns the Peter Allen House.

Kirtland, Lake County

(Also in Lake County: Painesville and Perry; together, the three offer an uncommon mix of early, Victorian, and modern buildings.)

Access: Kirtland Temple is on west side of State Route 306 south of I-90 (exit 193).

KIRTLAND TEMPLE, 1836

Joseph Smith, Jr. et al.
9020 Chillicothe Road, NHL, Kirtland, NRHP
Historic Mormon temple, with daily tours; check hours; 440/256-3318

Today Kirtland has become outer Cleveland; most of it has a suburban feel. But on the main north-south road this town has an extraordinary building from the 1830s, well before suburbs as we know them. The Kirtland Temple, begun just three years after prophet Joseph Smith founded the Church of Jesus Christ of Latter-day Saints in New York State, is an awesome structure. ¶ Attracted by a group of followers in Kirtland, Joseph Smith moved here in 1831; by the next year Mormons numbered 500 and Smith was receiving revelations calling for a large church. In summer 1833 his prayers brought a vision that described the temple's size and general structure; and that was how it was built. Smith apparently never had drawings made but approved ideas as work proceeded. ¶ Construction began in June, 1833, when Smith, Brigham Young, and others set off for the quarry with a wagon. During the next three years, perhaps 500 men worked on this building, 188 of them regularly. The temple is known for its interior wood carving, much done by carvers who, like their contemporaries elsewhere, used pattern books by New England architect Asher Benjamin. While Smith worked as a quarry foreman, Brigham Young and his brother made the windows; later Young painted the interior white. Surely, the Kirtland Temple had the most famous construction crew ever to lay hand to an Ohio building. ¶ The temple is 59 by 79 feet on the outside; the tower reaches a height of 110 feet. The design is a stylistic mix, mostly Greek Revival and Gothic. Both the first and second floors

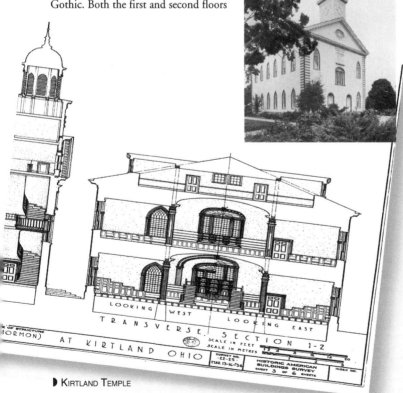

▶ KIRTLAND TEMPLE

▶ KIRTLAND TEMPLE INTERIOR

are large meeting rooms with multiple pulpits at both ends—four rows of three pulpits that are higher and more elaborate in the first-floor sanctuary, which also has a coved ceiling. Originally divided by canvas drapes hung from the ceilings, the second floor was used for classes. The third floor, lit by dormer windows, is partitioned into offices and meeting rooms. The exterior is mostly rough stone covered with a stucco painted to simulate bricks. ¶ After the panic of 1837 caused the Mormon bank to fail, Joseph Smith fled west, abandoning the still new temple. In 1862 his estate sold it to an individual linked to the Reorganized Church of Jesus Christ of Latter-day Saints, a Mormon offshoot, which has owned and cared for the building since 1880.

Lucas, Richland County

(Also in Richland County: Bellville, and Mansfield; the three make a loop tour. State Route 13 connects Bellville and Mansfield. To reach Malabar Farm from Bellville, drive east on State Route 97; at intersection with State Route 95 turn left/north to state park. From Malabar Farm take County 303/Pleasant Valley Road northwest to County 302; jog right to County 139/Hanley Road; turn left/west to State Route 13.)

Access: Malabar Farm is about 10 miles southeast of Mansfield. From I-71 take exit 169 and drive east, following signs to park (in reverse of routing above).

BIG HOUSE, MALABAR FARM, 1941

Louis Lamoreux, Mansfield, with consultant I.T. Frary, Cleveland
4050 Bromfield Road, Lucas, NRHP
The house at Malabar Farm State Park is open year-round; fee; 419/892-2784

When World War II threatened their long-time residency in France, author Louis Bromfield, his wife Mary, and their three daughters headed for his boyhood home in Ohio. Though he'd grown up in Mansfield, Bromfield treasured memories of the countryside around his grandfather's farm in southeast Richland County. That was where he wanted to settle—and where he wanted to show people how to farm without destroying the topsoil. Malabar Farm was to become the world's most famous farm. It didn't hurt that Hollywood and literary celebrities were regular visitors. But while James Cagney ran the roadside stand or Joan Fontaine attended the birth of a calf, Malabar Farm was also demonstrating agricultural techniques even today regarded as sound, like green manure, crop rotation, and contour plowing. So, along with the famous came farmers and curious tourists, at the rate of 20,000 a year. On summer Sundays Bromfield himself gave a tour that drew 100 to 200 people. Today Malabar Farm is less famous than it was in the early days, but as a state park and ongoing farm operation, it draws more people, 200,000 a year. Of those an impressive 80-90,000 tour the house. The white-frame house is where Humphrey Bogart, 45, married Lauren Bacall, 20, in 1945. Bogart and Bromfield had been friends since they met in New York in the 1920s, when Bromfield was a drama critic. The marriage to Bacall was Bogart's fourth, and his divorce had been finalized just 11 days earlier; Malabar Farm was chosen as a quiet, low-key place for the wedding. Perhaps it was less low-key than expected, for reporters arrived in full force. The couple spent their wedding night in a twin-bedded guest room, and the next day left by train for Hollywood.

▶ MALABAR FARM

The Big House: Ohio Revival Architecture—Louis Bromfield created Malabar Farm. The house and Malabar Farm's innovative, educational agriculture were his idea; the people who thronged to the place, a mix of relatives, local farmers, literary types, and Hollywood stars were all his guests. Ultimately, the strong, authoritarian personality that enabled him to realize Malabar Farm, also decreed its relatively short life as a working family farm.

Malabar Farm evolved from a romantic vision—an idealized notion of country living. In Mansfield the young Bromfield had seen the wretched lives of farmers who'd been forced off their land by exhausted soils. He proposed to show farmers how to revive depleted soils, so they could stay on their farms and lead the wholesome lives impossible in the city.

When he returned to Richland County, Bromfield expected to realize "the continuity which existed in France, the succession of generation by generation." He chose the farm he wanted to buy—it belonged to an older couple whom he remembered from childhood—and knocked at the door. Once he had bought their farm, he named it for hills near Bombay, India, which he had visited; his two novels set in India paid for the land. In spite of the exotic name, this place was to be an *Ohio* house. The 1830 farm house already on the property was to be expanded with additions that, though built all at once, used slightly different styles so as to seem from different times. The house was to look as though it had grown gradually through the previous century, as the farmer-owners prospered.

The author chose his architect, Louis Lamoreux of Mansfield, for his knowledge of Ohio's old houses, and for agreeing that if Bromfield changed his mind about something during construction, Lamoreux wouldn't object to tearing down and rebuilding. Lamoreux's friend I.T. Frary, of the Cleveland Museum of Art staff, helped too. Frary, author of *Early Homes of Ohio*, "knew his Ohio houses to the ground," Bromfield wrote. "The idea of building a house which was to be a kind of apotheosis of Ohio architecture appealed to him."

In 1939, 1940, and 1941, Bromfield bought four contiguous farms altogether, for a total of almost 600 acres. To pay for the house, he spent most of two years in Hollywood writing screenplays. When he reappeared at Malabar Farm for a visit, he often wanted something rebuilt, as he had anticipated, so construction stretched out over 18 months. Floor space tripled. Bromfield wanted space to accommodate his family, the governess, his agent, his parents, and friends. It was the Big House.

The outside of the house copied details from originals all over Ohio. The cast iron pillars on the front porches took a grapes-and-leaves design from houses on the Ohio River. The front-door area used designs from Norwalk and from Kirtland— Bromfield speculated that Brigham Young himself might have designed it in his early carpentering days in Kirtland. Bromfield wrote that the dormer windows came from the Zoar Hotel (see also); the front door was from a Chagrin Falls house that had burned; the chimneys were like those of Western Reserve taverns; and door and window ornamentation emulated that of Cincinnati's Baum-Taft House.

Though the interior used early Ohio moldings and black walnut doors, it otherwise went farther afield for inspiration. Bromfield described the front hall's double stairway as Classical in style, while the livingroom and

▶ MALABAR FARM, BIG HOUSE

diningroom were French, with doors leading outside. The livingroom was big enough to serve as a ballroom; the adjacent front hall, big enough to accommodate the 42-piece Lucas High School band. A second "country" diningroom was sometimes for the children and always for farm workers or boys interested in agriculture. Not counting visitors, in summer 20 people ate at Malabar Farm every day.

In his study Bromfield wanted space for bookcases, for a big desk (his 29-drawer desk was too high for typing so he put the typewriter on a card table) and for the five or six boxer dogs always around him. On the second floor, above the study, his secretary, agent, and frequent visitor, George Hawkins, who scorned what he called the "humus, mucus, retch and vetch" of farming, had a room designed to make him feel as comfortable as he was in his suite at the Hotel St. Regis in New York. It had cypress paneling and Richland County's only white Italian marble bathroom. Bromfield's

wife, Mary, had a bedroom in the original house, while their three daughters were at the building's other end in the wing with the dormers. The Humphrey Bogart-Lauren Bacall honeymoon guest room was over the front door.

Today the house seems a perfect period piece: a complete recapturing of the 1940s in its colors and furnishings. As that was the era of my own earliest memories, it gave me goose bumps. And the house looks marvelous on its site, where it nests among the green hills. It has achieved exactly the settled, enduring, and lived-in look that Bromfield wanted it to have. But perhaps not in the way he expected.

Malabar Farm was, really, a short-lived enterprise, lasting only about 15 years. Though it flourished in the 1940s, by the 1950s Bromfield's reputation had declined. His crony George Hawkins died in 1948; and Mary died in 1952. With a view to carrying on Malabar Farm, two of Bromfield's daughters studied agriculture at Cornell. One bought a nearby farm with her husband; the other hoped to take over the management. But Bromfield wasn't called The Boss for nothing. He yielded not an iota of responsibility, and the daughters, understandably, moved away. When Louis Bromfield died at Malabar Farm in 1956, his early dream of Malabar Farm's continuing as a family enterprise, was doomed.

In 1958, the daughters sold the farm to a foundation that intended to keep running it as a demonstration farm. That was not a successful venture. Ultimately, in 1972, the State of Ohio took title; in 1976 it opened Malabar Farm State Park. So the farm goes on; and largely through it, so does Louis Bromfield. Besides, the park takes good care of the world's only Ohio Revival house.

Mansfield, Richland County

(Also in Richland County: Malabar Farm at Lucas, Bellville, and Mansfield make a loop tour. See routing at Lucas.)

¶ "We met three good people today," Doug Graf said, as he reflected on a Sunday afternoon trip to Mansfield, to look at two buildings there. He was measuring goodness by how these three people related to buildings—old buildings, as it happened—and he pointed out that the three were of varying ages. The youngest was the manager of Brunches Restaurant and Gourmet Coffee. He's been keeping his downtown restaurant open on Sundays since 1996. It's succeeded, for he's always been busy, but he wished others would follow his lead.

▶ OAK HILL, INTERIOR

Brunches is at 103 North Main Street, in Mansfield's resurgent downtown Carrousel District. ¶ Then there was the middle-aged pastor at St. Luke's Lutheran Church. He loves the church building. He's thought about its woodwork; he knows its architect and history; and he's happy to show it off—even the attic that's accessible only by ladder. ¶ And the third good person was an older woman, a volunteer guide at Oak Hill, a Gothic Revival house museum. An enthusiastic and well informed host, she herself had helped restore the house.

Access: Mansfield is just west of I-71. Take U.S. 30 west to State Route 13/Main Street and drive south to Surrey Road; turn right/west to Oak Hill Place and then right/north short distance to Oak Hill Cottage.

▶ Oak Hill cottage

OAK HILL COTTAGE, 1847

310 Springmill Street, Mansfield, NRHP
Richland County Historical Society house museum; open Sunday afternoons April
through December; fee; 419/524-1765

A brick Gothic Revival house, Oak Hill abounds in pointed arches, some
frosted in Carpenter Gothic bric-a-brac, as is the porch that runs across the
front of the house. The ultimate in Gothic detailing is found indoors, in the
front hall, where slender round columns have a delicate crenellation at the
top. A railroad man built Oak Hill, but Dr. Johannes A. Jones, who bought it
in 1864, is better known today because his family remained in the house a
hundred years and then left almost all the contents. An itinerant eye doctor
and patent medicine inventor, Jones settled in Mansfield after marrying a
local woman. He was the owner who installed the Italian marble mantles; he
and his family made Oak Hill one of the city's show places. Mrs. Jones's
nephew was author Louis Bromfield, who in the 1920s wrote two novels set
in this house, *The Green Bay Tree* and *Shane's Castle*. The Richland County
Historical Society bought Oak Hill after the youngest Jones daughter died in
the mid-1960s, but it took almost a decade to muster paperwork and money
for the restoration. With the west wall bulging, the staircase sagging, and
termite damage severe enough to leave a 2-inch gap between floor and
baseboard, the Historical Society spent most of another decade stabilizing the
structure and then restoring it. Guide Pat Horchler recalls that interior
restoration began in 1983; one Saturday that February she was washing the
stairs with cold water. Ten months later, in December, the museum was
ready.

**Access: From Oak Hill take Main Street/State Route 13 south to
downtown.**

105-109 NORTH MAIN STREET, MANSFIELD
BETWEEN FOURTH AND FIFTH STREETS, 1870s
Shops and offices

The building at numbers 105-109 was built during an 1870s boom, but the jaunty three-story iron porch over the sidewalk was added about 1914, when the Overlook Bakery and Restaurant was at this address. The porch was almost entirely rebuilt in the 1980s. The building is part of a little mecca of delights between Fourth and Fifth Streets on North Main Street. Here, on both sides of the street, rehabbed red-brick Italianates, two and three stories high, house inviting first-floor shops. It's possible to eat, or to visit a gallery or bookstore. It's even possible to buy a meal on Sunday. This neighborhood is called the Carrousel District. There is a carrousel, a non-profit operation in

a new building at Fourth Street. Now open year-round, except Mondays, it was installed in 1991 to give the neighborhood a focus and a prime draw; it also helped attract two carrousel companies to Mansfield. The driving force here has been Engwiller Properties, a for-profit development company launched in 1985, when a group of local investors realized that the worst downtown neighborhood had many of the best buildings. They bought up most of them, including 105-109 North Main, so that now Engwiller

▶ 105-109 NORTH MAIN STREET, MANSFIELD

owns 25 structures in the Carrousel District. Development manager Chris Buchanan says the company has been renovating three to four buildings a year as retail and office space; the hope is to add apartments too. Even though other property owners in the area have also been rehabbing, the Carrousel District, says Buchanan, "is a very long-term turnaround." The turnaround in neighborhood quality already is beyond measure. The day before the carrousel opened, two massage parlors closed.

Access: Mulberry Street, one way northbound in downtown, is two blocks west of Main.

DR. JAMES H. CRAIG HOUSE, NOW MANSFIELD CHAMBER OF COMMERCE, C. 1886

Levi T. Scofield, Cleveland
55 North Mulberry Street at West Third Street, Mansfield
Chamber of Commerce offices

Finding the architect who designed the Dr. James H. Craig House was a real success for Cleveland Victorian house buff Craig Bobby. At the Western Reserve Historical Society in fall 1998, he went through architect Levi Scofield's drawings, and among them, he recognized this house. As for the date it was built, the 1886 estimate coincides with a time when Scofield was in the vicinity, working on the Mansfield Reformatory. The house is a two-and-a-half story red brick that Bobby has long admired for its octagonal cupola and the unusual mix of Italianate, Second Empire and Gothic Revival styles. Inside the woodwork and stairs are wonderful; the dropped ceilings, a disappointment.

Access: Take Main Street south to Park Avenue West and turn right/ west. Within half a mile St. Luke's is on the left, where Marion Avenue veers southwest. At the same place, Sturges Avenue is a left/south turn; Bushnell House is near corner. Then continue west on Park for Bissman House and Kingwood Center.

ST. LUKE'S LUTHERAN CHURCH, 1891, 1927

William Gibbons Preston, Boston
2 Marion Avenue at Park Avenue West/State Route 430, Mansfield
Church; may be seen during weekday morning office hours or by prearrangement; 419/522-0943

Doug Graf was the one who spotted St. Luke's Lutheran Church, set on a triangle of land formed by Marion Avenue angling off Park to the southwest. The building faces east, so westbound traffic has a view of the full facade.

This is not your usual Ohio church. Though it has Richardsonian Romanesque features, Graf calls the style Arts and Crafts. The facade, like the site, is triangular, with a stout square tower on the left, adjoined by the peak of a gable descending, hypotenuse-like, on the right. Below, strong horizontals—the red roof of a vestibule and a row of four windows—complete the triangle. Details on the front include a single buttress, a single bracket, a tower clock not centered but at the side. The material is a roughly-cut gray limestone, with trim in a light brown sandstone; the roof, flat

▶ St. Luke's

▶ St. Luke's Lutheran Church

red tiles. The Arts and Crafts interior is spectacular, in part because of the ceiling beams ("Working beams," Graf reported, after he'd followed the pastor, Rev. Stephen Patrick, up a ladder and into the attic). Carved and paneled woodwork includes wainscoting, pews, and altar pieces; windows, round-arched, have leaded and stained glass. The rosettes on the round arch in front of the altar originally held small lights, an approach popularized by Louis Sullivan's 1890 Chicago Auditorium. Originally also, all this white oak woodwork had a golden finish that was later darkened, probably in 1926, when St. Luke's built a large Sunday school addition at the back of the church, beyond the altar. Steel industrialist Michael Harter donated St. Luke's site. He also picked the architect, though how he found Bostonian William Gibbons Preston (1844-1910) is unknown. Preston, who attended the École des Beaux-Arts in Paris, started in practice with his architect father in 1861. For St. Luke's, he designed not only the building, but also the interior, including the windows and woodwork. Preston is known mostly for Boston buildings, but pastor Patrick also found some of his work in Savannah. "If you stand back and look at their county courthouse," he says, "it's a lot like our church."

MARTIN BUSHNELL HOUSE, 1893
34 Sturges Avenue, Mansfield, NRHP
Private offices

Around the turn of the century, Mansfield quarries were the source of a marvelous red sandstone. Six Ohio Presbyterian churches used this stone; three, in Napoleon, Dayton, and Barnesville, are in this guide; another fine one is in Upper Sandusky. But extraordinary as the stone of those churches is, the Martin Bushnell House offers the best display of all. The whole house is done in this sandstone, with the most astonishing samples on the front porch. While the churches' stone is red with gold, gray, and tan, here the color is all in shades of red, from pale pink to dark. The paired red columns above the porch balustrade have marble-like patterns—a real stunt in sandstone. On the porch walls dark lines in the stone form exuberant and shimmering clouds: rapturous sunsets forever and ever. ¶ Interestingly too, though the stone was laid in straight rows at the back of the house, at the front sides and on the walls over the porch, it was laid in patterns of diamonds or triangles or swirls. No wonder builder F.D. Webber used a picture of this house on his business letterhead. ¶ Richard Hull, a Mansfield man who for 40 years has traded in rocks for, say, classrooms, has heard stories about the red sandstone. One was that what was in demand originally was pink stone. "Then," he says, "somebody thought they ought to save those lined ones too." The stone wasn't recovered successfully until workmen were brought in from an Italian quarry that had a similar rock. Even then, seams were often too small to use, or the material broke during quarrying. The best of the sandstone, probably including that on the Bushnell House's porch, came from northeast Mansfield's Fifth Avenue quarry, today in the area of Fifth Avenue and U.S. 30. ¶ The other good news about this house is the first floor woodwork. It's sycamore

▶ MARTIN BUSHNELL HOUSE

in the front rooms, in designs that are a rectilinear Art Nouveau variant carved by German craftsmen. The rest of the woodwork, like the oak in the hall, is Ohio Victoriana. ¶ The Bushnell House's architect is unknown, but he provided an interesting Richardsonian Romanesque design. Though a porte-cochere has obviously been lopped off the south wall, the exterior appears largely intact and is readily visible. Inside, as part of a remodeling about 1950 to permit apartments upstairs, the house was mutilated by the removal of its 14-foot-wide stairway. ¶ Martin Bushnell, only a distant relative of Ohio Governor Asa Bushnell of Springfield, was a Mansfield businessman; his descendants stayed in the house until 1948. Later, the Ohio Genealogical Society was here from 1988-1998. Their office manager, Tom Neel, researched the house; he even sent me a copy of Webber's letterhead.

BENJAMIN F. BISSMAN HOUSE, 1890

George Franklin Barber, Knoxville
458 Park Avenue West, Mansfield, NRHP/Park Avenue West MRA
Private house

Craig Bobby says that this exuberant brick and stone Queen Anne is based on a design by Knoxville-based mail-order architect George Franklin Barber. Barber was so successful in designing Queen Annes, which typically had the fancy detailing seen here in the porches, tower, and gables, and then selling them by mail, that thousands of examples of his work were built across the country.

KINGWOOD CENTER, 1926
Clarence Mack, Cleveland
900 Park Avenue West, Mansfield, NRHP
Garden center and house museum; open year round; 419/522-0211

In the 1920s Clarence Mack was a popular Cleveland architect; he did houses in Rocky River, Shaker Heights, and Lakewood (see also Lakewood). They're still private houses. If you don't happen to know someone who owns one, the way to see the inside of a Mack house is to go to Mansfield, where the architect's biggest Ohio house was built for manufacturer Charles King. Mostly French Provincial, Kingwood is attractive enough to show what the fuss was all about. Mack usually also decorated and furnished his Cleveland houses, but he didn't do that

▶ KINGWOOD CENTER

here. The house has 47 acres of gardens, open to the public. The landscape architects were William Pitkin, Jr. and Charles Mott.

Mantua, Portage County
(Also in Portage County: Hiram is nearby.)
¶ While in and near Mantua village, be sure to see Mantua Center, a picturesque Western Reserve green with adjacent buildings. It's a mile north on State Route 44, then less than a mile west.

Access: State Route 44, which is an exit from I-76 to the south or U.S. 422 to the north, bisects Mantua and becomes Main Street in town. Hine House is on Prospect Street a little west of Main.

HORACE L. HINE HOUSE, C. 1895
Fenimore C. Bate, Cleveland
4624 West Prospect Street, Mantua, NRHP
Residence and Mantua Manor Antiques, open daily except Monday and holidays; check hours; 330/274-8722

Gail Shuss, who owns the Hine House, is an ordinary person, in the financial sense, with an extraordinary house. She's a resourceful do-it-yourselfer who has managed to keep her house in reasonable condition, but she has had a paint problem. For years the house has needed painting; its boards became a weather-worn gray. When I visited in spring, 1996, a hardware store that had agreed to give her the paint, had just gone out of business. Three years later, painting and related repairs finally began but in fall 2001 had a long way to go. Colors—a base of gray green with accents in teal and plum—were

▶ HORACE HINE HOUSE

suggested by a Denver company that sells color recommendations for Victorian houses. ¶ This is a wonderful house, readily visible from the road. You'll see a wrap-around porch, a three-story octagonal tower, a recessed balcony in the front gable and another on the east side, bays, and all kinds of windows—a mix of stained glass, leaded glass, and plain glass, which Shuss says is a thick triple-plate. Don't miss the fourth-floor dormer with a low conical roof, visible from the west; Shuss says that Horace L. Hine, who built the house, liked to sit on the window seat in the little room up there. The siding is a mix of shingles and clapboard with carved wooden panels, many containing recessed squares. Squares are a recurring motif; Shuss calls them the house's theme. ¶ The architect was unknown until Craig Bobby found his name at the Cleveland Public Library, where he was reviewing the 1880-1900 Building Synopsis columns in the magazine, *The Inland Architect and News Record*. Bate did Grays Armory on Bolivar in downtown Cleveland, as well as many houses for upper-middle class clients like Horace Hine, who owned Mantua's Crafts & Hine bank with W.H. Crafts. Hine built this house to be showier than Crafts's house across the street. He succeeded, though you'll have no trouble spotting the competition. ¶ The house helps support itself. Roomers live on the second floor and Shuss and another women run Mantua Manor Antiques downstairs. The house is open during business hours, so visitors may see the hall, parlors, and diningroom, every one in a different wood—Hine owned a lumber yard too. Later he lost his fortune and the house was vacant 20 years, until acquired in the late 1930s by Jim Haylett, who turned it into an auction house.

▶ ZIMMERMAN OCTAGON HOUSE

Marshallville, Wayne County

(Also in Wayne County: Wooster.
This guide lists octagon houses in Monroeville, listed
with Norwalk in Northwest Ohio; Kinsman; and
Hamilton in southwest Ohio.)

**Access: From U.S. 30 between Wooster and Massillon, take State
Route 57 north; house is on right/east side north of Orrville and just
before State Route 585.**

ZIMMERMAN OCTAGON HOUSE, 1883
Ezekiel B. Zimmerman, builder
State Route 57, Marshallville, NRHP
Private house; best visible in winter

Wayne County's Ezekiel Zimmerman Octagon House was among those
inspired by Orson Squire Fowler, a mid-nineteenth-century character who
promoted eight-sided houses as better and cheaper for ordinary people. Set
on a country road, the red brick example that Zimmerman built for himself
retains its distinctive look. Alternating sides have pointed gables, a pattern
echoed in the eight-sided cupola, which also has round-arched windows.
Each wall is 17.5 feet wide. Bricks, installed three deep, were made on the
premises. Eric Johannesen, who prepared the National Register form,
reported that special wide-angle (135-degree) bricks were made for the

corners. He found also that the floor plan was based on one that appears in Section V of Fowler's book, *A Home for All*. The porch pillars once had ornate Eastlake trim. ¶ In 1853 Fowler proposed a cheap and rugged new building material, a type of concrete molded in wooden forms. While that idea is the one that now seems prophetic, in his own day Fowler's name was associated with octagon houses, which he began promoting with the publication of *A Home for All* in 1848. He argued that the eight-sided house was closer to the circle, the form Nature preferred for dwellings. By simplifying ventilation, illumination and heating, the design kept costs down. *A Home for All* inspired hundreds of octagon houses besides the Zimmerman House, a relative latecomer. Ray Luce, formerly Ohio historic preservation officer, described the eight-sided house as particularly American, a distinctive contribution to Western architecture; Europe, Luce wrote, had octagonal structures but never residences.

Massillon, Stark County

(Also in Stark County: Alliance and, in Vol. I, Canton.) ¶ In the eyes of the world, Massillon is famous for high-school football; but it could well be more famous architecturally. For one, Massillon was where architect Herman J. Albrecht (1885-1961) practiced, though he later had a Cleveland office as well. We know about Albrecht today mostly because he's been championed by Akron architectural historian James A. Pahlau, himself a Massillon native. Pahlau's interest in architecture was first piqued when he was a youth walking home along Massillon's Fourth Street, where he passed five blocks of exceptional houses, including good early twentieth-century examples of Georgian and Tudor Revival styles. And finally, this city has one of Ohio's best houses, the Massillon Woman's Club. Not only is the house terrific, but its proprietors, the Massillon Woman's Club, are among the state's best preservers of a historic property.

Access: From U.S. 30 west of Canton take State Route 21 north to Lincoln Way; turn right/east; library is within half a mile at 2nd Street. Five Oaks is two blocks further on, on 4th Street; turn left/north to North Avenue, where house is on the corner.

MASSILLON PUBLIC LIBRARY, 1937

Herman J. Albrecht, Massillon
208 Lincoln Way East at 2nd Street N.E., Massillon
Public library open daily except summer Sundays, 330/832-9831

In the 1930s, Massillon attached a Georgian Revival library to a side of city founder James Duncan's 1835 Federal-style house. The Duncan House became the museum wing of the L-shaped complex that architect Herman J. Albrecht designed. The other wing is a reading room; and between the two is a rotunda, with a dome above and a porch facing the street below. An octagonal auditorium is under the rotunda. In 1963, the dome was cut off by a dropped ceiling, and the reading room, which had tables with reading lamps and a marble fireplace, got an acoustic-tile ceiling and fluorescent lights. Without these alterations, this library could be a gem; Director Camille Leslie says she dreams of opening up the rotunda's dome. In 1996, the museum moved away and the library expanded into the Duncan House.

FIVE OAKS, NOW MASSILLON WOMAN'S CLUB, 1894

Charles F. Schweinfurth, Cleveland
210 4th Street N.E. at North Avenue, Massillon, NRHP
Private club for Massillon women; group tours available by prearrangement; fee;
330/833-4896

Five Oaks is a voluptuous house. It was executed by craftsmen who could carve leaves in sandstone, cherubs in mahogany, or lions in oak—five different lions pose atop stairway posts. Named for five oak trees that grew in the yard (and before long dubbed "Four Oaks and a Stump"), the house is Richardsonian Romanesque. The rough-cut sandstone is local, from a quarry at the north edge of Massillon. A massive one-story porch, with open round arches, is on the left front; a three-story octagonal tower, on the right. Between the porch and the tower a wide, deep-set window offers a close look at the detailing, for a band of carved foliation frames the entire window.

▶ FIVE OAKS, ARCHITECT'S DRAWING

As for the interior, the third floor has a ballroom and servants' rooms—their bathroom had no toilet, which gives us an insight into the 1890s. The second floor has birdseye maple woodwork and a beautiful Tiffany window in a bathroom. The first floor is the high point, especially the hall and stairs, the south parlor's octagonal alcove, and the billiard room. The wood trim, initially swaddled in a dozen coats of varnish, remains bright and extraordinary. The first floor hall has quartersawn white oak (including columns with fleurs-de-lis in relief and ceiling beams that end as the heads of nymphs), while the parlor and adjacent library are in a sensuous gold-colored rose mahogany that almost seems illuminated from behind.

Fame, Money, and Maintenance—Five Oaks is a hundred-year-old house so good that it is still making reputations—those of its builders and now of its tenders. It also offers insights into money and architecture.

Charles Schweinfurth, Cleveland's leading architect in the 1890s, did many of that city's great buildings. When he designed Five Oaks in 1892, he hadn't yet done Trinity Cathedral or 15 rich men's castles, of which only one survives, on Euclid Avenue's Millionaires' Row. Five Oaks proves his skill, though it may also make us miss Euclid Avenue all the more.

Even if Schweinfurth had never done Five Oaks, his name would be known to everyone interested in Ohio architecture. Not so the name of J. Walter McClymonds. Were it not for this house, McClymonds, rich though he was, would be safely obscure, at least outside Massillon.

Five Oaks cost McClymonds $200,000—in today's money that would be about $3 million—and it's surprising it didn't cost more. Schweinfurth gave McClymonds a good design and he also used his client's money well. The sandstone still looks superb, but it was local stone. The hall could hardly seem more luxurious, but its white oak could be harvested locally. The house has exotic, imported materials, precious-metal detailing, Tiffany windows, beautiful carving; but expensive features were used selectively for impact—they gave bang for the bucks.

For seven years after McClymonds died in 1912, no one lived at Five Oaks. Then in 1919 the McClymondses' two daughters offered it to the Massillon Woman's Club to use as a meeting place. Five years later, they gave the house to the club, which has occupied and tended it for over 80 years. Maintenance hasn't always been easy. For instance, the octagonal tower in front has had chronic drainage problems and leaks. In 1993, in a pile of junk, the Woman's Club found a sketch Charles Schweinfurth did of Five Oaks. That drawing shows the tower roof designed in a way that would have prevented leaks. Why it was built differently, no one knows.

The billiard room is Five Oaks' most distinctive room. It's where the bridal party ate when the McClymondses' daughter Edna married Arvine Wales in 1900. Her wedding, at home with 400 guests, was delayed an hour because President and Mrs. McKinley were late arriving from Mansfield, where they'd attended Senator Sherman's funeral. An old friend of McClymonds, McKinley and his wife joined the wedding party in the billiard room. There they could enjoy woodwork of unfinished black walnut; Moroccan leather, studded with brass nail heads, on the walls; and a Tiffany chandelier. The ceiling, also by Tiffany, is extraordinary: a leaded translucent glass barrel vault, with light from a roof skylight two stories above.

For the Woman's Club, the billiard room's beautiful glass barrel vault represents a dilemma. It's accessible from the light shaft above, but the club can find no one who will clean it.

But, though the billiard room ceiling may be dingy, Five Oaks could hardly have better proprietors than the Woman's Club. Open to any woman resident, the club has over 600 members. One way to see just how well this group serves the house is to look at the wheel-chair lift, outside near a back door on the north wall. It is a perfect example of how to provide.

▶ MEDINA SQUARE

Medina, Medina County

(Tour with Lorain County's Wellington and Oberlin to the west, or with Akron to the east [Vol. I].)

Access: Medina Public Square is about three-and-a-half miles west of I-71 on State Route 18; it's at the junction of U.S. 42 and State Routes 18, 3, and 57. The Medina Community Design Committee provides free walking-tour brochures; 330/725-7516

PUBLIC SQUARE, 1818
Liberty Street/State Routes 3 and 18 at Court Street/U.S. 42, NRHP/Medina Public Square Historic District
Public park, band concert venue

What's most remarkable about Medina's Public Square is its late twentieth-century history, for, starting in 1968, it was the beneficiary one of the country's earliest community-based preservation efforts. Certainly it was worth saving. Because an 1870 fire destroyed most earlier structures, the square's buildings were "one of the most complete collections of late nineteenth century or 'Victorian' architecture in the region," as Eric Johannesen wrote in the National Register form. Thus almost everything on the square dates from between 1870 and 1900, so that style and scale are relatively consistent. The result is so attractive that people move to Medina because of Public Square. ¶ The square's park is just over two acres, with trees and a 1975 bandstand that's a copy of Bellville's (see also), except that Medina still has a band that draws up to 2,000 people to summertime concerts. What roused the preservationists in 1968 was a judge's suggestion that the courthouse, which faces west into the square, be torn down. That suggestion was never taken up, but it stimulated a group of volunteers, including artists and architects, who formed the Medina Community Design Committee. Worried about the decline of the buildings around Public Square, where dilapidation, sheet siding, and cluttered signs were becoming too common, they promoted three showcase renovations to inspire others: a firehouse, a department store, and a bank. The firehouse, conspicuous on the south side of the square with its restored red tower, was in that first crop of rehabs. Now, says CDC coordinator Janet Senkar, it's being turned into a museum. ¶ Public Square was platted in 1818, back in the days when Medina was still Mecca (it had to change its name because there's another Mecca in Trumbull County) and when clearing trees had to be the first order of business. Public

buildings on the square's east side today include a relatively new 1969 courthouse, red-brick, and the still-standing old courthouse, whose wonderful Second Empire facade was an 1873 updating of a Greek Revival predecessor. (Alas, the 1952 interior is awful.) ¶ In 1841 the Greek Revival building had replaced a 20-year-old courthouse whose sandstone was crumbling. The funny thing is, that supposedly collapsing building from the 1820s is still there—it's on the west side of the square, where for years it's housed an army-navy store. Which goes to show that in buildings, even crumbling may not be fatal. What makes old buildings fall down is people.

▶ MEDINA TOWN HALL

▶ MEDINA SQUARE, SOUTH SIDE

▶ MAHONING VALLEY PUMPING WORKS, ARCHITECT'S DRAWINGS

Mineral Ridge, Trumbull County

(Mineral Ridge is on Mahoning Valley tour; for routing see Warren.)

Access: From State Route 46 just north of the Mahoning County line, take Ohltown-McDonald Road west. Go half a mile to the entry gate, on the right at a bend in the road; inside the gate follow the road, which first provides a plant overlook and then leads to the buildings. A complex of new structures will appear on the left; continue to see the three original buildings facing onto a lawn.

MAHONING VALLEY SANITARY DISTRICT, PURIFICATION AND PUMPING WORKS, 1932

Charles F. Owsley, Youngstown; William H. Dittoe, chief engineer
1181 Ohltown-McDonald Road, Mineral Ridge
Water plant; 330/652-3614

Once, harnessing a river and purifying its water for cities and towns seemed triumphs worthy of celebration. Few places show that better than the three original buildings in the Mahoning Valley Sanitary District's Purification and Pumping Works, which took six years to construct. There a formal layout and spectacular tower combine to give the place a heroic dimension; it is one of Ohio's architectural high points. ¶ At one end of a rectangular green, a 100-foot tower stands flanked by two lower buildings that face each other across the green. Art Deco in style, all in iron-flecked buff brick with limestone coping, the buildings are related but not the same, though some patterns, like the design in the metal doors, recur. Intricate brickwork, different for each building, enlivens facades that seem plain from a distance. ¶ In spite of its grandeur and urban look, this complex is off by itself, next to the Meander Creek Reservoir spillway and well apart from its 300,000 water users in Youngstown, Niles, and smaller communities. An 86-inch conduit brings reservoir water to the Pump Station, on the right when facing the tower. From there it flows to the central building, the Water Purification Works; the tower was designed for chemical storage, while its wings contain settling basins. Finally, the water passes through the filtering facilities behind the third structure, the Administration Building, whose third story was designed to store 165,000 gallons of water—that accounts for heavy columns in the walls and in the circular lobby at the front. The storage is no longer needed; Chief Engineer David G. Tabak hopes to install labs and offices. ¶ That the Sanitary District values its original buildings for their architecture is evident in several structures added in the 1990s. Seen on the left when driving in, they emulate the older ones with the same buff brick, though copings, Tabak says, had to be precast concrete rather than limestone. ¶ On leaving the plant, my companion, Warren planner Alex Bobersky, turned right outside the gate and drove west on Ohltown-McDonald to Ohltown-Mineral Ridge, where he turned right and then right again onto Trumbull County 67A, a bridge across the reservoir. From that bridge, it's possible to look north, across almost two miles of water, and see the waterworks, the only break in the forest that outlines the reservoir banks.

▶ McKinley Birthplace Memorial

Niles, Trumbull County

(Niles is on Mahoning Valley tour; for routing see Warren.)

Access: South of Warren and north of I-80, Niles is on State Route 46, which passes the McKinley Memorial.

MCKINLEY BIRTHPLACE MEMORIAL, 1917

McKim, Mead & White, New York
40 North Main Street, Niles, NRHP
Private memorial, public library, auditorium, and museum complex; open daily; ask for museum key in library; 330/652-1704

The famous and prolific firm of McKim, Mead & White did nothing else like the National McKinley Birthplace Memorial. Enclosed by a colonnade, an open central courtyard focuses on a full-size statue of McKinley, while busts of his principal cohorts line the wall behind him. Of the two adjacent wings, one is a public library and the other, an auditorium with McKinley artifacts on display in the balcony. The complex is planned well. For instance, the front columns are spaced so the statue can be seen as one approaches. Or, the library has a round bay in which book stacks, on three levels separated by glass-brick floors, radiate out toward the wall. The exterior is all in white Georgia marble.

**McKinley Memorial:
Immodesty**—A Neoclassical temple afloat on its own expansive lawn, the McKinley Memorial contrasts with its setting, for Niles is a gritty, blue-collar steel town. Even though the memorial incorporates community facilities, including the local public library, it seems remote; it looks as though it was planted here by outsiders—as it was.

President William McKinley was assassinated early in his second term, in 1901. This memorial was the idea of Joseph G. Butler; it struck him while he was giving a speech to the Niles Board of Trade in 1910. Butler, a steel tycoon and boyhood friend of McKinley, checked out his idea with a few friends, including the head of United States Steel, a cardinal, President William Howard Taft, and Henry Clay Frick, another steel tycoon, who promptly pledged $50,000 for a library. Soon Butler realized the memorial could be far more ambitious than he originally imagined. Moreover, it could honor not only McKinley, but also the most generous donors. Their busts are on display in the auditorium; those who gave less got bronze plaques. The bust that sculptor John Massey-Rhind did of Frick has a place of honor—under a skylight right inside the library door.

McKim, Mead & White were chosen as architects from six entries in a blind competition. In the decades before and after the turn of the century, this influential firm designed buildings for the nation. Just when the city was most important, McKim, Mead & White, as historian Leland Roth says, was devoting "its greatest energy to urban and public buildings." Ohio has two examples, both initiated by Joseph Butler: Youngstown's much-altered Butler Institute of American Art and this little-changed McKinley Memorial. Both were designed after the deaths of

▶ McKinley Memorial

two of the original partners, Charles McKim and Stanford White, but before the 1919 retirement of the third, William Mead. Roth claims that though a McKim, Mead & White design meant high quality even into the 1920s, the firm lost some of its "sheer élan" after 1909.

But Rebecca Rogers admires the McKinley Memorial unabashedly. "To me it's a gem," says Rogers, an architect and Youngstown preservation consultant. "You don't expect it to be there, and then when you're in it, you're in it. It wraps around you." To her, it succeeds fully because it celebrates not just McKinley, but his era and his place—it uses Ohio tiles and terra cotta. He is shown surrounded by his cronies, rich industrialists, like Mark Hanna, and politicians, including Taft and Theodore Roosevelt. "It embodies that whole 'us-guy' crowd," says Rogers. "They knew what they were doing. They have no modesty."

North Bloomfield, Trumbull County

(See Western Reserve for rural loop tour including North Bloomfield, pages 143-145.)

BROWNWOOD, 1819

Amos Stockwell, North Bloomfield
8774 State Route 45, just south of State
Route 87, North Bloomfield, NRHP
Private house

▶ BROWNWOOD

Little more than a highway intersection with a green and a few buildings, North Bloomfield has a house that puts it on the map: Brownwood is one of Ohio's finest early houses. Owner Judith Sheridan has a two-foot stack of books and magazines that have featured it; and in I.T. Frary's book *Early Homes of Ohio*, its picture appears opposite the title page. ¶ Just south of North Bloomfield's square, Brownwood overlooks State Route 45 from a hillside of flowers and trees. White frame, two stories with the gable end facing the street, it's an 1819 farmhouse, but a squire's farmhouse, with an elegant Federal facade. The squire was Ephraim Brown, who came from New Hampshire in 1815 and brought a carpenter, Amos Stockwell, who built this house four years later. Some elements of the design appear in Asher Benjamin's 1814 builders' manual, while the arch over the door is like ones found in New Hampshire. ¶ In his forties when he migrated, Ephraim Brown owned all 16,000 acres of Bloomfield Township and, with his wife, he proceeded to populate it. They had nine children, so the south parlor was added just a few years after the house was built. Another addition, a two-story wing at the rear, was built in 1840. Since then this 17-room house has had no further accumulations, though it does have plumbing and electricity. It is surely among Ohio's most pristine old houses—on its walnut corner posts, an upstairs bedroom has the *original* red paint. ¶ The Brown family owned the house for 150 years, though by the early twentieth century, they were prospering in Cleveland and used Brownwood only in summer. Around World War I, a grandson developed a dairy herd. In 1958 another descendant arrived with his bride and left shortly after a grand piano fell through the floor. (They were the ones who installed the structural steel in the basement.) The Western Reserve Historical Society inherited the property in 1969, then took the 1823 bedroom wallpaper for a house at Hale Farm and Village museum. When Judith and Terrence Sheridan moved in in 1974, they became the second family to own and live in Brownwood. ¶ But by then, the house had lost its 17 front windows when a building on the square exploded; for a long time, the Sheridans spent their time digging shards of glass out of doors. Outside they cleared away six-inch poison ivy roots, while inside they dealt with mold hanging like stalactites in the basement. For Terrence Sheridan, working on an old house initially seemed like a good escape from the office. Now he says, "Restoration once is fine, twice is a bore, and the third time ..." He shrugs.

Oberlin, Lorain County

(Also in Lorain County: Wellington; Medina is nearby.)
¶ Oberlin has one of Ohio's best collections of twentieth-century buildings—indeed, the best in a compact, walkable area, with the bonus of a Frank Lloyd Wright Usonian house only a short drive away. Except for that house, these buildings face or are near the 13-acre Tappan Square, which was Oberlin College's original site. Early in the twentieth century, the Olmsted Brothers developed a plan that razed the college buildings in the square and in 1914 made it a landscaped green space. ¶ The aggregation of notable twentieth-century buildings here is no accident. Since World War II the college has sought name architects for its new buildings. Earlier, for 30 years starting in 1903, Cass Gilbert was the college's consulting architect. Though an Ohio native, Gilbert (1859-1934) grew up in St. Paul and practiced in Minnesota for 20 years. Then he moved to New York, where in 1913 he did the Woolworth Building, a glorious skyscraper with Gothic detailing. It was such a great success that afterwards "a faint trace of condescension entered his correspondence with the college." So observed Oberlin history professor Geoffrey Blodgett, citing a 1916 letter in which Gilbert described his Oberlin work as "small and relatively unimportant." Altogether, by the 1930s Gilbert had done five buildings for the college, a group that Blodgett

▶ PETERS HALL

Elm St. looking west, Oberlin, Ohio

believed is the "finest
cluster of Cass Gilbert buildings anywhere.
Blodgett became so entranced that before his death in
November of 2001, he published the first volume of his
biography, *Cass Gilbert: The Early Years*. ¶ Oberlin is also
the site of the only U.S. house by Dutch architect Gerrit
Thomas Rietveld (1888-1964), who in the 1920s helped
develop the International Style. While on a Fulbright in
Utrecht in 1956, Charles Parkhurst, who taught art at
Oberlin, met Rietveld and asked the architect to design
his house. Just west of Oberlin, the Parkhurst House,
1961, is not visible from the road. ¶ For further information, see Geoffrey Blodgett's book, *Oberlin Architecture,
College and Town: A Guide to Its Social History*, or his
brochure, "Oberlin College Architecture: A Short History", available from the College Relations Office, 153
West Lorain Street, Oberlin 44074, 440/775-8474; open
weekdays during business hours. All campus buildings
have signs giving their name, architect, and date. ¶ This
tour starts with the Allen Memorial Art Museum at the
northeast corner of Tappen Square, and then goes clockwise around the square. Oberlin College is a National
Historic Landmark and all the pre-1940 buildings here
are on the National Register. For best touring plan for a
day when the Frank Lloyd Wright Weltzheimer House
(see below) is open.

Access: Oberlin and Tappan Square are at the intersection of State Routes 58/Main Street and 511/Lorain Street. From Cleveland take I-480 west; it becomes State Route 10 and then State Route 20; exit at State Route 511 and drive west into town.

ALLEN MEMORIAL ART MUSEUM, 1917

Cass Gilbert, New York
87 North Main Street/State Route 58 at East Lorain Street/State Route 511, Oberlin, east side of Tappan Square
College art museum, open daily except Monday; donation requested; 440/775-8665

Of all Cass Gilbert's buildings in Oberlin, the Allen Memorial Art Museum—which houses one of the country's best college art collections—is the most successful. The Beaux Arts design, with a central, recessed and arcaded porch, is lovely if not very radical, but the colors and materials—the red tile roof, the walls in buff sandstone ornamented with rectangles outlined in red sandstone—seem more daring. In fact, Blodgett says Gilbert worried that the color contrasts might be too sharp, though he knew that time and weather would soften them. Two other architectural features are worth looking for. One is inside: the central atrium that extends the full height of the structure to clerestory windows. The other is at the back: an outdoor courtyard enclosed on two sides by rows of red columns. The benefactor, Dudley Peter Allen, grew up in Oberlin, studied medicine at Harvard, and became a Cleveland surgeon; his wife was oil heiress Elisabeth Severance. Allen wanted to donate the museum to the college, but then died, and his widow took it up as a memorial to him. Dudley Peter Allen's name comes up elsewhere in this guide, in connection with the Peter Allen House in Kinsman. He was the grandson who bought the carved woodwork from a later owner of his grandfather's house and carted it home to Cleveland. Ultimately the woodwork was returned to Kinsman, where that story is told here.

▶ ALLEN ART MUSEUM

ALLEN MEMORIAL ART MUSEUM ADDITION, 1976

Venturi & Rauch, Philadelphia
91 North Main Street, Oberlin, adjoining the art museum
Gallery, offices and
classrooms, conservation
studios, library

In 1966, architect Robert
Venturi published a book,
Complexity and
Contradiction in
Architecture, and thereby
became the country's
leading architectural
theorist. He argued for
ambiguity and tension
and for complexity and
contradiction in design;
he challenged the "less is
more" approach of Mies
van der Rohe and the

▶ ART MUSEUM ADDITION

International Style. ¶ Influential though Venturi was, relatively few of his
designs were built before the mid-1980s; thus this building is a rare example
of how he practiced what he was preaching. Venturi also had something to
say about doing a modern addition for a traditional building. It is, he said,
"like drawing a mustache on a Madonna." ¶ Certainly, his addition for the
Allen Art Museum doesn't look like still more Cass Gilbert. The front part,
housing a gallery, has walls in a checkerboard of buff and red sandstone; the
less visible back, for classes and offices, is buff brick. Black-banded, black-
mullioned windows tie the two sections together. Although the addition
doesn't try to match the older building—for instance, roof lines are at
different levels—it deliberately relates to it. ¶ The new part uses the same
stone—in fact the red, Blodgett says, was from the original quarry, even
though only defective stone was left. Roof overhangs are the same depth, and
both use rectilinear designs. Another old-new link, out of sight from the
front but part of an outdoor walkway connecting the buildings at the back, is
a fat, wood-covered, stripped-down column with Ionic volutes, or scrolls,
supporting an overhang. Also, from the rear alley a connecting roof is visible
over receiving docks. From a distance it could almost be the red tile used in
the rear courtyard; close up, it's corrugated metal, painted to match, exactly.
¶ The most controversial campus building ever, the addition does not have
the jarring effect of a mustache on a Madonna. Much like the contrasting
stones that Gilbert worried about when he designed the Allen, it has
mellowed into looking just right.

HALL AUDITORIUM, 1953

Wallace Harrison, New York
67 North Main Street, Oberlin, next door south to the Art Museum
College theater auditorium

Hall Auditorium was built with a legacy from Oberlin alumnus Charles
Martin Hall, who founded a fortune on his 1886 discovery of an inexpensive
way to process aluminum. The curiosity is that though Hall died in 1914, his
auditorium wasn't built for 40 years. Cass Gilbert designed one, but

construction was stalled by World War I, then by the Depression, and then by Homer Johnson, Hall's executor, who hoped his fledgling architect son Philip might get the commission. Finally the job went to Wallace Harrison, with Philip Johnson as a consultant. Harrison had done the United Nations building in New York and later would do the Metropolitan Opera House at Lincoln Center. There's a lot going on in this building—a curve or slanting line at every turn. Stand across the street and look at the facade, with its undulating marble curtain. The slight tapering of the outer walls and the immense curtain make it seem as though you're looking up at a monumental stage. The auditorium seats only 500, which limits its usefulness.

CONSERVATORY OF MUSIC, 1964
AND KING BUILDING, 1965
Minoru Yamasaki, Detroit
Conservatory, 77 West College; King Building, 10 North Professor, Oberlin;
both at southwest corner of square
Classroom buildings, open daily

These white, three-story buildings seem an architectural tour de force with no particular cognizance of the preexisting setting, which was often how

things were done at the time. With the likes of pointed windows, pinnacles, and crenellations, architect Minoru Yamasaki's detailing has Gothic references. The material used was a newly developed steel-reinforced, machine-molded quartz aggregate. It turned out to be permeable, so that after some years the steel inside oxidizes, expands, and puckers the outside. The college, Blodgett points out woefully, has spent millions of dollars repairing these buildings.

▶ TALCOTT HALL

TALCOTT HALL, 1887
Weary and Kramer, Akron
2 South Professor Street at
College Street, Oberlin
Dormitory; not regularly
accessible to the public

Both Talcott Hall and Baldwin Cottage next door are dormitories originally built for women by Weary and Kramer. Both buildings are unusually interesting. Talcott, which looks wonderful on its corner site, has seven gables. Baldwin has a pair of round arches in front on its porch and a fat octagonal tower under a bell-shaped roof. Rooms inside both are all distinctive.

▶ PETERS HALL

PETERS HALL, 1887

Weary and Kramer, Akron
50 North Professor Street, west side of Tappan Square, Oberlin
Office and classroom building; open daily

Weary and Kramer did three of the four older sandstone buildings at Oberlin
College — Blodgett calls them "the stone elephants". Peters Hall, the one
with the high conical tower roof, has a wonderful interior hall, two stories
high, with a massive brick fireplace opposite a double stairway; ceiling, stairs,
and wainscoting are red oak. Cass Gilbert thought so little of Peters Hall that
he wanted it razed. It survived to receive a $4 million renovation for its 110th
anniversary.

FINNEY CHAPEL, 1908

Cass Gilbert, New York
90 North Professor, west side of Tappan Square, Oberlin
Concert hall

Finney Chapel was Cass Gilbert's first contribution to the Oberlin campus.
Improbably, it combines ideas from twelfth-century French Romanesque
churches and the college's 1901 Warner Gym (now Warner Center, behind
Peters Hall) by Normand Patton, Chicago—Gilbert thought the gym was the
best existing building on campus.

To see more Cass Gilbert work: Next door to the
south of Finney Chapel is Gilbert's second Oberlin
building, Cox Administration Building. Two stories and
relatively compact, Cox is Mediterranean in style.
Gilbert's third project was Allen Art Museum, above; his

fourth, in the 1920s and not on Tappan Square, was the
Allen Memorial Hospital (much altered since); and his
fifth, Bosworth Hall on Tappan Square's north side.
Bosworth, built in 1931 for the Graduate School of
Theology, was part of a Quadrangle that encompassed
chapel, classrooms and residential quarters. Though it
retains the red tile roof and Mediterranean look,
Bosworth Hall, which has a central tower with the chapel
behind, was the only Gilbert building here in limestone
rather than sandstone. At the rear red-brick dormitory
wings connect with arcades to form a courtyard. The
theological school left in the 1960s, and the building now
houses Alumni Affairs and Asia House.

FIRST CHURCH, 1844, TOWER ADDED 1845
Richard Bond, Boston
106 North Main Street, kitty-corner from the art museum, Oberlin, NRHP
Church; interior accessible by office entrance from the parking lot in back,
weekdays during business hours; 440/775-1711

First Church is Oberlin's true venerable—how surprising that a college with
so impressive an early nineteenth-century history has only one large building
from that era. For almost four decades it was the home church of Charles G.
Finney, an evangelist who was also president of the college from 1851 to
1866. Above front stairs wide enough to hold 250 people for a photograph,
as it did when Blodgett's daughter was married, the building presents a
balanced Greek Revival facade in red brick and limestone. Fortunately the
interior is accessible.

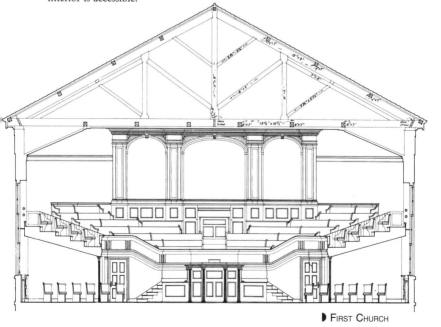

▶ FIRST CHURCH

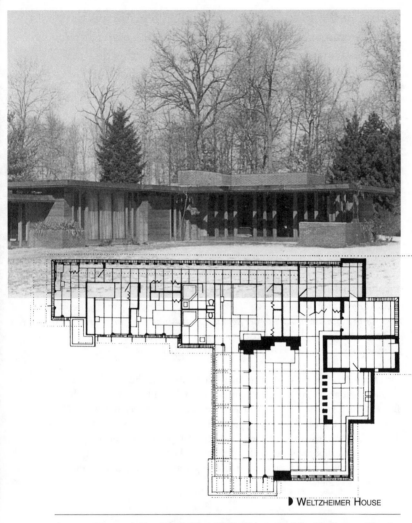

WELTZHEIMER HOUSE

Access: To reach the Frank Lloyd Wright house, take Professor Street south from Tappan Square a few blocks to Morgan Street; turn right/ west and drive to house, set far back from the road but readily visible on the right after Fairway Drive. To see the back of the house continue on Morgan to the corner, Pyle-South Amherst Road; turn right, right again at first turn, Glenhurst Drive; and right again at first turn, Woodhaven Place.

WELTZHEIMER HOUSE, 1950
Frank Lloyd Wright, Spring Green, Wisconsin
127 Woodhaven Place, rear entrance; front faces Morgan Street, Oberlin
House is open for one-hour public tours, afternoons of first Sunday and third
Saturday of every month; reservations advised; tickets for sale in Allen Art
Museum lobby on tour days; 440/775-2086

In the middle of the 1930s Depression, Frank Lloyd Wright began to think about designing affordable houses that he dubbed "Usonian". He proposed to economize by eliminating visible roofs, basements, garages, radiators, painting, and plaster. Instead, Usonian roofs would be flat, cars in carports, walls of unfinished wood, and heating in the concrete floors. Though some of these economies later backfired (it's hard to fix a pipe that's embedded in concrete), at the time they sounded reasonable to many people, including nine Ohioans who built Usonian houses between 1948 and 1957. This, the Charles Weltzheimer House, was the first. Today it is the only Wright house in Ohio that has regular public tours. ¶ The Weltzheimer House is a fairly typical Usonian: one story, L-shaped, with the kitchen near the hub, storage cabinets lining the bedroom wing hall, a massive livingroom fireplace, large windows, and broad cantilevered eaves. Walls are mostly of plywood with redwood veneer. Ceiling heights vary; they're lowest, 6 foot 6 inches, in the hall, and highest, 11 feet 6 inches, in the kitchen and utility room. The house is set back 500 feet from Morgan Street, at a 45-degree angle to the street, so that the bedroom wing has morning sun, and the livingroom, afternoon sun. ¶ Weltzheimer's job brought the family to the Oberlin area in 1946, and early the next year his wife, Margaret, wrote to Frank Lloyd Wright describing the three-acre cornfield they'd bought and mentioning that they could spend up to $15,000 on a house. That summer the family visited Wright in Wisconsin, but it was July, 1948 before they had their final plans in hand. Construction proceeded under the supervision of a Wright apprentice, Ted Bower, who lived with the family for nine months. Though Wright never visited the site, Bower's relatively long stay assured design consistency. ¶ Final costs, perhaps three times the original budget, were a strain for the family. The Weltzheimers were divorced in the 1950s and in 1963 Margaret Weltzheimer had to sell the house. The next two owners were contractors who tried to modernize it; in 1968 Ellen Johnson, an Oberlin art professor, bought it and began restoration—which meant the likes of removing white paint from everything. She died in 1992 and by her will the house went to the college, which uses it as a residence for art lecturers.

Frank Lloyd Wright's Ohio Buildings

William Allin Storrer, who's done the definitive catalogue of Frank Lloyd Wright work, lists 11 buildings in Ohio; except for one medical office building, they are all houses. Two, including the Weltzheimer House and the Westcott House in Springfield, are listed in this guide. Though the Medical Clinic may be visited, all the homes are private and should be viewed from the street. Buildings are listed here with original owners' names:

1. Staley House, 1950, 6363 West Lake Road, North Madison
2. Rubin House, 1951, 518 44th Street, N.W., Canton
3. Boulter House, 1953, 1 Rawson Woods Circle, Cincinnati
4. Dobkins House, 1953, 5120 Plain Center Avenue, N.E., Canton
5. Penfield House, 1953, 2203 River Road, Willoughby Hills
6. Feiman House, 1954, 452 Santa Clara Drive, N.W., Canton
7. Tonkens House, 1954, 6980 Knoll Road, Amberley Village
8. Meyers Medical Clinic, 1956, 5441 Far Hills Avenue, Dayton
9. Boswell House, 1957, 9905 Comargo Club Drive, Indian Hill

Painesville, Lake County

(Also in Lake County: Kirtland and Perry.)

¶ Painesville is a famous Western Reserve town, seat of the state's smallest county, Lake, which separated from Geauga in 1840. Painesville has a lovely square, where the substantial buildings on the perimeter include two Lake County Courthouses. The present courthouse dates from 1909; the old one, 1852, is now Painesville City Hall.

Access: From I-90 east of Cleveland take exit 200, State Route 44; take 44 north to State Route 84; turn right/east; make an immediate left onto Chestnut Street; drive north until Chestnut ends at Mentor Avenue/U.S. 20; turn right/east. In a few blocks Lake Erie College is on the right, facing Washington Street, which at that point forks off U.S. 20 to the right. To reach the old depot return to U.S. 20, now Erie Street, and drive right/east through downtown to State Street; turn left and drive one block to railroad. Square is downtown, at Liberty Street a block south of Erie Street.

LAKE ERIE FEMALE SEMINARY, NOW LAKE ERIE COLLEGE HALL, 1859

Charles W. Heard, Heard & Porter, Cleveland
391 West Washington Street, Painesville, NRHP
Classroom and office building for college with 700 men and women students; building open and accessible weekdays; 440/942-3872

For 40 years, this was Lake Erie Female Seminary's only building, accommodating students, offices, classes, and religion. It's an imposing 180 feet in length, four stories plus a raised basement in height, with a central

▶ LAKE ERIE COLLEGE HALL

▶ LAKE ERIE COLLEGE HALL

tower that rises one story more. Red brick with white trim, the Italianate facade has "180 hooded windows" altogether, as noted by Lake Erie College chronicler Margaret Gross. Eric Johannesen especially liked the arcaded porches between the tower and the end wings. They are, he wrote, "an especially fine detail... [They] give the building a hospitable and gracious look that suggests the resort architecture of the lake area in the latter part of the century." Architect Charles W. Heard (1804?-1876) represented the best traditions in Western Reserve design. After apprenticing with Painesville architect-builder Jonathan Goldsmith, one of whose daughters he married, Heard practiced in Cleveland with Simeon Porter, son of Lemuel Porter, who designed Tallmadge Church. Simeon Porter did Mount Union College's Chapman Hall in Alliance (see also).

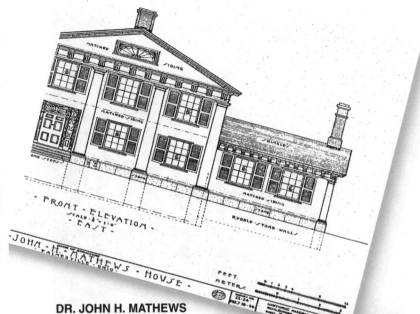

DR. JOHN H. MATHEWS HOUSE, 1829

Jonathan Goldsmith, Painesville
309 West Washington Street, Lake
Erie College campus, NRHP
The Mathews House is east
of College Hall, readily visible;
to see interior, call the college; fee;
440/942-3872

▶ MATHEWS HOUSE

At least in the annals of Ohio architecture, the name of the early architect-builder Jonathan Goldsmith (1783-1847) is ever linked with Painesville; and the Dr. John H. Mathews House there is arguably the best of his few surviving works. Partly because Talbot Hamlin wrote about him in his book on Greek Revival architecture, Goldsmith has become the best known of early Ohio architects. His reputation is in inverse proportion to his extant work; the buildings Hamlin was most enthusiastic about, Painesville's Bank of Geauga and Goldsmith's house, are gone. Some Goldsmith drawings and business accounts survive. So does a memoir by his daughter Lucia, who in 1900, when she was 82, wrote about her family and her father. ¶ Born in Connecticut, Goldsmith was apprenticed to a shoemaker at the age of 11, but he hated the work and six years later bought his way out and apprenticed himself to a carpenter. In 1811 he brought his family to Painesville, a frontier community where, at least at first, his shoemaking skills proved useful. Ultimately Goldsmith worked extensively as an architect-builder in Cleveland and Painesville. He might have moved on to Michigan or Texas or Wisconsin, but his wife Abigail liked Painesville and kept him there. ¶ In 1973 Goldsmith's William P. Robinson House was moved, in eight pieces, from Willoughby to Hale Farm and Village in Bath, where it was reassembled and put on exhibit. The Mathews House had been moved even earlier, in 1951, but it traveled only half a mile from its original location on State Street. When the house was threatened with razing, 339 contributors gave $15,000 for the move, which came in three stages: one for the main house, and one for each wing. But now the exterior of the Federal and Greek Revival house is always accessible for a close look at the carving, which Goldsmith did himself.

LAKE SHORE & MICHIGAN SOUTHERN
RAILROAD STATION, 1893

Shepley Rutan and Coolidge, Boston
475 Railroad Street, Painesville
Former station under renovation for a
museum; for information e-mail Western
Reserve Railroad Association:
nycdepot@ncweb.com

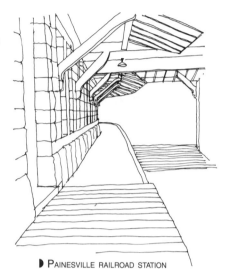

▶ PAINESVILLE RAILROAD STATION

When I saw this Richardsonian Romanesque railroad station in spring, 1997, it was boarded up. The inside, largely gutted, housed a group of radiators (some round) and a pile of stone—what was left of the chimney that toppled in 1994. Even chimneyless, it was a wonderful building, round at one end, with a roof sweeping down into 12-foot overhangs supported by oversized wooden brackets. Like a ship's bow, the round end pointed up the track.

The designer was Boston architect H.H. Richardson's successor firm, Shepley Rutan and Coolidge, who did many railroad stations, including one in Sandusky (see also). As the new station went into service in February 1893, the Painesville *Telegraph* reported that the building was 111 by 33 feet. The semicircular end held a ladies' waiting room separated from the main waiting room by the ticket office and restrooms. On the track side of the building, the telegraph office occupied a bay under an eyebrow dormer, while baggage and express rooms were at the far, squared end. The article lamented that the lavatories, finished in marble and equipped with quality plumbing fixtures, could not be used because the sewer line had yet to be installed. What to do with an unused railroad station is not always easy to figure out. In 1993 Ed Dunlap, a Painesville native and Pittsburgh roofing magnate, bought the station from the railroad to develop . as a restaurant. When that proved impractical and the   Lake County Historical Society decided it didn't   have the wherewithal to take on

▶ PAINESVILLE RAILROAD STATION

the depot, station stalwarts formed a separate nonprofit. Called the Western Reserve Railroad Association, it plans to transform the station into a museum and rental facility. In 1997 Dunlap gave the building and $50,000 to the association, which was likely to need another $700,000 for a complete rehab. By early 1999, president Mark Welch reported that repairs to the slate roof were complete—a $154,000 job. Welch was delighted with the new copper ridge caps and restored cupola. He postponed the targeted finish date to 2003, and resumed looking for money.

Peninsula, Summit County

(Peninsula, Hudson, and Twinsburg, linked by State Routes 303 and 91, make a northern Summit County tour. This guide has three old rural schools—all very different—in this region; others are in Southington and Cadiz (listed with Southeast Ohio.)

¶ The tiny, picturesque town of Peninsula is surrounded by the Cuyahoga Valley National Park. Virtually a clearing in the forest, the village comes right out of a fairy tale. A modern fairy tale, for there's now a historic architectural tour on line: *www.explorepeninsula.com*

Access: From I-271 exit at State Route 303; Peninsula is just to the east; Township Hall is on north side at Riverview Road.

PENINSULA HIGH SCHOOL, NOW BOSTON TOWNSHIP TOWN HALL, 1887, REHAB 1999

1775 West Streetsboro Road, Peninsula, NRHP/Peninsula Village HD
Township and rental offices, community rooms; 330/657-2842

In 1988 Randy Bergdorf, archivist and historian at the Peninsula Library, went into politics to save a vacant, moldering building with tall windows and a tower, the Boston Township Town Hall. Being elected township trustee turned out to be the easy part. ¶ The problem was money, of course. With 90 percent of the township's land in what's now the Cuyahoga Valley Park, Peninsula is surrounded mostly by forest—though spared from sprawl, it has almost no tax base. It did have money about 1980, when it came into a $4.1 million inheritance tax windfall, but that whooshed into potholes and other routine expenses. Fortunately, the township reserved $350,000 for the hall; unfortunately, estimates by the 1990s approached $1 million. So in 1990 Bergdorf led in founding the Boston Township Hall Committee, a nonprofit fund-raising entity that qualified for substantial grants by taking a long-term lease on the hall. Rehabbing began in fall 1996 and took three years. The building is supporting itself with rentals. ¶ The Town Hall is a Stick style, with exposed frame construction and some boards set diagonally or vertically. A bell tower rises above on skinny posts, though the bell fell out while

▶ Boston Township Town Hall

celebrating the end of World War II. ¶ Originally the hall was Peninsula High School, built by the village in 1887 because the township school was too expensive. Two classrooms up and two down, the new school had all 12 grades; calling it "high school" added status. It housed a school until 1939, when the township became owner and turned it into the Grange Hall and a community building. Scouts met there for years. That was how Randy Bergdorf came to know the building in his youth, in the late 1970s and early 1980s, before it was closed for fire violations in 1985. Will Scouts meet there again? Bergdorf is working on that.

Perry, Lake County

(Also in Lake County: Kirtland and Painesville.)
¶ Once upon a time this area was all plant nurseries and garden stores. It still was when the Perry Nuclear Plant was completed in 1988, but then in the 1990s, as the power plant's property taxes permitted construction of a fabulous new school, people rushed to move in. So what's growing now are suburbs.

▶ Perry Education Village

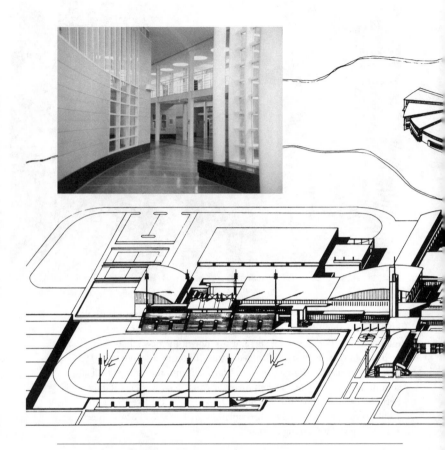

Access: From I-90 take State Route 44 (exit 200) north to State Route 2; drive east; road becomes U.S. 20; at second light turn right onto Center Road; school is on left in half a mile.

PERRY COMMUNITY EDUCATION VILLAGE, 1993, 1995
Ralph Johnson, Perkins & Will, Chicago; Burgess & Niple, Columbus
1 Success Boulevard, Perry
Public school, K-12; visitors wanting to look around should check first in office; tours may be arranged beforehand; 440/259-3511

The first time I visited the Perry Community Education Village, I stood near the entrance and looked north, up the length of the football field. There the Perry Nuclear Plant's cooling towers, actually two miles distant, appeared between the goal posts. Alas, when I went back a year and a half later, a scoreboard blocked that symbolic image: the triumphant intertwining of this school and the power plant whose taxes made it possible. ¶ The windfall from Centerior's 1988 plant gave Perry the kind of opportunity that, says retired Superintendent E. Edgar Goodwin, comes "once in ten lifetimes." School officials saw and seized their uncommon chance to set high educational, technological, and architectural goals for their new building. Perry became ambitious. ¶ It determined on "a cathedral for education, the

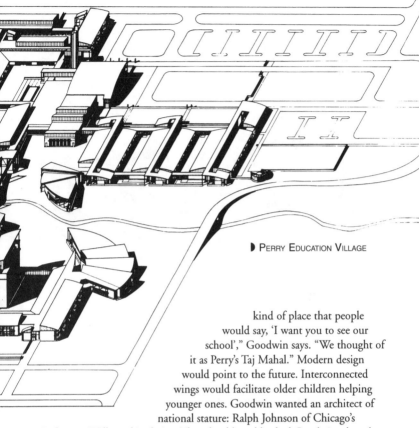

▶ PERRY EDUCATION VILLAGE

kind of place that people would say, 'I want you to see our school'," Goodwin says. "We thought of it as Perry's Taj Mahal." Modern design would point to the future. Interconnected wings would facilitate older children helping younger ones. Goodwin wanted an architect of national stature: Ralph Johnson of Chicago's Perkins & Will was his choice. The school board backed Goodwin, though he acknowledges that not having to pass a levy made that easier. ¶ Because later other localities began sharing the power-plant tax revenues, Perry was really flush only for the first part of the $100 million project. That was the 1993 west wing, for which $70 million in cash was lavished on the high school, theater, main kitchen, and athletic facilities the community shares. An extraordinary quarter-mile hall bridges a creek to connect that wing with the more cost-conscious elementary and middle schools to the east, finished in 1995. ¶ All the buildings are mostly low and sprawling, with some 30-foot-high spaces showing on the outside as arcs or angles rising above the roof line. Higher still are the bulky 90-foot theater flyloft and a slender 100-foot tower whose clock is visible only from the football stadium. All three schools have appendages with fan-shaped footprints for libraries, music, and art rooms. Of course, the whole place is wired—blackboards are out, so chalk dust won't gum up the electronics. Classrooms have glossy white boards that take markers, easily erased. ¶ This school has design awards in its trophy case, but it's not perfect. Some students call it "the jail". A high-school staffer complains that classrooms are too small, landscaping was too slow in completion, nooks and crannies too many for supervising adolescents. But he adds a high compliment: "Whether you like the looks or not, it works educationally." Steven Litt, *Plain Dealer* architecture critic, had very high praise. This complex, he wrote, "deserves to be treasured and studied as an architectural masterpiece."

▶ CHALKER HIGH SCHOOL

Southington, Trumbull County

(This guide has three old rural schools—all very different—in this region; others are in Peninsula and Cadiz
[listed with Southeast Ohio].)

CHALKER HIGH SCHOOL, 1906

4432 State Route 305, Southington, just west of State Route 534
School building and administrative offices; open weekdays; 330/898-1781

Because Southington is a small place, this school is a surprise—the last thing
you expect in this Western Reserve countryside. It's a flamboyant building,
two stories in orange brick with brown trim. In front it has a formal porch
with tall white Ionic columns. It even has an intact porte-cochere,
balustraded on top. And two recumbent lions flank the doorway, their heads
raised. Much like this building, they look very proud. Native son Newton
Chalker made lots of money as an Akron lawyer, and then donated this
school, with an endowment, to his home town. Surely, he hoped it would
make education more convenient than his own had been. In 1856, at 14, he
had had to travel seven miles to the nearest high school, in Farmington. That
was just the first step in his pursuit of an education, which from high school
on he paid for mostly by stopping to work as a school teacher; he didn't finish
law school until his late twenties. Little wonder that when he provided a
school for Southington, the building would look triumphant. Southington
Local Schools, serving the township, have fewer than 700 students altogether;
some are in adjacent buildings just to the east. Chalker High School still has
classrooms in use on the second floor and in the basement, while offices fill
the first floor. The interior has been altered. Photos in the lobby all show
Newton Chalker, except for one of George Washington and another of an old
man in a black hat. That's Newton's grandfather James Chalker, from
Connecticut, a founder of Southington.

Tallmadge, Summit County

(Western Reserve Church tour; for routing see Twinsburg.)

¶ Tallmadge is famous for one building, an old church. It's set in a green, the hub of a traffic circle whose rushing cars make the road seem like a moat, keeping the green separate from the auto service and fast food shops on the other side. All this is a far cry from the early days, when the eight roads coming to the circle were all leading to the church.

Founded in 1806 by Congregational missionary David Bacon, Tallmadge was a theocracy under which residents paid two cents an acre for the church until 1814. By then Bacon, encumbered by debt, had gone back to Connecticut. In 1853 a second building joined the church in the green, a Greek

▶ FIRST CONGREGATIONAL CHURCH

Revival Town Hall, which had a school upstairs. It now houses the Tallmadge Historical Society and its museum; 330/630-9760.

Access: Tallmadge Circle is northeast of Akron at the intersection of State Routes 91 and 261

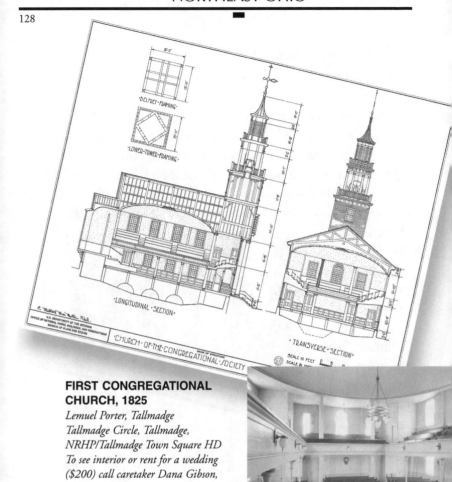

·BELFREY·FRAMING·

·LOWER·TOWER·FRAMING·

·LONGITUDINAL·SECTION·

·CHURCH·OF·THE·CONGREGATIONAL·SOCIETY·

·TRANSVERSE·SECTION·

SCALE IN FEET

FIRST CONGREGATIONAL CHURCH, 1825

Lemuel Porter, Tallmadge
Tallmadge Circle, Tallmadge,
NRHP/Tallmadge Town Square HD
To see interior or rent for a wedding
($200) call caretaker Dana Gibson,
330/733-5879

The First Congregational Church of
Tallmadge is a beautiful building. It is
the masterpiece of Lemuel Porter
(1775-1829), who had apprenticed

▶ FIRST CONGREGATIONAL

and established himself in Connecticut and then came to Ohio at 42. Five
years later, with help from Archer Benjamin's builders' manual, he began
work on this church, which has been linked securely to New England ever
since. That hasn't been to the Tallmadge church's advantage. For instance,
while surveying American architecture G.E. Kidder Smith averred that it
"would be a capable but unremarkable example in the East." Ohio authority
I.T. Frary was more generous, claiming that it "compares favorably with all
but the very best examples in New England."
¶ Porter, a skilled carver, did both the interior and exterior. The columns are
the solid trunks of walnut trees, not fluted but reeded, or carved with slender
convex ridges rather than grooves. The shallow central porch and its
pediment have a flush-matched siding that contrasts with the clapboard on
the rest of the building. Porter unconventionally mixed Greek orders—he
used Ionic columns and a Doric frieze. That was probably to achieve a
"visually active" facade, as Hiram College scholars John Strassberger (who has
since left for Pennsylvania) and David Anderson wrote. They added that the
church's design refuted any notion of the "frontier as a place of mere
primitive squalor." ¶ After Lemuel Porter finished Tallmadge church in 1825,

he was summoned to Hudson to build Middle College for Western Reserve College. The Porter family moved to Hudson in 1829, but Porter died that fall. His Middle and South Colleges are long gone, but a few of his houses can still be seen in Hudson. "He's an original talent," says Priscilla Graham, an architectural historian in Hudson. "He didn't do the same thing over and over. And there's no question he was important. He was a deacon in the church, a colonel in the militia. When he died they had a procession walking ten miles from Hudson to Tallmadge. That's what they thought of him." ¶ And Graham, who herself has seen most of the famous New England churches, affirms that Tallmadge's is on a level with the best. ¶ But about 1970, its congregation abandoned Tallmadge church. They built themselves a bigger brick building not far away on Heritage Drive, where everything is relatively new. So the Ohio Historical Society manages Tallmadge Church. The crown jewel of Ohio's Western Reserve churches, is no longer a church.

Twinsburg, Summit County

(Western Reserve Church tour: Start with Twinsburg Congregational Church; take State Route 91 south to Hudson's Western Reserve Chapel, and then on to Tallmadge Church. Continue south on 91; after I-76 turn left/east on U.S. 224, which after 14 miles reaches Atwater.)

¶ Since 1976 Twinsburg has been hosting a festival for twins; one of the highlights is the Double Take Parade. Twinsburg has two architectural sites of interest here, but they certainly wouldn't qualify for that parade.

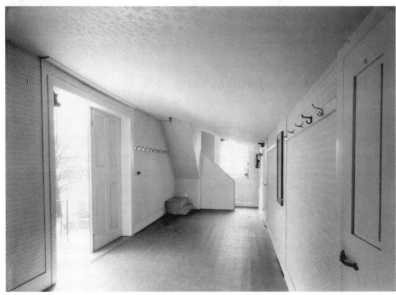

▶ TWINSBURG CONGREGATIONAL

Access: Twinsburg Square and the Congregational Church are at the intersection of State Routes 91 and 82. East of Cleveland, I-480 has an exit at State Route 91/Darrow Road; exit is south of square and just north of Crown Hill Memorial Park.

TWINSBURG CONGREGATIONAL CHURCH, NOW FIRST CONGREGATIONAL CHURCH, UNITED CHURCH OF CHRIST, 1848

Simeon Porter, Cleveland
9050 Church Street, Twinsburg Square, Twinsburg, NRHP
Church; 330/425-2181

The very model of classical serenity, this white church faces into a beautiful square; it looks splendid in the morning sun. Of frame construction and Greek Revival style, it was built from a mail-order plan Simeon Porter sent from Cleveland. The spire was replaced in 1857.

▶ Twinsburg Congregational Church

CROWN HILL MEMORIAL PARK, 1929

L.E. Blue, Cleveland
8592 Darrow Road/State Route 91, Twinsburg,
above Highland Road Cemetery; 330/425-8128

In contrast with Simeon Porter's classical church downtown, Crown Hill Memorial Park has two romantic cemetery buildings. They're readily visible from the road; close up they're even better. The one with the square tower is the chapel—Akron architectural historian James A. Pahlau dubs it late Gothic Revival—and the other, an administration building with a round tower and conical roof, he calls Norman Cottage style. Behind the buildings and fronting the burial grounds, a long wall has some little turrets of its own.
  ¶ This cemetery complex has several remarkable features. One is that both buildings have essentially unaltered interiors, excepting only the chapel's carpet. Secondly, the exterior masonry, used in both buildings and the wall, is

very unusual. It is basically bricks, some swollen, warped, or blackened; some laid with the long side vertical and others in the usual way. Ohio State's Douglas Graf says they are "clinkers", or spoiled, overcooked bricks. They are so varied, so active, so restless and uneasy in effect, that they seem a Sturm-und-Drang siding. ¶ What particularly impressed Graf about these buildings was the crenellation on top of the chapel tower. It seems to be crumbling away, as if in ruins. That's deliberate, symbolic of the business of the cemetery. Graf called the style Arts and Crafts. ¶ So Doug Graf and Jim Pahlau, both experts, had different initial takes on the style of Crown Hill's buildings. Of course, they are both right, but they were focusing on different aspects. Graf called it Arts and Crafts because of the clinkers and the symbolism of the eroding crenellation. Pahlau cited revival styles because of the forms the architect used. Unlike the atomic weights of elements, architectural styles can be a matter of interpretation.

¶ Another thing about this cemetery: it's said to have a twin. It's a cemetery in Oklahoma, designed by the same architect and built of the same material.

▶ CROWN HILL, ADMINISTRATION BUILDING

▶ TRUMBULL COUNTY COURTHOUSE

Warren, Trumbull County

(For Mahoning Valley tour of sites in this guide, just east of downtown Warren, turn off U.S. 422 onto State Route 169/Niles Road, which continues south to Niles, where it joins State Route 46, which continues south to Mineral Ridge. After that, 46 intersects I-80, which just to the east links with I-680 and Youngstown, Vol. I.)

¶ Warren has a radical city planner, Alexander T. Bobersky, who sees old buildings as valuable assets; razing them, he says, is "throwing away your inheritance." So it's no accident that lately Warren has been in the throes of an impressive spurt of city-stimulated redevelopment of old buildings. By late 2001, the 1923 Robins Theatre was moving ahead with restoration. The handsome and previously shabby 1832 Kinsman House was now city-owned and being restored. A non-profit agency had a city loan to rehab three downtown commercial buildings, and vocational students were renovating an 1854 Italianate house on Mahoning Avenue.

Respinning Warren—On his way to the future, Warren city planner Alexander T. Bobersky has come up with a new spin on Warren's past. For starters, he's knocked Henry B. Perkins, the legendary patriarch, off his pedestal.

Perkins, who's been generally revered in Warren, and whose house is now a splendid city hall, started out well as a son of General Simon Perkins from Connecticut. Simon made Warren the seat of Trumbull County when that really mattered, for it included all the Western Reserve. But by 1845 Simon was gone and the county had been chopped up into all the counties of northeast Ohio, and by 1863 Henry had taken over his father's bank, only to spend the rest of his life making sure Warren stayed a bucolic backwater.

Henry was the youngest of Simon Perkins's sons. The oldest went off to develop Akron on land his father owned. Another settled in Cleveland and still another, Jacob, built the Cleveland and Mahoning Valley Railroad. "Unfortunately for Warren," Bobersky says, "Jacob, who believed in railroads and industry and progress, died early in life." Henry, 39 when he took over the bank, was the only one left in Warren. And in fact, he was a very good banker—so successful that during the Civil War Lincoln's Treasury secretary consulted him. What Bobersky takes issue with is the way Henry stymied progress in Warren. For instance, to make sure that Warren stayed a bucolic county seat, he turned down the Packard brothers when they wanted a loan to make cars. The Packards ended up in Detroit, where bankers were more receptive.

Traditionally Warren has exalted Henry. Harriet Taylor Upton, a resident, suffragette, and the author of a two-volume Trumbull County history, wrote of his "justice and unimpeachable integrity," how handsome he was, and how he saved the library from bankruptcy. But Bobersky takes a more critical view of Henry's civic generosity.

Alex Bobersky's appearance—he is bearded, rugged-looking, self-effacing—belies his astuteness. Not only is he a planner by profession, but he is also, by avocation, a cultural geographer. With co-author David Stephens, he has traced Ohio settlement patterns through roof designs in slates of contrasting colors. They've also studied Western Reserve town squares. They found that of the 96 pre-1825 towns, only seven were true New England theocracies, with a single building as meeting house, church, and school. Though Warren has always thought of itself as a New England town, it was never a theocracy.

Nor was it founded by New Englanders, as Bobersky can tell from the layout of Warren's square, which is characteristically mid-Atlantic—the clue is that the courthouse is in the green, rather than at the side facing into it. That observation led Bobersky to rediscover forgotten town founder Ephraim Quinby, a Pennsylvanian. Quinby had become obscure because later arrivals, richer and better educated New Englanders, took charge and conveniently forgot the initial wave from Pennsylvania.

Cultural geography also led Bobersky to discover that in Henry Perkins's late nineteenth-century era, Warren was essentially a landed aristocracy, far removed from the egalitarian American ideal. The 1874 atlas shows a ring of large farms around Warren, all owned by gentlemen who lived in town; Henry Perkins alone owned or controlled almost 1,800 acres of prime farmland. Progress would have threatened the landed aristocracy's power and way of life. Sums up Bobersky: "Industrialization, urban growth, and foreigners all had to wait until Henry was gone.

"Henry Perkins made one mistake," he continues. "He let his children go to Yale and then made them come back to Warren." Being tied by your father's purse to a small country town may be an unhappy experience. One son killed himself; another drank himself to death. One daughter married an itinerant salesman; the other, a Cincinnati judge. In 1902, grieving after his son's suicide, the old man hung himself in the office building stairwell next to his house.

Bobersky values civic generosity, which gives cultural enhancement to places. Founder Ephraim Quinby laid out courthouse square and then donated it to Warren. That, in Bobersky's view, was "the most significant act of civic leadership" in the city's history. Henry Perkins was never so generous. He did save Warren's library from bankruptcy; he did support local schools; but, says Bobersky, "he left no civic institutions, foundations, or grandchildren." His money and power were for his own benefit, while the Packards, like Quinby generous to the community, gave Warren both a landscaped park and Packard Music Hall. Perkins's daughter donated the land behind the mansion, but it's a flood plain under water every year or two. As for the house, she *sold* that to the city.

The reaction to decades of barring progress set in after Henry Perkins's death. Liberated from the ban on industrial development, Warren's Board of Trade pulled out all the stops in its push for progress and industry. Starting in 1906 it lured 40 industries to Warren in 20 years; 20 others came with the flow. The bucolic county seat vanished forever, succeeded by an industrial town that prospered until the 1980s recession, when it lost 30 industries and unemployment percentages climbed into the mid 20s. Directly and indirectly, says Bobersky, Henry Perkins shaped the economic extremes of 150 years of Warren history, and neither extreme succeeded.

But by 2001, new tenants had those old factories back in use, though with lower-paying jobs; unemployment was down to 6.5 percent. With Packard Electric and Lordstown assembly, General Motors still accounted for a high 60 percent of local manufacturing employment, but the percentage was drifting downward. Bobersky regrets that Warren is "a twentieth-century branch-plant industrial town, which means a lack of leaders. Our hospitals, our newspapers, all are becoming owned by someone else." Some Community Development projects he helped with, such as recruiting a state prison (jobs, Bobersky notes, "with salaries and benefits that nobody in Detroit is going to take away") were, he realized, ironic victories.

Another of Bobersky's Community Development projects was one that may not sound like much outside Warren: the county's first parking garage. A parking garage is progress? It is in Bobersky's eyes, for he sees it as preserving downtown around Courthouse Square, by forestalling the razing of buildings for parking lots and keeping the streetscape intact. "What little urbanity we have is tied up with the square," he says.

And along with a reviving economy, a little urbanity augurs well for Warren.

▶ TRUMBULL COUNTY COURTHOUSE

Access: En route from I-271 near Cleveland to Youngstown, U.S. 422 passes through downtown Warren. From it turn north on Main Street to Courthouse, a building you can't miss. At the northwest corner of the square Main veers to the northwest, becomes Mahoning Avenue and, north of City Hall, State Route 45.

TRUMBULL COUNTY COURTHOUSE, 1897; RESTORATION 1996

LaBelle and French, Marion, Indiana; restoration by van Dijk Pace Westlake, Cleveland
160 High Street, Warren, NRHP
Open weekdays; 330/675-2557

This Richardsonian Romanesque courthouse has a fine site: a central downtown square that is still the city's focal point. The courthouse has a high central domed clock tower, load-bearing sandstone walls, and 12-foot copper statues of justice atop central gables on four sides. The roof of copper sheeting over ceramic tiles used to seem like acres of green. Several years later it looked brown, as the new roof of the same materials mellowed on its gradual way to greenness. The third floor Common Pleas Courtroom No. 1 was fully restored; interior halls are handsome.

HENRY B. PERKINS HOUSE, NOW WARREN CITY HALL, 1871
Joseph Ireland, Cleveland
391 Mahoning Avenue, Warren, NRHP/Mahoning Avenue HD
City hall, open weekdays; 330/841-2601

The rich and influential Henry B. Perkins hired a distinguished Cleveland architect, Joseph Ireland, to build his Italianate mansion. The end result was worthy of his station and of his guests, who included five former and future presidents: Ulysses S. Grant, James A. Garfield, Rutherford B. Hayes, Benjamin Harrison, and William McKinley. The grounds extended back half

a mile to the Mahoning River; no other Western Reserve town, says Warren planner Alex Bobersky, had so large an estate just a block from the Courthouse Square. Though most of Perkins's varied plantings have been lost, Bobersky says that the number of different trees remaining could provide the basis for a

small arboretum. In 1931 a Perkins daughter sold the 20-room house to Warren for $75,000, and it's been City Hall ever since. French mirrors reflect municipal business conducted in front of Italian marble fireplaces. The mayor is in the library; the Public Service director, in the parlor; Human Resources, in the kitchen. The assortment of color family snapshots, metal office furniture, and computers shows that the city is down to business and at home. Structural changes have been relatively few—Henry B. Perkins would know the place. The City of Warren has honored its premises far better than Ohio colleges, which have routinely gutted old buildings to modernize the interiors with dropped ceilings and paneling. The changes that the city has made, sit uneasily with Mayor Henry J. Angelo. In the mid-1970s, the city sandblasted the brick (not too badly, but that's now a preservation taboo); painted the stone, leading to water problems; and put seven air-conditioners through the 14-inch walls. Angelo hopes someday to find the money to make amends for all these, as well as take out the radiators, which aren't original, and banish hanging fluorescents. Says the mayor, "I have a real love for this building."

EVATION.

T TO THE INCH.

▶ PERKINS HOUSE, ARCHITECT'S DRAWING

▶ WELLINGTON TOWN HALL

Wellington, Lorain County

(Also in Lorain County: Oberlin; tour also with Medina to the east.)

Access: Wellington is nine miles south of Oberlin on State Route 58, at the intersection with State Route 18.

WELLINGTON TOWN HALL, 1885

Oscar Cobb, Chicago
115 Willard Square, on State Route 58, NRHP/Wellington Center HD
Town hall and gym

This is the Town Hall that cheese built, and as the "Cheese Empire of the Nation," Wellington was not about to settle for anything cheesy. A Chicago theater architect drew up plans for a combination town hall/opera house dramatically crowned with ogee-shaped gables rising above the roof. Atop the three-story red-brick building, these decorative wooden gables are all painted white, as is an open cupola under its own ogee-shaped roof. To complete the exotic fillips, the central third-floor window has a large round Moorish-seeming arch. ¶ The building is a mixture of styles that one source lists as Byzantine, Greek, Gothic, and Spanish. That's too many for some scholars. At Westerville's Otterbein College, an art teacher used to show her classes a picture of Wellington Town Hall as an example of bad architecture; she believed that good architecture sticks to a single style. It's true that a stylistic hodgepodge takes risks, and that uniqueness is no guarantee of merit. But this Town Hall succeeds. It's fun, ambitious, distinctive: a Town Hall Wellington is justifiably proud of. ¶ Wellington's reign as Cheese Empire came between the Civil War and 1900. The place had 40 cheese factories; in

1878 alone it shipped 6.4 million pounds of cheese and 1 million pounds of butter. Cheese and other commerce also gave the town the impressive row of manses visible on State Route 58 south of downtown. ¶ As for changes in the Town Hall, the 1,000-seat opera house does not endure. Its top was lopped off and the bottom converted to a gym in the 1950s, according to Charles Oney of the Southern Lorain County Historical Society. A more recent alteration affected the third floor, which has high ceilings and stained glass in the windows, but low-ceilinged modern offices were thought a necessity. So rather than block off the windows, the designer ran the corridor around the wall and in the center built a low-ceilinged windowless hut for office space. ¶ The building facade has a wonderful iron balcony in front of the second floor's big arched window. For about 30 years, the balcony, removed in a 1950s remodeling, wasn't there. But it happened that instead of selling it for scrap, the contractor took it home and planted flowers in it. In 1985 when everybody was looking at old pictures and wondering if the balcony could be replicated, the contractor hauled it out of his garden and sent it back.

▶ WELLINGTON TOWN HALL

West Andover, Ashtabula County
(See Western Reserve for rural loop tour including West Andover, pages 143-145.)

Access: From I-90 turn south on State Route 7, which U.S. 6 joins. Stay on 6 when it turns right/west at Andover. West Andover is two miles farther; John Henderson House is on the east side of Stanhope-Kelloggsville Road just north of U.S. 6.

JOHN HENDERSON HOUSE, C. 1850
5248 Stanhope-Kelloggsville Road, West Andover, NRHP
Private house

The John Henderson House, a small Greek Revival dwelling, comes as a surprise, for its design is so sophisticated and its location, so remote. Architectural historian Eric Johannesen pronounced it "one of the masterpieces of the Greek Revival architectural idiom in all of northeastern Ohio." ¶ The house is partly Doric detailing from an Asher Benjamin builders' guide, and partly Jeffersonian. The Smithsonian Institution's Roger Kennedy, who included it in his book on Greek Revival in the United States, pointed out that the house resembles Thomas Jefferson's first plan for

▶ JOHN HENDERSON HOUSE

Monticello. Kennedy suggests that both Jefferson and this builder were working from Palladian drawings. ¶ As in Jefferson's plan, done about 1772, the Henderson House has two stories in the middle, both with recessed porches and four columns framing a door and two windows. At the sides single-story wings here are just wide enough in front for one window and a pilaster; pilasters continue around onto the sides. John Henderson, a builder, is the earliest documented owner; he probably constructed his own house. ¶ When I saw the house again in 2001, not only was it for sale, but major construction was underway on the facade. It turned out that, after ten years in the house, owner Lauren Zack had moved to Virginia, but she reported from there that she was still having work done on the house. The project I'd seen, she said, was restoration of a copper pan in the upper porch's floor. She also planned to repaint. She said, "I keep telling people, '*No, you can't put vinyl siding on it.*'"

Wooster, Wayne County

(Also in Wayne County: Marshallville)
¶ One time when I was in Wooster the old Tudor Revival high school was being torn down; its successor is a new shopping-mall-style building on the outskirts—everyone has to drive to reach it. But Wooster does have a wonderful downtown whose revitalization received national recognition. And it has the Wooster College campus.

Access: Wooster College is a little north of downtown Wooster; central campus is bordered on west by Bever Street, on north by Wayne Avenue, on east by Beall Avenue, and on south by University Street. From U.S. 30 eastbound take Madison Avenue exit; turn right/north; road becomes Bever. Coming from the north, from I-71 take State Route 83 south; in Wooster turn right/south on Friendsville Road; road becomes Burbank, then Bever. For more information check online: *www.wooster.edu*

WOOSTER COLLEGE CAMPUS, 1902-1937
NRHP
College campus; 330/263-2000

Wooster College has a lovely campus. That's due in part to the hilltop site, the grounds, the mature trees, and in part to the buildings, a group of large solid-looking structures with Medieval detailing and light-colored masonry. They are an early twentieth-century ensemble, more important for their overall impact than for the individual units. ¶ They are here because in 1901 a fire destroyed Wooster's six-story monster of an Old Main. Only two years at the helm and suddenly all but bereft of his institution, President Louis Edward Holden proceeded to prove himself in fundraising—once he had convinced Andrew Carnegie to offer $75,000, Holden replied that what he was expecting was $100,000. He got it, on condition that he raise another $150,000 within 60 days. Of course Holden did, so that where one building had been, five went up. ¶ Two fortuitous strokes helped this campus rise above the ordinary, and the first was consulting Chicago architect Daniel H. Burnham before reconstruction began. Though President Holden wanted every new building in a different style, Burnham, then the nation's preeminent planner, urged Wooster to use just one style in the new buildings, to give the campus cohesion and harmony. So the buildings are a consistent Collegiate Gothic, and all the initial group were in a vitrified gray brick. ¶ The principal architect was

▶ EBERT ART CENTER

Holden's brother, Lansing, of New York, who designed four of the five buildings finished a year after the fire. His included the new old main, Kauke Hall, and Ebert Art Center (originally Severance Hall), to the north. Later Lansing Holden provided Wooster with an attractive pair of dormitories, done perhaps when he had more time: Kenarden Lodge, 1911, and Holden Hall, 1907. Another campus architect was Daniel Everett Waid, also of New York, whose designs included Douglass Hall, 1929, a dorm, and Galpin Hall, 1933, the administration building. As

▶ GALPIN HALL

for the grounds, the Oak Grove, used for commencements, is between Kauke and Ebert; and behind Ebert there's the Quad, a long open green loosely enclosed by buildings. ¶ Then there's the second fortuitous stroke: the arch, called the Delmar Archway, through Kauke Hall's first floor. It's so right that it looks as though it must have been there forever, but in fact the arch was added in 1962, and has been enmeshed in campus traditions, such as commencement processions, ever since. From the front it's an enticing entry to the campus. On a grander scale, it opens up a splendid north-south axis that runs through campus toward hills so far off that they're faint on the horizon. Stand on the steps in front of Ebert and look south, through the archway. It's a marvelous vista. By design.

▶ KENARDEN LODGE

Spotting New England: Ohio's Western Reserve

No region of Ohio has so much the stamp of another place, as some rural parts of the Western Reserve. Originally a Connecticut colony of sorts, Ohio's northeast corner was settled by New Englanders who brought New England with them. The Western Reserve area they came to was bounded on the north by Lake Erie and on the south by the 41st parallel—roughly where U.S. 224 runs now; then it extended west through what are now Erie and Huron counties. All the land was sold to developers to endow Connecticut's public schools except for the westernmost strip, the Firelands, which was reserved for people who had Connecticut property that the British burned during the Revolutionary War. Today the Firelands make up almost all of Erie and Huron Counties (listed in this guide with Northwest Ohio.) ¶ The key to spotting New England influence is the town layout: a green with public buildings at the periphery. So says Ohio State's Douglas Graf, who goes on to point out that a surrounding grid of streets confirms that this is nineteenth-century Ohio rather than the seventeenth-century prototype. "New England towns tend to be ridiculous in layout," he says. "That gets dumped in Ohio. Even in the Western Reserve where they're duplicating New England towns, they don't really. They're rationalizing them into a grid." So Ohio has none of the picturesque streets going off in odd directions—the "cowpath" streets of Massachusetts's Marblehead or New York's Greenwich Village. ¶ But if the ridiculous layouts of New England towns never made it to Ohio, at least the New Englanders who settled the Western Reserve cared about how their communities looked. They "placed a high value on beauty and order along with due regard for possible speculative profits from the sale of town lots," writes John Reps, an authority on town planning. Some of the settlers from New England were older, established individuals with enough money to buy a whole township for development. When they moved west, they brought the best builder from home along with them; some New England-trained carpenter-builders did very fine work in Ohio. The Western Reserve became the prime area for designs from builders' handbooks by New England architect Asher Benjamin. ¶ What we usually think of as typical Western Reserve architecture is a white Federal or Greek Revival house or a white church with a tower, built of wood by a New England-trained

▶ ATWATER CONGREGATIONAL CHURCH

carpenter-builder. Such structures have virtually all disappeared from cities, though even in cities a New England green or square may remain—the premier example is Cleveland's Public Square. ¶ Today the best places to find a still intact Western Reserve look, complete with green and buildings, are rural ones. The following tour, in southern Ashtabula and northern Trumbull counties, is an especially good one—it's generally consistent and unspoiled; it includes some sites described more fully with their town listings in this guide. To see Western Reserve churches, the itinerary for a tour of the best is listed with Twinsburg, the starting point. Between them, these two itineraries include the work of the leading Western Reserve builders, except for architect Jonathan Goldsmith, best represented today by the Mathews House in Painesville. ¶ Early New England influence in Ohio was not limited to the Western Reserve. To their enduring benefit, both Granville and Marietta, also in this guide, were founded by New Englanders.

Loop Itinerary for Touring Western Reserve, Ashtabula and Trumbull Counties—Start in Mesopotamia, a tiny Trumbull County town at the intersection of State Routes 534 (an exit from both I-90 and I-76) and 87. Mespo, as the locals call it, has an idyllic 1600-foot-long one-time common surrounded almost entirely by nineteenth-century buildings, mostly houses, but including a few public buildings as well. One fine Sunday afternoon, while showing America to visitors from Ireland, we drove through Mesopotamia. Several motorcyclists in full regalia were picnicking on the green, while on the periphery two horse-drawn carriages full of Amish teen-agers, also in full regalia, were racing each other.

Drive east on 87; North Bloomfield (see also), a still smaller place, is at the intersection of State Route 45. Here the square is north of 87; a famous early house, Brownwood is at the southeast corner.

Continue east on 87 to the hamlet of Gustavus Center, an enchanting place about 11 miles distant. Gustavus Center has a square with adjacent church and houses; all buildings have signs identifying them and giving dates. Builder Willis Smith of Kinsman did the brick George Hezlep House, 1832. A Victorian Town Hall, 1890, faces the highway. This square and its buildings are on the National Register as the Gustavus Center Historic District.

▶ GUSTAVUS CENTER TOWN HALL

Continue east on 87 about five miles to Kinsman (see also), which has two especially noteworthy Willis Smith buildings. The square, a traffic roundabout, is a block south of the church at State Street and State Route 7.

From Kinsman, take State Route 7 north into Ashtabula County; at U.S. 6 in Andover, turn left/west to West Andover and the Henderson House (see also).

Continue west on U.S. 6 to State Route 45; drive nine miles north to Jefferson (see also), which has two squares and an early law office. Then return to U.S. 6 and continue west, especially to see Rome, whose 1836 Presbyterian Church is visible across the cornfields, and Harts Grove, which has, even in spite of the gas station, an idyllic green.

Tour may end at State Route 534, Harts Grove. Or, continue to a more developed Western Reserve county seat, Chardon, 14 miles further east on U.S. 6. There the Geauga County Courthouse, 1869, faces into a picturesque green. Designed by Cleveland architect Joseph Ireland, this red brick Italianate courthouse with an octagonal tower is among Ohio's best on the outside, which makes the inside, a 1970s rehab, all the more disappointing.

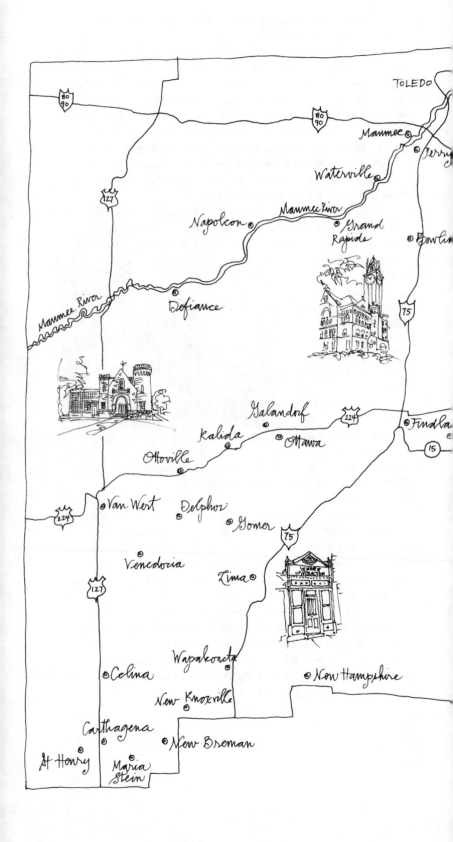

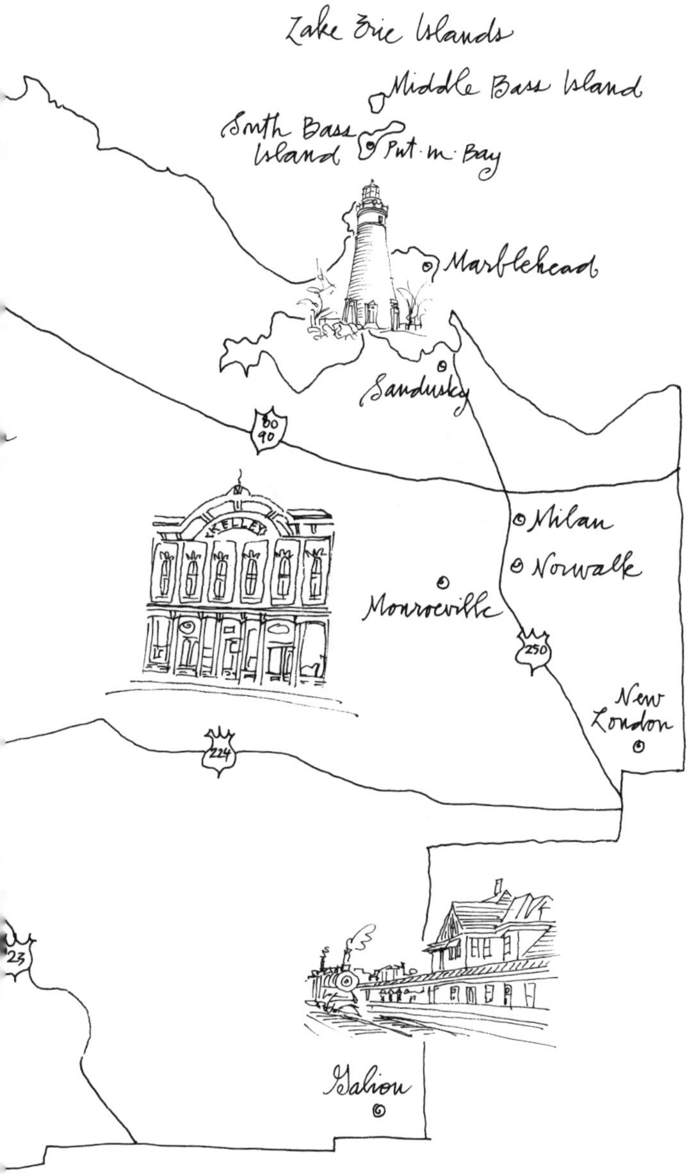

Lake Erie Islands

Middle Bass Island

South Bass
Island   Put-in-Bay

Marblehead

Sandusky

80
90

KELLEY

Milan

Norwalk

Monroeville

250

New
London

224

23

Galion

Northwest Ohio

Northwest Ohio has a flat landscape that for architecture, becomes a stage. It flaunts a nearby building and gives allure to the distant. Here, landscape and architecture can interact for the exaltation of both. ¶ Before settlement Northwest Ohio had the state's only vast uninhabitable, even unimpenetrable region, the Great Black Swamp. Fifteen-hundred square miles of dense wet forest, where early in the season trees stood in water, where soil was mud and the air, dense with mosquitoes, it was slow to be cleared, with half done only by 1870, and all, not until 1900. Not only did the swamp delay settlement, but it determined where towns are—or, are not, as author Louis W. Campbell pointed out. We can tell where the Black Swamp was because of towns built along its edge, encircling it. Going counterclockwise, they are Toledo, Maumee, Napoleon, Defiance, Fort Wayne, Indiana, Van Wert, Delphos, Findlay, Fostoria, Fremont, and Port Clinton. Only Bowling Green was in it. ¶ Once a lake bottom, much of Northwest Ohio land has a slope of only a foot or two every mile, so it could be farmed only with underground drain pipes to carry away excess water. The soil was worth the trouble. It's so productive that Maumee River basin farmers collect 25 per cent of the state's agricultural income from only 11 per cent of its land. Nor was soil the only source of wealth underfoot. In the 1880s and 1890s, Northwest Ohio—Lima, Findlay, Toledo, Wood County—enjoyed the nation's second oil boom. Enriched by productive farms and especially by oil, people could afford good buildings. ¶ Before 1830 Northwest Ohio had no place that could be called a town. The swamp wasn't the only hindrance to settlement; into the 1840s this was the last part of Ohio with Indian reservations. Then when settlers did come, they were less likely to be the New Englanders or Pennsylvanians or Virginians who arrived earlier in other parts of Ohio. These people were newcomers from France, Wales, and especially, Germany. Starting in the 1830s Germans came up the canal from Cincinnati; Catholics settled one town, Protestants the next. In some places, the twain have never met. Immigrants inhabited towns like Frenchtown, Gomer (which has welcome signs in Welsh), and Minster; some of their buildings were characteristic of the old country. ¶ But what most distinguishes Northwest Ohio architecture is the setting, that flat terrain. See from miles away court-house towers like those of Napoleon and Bowling Green; see the

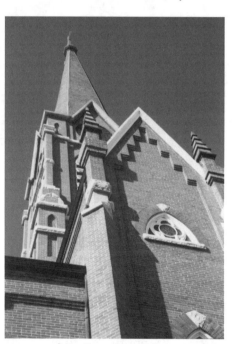

▶ ST. HENRY, MERCER COUNTY

mosque at Perrysburg that's so astounding from I-75; see the steeples of churches, especially in Putnam and Mercer and surrounding counties, where, almost always in sight, they become an awesome array.

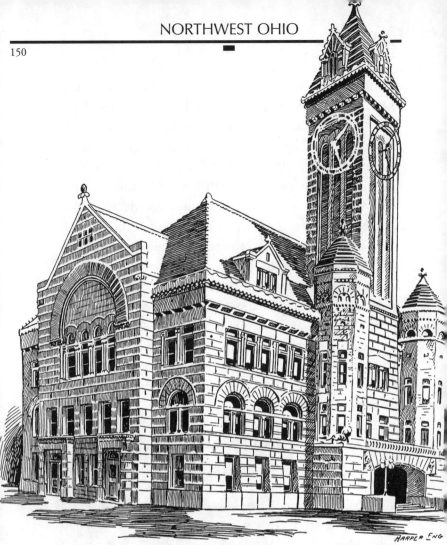

▶ WOOD COUNTY COURTHOUSE

Bowling Green, Wood County

(Bowling Green and Findlay, 25 miles apart off I-75, both
show what oil built.)

¶ County seat and college town, Bowling Green has
Bowling Green State University and its 17,000 students,
who, as in many university towns, have helped keep Main
Street alive. But the key to architecture here is the historic
turn-of-the century oil boom, which left wealth behind in
buildings. Examples include both the Millikin Hotel and
the Wood County Courthouse, where one of the murals,
painted by I.M. Taylor, also mayor in 1910-11, depicts
county oil wells.

Access: From I-75 exit at State Route 64/Wooster Street and drive west into town. Clough Street, where the windmill is between South College Drive and Troup Avenue, parallels Wooster Street a block to the south. The Wood County Courthouse is a block north of Wooster on Court Street between Prospect and Summit streets. Hotel Millikin is at southeast corner of Wooster and Main Street/State Route 25.

WINDMILL, 1939

Birtis H. Urschel, builder, Bowling Green
722 Clough Street (name rhymes with "rough"), Bowling Green
Private apartments

This Windmill was originally an outbuilding, designed by industrialist Birtis Urschel to house a heating plant that served the eight dwellings across the street. It's 45-feet high and hexagonal, with the top two stories covered in wood shingles and the first floor in stone from the adjacent quarry, later a swimming pool. Now two apartments, the windmill looks like an attractive place to live.

WOOD COUNTY COURTHOUSE, 1896

Yost & Packard, Columbus;
1980 restoration by Munger Munger & Associates, Toledo
1 Courthouse Square, East Court Street at North Prospect Street, Bowling Green, NRHP
Courthouse open weekdays;
419/354-9000

Tower of Justice or no, the Wood County Courthouse began as a scandal. During construction all three commissioners and a former one, the architects, and the builder were indicted for attempted bribery, proposing inflated bids, and other chicanery. This story comes from

▶ WOOD COUNTY COURTHOUSE

retired newspaper editor Paul Willis Jones, who prepared his "courthouse capers" speech in 1994 and then gave it 17 times. ¶ Akron architect Frank O. Weary testified that two commissioners promised him the job if he'd give them each $1,500—an amount they upped to $3,000 later the same day. Weary agreed to nothing, and the two commissioners left for Columbus, to talk to Yost & Packard. Whether the bribe was proposed again will never be known, but Yost & Packard did get the job. They were indicted not for bribery but for permitting the builder to substitute a cheaper stone. ¶ Nine months later all indictments were dropped. It was, mulls Jones, an era of lax morality. But aesthetic sensibilities were perfectly intact; this is one of Ohio's best courthouses. Richardsonian Romanesque, three stories, the building has load-bearing stone walls. It has the state's tallest courthouse clock tower, 185

▶ DETAIL, WOOD COUNTY COURTHOUSE

feet high, visible for miles in the flat country of northwest Ohio. The interior has a splendid central stairway, Italian tile floors whose patterns have mostly walked away, and, above the third floor, a stained-glass barrel vault that's over 20 feet high. Courtroom No. 1, occupied since 1974 by Judge Gale Williamson, was finished originally with seven different kinds of oak. ¶ The judge was sorry that the restoration architects replaced the undulating spectator rail with a straight one; he rues that the marble water fountain on the stairway wasn't repaired; he questions a "Virginia style" courtroom added in 1980, the style chosen by a then incumbent judge who wasn't reelected because voters deemed the furniture he picked too expensive. ¶ Judge Gale admires the courthouse's stone carvings, done by Dayton's Whyte and Priest, with W.D. Priest supervising. These carvings incorporate 50 to 75 different faces, a few gargoyles, a dragon of evil, and fruits that look like pineapple and coconut but, the judge learned, aren't. He likes the diversity of carved faces— some with shawls, others with beards, or mustaches, or hats, or bald heads. He especially admires the carving in the east gable: Law, between Agriculture and Commerce. Law's fist rests on Commerce's shoulder, while Agriculture gets a friendly pat. ¶ The judge isn't the only one to admire the carving. Cleveland architect Robert C. Gaede, who calls this courthouse "the handsomest in the state," says he could sit all day and admire the stonework.

HOTEL MILLIKIN, 1896
Bacon and Huber, Toledo
101 South Main Street, Bowling Green, Main Street HD
Former hotel; now ground-floor shops only

This old hotel retains some of the elegance it had originally, when William H. Millikin built it fancy to show his appreciation to Bowling Green, whose oil boom provided him what a county history calls a "snug fortune". A man who spent most of his life following oil booms around the country, Millikin arrived here in 1889, a veteran of western Pennsylvania oil fields. Granddaughter Virginia Nader, who still lives in the house he bought, says the hotel was very luxurious for its time and place. It was built with running water and had its own electric generator—so it was well lighted, had an elevator, and sold extra power to Main Street merchants. When Millikin went on the road to newer oil fields, his family stayed in town, where his wife kept an eye on the hotel. Nader says that when her grandfather was in Kansas, he'd come home by train for weekends. In the 1930s and 1940s, when this area had the country's best pheasant hunting, Clark Gable and Ernest Hemingway stayed here. The hotel stopped renting rooms in 1958, and in 1993 Nader and her brothers gave the building to Bowling Green State University, which by the end of the decade had sold it to a lawyer and his wife, Robert and Patricia Maurer. In late 2001 the Mauers planned to start renovating the upper floors as apartments for graduate students.

▶ HOTEL MILLIKIN

Access: To reach Wood County Historical Museum, the former county home, drive south on State Route 25 to U.S. 6; turn east; take first right after I-75, County Home Road.

**WOOD COUNTY INFIRMARY, NOW WOOD COUNTY
HISTORICAL MUSEUM, 1868, 1898**
1898 wings by E.O. Fallis, Toledo
13660 County Home Road, Bowling Green, NRHP
Museum and Wood County Historical Society office, open Tuesday to Friday;
guided tours summer weekend afternoons; donation; 419/352-0967

This is a good, quirky local history museum in a former county infirmary.
The old, original building is a two-and-a-half-story Italianate brick, but the
real architectural interest is in the easternmost wings added by Toledo
architect E.O. Fallis. How lovely they are, with porches fronting both first
and second floors, and white balustrades built with designs that stand out
against the dark recesses behind.

Carthagena, Mercer County

One of Ohio's architectural high points is an ensemble of
German Catholic churches in four western counties.
They're arrayed on flat, rich agricultural land, where the
number of silver-domed silos—one, two, three, or even
four—broadcasts a farm's relative wealth, just as a spire
every few miles broadcasts a well-anchored religion.
Those steeples, often visible for miles, inspired the name
used for the National Register nomination: Cross-Tipped
Churches of Ohio. What makes these churches important
is their large number. While some are architecturally
worthy by themselves, together they achieve an impact
that is breathtaking. ¶ The architectural display is most
concentrated in Marion Township, in the southeast
corner of Mercer County. In a three- by six-mile area,
Marion Township, whose 1990 population was 2,784, has
five active churches and a total of three chapels at St.
Charles, a former seminary, and Maria Stein, a former
convent. On Olding Road in Marion Township I saw
four spires on the horizons. Thomas J. Wehrhahn of
Celina, says that from Stelzer Road, behind St. Charles,
it's possible to see seven. ¶ To see church spires on every
horizon is an exhilarating experience. It's proof of triumph—secular as well as religious—in a new country. It
exalts this place.

The Cross-Tipped Churches—The Cross-Tipped Churches are the legacy of a priest and an architect, both from Switzerland, and both arriving, though not together, in Ohio in the 1840s. That we are now aware of the churches is largely due to Mary Ann Olding, who put them on the National Register. Given that this is a rural place, it is miraculous that almost all the 29 churches that went on the National Register in 1979 survive as active parishes, at least for the moment. Frequently one priest serves two churches, which is simple enough when they are two miles apart.

Now a Cincinnati preservationist, Mary Ann Olding grew up in Mercer County's Fort Recovery, but her father's home was Carthagena in Marion Township. There Olding farms claimed both sides of Olding Road; her grandfather's was on the south side, her aunt and uncle's on the north. As a place she knew in childhood, Marion Township had for her the familiarity of home. She says, "I had no idea this place was different from anywhere else."

But as an adult, Olding realized that it's like nowhere else. While head of the regional preservation office in Celina, she tried a more objective look at southern Mercer County and its history, and discovered that within 22 miles of Maria Stein, in four Ohio counties and eastern Indiana, there were 68 historic religious buildings, including the 29 churches, all administered by one religious order, the Missionaries (then Society) of the Precious Blood. That insight gave her the link she needed to assemble a thematic National Register nomination. She, Marilyn Niekamp, and Lois Rock surveyed not only churches, but also schools, rectories, convents, and the seminary. Olding traveled to compare other German settlements in Minnesota, Wisconsin, Missouri, Texas, and Indiana. She found nothing like the cross-tipped churches of Ohio—nothing, as she says, "so fabulous."

The churches are enduring testimony to the zeal of the Rev. Francis de Sales Brunner, Swiss-born head of the Missionaries of Precious Blood, who in 1843 sailed from Europe and came to northwest Ohio, then a relatively undeveloped area where many Germans were settling. Bringing with him seven priests and seven brothers, Brunner, who was ever the single-minded missionary, went on to build ten northwest Ohio convents by 1857; each one was a self-supporting farm community housing the priests, lay brothers, and nuns who taught and ministered to German immigrants. "There was no hostile government to thwart his plans and no envious clergy to deter him. Land could be had at a low price, building material was abundant, help was willingly proffered by the grateful inhabitants." So Sister Octavia described Brunner's building program in her 1945 history of the Sisters of the Precious Blood.

An adept linguist, Brunner could do whatever he wanted because the bishop of Cincinnati knew no German and was relieved to have Brunner take over. The bishop might delegate, but Brunner never did, even though he was often away. Between 1845 and his death abroad in 1859, he made four trips back to Europe, some of them prolonged; and even while absent he insisted on sole authority. Sister Octavia wrote that he was accused of parsimony, harshness, lack of interest; he was dictatorial. But she concluded that there was no arguing with what he accomplished: he brought the Missionaries of the Precious Blood to America, and established them so securely that, in the decades after his death, area parishes exultantly built one cross-tipped church after another.

As it happened, Brunner's early charismatic success was given more momentum by an American priest, the Rev. J.M. Gartner, on a mission in Italy in 1872. At a time of widespread plundering by Italian bandits, Gartner rescued a large collection of church relics, or articles linked with saints, and brought them back to America. After exhibiting them in New York, Cincinnati, Baltimore, and other cities, Gartner selected a permanent repository: the convent chapel at Maria Stein, where the nuns would tend his treasures at a place that to him seemed a perfect destination for pilgrimages. He deposited the relics there in 1875. The second largest collection of relics in the United States, they still attract pilgrims.

Though the cross-tipped churches are most significant architecturally as an ensemble, some are especially well designed. That's chiefly because of the DeCurtins family, architects, artisans, and builders whose work was exceptional. The patriarch was Anton DeCurtins (c. 1830-1895), who as a youth in eastern Switzerland apprenticed in carpentry; about 1850 he settled in Carthagena. There he and his wife Mary raised eight children, most of whom followed him into the building business. Remembered especially for churches, the DeCurtinses were a complete construction team. Anton and his son Andrew (c. 1865-1940), who after his father's death practiced in Celina and Lima, were architects. Son John was a contractor; son Frank was an artist trained in Munich; and all the women in the family did decorative painting, with daughter Agnes the creator of the gold leaf designs in the Maria Stein relic chapel. Thus the family offered turnkey jobs: designs, lumber, construction, frescos, painting, pews, and pipe organs.

Anton DeCurtins did his home parish church, St. Aloysius in Carthagena, completed in 1878. Simple and elegant, it is the very model of a cross-tipped church.

▶ St. Augustine, Minster

Touring the Cross-Tipped Churches Area—The most impressive cross-tipped churches are the rural ones, whose isolated sites enhance their impact. Also, for a sense of the architectural ensemble—of the sheer numbers—try to see more than one or two churches. That's relatively easy just in Marion Township, where the villages of Carthagena and Maria Stein are. There, in a two-and-a-half-mile radius, you can see St. Charles, the

former convent of Maria Stein and its glorious chapels, and five churches.

After Marion Township, an extended four-county cross-tipped churches tour, below, takes in eight more churches: three in Mercer County west of U.S. 127, one in Darke County, one in Shelby County, and three in Auglaize County. For the insatiable, I'll end with a list of the remaining cross-tipped churches. All these buildings are on the National Register in the Cross-Tipped Churches of Ohio TR.

For a map and suggested tour, and for information on guided tours, call the Auglaize and Mercer Counties CVB, 800/860-4726. Thomas J. Wehrhahn offers tours in conjunction with the Marion Community Development Organization; call him at 419/586-2051.

Access—Marion Township: This tour makes a loop, with U.S. 127 the western edge. St. Charles is on the east side of U.S. 127 just below State Route 274; St. Aloysius Church faces 274 just east of U.S. 127. Proceed east on 274 to County 716A, which will take you half a mile left/north to St. Sebastian—head toward the spire. Then continue east on 274 past Chickasaw to St. Johns Road; turn right; Maria Stein will be on the right. Then continue south to State Route 119, where St. John's Church is just to the left, and St. Rose and Cassella are up the road to the right, at two-mile intervals. Stelzer Road, from which seven spires are visible, runs behind St. Charles; turn right from 274.

ST. CHARLES SEMINARY, NOW ST. CHARLES, 1922, AND CHAPEL, 1906

Hermann J. Gaul, Chicago, seminary; and Andrew DeCurtins, Lima, chapel
U.S. Route 127, Carthagena
Private retirement home; motherhouse of Cincinnati Province of the Missionaries of the Precious Blood; only the chapel is open to the public, who may use the main front entrance

From the highway St. Charles is a spectacular sight. That's partly the setting, a quarter mile back from the road, at the end of an allée of trees. There, the building's central section rises six stories to a dome whose segments become alternating wedges of light and shade on a sunny day. Three-story side wings have turrets to provide a little heft on the end pavilions—heft that a 371-foot-long facade needs. The building footprint is U-shaped, with a preexisting chapel enclosed in the U. When the chapel was remodeled in 1961, paintings by a member of the order were lost; a gold mosaic in the apse behind the altar was gained. Built as a seminary to train priests and brothers of the Precious Blood, St. Charles had student rooms on the third floor, classrooms on the second, a library on the first, and billiards and a gym in the raised basement. At one time a hundred seminarians were enrolled. Supporting farm buildings are to the east; four brothers continue to farm St. Charles's thousand acres of crop land.

ST. ALOYSIUS CHURCH, 1878

Anton DeCurtins, Carthagena
State Route 174, Carthagena

▶ ST. ALOYSIUS

Of all the Cross-Tipped Churches, Mary Ann Olding describes St. Aloysius as her favorite, "because of the way it sits on the land." Though it's not an especially large church, it gains stature by claiming a slight rise in the terrain. This was the home church of architect Anton DeCurtins, who built the altar himself. That was not enough to assure its place in the 1970s, when the interior was remodeled and the DeCurtins altar put in storage. Though stripped of its original ornament, St. Aloysius's interior is elegant, with features like a vaulted octagonal apse. Romanesque Revival, red brick, the rectangular church has a gable roof. The tower has an

▶ ST. SEBASTIAN, CHURCH AND COMMUNITY

octagonal white belfry and a high pointed steeple. The first of the cross-tipped churches to have a spire, it became the prototype, inspiring both new churches and the addition of steeples on older ones. Originally, in 1835, Quakers founded Carthagena as a haven for freed slaves; they named it Carthage for the African city that challenged Rome for world supremacy. By 1857 white settlers had purchased most of the land the blacks owned; in 1860 the Missionaries of the Precious Blood bought the buildings the Quakers had built for a school, Emlen Institute, whose chapel served St. Aloysius parish before it built this church.

ST. SEBASTIAN CHURCH, 1904

Andrew DeCurtins, Lima
Sebastian Road at County 716A, Sebastian

▶ ST. SEBASTIAN

In the middle of a place as big as a minute, St. Sebastian majestically faces a green. Church is High Victorian Gothic, red brick with sandstone trim and a front central tower.

MARIA STEIN CONVENT AND RELIC CHAPEL, NOW MARIA STEIN CENTER AND NATIONAL MARIAN SHRINE OF THE HOLY RELICS, 1892, 1900

Anton DeCurtins and sons, Carthagena
2291 St. Johns Road, Maria Stein
Former convent and two chapels, one housing relics; gift shop; museum open in summer; chapels all year except Mondays and holidays; 419/925-4532

The nuns working here number only five, but nowadays that seems like a lot. They live elsewhere because this is no longer a convent, but it still has a shrine with the country's second largest collection of relics, or articles associated with saints. The two chapels, both well worth seeing, are accessible from the old convent building. The larger one is the convent chapel, which has three unpainted wooden altars and wainscoting. From it a door leads to the smaller, more elaborate relic chapel, which has exquisite carving in its three altars and railing. The relics are kept in niches in the altars. Michael Leach, parish historian at St. John the Baptist Church in Glandorf, Putnam County, says the carving in both chapels was done by Cincinnati's Schroeder Studio.

HOG BARN, 1850s
Barn razed in 1998

From a shrine to a hog barn? Remember, this is an architectural tour. The barn no longer houses hogs, though it makes a still sound storage shed for a man in the construction business, who rents it. The man, now well into middle age, grew up on the adjacent farm; in sunny 90-degree weather, he used to see the nuns out shucking wheat in their habits. From far away they must have seemed bits of black fluttering amid the gold. They were following the founder's edict, farming to support their convent, which was tending the relics. This rectangular wooden barn has a gable roof that extends to form broad eaves, and three windows set in the front gable at the points of an equilateral triangle. The barn is interesting because it's unusual, but while Mary Ann Olding was at the regional preservation office in the 1970s and 1980s, she found that its type is not at all unusual around here, for she counted 137 similar structures in Marion Township alone. She calls it a Saxon barn, characteristic of northwest Germany, where the settlers here came from. In Saxony, the three windows were important because people lived in that end of the barn and needed them to let smoke out.

ST. JOHN THE BAPTIST CHURCH, 1889
Anton DeCurtins,
Carthagena
8533 State Route 119,
Maria Stein

What I especially remember about St. John the Baptist Church is the organist at practice, so the church resounded with music. This is one of the larger cross-tipped churches, Romanesque Revival, brick, with a very tall central tower topped by

▶ ST. JOHN THE BAPTIST

a pointed spire and a fine interior, with side aisles and ceiling vaults.

ST. ROSE CHURCH, 1911
7428 State Route 119, St. Rose

St. Rose also has a high steeple. Brick with sandstone trim, late Gothic, cruciform in plan, it has a particularly fine old altar.

NATIVITY OF THE BLESSED VIRGIN MARY, 1858, 1888
6524 State Route 119, Cassella

This is a simpler, earlier church, with Gothic Revival motifs. It was rebuilt after an 1888 fire, and in 1915 the church hired itinerant workmen who hid the scorched brick walls with a gray stucco molded to look like stone.

Access: Extended Four-County Cross-Tipped Churches Tour in Three Parts: Part I, Western Mercer County—Of the ten active Mercer County cross-tipped churches west of U.S. 127, this itinerary takes in three. Continue west from 127 on State Route 119; after half a mile, turn left/ south on Cranberry Road. After seeing the church at Cranberry Prairie, return to 119 and continue west to St. Henry. From St. Henry take State Route 118 south to Burkettsville.

ST. FRANCIS CHURCH, 1906

Andrew DeCurtins, Lima
1509 Cranberry Road, Cranberry Prairie

Marion Township has five active churches of its own, plus St. Francis half a mile into the next township. One of my favorites, this red brick church has a good site, Gothic arches, Greek cross layout, a tower, carved altars, vaulted ceilings and stained glass. It's almost all there is to Cranberry Prairie, but it seems sufficient to justify the place.

▶ ST. FRANCIS

ST. HENRY CHURCH, 1897

Adolphus Druiding, Chicago
272 East Main Street, St. Henry

After Cranberry Prairie, St. Henry (pop. 2,000) is a booming metropolis; its High Victorian Gothic church is proportionately substantial. The DeCurtins Brothers didn't have the design job, but they built the church and decorated it. The tower is 196 feet high, and a niche over the front door holds a granite statue of St. Henry himself.

ST. BERNARD'S CHURCH, 1924

J.F. Sheblessy, Cincinnati
75 West Main Street, Burkettsville

St. Bernard's Church looks different because, instead of a central spire, it has two front towers, one on each side, and its brick is brown, not red. Style is Romanesque Revival, designed in 1900, but not built until 1924.

Extended Four-County Cross-Tipped Churches Tour: Part II, Darke County—Access: Darke County: From Burkettsville, return to U.S. 127 on street in front of church, which becomes County Line Road; drive south and turn left at State Route 185 which goes south and east to Frenchtown.

HOLY FAMILY CHURCH, 1866
14 East Wood Street, Frenchtown

Holy Family Church has a small building exalted by its open belfry and marred by a 1964 vestibule that takes over the facade. A nineteenth-century French-immigrant community, Frenchtown was of particular interest to Mary Ann Olding because it was the home of her mother's family. When Olding first began thinking about ethnic settlement architecture, she looked for what seemed French in Frenchtown, and her eye lit on some cute little cottages with steeply pitched gables. But when she went to the settlers' town in eastern France, Hannonville, such cute cottages were not what she found. Traveling with an Ohio Arts Council grant (itself an achievement, she says: "They weren't even eager to send you out of the state"), she found that the houses of Hannonville were plain two-story row houses. So she looked again at Frenchtown. She realized that "those doll houses" with steep gables had been built by earlier settlers from Virginia; what the French built were plain, two-story houses. The plain houses not only made immigrants from Hannonville feel at home, they also reflected the fact that these Ohio French weren't so rich as the Mercer County Germans.

Extended Four-County Cross-Tipped Churches Tour: Part III, Shelby and Auglaize Counties—Access: From Frenchtown, continue southeast on State Route 185; in Versailles turn left/northeast on State Route 47, which connects with State Route 66; turn left/north; in Fort Loramie church is just to the east on State Route 705. To reach Minster, continue north on State Route 66 (you'll see the upcoming spire while the one behind is still in your mirror.) Church is on Hanover Street, two blocks west of highway.

▶ Sт. Michael

ST. MICHAEL CHURCH, 1885
Anton Goehr, Minster
33 Elm Street, Fort Loramie, Shelby County

St. Michael could be a textbook example of High Victorian Gothic, a style not known for restraint. At the back a door leads to the earlier, much altered 1851 church.

ST AUGUSTINE CHURCH, 1849, 1874
Anton Goehr, Minster (1874)
48 North Hanover Street at Fifth Street, Minster,
Auglaize County

▶ ST. AUGUSTINE

Architect Anton Goehr added the two towers,
which are topped by octagonal copper cupolas
and high pointed roofs; they're an area
landmark.

Access: Rural Auglaize County: From Minster drive north on State
Route 66 through New Bremen (see also) and St. Marys; a few miles
northeast of St. Marys turn right/east on Glynwood Road to
Glynnwood. Fryburg, south of Wapakoneta (see also), is tricky. From
Glynnwood continue east on Glynwood Road into Wapakoneta; in
downtown turn right/south at State Route 198, which becomes Willipie
Street, which south of U.S. 33 becomes County 25A/Dixie Highway and
in a few miles intersects Fryburg Drive/Township 110; turn left/east
into Fryburg. These churches are worth the trouble.

ST. PATRICK CHURCH, 1884
06959 Glynwood Road, Glynnwood (Road has one n; place, two)

St. Patrick is red brick, Gothic Revival, with a tall projecting central tower. Interior is simple but very nice. This was the parish of the Irish workers who came to the area to build the canal. "Years ago," says parishioner Albert Reier, "the Irish used to kid that Canada thistles and the Germans were taking over the community." When his parents were married here in 1924, there was a pot-bellied stove in the middle of the sanctuary.

ST. JOHN CHURCH, 1850
112219 Van Buren Street, Fryburg

Oldest of all the cross-tipped churches, St. John is small, of stuccoed brick. The sanctuary has a large round arch fronting the altar, wall frescoes and stenciling, and a fine reredos at the back of the altar. The handsome building next door, now the parish hall, was built as a school.

List of Other Cross-Tipped Churches (adapted from handout issued by the Marion Community Development Organization)

Mercer County:
1) Holy Trinity Church, 1899, 116 East Main Street, Coldwater
2) Immaculate Conception Church, 1903, 229 West Anthony Street, Celina
3) St. Anthony Church, 1869, 471 St. Anthony Road, St. Anthony
4) St. Joseph Church, 1866, 1689 St. Joseph Road, St. Joseph
5) St. Mary Church, 1871, 3821 Philothea Road, Philothea
6) St. Paul Church, 1888, Sharpsburg Road, Sharpsburg
7) St. Peter Church, 1904, 1477 Philothea Road, St. Peter
8) St. Wendelin Church, 1870, 2980 Ft. Recovery-Minster Road, Wendelin
Darke County:
9) St. Louis Church, 1914, 15 Star Road, North Star
10) St. Nicholas Church, 1908, 128 Church Street, Osgood
Shelby County:
11) St. Patrick Church, 1915 (CLOSED), Hoying and Wright-Puthoff Roads, St. Patrick
12) St. Remy Church, 1890, 108 East Main Street, Russia
Auglaize County:
13) St. Joseph Church, 1887, State Route 364, Egypt
14) St. Joseph Church, 1911, 101 West Pearl Street, Wapakoneta
Indiana:
15) Trinity Church, 1885, State Route 67, Trinity

▶ Main Street, Celina

Celina, Mercer County

(Also in Mercer County: Carthagena and Cross-Tipped Churches tours.)

¶ Given where it is, Celina is exceptional in having a waterfront—on Grand Lake, a canal reservoir built in 1845. Just as unusual is the downtown movie theater showing current movies on five screens.

Access: Main Street is also U.S. 127.

101-125 SOUTH MAIN STREET, 1895-96

*South Main Street, west side, between West Market and West Fayette Streets,
Celina, NRHP/Celina Main Street Commercial HD*
Private commercial buildings

Completely rebuilt after a 1894 fire, this block has one of Ohio's best groups
of Main Street commercial buildings. Altogether, it has nine two- and three-
story structures. Several are elaborate and stylized, while others are simpler.
It's not a perfect block because of the gap in the middle—a building was
razed in the 1960s. Materials are predominantly brick, with some wood and
stone trim. The block also has historical continuity: a drugstore has occupied
the corner location since 1866; a cafe and bar have always been where Club
Cafe is, as has a bakery, where Charlie's Tasty Pastries is. ¶ From north to
south, these are the block's

buildings. Bair Pharmacy,
101 South Main, is at the
first corner. In old
photographs the corner
turret's conical roof with
flared eaves sticks out like the
landmark it is. The next two
two-story buildings have
mansard roofs. Then comes
the bakery, which has a
second-floor bay and an
elaborate, ornamented
cornice. According to the
National Register form, the
building that was razed,
forming the parking-lot gap
next door, was a twin of this
one. ¶ The buildings just
south of the gap have turrets
of different shapes, a steep
gable, a steep conical roof,
and, overall, a romantic
European flavor. At street
level the next one has a
recessed porch with two
columns and a stairway.
Insurance agent Chuck
Stammen bought these three
buildings in 1993; the first

▶ MAIN STREET, CELINA

two have now been joined into one. They look so good because he restored
the facades, which before he came along had boarded-up windows and a
tilting turret. The remaining structures used to be a department store. The
first one, now an insurance agency, has a round two-story bay that's missing
its original conical roof. The last building has a round corner turret and
decorative brick work, especially in the round arches over the second-floor
windows.

▶ MERCER COUNTY COURTHOUSE

MERCER COUNTY COURTHOUSE, 1923
Peter M. Hulsken, Lima
101 North Main Street, Celina, NRHP/Celina Main Street Commercial HD
Public courthouse, open weekdays; 419/586-3178

Set in the middle of a one-block square, the Mercer County Courthouse is
the picture of dignified restraint: Neoclassical Revival, Ionic columns, gray
limestone. Thus the interior flamboyance is unexpected—the immense
central rotunda dominated by a double stairway under a round dome.
Ribbons of black marble balustrades ring the rotunda and outline the stairs.
The building is well maintained and little altered.

CITY HALL, 1890
North Main Street at East Livingston Street, Celina, NRHP/Celina Main Street
Commercial HD
Public building; open weekdays

The Celina City Hall's most impressive feature is an octagonal corner tower,
slightly tapered, open at the top level. The tower was intended to resemble a
lighthouse, given the proximity of Grand Lake. The building is
Richardsonian Romanesque, in a mix of rough-cut stone and brick. Interior is
altered, with a one-time theater converted to a gym.

IMMACULATE CONCEPTION CHURCH, 1903
Andrew DeCurtins, Lima
229 West Anthony Street at Walnut Street, one block west of North Main Street,
Celina, NRHP/Cross-Tipped Churches of Ohio TR
Catholic church; 419/586-6648

The large Immaculate Conception Church is a major event in Celina's
streetscape, even though it's not on Main Street. Romanesque Revival, red
brick, the church has a large central dome and two on front towers, all
copper green and slightly bulbous.

Defiance, Defiance County

(Maumee Valley tour includes Defiance; for routing, see Maumee.)

¶ At the place where the Auglaize River flows into the Maumee, General "Mad" Anthony Wayne built Fort Defiance in 1794. Today the site is an especially lovely park, stretching out next to the city's library and offering fine old trees and a wonderful view.

Access: Prettiest access is Maumee Valley tour route, State Route 424, which winds its way into town from Napoleon to the east. At State Route 66/Clinton Street turn left-south to cross river, then immediately left onto Fort Street for library. To reach the cemetery go south/left from Fort onto Clinton, which becomes State Route 111; cemetery is about a mile and a half.

DEFIANCE PUBLIC LIBRARY, 1905

Wing and Mahurin, Fort Wayne
320 Fort Street, Defiance, NRHP
Library; 419/782-1456

Set next to the site of Fort Defiance, the library has a location of honor. This exotic Carnegie library uses distinctive red sandstone from a Mansfield quarry in an Arts and Crafts style, with flared roof eaves, crenellated parapets, half-timbering. Though the original building was quite wonderful, much of it has been obscured by additions.

RIVERSIDE CHAPEL, 1890

Jonathan I. Hale, Ottawa, Ohio
Riverside Cemetery, 1417 South Clinton
Street, Defiance, NRHP
Cemetery chapel

"A Gothic Revival gem" is how Toledo preservationist Ted Ligibel describes this small cemetery chapel. The materials are striking: rough-cut limestone with trim in smooth limestone and red sandstone. The porch has lacelike carving, mostly done during the winter before construction. Originally, before machines could dig in frozen ground, caskets of people who died in winter were stored here in the basement until spring; a chapel is upstairs. The local

▶ RIVERSIDE CHAPEL

chapter of the Daughters of the American Revolution restored the chapel in the late 1970s.

West Sandusky Street Findlay, Ohio.

Findlay, Hancock County

(Bowling Green and Findlay, 25 miles apart off I-75, both show what oil built.)

¶ Though Findlay has been reviving its downtown and Hancock County has refurbished the courthouse, the town's standout architecture is Victorian houses. Many sprouted up during the 1880s gas boom, when businesses, lured by offers of free sites and free fuel, rushed into Findlay. ¶ Since 1982, resident Rosalinda Paul has been researching Findlay's old houses. She keeps track of their appearances in nineteenth-century picture books, their alterations and restorations. Hardest to track were architects' names. It's helped that Paulette Weiser, an archivist at the Hancock Historical Museum, has been going through old newspapers. Weiser turned up W.L. Kramer as architect of the William L. Carlin House because the paper reported on a feud between architect and owner. ¶ Finding H.O. Wurmser, architect of the Charles Bigelow House, was more serendipitous. Craig Bobby of Lakewood, a dedicated Victorian-house fan, discovered the name when he recognized a picture of the Bigelow House in a 1903 issue of *Ohio Architect and Builder*. Born in Findlay in 1861, Henry Oswald Wurmser practiced there until 1893, when he moved to Lorain.

❡ Rosalinda Paul says that Findlay's best streets for houses are South Main from downtown to 6th Street and Sandusky Street from Western Avenue on the west to the creek on the east. It seemed to me that I was seeing good things in every older neighborhood, so this itinerary, starting on North Main and proceeding south, includes houses on other streets. ❡ These houses are private but may be seen well from the street. In May of even-numbered years the Historic Preservation Guild of Hancock County offers Findlay old-house tours. Write P.O. Box 621, Findlay 45839 or call Rosalinda Paul, 419/422-8592. She gave me almost all the house names and dates used here.

Access: To reach downtown Findlay from the east or west take U.S. 224 to Main Street; or, from I-75 exit at State Route 12/Main Cross Street and drive east to Main Street. Sandusky Street parallels Main Cross two blocks to the south. Houses here are in order for a tour from north to south.

CHARLES BIGELOW HOUSE, 1889

H.O. Wurmser, Findlay
2816 North Main Street, just north of West Bigelow Street, Findlay

This wonderful Queen Anne never misses a chance for another turret or arch, open porch or bay, or for a different pattern in a different gable. Owner Janice Sartore says the house has never been neglected or undergone a major alteration, though a garage has been attached at the back. When she and her husband bought the house in 1988, they became only the third family to own it. Inside, the highlight is a spectacular carved butternut stairway that starts with a bronze dragon holding the newel-post lamp; it rises to a round, pulpit-like landing overlooking the hall and then ascends in a curve that echoes the arch over the landing window. For Charles Bigelow, that was one of the rewards of leaving the farm and going into the sawmill business with his father-in-law. The house he built has three-and-a-half stories; the outside is red brick with stone and wood trim. See also the Newton Adams House below: originally it was a mirror image of the Bigelow manse.

ELI G. DEWOLF HOUSE, C. 1874

226 West Sandusky Street, Findlay

This Italianate house with a mansard-roofed tower is earlier than most in this town; it appeared in an 1875 atlas. Roof and dormer brackets are so close to each other that from a distance they almost look like dentils. The distinctive tower window combines a trefoil and a triangle. Rosalinda Paul says that in 1900 the house was moved here from its original site two blocks away on West Main Cross Street.

▶ CHARLES BIGELOW HOUSE

JOHN SCOTT HOUSE, 1887
500 West Sandusky Street, Findlay

This glorious Queen Anne's reign as the Unpainted Lady of West Sandusky Street ended in 1998, when the house reemerged in brilliant colors. It has porches, bays, nooks galore, and, at the summit, a tower with an open porch in front.

JOHN POE HOUSE, 1888
904 South Main Street, opposite Hancock Street, Findlay

This brick Queen Anne has a remarkable second-floor porch, open under a round roof that has no support posts. Rosalinda Paul says the owners have done a museum-quality interior restoration.

HORACE VANCE HOUSE, C. 1888
201 Elm Street, one block right/west of South Main, Findlay

This is a favorite of mine—a smaller house with Stick style detailing in a pattern of curves on the facade, and a strong diagonal line from the gable down through the porch roof.

▶ WILLIAM CARLIN HOUSE

NEWTON ADAMS HOUSE, 1888

H.O. Wurmser, Findlay
1110 Hurd Avenue, Findlay, reached from South Main by turning right/west on
Locust Street and driving three blocks; turn left on Hurd

This is the house that's a mirror image of the Bigelow House at 2816 North
Main, though here the tower and carriage entrance have been removed. But,
says Rosalinda Paul, it does have the great staircase. The Adams House is the
southernmost in a row of three interesting Victorians.

WILLIAM L. CARLIN HOUSE, 1888

W. L. Kramer, Findlay
1109 South Main Street, southeast corner at 2nd Street, Findlay

The Carlin House is so imposing that it looks like a courthouse—it's the
massive square tower with a dome roof on the corner. Red brick with trim in
stone and wood, the house also has a full complement of bays, round-arched
windows, and, balancing the tower on the other side of the facade, porches at
three levels. The interior has been remodeled, partly because the house once
accommodated two families, and partly because in 1916 the owners wanted
to be more up-to-date. William L. Carlin, lawyer, real estate agent, and state
senator, built the house. The architect's name comes from an 1894
newspaper report that Carlin was suing W.L. Kramer, who had prepared the
house plans and specifications, for failing to oversee the construction
properly. (Otherwise unknown today, Kramer is listed in the 1888 city
directory as an architect and construction superintendent.) Carlin didn't live
in the house very long. The story goes that he lost it in a card game.

Galion, Crawford County

(Galion is between Mansfield to the east [see Northeast Ohio] and Marion to the southwest [Central Ohio], all three linked by State Route 309.)

¶ With one of Ohio's earliest Main Street programs, Galion has revved up a downtown that spent 20 years as a string of mostly empty stores. In less than ten years, 70 downtown buildings were brought up to code, and to the delight of Chamber Director Dave Dayne, by late 2000 vacant retail space was in short supply. New projects on the drawing boards were rehabbing a long-derelict downtown hotel and the Big Four Depot.

¶ In Galion and its environs, I noticed a local quirk on some nineteenth-century houses: an appurtenance that looks like a flat box set on top of the roof. Originally devices for improving ventilation, now they're a regional curiosity.

Access: From the east, State Route 97 arrives from I-71; or State Route 309 comes west from Mansfield. In Galion the main east-west road is Harding Way/State Route 309, which just east of downtown intersects Washington Street, where depot is half a block north. Just west of downtown, Union Street leads a block south to Brownella.

▶ Big Four Depot

BIG FOUR DEPOT, 1900

127 North Washington Street, Galion, NRHP
Former station; vacant

This fancy station was built to house the division headquarters of the
Cleveland, Chicago, Cincinnati and St. Louis Railroad, called the Big Four.
Thus the depot became unusually grand: two-and-a-half stories high, with
rough-cut stone at the ground-floor level and festively painted green and
white wood above. Flared at the eaves, the roof shapes third-floor gables and
dormers. ¶ Were it not for Robert Meek, the Big Four Depot would not be
standing today. Meek first boarded a train here in 1923, when he was six, to
go 20 miles to Shiloh, where his father had a sawmill. In those days 40 trains
a day came through Galion; Meek remembers seeing as many as three
standing outside town, waiting to take on water and coal. But ultimately the
railroad went out of business; the last passenger train came through Galion in
1968; and the station was sold. ¶ As an adult Meek became a contractor, and
when he heard the station was going to be torn down in 1984, he went for a
last look. The owner was there; his asking price was $75,000. "As I walked
away out the door, the price came down," Meek recalls. "Fifty, forty and then
lower. $25,000. 'Well dang,' I said. 'Any fool would do that.' I thought it
was a joke. But the next Tuesday we were working on a roof and the man
came over to the job with papers for me to sign. 'You bought the depot,' he
said. When he'd told me four times, I got a little shaky." ¶ Meek put glass in
all the windows, fixed the roof, replaced buckled floors, and stripped green
paint from wooden stair banisters. He had some tenants, including a
restaurant, a deli, a ballet school. But ultimately Meek too put the depot on

the market, and this time, in August 2000, the buyer was the City of Galion, whose initial steps included repairs and planning for a new use. "We want it to anchor the uptown area," said the Chamber's Dave Dayne. One possibility was as new quarters for the Chamber and the Main Street program.

BROWNELLA COTTAGE, 1887

Clarence O. Arey, Cleveland
132 South Union Street at West Walnut Street, Galion, NRHP
House museum; open Sunday afternoons in summer, with first tour at 1:30; fee;
for group tours call 419/468-9338

When Galion's Miriam Sayre gives tours of Brownella Cottage, she hates to take young children. "They don't know what a bishop is," she says. "And you can't tell little children that he didn't believe in Jesus." Sayre, born in 1908, is one of the few in Galion who still remember the once notorious Episcopal Bishop William Montgomery Brown, who in his later years questioned Jesus's divinity. ¶ Bishop Brown, who died in 1937, is remembered today mostly for his Communist beliefs. When he was an old man and Mim Sayre a young woman, she used to read to him—newspapers like the *Daily Worker* and *New Masses*. Among radicals of that era, he was a celebrity; people like socialist Eugene Debs and communist Earl Browder came to Galion to see him. Communist or no, doubting Christian or no, Sayre insists he was always a regular at the Episcopal church across the street. That church was his first parish as a priest and the reason he came to Galion, where his mother-in-law built him and his bride this "cottage", Brownella, as a wedding present. ¶ In the house's back yard are covered, enclosed walkways, perhaps 100 feet long altogether, that were added in the 1920s because Brown's doctor didn't want him walking in rain and snow. These

▶ BROWNELLA COTTAGE

arcades, with multipane windows over stone-simulating block and a low wooden balustrade along the roof edges (since removed, alas), connect the house, the study, and the carriage house; Brown walked miles and miles in them, Sayre says. They are probably architecturally unique. They are also at least unusual in having a hammer and sickle painted on the sidewalk. ¶ The house has Queen Anne features, including a two-story octagonal tower. It has a dozen rooms, including four parlors. Much of the siding is a brick veneer attached to the walls with iron bolts in the shape of Maltese crosses. Though "a Cleveland architect" has been credited traditionally with the house, his name was misplaced until 1996, when Dr. Bernard Mansfield of the local Historical Society found it on blueprints for the carriage house.

On Becoming a Communist Bishop—Nothing was ever ordinary about William Montgomery Brown. For one, he was in his twenties before he learned to read; and then he moved away so as to be among strangers while he raced through elementary school. Born in Orrville in 1855, Brown lost his father in the Civil War, and his mother had him bound into service to a farmer who gave him much work and no education. The youth was so mistreated that neighbors complained to county authorities, who rescued him; by then he was 16. At 25, he met Mrs. Mary Scranton Bradford in Cleveland. She encouraged him to become an Episcopalian and helped him catch up academically so he could attend seminary. Brown later married Mrs. Bradford's adopted daughter, Ella, and the young couple moved into Brownella in Galion.

As an established priest, Brown became so zealous that he founded or revived a hundred Episcopal churches in Ohio; his reward was being named Bishop of Arkansas in 1898. It was not a successful appointment. He called for integration in churches, which stirred up so much controversy that he finally resigned and, in poor health, fled back to his home in Galion. There, at the suggestion of his doctor, he began reading Charles Darwin's *Origin of the Species.* "Science," Brown wrote later, "simply left me floored. My old theological universe vanished. I found myself in a world of reality instead." After science, he found socialism and Karl Marx. He published *Communism and Christianism,* a 1920 book that set forth his doubts about Jesus's divinity. His late and accelerated education left him "naively orthodox," he wrote; it left him vulnerable to being bowled over when he found Darwin at 57. Gradually he exchanged orthodox religion for Darwin, Karl Marx, and likely a deeper but less literal faith.

But when he was in his late sixties, and because he never could hold his tongue or his pen, he was tried for heresy in Cleveland's Trinity Cathedral. There "eight bishops in full regalia," as he wrote in his memoir, *My Heresy,* convicted him, and the national press looked on.

Ultimately Mrs. Bradford, the mother-in-law, gave Brown not only Episcopalianism and her daughter, but also her fortune, principally land in Cleveland, including much of the Flats. Communist though he was, Brown had no problem with being rich too. Before Cleveland built Union Terminal in the 1920s, the bishop and his wife owned the site. He was delighted to receive $80,000 for "the wealth which American workers created in the process of producing Cleveland."

When Brown died, childless, he left Brownella and half a million dollars, which multiplied through the years. For decades his estate disbursed bequests to individuals, Galion Hospital, and Kenyon College. Finally, 50 years after the bishop's death, the Crawford County probate judge directed Galion attorney Kenneth Miller Petri to settle the estate within two years, which Petri did. After a $250,000 restoration, Brownella became the Galion Historical Society's museum.

▶ BROWNELLA CARRIAGE HOUSE

Glandorf, Putnam County

(Ottawa is just to the east on U.S. 224.)

¶ Country Churches tour: All these churches dominate their villages; except for the Presbyterian church in Venedocia, they are all Catholic. Start at Glandorf, here, off U.S. 224 west of Findlay. Continue west on 224 to Kalida (St. Michael Church, 1926, a large Romanesque Revival structure with a separate 135-foot campanile, or bell tower) and Ottoville (Immaculate Conception Church, 1923, has twin towers on the facade); then turn south on State Route 66 to Delphos (St. John Church, 1880, S.W. Lane, Cleveland, which has a 200-foot tower). From Delphos drive west on State Route 697; at State Route 116 turn south/left to

▶ St. John the Baptist

Venedocia (see also). ¶ The village of Glandorf, a suburb of the village of Ottawa, may not be very populous, but it surely passes muster in architecture.

Access: Glandorf is just west of Ottawa off U.S. 224; take State Route 694 north.

ST. JOHN THE BAPTIST CHURCH, 1878

Cudell and Richardson, Cleveland
Main Street and State Route 694, Glandorf, NRHP
Catholic church; usually open daily; "A Visitor's Guide", a brochure by parish historian Michael Leach, is available near the front door; 419/538-6928

Glandorf takes some finding, but once you're there it's impossible to miss St. John the Baptist Church and its high central tower. The domination is not just physical. In this village of under 1,000 people, the parish has 2,700 members (and Ottawa has its own Catholic church.) St. John the Baptist is red brick with stone trim, cruciform in plan with side aisles, High Victorian Gothic in style. It has a good interior, with Gothic vaults high overhead and stained-glass windows for daytime light. In many ways the building is similar to Cleveland churches that Eric Johannesen describes in *Cleveland Architecture, 1876-1976*—city churches that the German Frank Cudell and his Scottish-born partner, John Richardson, were doing about the same time they did this one. But no Cleveland church has the setting this one has, towering at the end of a country highway.

The Parish Historian—St. John is unusual in having a parishioner, Michael Leach, who is so interested in his home church that at Bowling Green State University in the 1970s, he wrote a master's thesis on its history. Though Leach, a teacher, is a fifth-generation Glandorf resident, he was born in New Jersey. "My mother left this German Catholic ghetto and met an Irishman in Erie, Pennsylvania," he explains, joking. But later his family resettled in Glandorf, and Leach's fascination with the church and place grew as they might not have, had he had just another German name.

▶ ST. JOHN THE BAPTIST

Glandorf, both town and parish, was founded in 1834 by a priest who came from Glandorf, Germany, to recreate his home community in America. Only 40 years later this church building was begun. The largest Catholic church in northern Ohio when it was built, it celebrated triumph: the successful implantation of German culture in the American wilderness. So says Leach, who goes on to point out particularly German features, like the prominent site in the community, or the appearance of not only blue but also red in Mary's dress, or the use of a horse, elephant, and camel accompanying the magi in the nativity set. While this church has the same patron saint, John the Baptist, as the mother church in Glandorf, Germany, it is a more spectacular building than the older one, which was burned repeatedly in wars. Leach is sure of that. He's been to the original Glandorf ten times.

Like other northwest Ohio churches (see also Carthagena), this one was associated with Father Francis de Sales Brunner, head of the Society (now Missionaries) of the Precious Blood. Though at the time of its founding in 1834, Glandorf's parish included all northwest Ohio, from Mercer County north to Michigan and west to Indiana, it might not have survived if the Missionaries of the Precious Blood had not taken over in 1848. Brunner, who was from German-speaking Switzerland, had two convents and two mission houses built at Glandorf. Though he died in 1859, his influence, Leach says, lived on in the building of this church. The parish is still administered by the Missionaries.

St. John the Baptist's transepts have circular paintings by Johann Schmidt of Covington ("America's finest nineteenth-century ecclesiastical painter," Leach says); the elaborate carved pulpit, in walnut, oak, and basswood, was by Schroeder Studio of Cincinnati. The pulpit won a gold medal at the Philadelphia fair in 1876; then it was purchased for this church.

In August, 1992, St. John the Baptist had a $1.2 million fire after two boys found the candle lighter in the sacristy. Leach, as historian, oversaw the subsequent restoration, which brought back paintings and statues that had been removed in a 1960s renovation, and returned the pulpit, which had been moved to the side, to its original location. "All my life," Leach says, "I'd hoped to see this church restored. When the fire happened, God opened a window."

Gomer, Allen County

(Also in Allen County: Lima)

¶ Gomer now is a typical country village, but it used to be a Welsh town. The Welsh believed they were descended from Gomer, a grandson of Noah. Today the village keeps up tradition with "welcome" signs in Welsh.

Access: From State Route 309 between northwest Lima and Elida turn north on Eastown Road; at Gomer Road turn left/north and drive into Gomer village, at the intersection of Lincoln Highway.

DR. JONES'S BARN, 1890s

Lincoln Highway at Gomer Road, southeast corner, Gomer
Vacant one-time horse barn; private; view from the back of the Gomer United Church of Christ's parking lot off Gomer Road, or from Lincoln Highway around the corner

Even though it's unused and weathered gray, this remains a splendid barn. Dr. Richard Jones built it behind his house; Cincinnati-based preservationist Mary Ann Olding says that it was meant for the thoroughbreds he imported from Europe. Outbuildings often were more flamboyant than the house; this one is Queen Anne, with both a pointed tower roof and a double gable on the facade. Urbana, listed under Southwest Ohio, also has a fancy in-town barn, the Chance Stable, c. 1895 (see also).

▶ DR. JONES'S BARN

▶ NAZARETH HALL

Grand Rapids, Wood County

(Maumee Valley tour includes Nazareth Hall and Grand Rapids; for routing see Maumee.)

¶ History-conscious Grand Rapids has a fine Town Hall downtown and, at Beaver and Third, a brick Queen Anne, the Kerr House, 1885, by Toledo architect E.O. Fallis. Most spectacular of all is Nazareth Hall, east of town.

Access: Nazareth Hall is on the south side of River Road/State Route 65 seven miles west of Waterville and about four miles east of Grand Rapids.

NAZARETH HALL, 1928

Lawrence Bellman of Mills, Rhines, Bellman & Nordhoff, Toledo
21211 West River Road/State Route 65, near Grand Rapids
Private rental facilities for weddings, parties, meetings; 419/832-2900

From the beginning, Nazareth Hall was a grand building, set at the crest of a hill that slopes down toward the Maumee River. It's a Spanish Colonial Revival, with bricks in shades of brown, terra cotta trim, red tile roof, arcaded windows. It's so grand that it's a little surprising that it was originally a school for 6- to 14-year-old boys; it almost seems more fitting as the setting for weddings, parties, and meetings that it's become. ¶ The Ursuline nuns built it as a boys' boarding school; after 1935 it was a military school, with girls arriving in summer for Lady Glen Camp. But when the Vietnam War led to the anti-militarism of the 1970s, enrollment plummeted; at the end of the 1981-82 school year, Nazareth Hall closed its doors. An auction disposed of the contents, including the howitzers that had been sitting out front. The "For Sale" sign went up; but for ten years, the building sat empty while vandals broke the windows. ¶ Traveling on the way to their river cottage, Perrysburg's Bob Bettinger, a businessman, and his family drove past often, so they were always aware of Nazareth Hall. Ultimately Bettinger began wondering what the building would cost. He arranged a tour, dickered over the price, and finally agreed to buy the place for $35,000. "Then," says his son Rob Bettinger, who manages Nazareth Hall, "everybody started saying, 'If I'd known I could have had it for that, I'd have bought it myself.'" But the building was in such a state of dilapidation that it has since soaked up well over ten times the purchase price. ¶ Initially, Bettinger had no idea what to do with his new purchase. But one day when he was mowing the lawn there, a woman stopped by and hailed him. She explained that she used to go to camp here, and now she'd like to get married in the chapel. Bettinger demurred. There were no restrooms, for instance. But the woman persisted, saying that her happy memories would easily overcome any inconveniences. So that's how the party facility began evolving, though the portable-toilet phase ended after that first occasion.

Lake Erie Islands, Ottawa County

(Lake Tour includes Sandusky, Marblehead, and Lake Erie Islands; for routing see Sandusky.)

Access to Put-in-Bay: Boat service is available from April to October. From Port Clinton to Put-in-Bay, Jet Express (800/245-1538) offers faster, more frequent, and more expensive passenger service than Miller Boat Line (1800/500-2421; 419/285-2421), which runs ferries from Catawba (end of State Route 53 north of State Route 2). For more information contact the Put-in-Bay Chamber at 419/285-2832.

▶ ROUND HOUSE BAR

Put-in-Bay, South Bass Island

People usually go to Put-in-Bay for relief from mainland hustle or for roistering; but they could include an architectural tour as well. Downtown has a fine waterfront park and the vintage Park Hotel. Two sites of statewide interest follow here, and for even more architectural suggestions see the little book *Island Heritage: A Guided Tour to Lake Erie's Bass Islands* by Toledo architectural preservationist Ted Ligibel and Richard Wright.

COLUMBIA RESTAURANT, NOW ROUND HOUSE BAR, 1873

60 Delaware Avenue facing Island Park, Put-in-Bay
Bar, open daily in season, 419/285-2323

"The most unusual commercial building in the state"—that's how Toledo historian Ted Ligibel describes the Round House Bar. This saloon does indeed occupy a round building, one story high, built of red-painted horizontal boards, which for a round building is odd; vertical siding might have been easier. The white metal roof has a small octagonal cupola on top. In May, 1873, the Sandusky *Register* reported that this building was manufactured in Toledo, dismantled, shipped, and then reassembled in Put-in-Bay.

Access: The Perry Monument is within half a mile east of downtown Put-in-Bay.

▶ PERRY'S VICTORY MEMORIAL

PERRY VICTORY MONUMENT, NOW PERRY'S VICTORY AND INTERNATIONAL PEACE MEMORIAL, 1912-15

Joseph H. Freedlander and A.D. Seymour, Jr., New York
Bay View Avenue/State Route 357, Put-in-Bay, NRHP
National Park Service monument with elevator to open observation platform at
317 feet; open daily late April to late October, other times by appointment; fee;
419/285-2184

If you're on foot in Put-in-Bay, Perry's Victory and International Peace
Memorial should be easy to spot; on clear days it's visible from 40 miles away
on the lake. It honors Commander Oliver Hazard Perry's Lake Erie naval
victory over the British—a battle well remembered because Perry put it well
afterward: "We have met the enemy and they are ours." Among those who
remembered was a savvy Put-in-Bay hotel owner, who in 1908 initiated the
idea of marking the 1913 centennial of Perry's battle. Within a couple years a
multi-state and Federal commission had formed, secured funding, and
announced a design competition for a monument: a tall shaft, with stairway,
elevator, high platform, visitor and maintenance facilities. The winners were
Joseph H. Freedlander and A.D. Seymour, Jr. of New York. Their design
called for a 352-foot high pink granite Doric column. Standing on a square

granite plaza, the column would have a diameter of 45 feet at the base, 35 feet near the top, where a 45-foot square observation platform would be set. At the very top, a 23-foot bronze urn would crown the world's largest Doric column. So it was built, with a domed rotunda enclosed in the base. The column has 78 courses of

▶ PERRY'S VICTORY MEMORIAL

granite blocks, each one curved for fluting and wedged for the circular wall. Three years after the 1912 ground breaking, the $600,000 monument was opened to the public, though the surrounding park wasn't finished until 1927, and the official dedication came only in 1931. The 1972 name change, adding "International Peace Memorial", recognized that from the beginning the monument was also intended to mark an 1817 peace accord between the U.S. and Canada.

Middle Bass Island

Access for Middle Bass Island: Miller Boat Line (1800/500-2421; 419/ 285-2421) runs ferries from Catawba (end of State Route 53 north of State Route 2). From Memorial Day to Labor Day, Sonny S, 419/285- 8774, offers boat service from Put-in-Bay.

LONZ WINERY, 1934
George Lonz and Henry Blocker, Middle Bass Island
Fox Road, Middle Bass Island, NRHP
Former winery closed summer 2000; now state park property

Lonz Winery is a folk-art castle. Dominated by its immense "LONZ WINERY" sign and its wacky tower, it rises above the beach, readily visible to people arriving by water. As intended, it looks very alluring. The castle was built on top of a limestone wine cellar dating from 1871, when Middle Bass Island's Golden Eagle Wine Cellars was one of the country's largest wine producers. In the late nineteenth century, Wehrle's Hall, serving wine and also offering a ballroom, billiards, and bowling, was built over the cellars; and in the early 1900s the Hillcrest Hotel went up next door. Both Wehrle's Hall and the hotel burned down in 1923, but by then Prohibition had begun and George Lonz was busy producing grape juice to meet the demand of home wine makers. Lonz Wineries built the castle in 1934, to celebrate the end of Prohibition. It's a long building with a high central tower and the big LONZ WINERY sign, which is set between short corner towers. The central tower, whose stages are outlined by buttress-like piers, improbably has the green copper dome of an observatory on top; it seems that George Lonz was a star

▶ LONZ WINERY

gazer. Building materials are block, stucco, stone, and brick. The castle uses some Gothic motifs—battlements and pointed arches outlined in brick. With all the masonry, the structure survived a fire that destroyed the interior in the early 1940s. The porch in front was added in the 1960s. Six weeks after the Ohio Department of Natural Resources bought Lonz Winery and 123 acres for a state park, in May 2000, tragedy struck. On the afternoon of Saturday, July 1, a concrete terrace behind the winery collapsed, dropping 100 people, picnic tables, and a soda machine 20 feet. One man died and 76 were sent to hospitals. The winery, which the state hadn't planned to keep as a wine vendor, never reopened. The next year, half a dozen meetings that made it clear to ODNR that people in the area wanted to keep the winery building. Most likely reuse, said project manager Phil Miller, would be as a restaurant, museum, and day-time conference facility; but all depended on a thorough evaluation of the building's structural integrity and, of course, upcoming state capital budgets.

Lima, Allen County

(Also in Allen County: Gomer.)

¶ Lima is an industrial town whose population peaked in 1925 and has been declining ever since. Between that and some pretty awful sprawl development on the outskirts, downtown has perhaps four times the space it needs. But this same Lima also has two of Ohio's most distinctive buildings: Kewpee Restaurant and a foundry roll shop, both dating from 1939.

Access: From the west or from I-75 just to the east, State Route 309 goes to downtown Lima, where it intersects both Market Street, the principal two-way east-west thoroughfare, and Main Street, the principal two-way north-south route. This tour of a few highlights starts from West Market Street between Baxter and Metcalf Streets.

HUGHES-RUSSELL HOUSE, NOW THE YWCA, 1870

649 West Market Street, Lima
YWCA

When Beatrice Russell died in 1947, after 24 years of widowhood, she willed her Second Empire house to the YWCA, which still occupies it. In the years after her 1904 marriage, Mrs. Russell herself added the showy round Neoclassical porch and later, the mirrored bathroom upstairs, while the front parlors remain true to the nineteenth century.

MACDONELL HOUSE, 1893

Frank Leech, Lima
632 West Market Street, Lima, NRHP
Part of the Allen County Historical Society museum; open year round except Mondays; hours vary; 419/222-9426

Eight years after oil was discovered near Lima, this lavish Victorian house was built for a man who was prospering in the candy business. The most unusual feature is the siding, part of which is red slate shingles. Be sure to see the 12-foot-high bay window on the east side.

THE TOP SANDWICH SHOP, NOW COURT CAFE, REMODELED IN 1952

312 North Main Street, Lima, north of the courthouse
Restaurant, 419/222-2233

What you see—an enameled steel building with a curving glass brick window—is a 1952 remodeling. That makes it late Art Moderne—the style in its "maturity", as Richard Francaviglia graciously put it in *Timeline*.

▶ KEWPEE RESTAURANT

KEWPEE RESTAURANT, 1939
111 North Elizabeth Street, Lima
Hamburger restaurant open daily, 419/228-1778

Architecture, insists Kewpee employee Nancy Strouss, is not the only
attraction here. Kewpee Restaurant has a menu offering hamburgers, chili,
malts, and soft drinks, plus two "new" items, French fries, added in 1975,
and yogurt, in the 1990s. Kewpee, Strouss emphasizes, does not prepare still
another frozen hamburger; every day it grinds and shapes fresh meat and
makes a new batch of chili. Every order is customized—even "degreased" is
an option. ¶ Kewpee's architecture—Art Moderne in its heyday—is also
noteworthy. Above the central door, over the red-letter KEWPEE sign, a fat,
naked Kewpee doll stands in a virtual nest of curved white setbacks. As
Richard Francaviglia wrote, the doll might be "lost as just another
commercial roadside icon if it were not given a kind of local immortality by
its niche-like setting." The one-story restaurant has a white enameled steel
exterior with horizontal bands of red for decoration. The interior, which has
booths, tables, and a self-service food counter, is in enameled white panels
with bands of stainless between them; the stainless bands are sometimes
simply decorative, as on the rest-room door at the rear. ¶ Taking their theme
from the popular Kewpie doll designed by artist and writer Rose O'Neill
about 1910, Kewpee Hotel restaurants (with no i in the name) flourished
after World War I; by World War II there were 400 of them. Stub and June
Wilson opened the Lima shop in 1928, and for a while they lived in an
apartment around the corner. This Kewpee was the new building they put up
in 1939. It proves that enameled steel can still look spiffy sixty years later.
¶ Strouss, who at times is bookkeeper, cook, and waiter, first arrived here on
Saturday morning, April 8, 1961, when she came for an interview and was
told to start working right away. She liked it so much that for seven years she
couldn't leave, not even for vacation. After about 15 years, she started
collecting Kewpie dolls—so far, she has about 75. Strouss likes the sense that
her work keeps her close to the pulse of Lima. "People coming home come
here first, before they go to see their family," she says. "This is Lima, right
here."

▶ City Loan and Savings

AMERICAN SAVINGS AND LOAN BUILDING, 1914, AND THOMAS BUILDING, 1927; TWO BUILDINGS JOINED AS CITY LOAN AND SAVINGS, 1937

Peter M. Hulsken, Lima
200 West Market Street and 101 North Elizabeth Street, Lima, corner location
County-owned office building, for county use (first three floors) and private tenants

In 1937 two buildings were combined into one, for offices, and given a handsome white terra cotta cladding. The corner building was originally a bank; the later Thomas Building, with balconies facing Market Street, was apartments over Harry Thomas's grocery store.

Access: To reach Whemco from downtown go south on Main Street; turn right/west on West 4th Street to McClain Road.

OHIO STEEL FOUNDRY ROLL SHOP, NOW WHEMCO OHIO FOUNDRY DIVISION, ROLL SHOP, 1939

Albert Kahn, Detroit
1600 McClain Road at West 4th Street, Lima
Private roll shop adjacent to foundry; to see from street continue west of McClain on West 4th; cross the tracks; at the bend in the road roll shop is visible on the left

People in Lima probably would be surprised to know that, judged by appearances in national architectural books, the city's most celebrated building is this factory. It's been pictured again and again, most conspicuously in Yale architectural historian Vincent Scully's book, *American Architecture and Urbanism*. Scully compared the factory's "simplicity of mass and continuity of surface" to that of American colonial architecture. Architect Albert Kahn was famous for his sleek factories; but he also did the likes of a Second Renaissance Revival library for the University of Michigan and a 1910 skyscraper in Youngstown (see also, Vol. I). Lima Locomotive Works, which early in the twentieth century helped make Lima famous, required steel parts; this foundry was a supplier. The roll shop was built of concrete, brick, and enough glass to insure interior daylight. Running the length of the building, a raised central section has clerestory windows along side walls that cant toward the center. All the glass expanses, even multi-story walls, are made up of relatively small rectangular panes framed in metal. After almost 60 years the vast stretches of small panes have become a maintenance challenge; they no longer glitter as they once did. That's typical in America, though Ohio State's Douglas Graf observes that in Germany, similar expanses of panes were cleaned and maintained so that they've never deteriorated. Troubled glass or no, the building, much like Kewpee built downtown the same year, still seems modern.

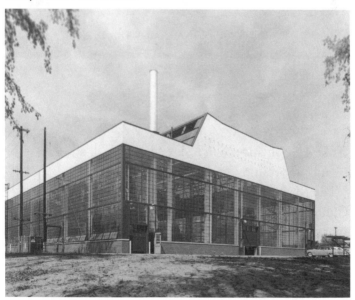

▶ WHEMCO ROLL SHOP

▶ MARBLEHEAD LIGHTHOUSE

Marblehead, Ottawa County

(Lake Tour includes Sandusky, Marblehead, and Lake Erie islands; for routing see Sandusky.)

¶ The Marblehead Peninsula extends east from Port Clinton, forming the north side of Sandusky Bay. It's a summer resort place, with bait shops and marinas.

Access: To reach Lakeside take East Harbor Road/State Route 163 east from Port Clinton or, if coming from Sandusky on State Route 2, after the bridge turn onto northbound State Route 269, which connects with 163; turn right/east. Lakeside is just east of Erie Beach Road on north side of road; watch for signs. For Marblehead Lighthouse, continue east on 163 through Marblehead village; Lighthouse Drive turns off to the left.

LAKESIDE, 1870s-1920s

State Route 163, NRHP/Lakeside HD
Private summer resort community and chautauqua; contact Lakeside Association, 236 Walnut Avenue, Lakeside 43440, 419/798-4461; in-season entry fee (nominal for brief visit); map provided

Lakeside, with its 200 acres and 800 cottages, is the largest and best known of Ohio's chautauqua camp grounds. In the chautauqua tradition, Lakeside offers, along with its Lake Erie site for recreation, a concert and lecture series. The historic Hotel Lakeside, 1875, 1879, 1889, at 150 Maple still functions as a hotel (see especially the porch overlooking the lake); Hoover Auditorium, 1929, Third Street between Central and Walnut, is in the Mission style. The two-story cottages represent many styles—including the typical porch-over-porch camp-meeting type—though winterization has transformed some into houses.

MARBLEHEAD LIGHTHOUSE, NOW MARBLEHEAD LIGHTHOUSE STATE PARK, 1821

Lighthouse Drive, Marblehead, NRHP
Marblehead Lighthouse became a state park in late 1998; tours offered most days in summer; check with Ottawa County visitors bureau: 800/441-1271 or 419/ 734-4386

Marblehead Lighthouse, the second on the Great Lakes, could hardly be more picturesque; it's not surprising that in recent years it's appeared both on a U.S. postage stamp and on Ohio license plates. Round, 25 feet in diameter at the base, the lighthouse has stuccoed white limestone walls that taper inward as they rise. Toward the top a red metal balcony rings the tower; at the summit, over the light, there's a red roof. The uppermost section was added in the late nineteenth century, extending the lighthouse's height to 65 feet.

▶ HOUSE OF FOUR PILLARS

Maumee, Lucas County

(The Maumee Valley tour, taking in several old river
towns that are in this guide, runs southwest from
Maumee to Defiance: In Maumee pick up Broadway,
heading southwest; it becomes River Road/Lucas County
1684 and goes to Waterville. At Waterville cross the river
and take State Route 65 southwest seven miles to
Nazareth Hall and another four to Grand Rapids [turn off
to see Grand Rapids south of the highway]; then continue
to Napoleon on State Route 65/110. From Napoleon take
State Route 424 west to Defiance. Of course, tour may be
done in reverse.)

¶ Maumee has many charms, including a beautiful
pedestrian path along the Maumee River and two uncom-
monly good porches.

Access: From Toledo U.S. 24/Detroit Avenue goes south to Maumee. From that road or from Ohio Turnpike exit 4, take U.S. 20/Conant Street south to Broadway; turn left/east to see House of Four Pillars. For Wolcott House continue east on Broadway, which bends and becomes River Road.

HOUSE OF FOUR PILLARS, 1835, 1844
322 East Broadway, Maumee, NRHP
Private house

One of Maumee's exceptional porches is on the House of Four Pillars. Originally, when built in 1835, this house was porchless, a deficiency the owner corrected nine years later by adding a Greek Revival porch with four two-story Doric columns. The house has sprawled out behind with modern amenities, like garages; but what we see from the street are these lovely fluted pillars. Perhaps they were the work of an itinerant column maker. The House of Four Pillars is famous for having been on the underground railroad; collapsed tunnels can still be seen at the rear. It's

▶ HOUSE OF FOUR PILLARS

known also for a one-time house guest. For a couple months in the summer of 1899 Theodore Dreiser and his new wife stayed here as guests of his friend Arthur Henry, a former city editor for *The Blade*. At the time Dreiser was a successful magazine writer, but that summer in this house, his host prodded him to try fiction, and Dreiser wrote his first story. After that initiation, in New York in September, Dreiser began working on *Sister Carrie*, a novel that shocked the nation when it came out the following year.

WOLCOTT HOUSE, NOW PART OF MAUMEE VALLEY HISTORICAL MUSEUM, 1827
1031 River Road, Maumee, NRHP
Museum, summer hours; fee;
419/893-9602

Maumee's second notable porch is that on the Wolcott House. It's a two-story porch on porch, Federal style.

▶ WOLCOTT HOUSE

▶ KELLEY BLOCK

Milan, Erie County

(Tour with sites in neighboring Huron County: from Milan take U.S. 250 south to Norwalk and U.S. 20 west to Monroeville, then U.S. 250 south and State Route 162 east to New London.)

¶ Having a founder named Ebenezer Merry must have been a good augury. Today's Milan is a pleasant and unpretentious place that's chock full of old buildings. A nineteenth-century canal port and ship-building center, the town is best known as Thomas Edison's birthplace;

the small house where he was born is now a museum open most of the year. (It's at the north end of Edison Drive; fee; 419/499-2135.) That Milan is today so good to look at, may be traced, alas, to its economic retrenchment after the canal's decline. ¶ Milan's charming Public Square is the site of the Second Empire Town Hall, 1876, 1888, where on my first visit I found the mayor presiding at a wedding. A free architectural walking tour and guide to the Public Square are available from the Visitors' Center gift shop of the Milan Historical Museum, 10 Edison Drive, P.O. Box 308, Milan 44846, 419/499-2968. (The shop is closed in January; from October-March, call for appointment.) ¶ For good, older houses see Center Street south of the Square.

Access: From Sandusky or the Ohio Turnpike to the north or from I-71 to the south, take U.S. 250 to Milan. At State Route 113/Church Street, turn east and drive a few blocks into the village and its Public Square.

KELLEY BLOCK, 1870
Public Square, Milan, NRHP/Milan HD
Row of shops and offices

Especially with its setting and its unaltered condition, the Kelley Block is easily one of Ohio's best Italianate commercial blocks. It was built by a civic worthy, Captain Henry Kelley, who began sailing on the Great Lakes at the age of 14 and 25 years later, in 1856, settled down in Milan to regale everyone with tales of his early adventures. He also built ships, invested in real estate, became a councilman, library trustee, and county commissioner, and lived well into his eighties. The two-story Kelley Block has a row of shops on the ground floor. The building is red brick, with iron Corinthian columns between shop windows, and cast-iron trim on the round-arched windows upstairs.

MILAN PUBLIC LIBRARY, 1912
H.F. Liebert, Lorain
Public Square, Milan
Public library

This is a Carnegie library, Prairie style, in stone, brick and multi-colored terra cotta, with a glazed red tile roof. It was designed by H.F. Liebert of Lorain. Liebert later moved to Wisconsin, where he designed a similar library for Ripley.

MILAN POLICE STATION, 1886
Church Street behind Town Hall, Milan, NRHP/Milan HD
Village police station

The Milan Police Station is in a tiny building. It's red brick with a sandstone base; in the front of the mansard roof, there's a single, round-arched dormer. The building looks like a spawn of the Town Hall, or perhaps, as Eric Johannesen suggested, a child's version of it. After telling the dispatcher inside what I was doing, I took a tape measure to the building's girth. It is 20 by 30 feet—I thought it was smaller, as it is inside, because the walls are over a foot thick. The interior has been remodeled. The dispatcher, who is also utilities clerk and cashier, said that the small quarters make for a "privacy problem." Everyone hears everything.

MITCHELL-TURNER HOUSE, 1848
128 South Center Street at Judson Street, Milan, NRHP/Mitchell HD
Private house

Here's Greek Revival opulence, with four two-story Ionic columns fronting a pedimented central porch and smaller columns on smaller porches on the flanking wings. The house was built for Zenas King, an iron-bridge pioneer.

Napoleon, Henry County

(The Maumee Valley tour includes Napoleon; for routing, see Maumee.)

¶ About eight miles east of Napoleon on State Route 110, which runs along the Maumee River, watch for two wonderful nineteenth-century Italianate farm houses, originally identical, one on each side of the road. The one on the north side, a little east of the other, is part of Red Gate Farm, a complex that includes a magnificent red barn. Well-kept, proud, unspoiled, the farm becomes a glimpse of an American dream.

Access: From I-75 exit 179, U.S. 6 goes west to Napoleon. For the scenic route, take State Route 65/110 from Grand Rapids, as on the Maumee Valley tour. Either way, take State Route 108/Scott/Perry Street to downtown Napoleon and the courthouse, at Washington Street. To see the Presbyterian Church take Washington two blocks west to Webster Street; church is on southwest corner.

▶ Henry County Courthouse

HENRY COUNTY COURTHOUSE, 1882, RENOVATION, 1998

David W. Gibbs, Toledo; renovation, Gaede Serne Architects, Cleveland
660 North Perry Street at Washington Street, Napoleon, NRHP
Courthouse; 419/592-5886

From its site on a high point above the Maumee River, the Henry County
Courthouse's white tower is visible from the surrounding countryside. In
1997-98 the Second Empire building received a $4 million restoration, both
interior and exterior; voters passed a levy to fund the project. This courthouse
was a hit when it was new too, for Union County built one like it.

▶ FIRST PRESBYTERIAN CHURCH

FIRST PRESBYTERIAN CHURCH, 1903

Harry W. Wachter, Toledo
303 West Washington Street, Napoleon, NRHP
Church; sanctuary open weekdays during business hours; 419/592-7736

Retired stone mason Maurice Graham so loves the stone on this church that he now shows up every Sunday; he attends the services and then walks around outside studying the walls. They were built of an extraordinary

sandstone, red from a distance, with tans and golds visible close up. Ohio has five Arts and Crafts Presbyterian churches in this stone, which used to be mined at the Will Heckler Stone Quarry near Mansfield; the others are in Upper Sandusky, Dayton (see also, Vol. I), Barnesville (see also, Southeast), and Shelby. Except for Shelby, these churches are similar enough to be siblings, though three different architects designed them. Glenn Harper, a Dayton preservationist who did the Napoleon church's National Register nomination, thought a single prototype unlikely: "Rather it appears that architects who received commissions for Presbyterian churches were simply designing in the fashionable style of the period." Harper deemed this example the best preserved of the five, and the most fully developed stylistically. Interior layout is on the Akron plan: an alcove off one side can be curtained. The sanctuary is octagonal, under a central stained glass skylight, with pews, curved to face the altar, in a lovely dark, reddish-brown wood. The alcove has two levels of Sunday-school classrooms with stained-glass windows. Outside the church has a tower and a turret with pagoda-style roofs in red tile.

New Bremen, Auglaize County

(Four-county Cross-Tipped Churches tour passes through New Bremen; for routing, see Carthagena.) ¶ The good news about New Bremen's old downtown is that it's still there. Almost all of it is owned by a flourishing local manufacturer, Crown Equipment Corporation, whose plants are on New Bremen's outskirts but whose handsome new stone headquarters building is in the middle of downtown (on Washington Street, State Route 66.) Crown has not only bought old downtown buildings, but it has refurbished them, converting most to company offices. As a result, downtown New Bremen looks as fresh as a new penny. ¶ The snag is, that when downtown becomes an office park, it doesn't seem like downtown anymore.

Access: New Bremen is at the intersection of State Routes 66/ Washington Street and 274/Monroe Street; about ten miles east 274 intersects I-75. To reach Reuben Thiesing's house take Washington Street a few blocks south of Monroe Street, to Plum Street; turn right/ west onto Plum; take the first left onto Canal, which is alley-like.

REUBEN THIESING HOUSE, 1980
Reuben Thiesing, New Bremen
214 Canal Street, New Bremen
Private house

Split-level in layout, Reuben Thiesing's house has three kinds of brick, flagstones, and wood shingles on its outside walls. It has stone sills and shutters—not the usual shutters, but abstractions made with stone blocks next to windows. The gables contain ornamental carving, the facade has bay windows, the structure is as solid as a fort. It is built almost entirely of scavenged materials, relics of one-time banks, houses, factories, and funeral homes. In this house, the demolished buildings of New Bremen reappear. It is house as folk art.

A Matter of Craft: Reuben Thiesing—Four times in Reuben Thiesing's life, which began in 1915, New Bremen has dredged the old canal that lies within the village. The first two times horses pulled the dredging scoop. The third time a backhoe replaced the horses. And the fourth time a bulldozer pushed a dredging blade—a combination powerful enough to reach all the way down to the underlying clay. There, from a hole scoured out by back eddies (here Thiesing interrupts his narrative with an aside: "I'm giving you a lot of stuff here. You don't know if you're frying eggs or what") the bulldozer found two enormous logs of white oak, felled beside the canal by axes and then stuck under water for over a century. After a struggle, the bulldozer dislodged the logs and set them on the canal bank. They were immense: 30 inches in diameter, one 18 and the other 14 feet in length.

Reuben Thiesing knows a lot about wood. A log, he says, will keep forever if it's not cut; but as soon as it's exposed to air, it has to be dried. When these intact logs were hauled up in the 1980s, Thiesing, long established as New Bremen's leading building materials scavenger, asked for them. The bulldozer operator agreed to drop them off at Thiesing's place nearby, but then the village interceded, blocking the request on the grounds that the logs were its property. So for a couple years they sat on the canal bank.

Then one day Thiesing noticed that they were missing. When he tracked them down, he found they'd been dragged to the dump for burning. So, Thiesing says, "I made a business of going to the dump and saying, in the right way, that I wanted the logs." Finally the town yielded. A friend who owns a sawmill collected the logs for him, cut them, and delivered them to Thiesing's property. While they dried in the air, the fragrance of the nine-teenth-century oak sap could be smelled for blocks around.

Later Thiesing used one of the logs for furniture for the New Bremen library, and he is still using the other.

Thiesing is a craftsman who is also creative. More specifically, he is a cabinetmaker, which means he has the skill to achieve both high accuracy and attractive appearance. Thiesing has done cabinets so fine that he's been called on to make them in three states. As for creativity, his father always told him to be original. That he is shows in all his work—his designs, his adapting of tools, his reuse of materials. His house, which he designed and built himself, has unique siding, shutters, gable decorations, and other features. Although he was a novice in masonry, he built a stone support for a bay window that was so innovative it prompted a mason to ask how he'd done it. In New Bremen, where Thiesing has a reputation as an eccentric, people acknowledge that his house is one of the local treasures.

Even in his eighties, Thiesing is over 6 feet tall and only slightly stooped. His face is long, with white curls wandering from under his cap; his glasses are sawdusty; his trousers, flecked with paint spots. His stories ramble, with fried eggs interspersed, or stray facts—for instance, that he was a drum major in high school or hauled ice for $6 a week.

But mostly, he has worked wood. Thiesing's teacher was his father, a cabinetmaker who learned from his father, a furniture maker. "My dad," Thiesing says, "is a gem in my life." At his father's urging, he bought a small house that once accommodated canal workers. Taking that house apart and putting it back together would be as good as a college education, his father said. The house was built of hand-hewn 8 by 8s and 4 by 4s; it has 12-by-12 oak sills and ash floor boards 9 inches wide. Just as people keep their diplomas, Thiesing still owns it. In 1997 he was working on it again, he said, "bringing it up to modern."

For 11 years, mostly during his twenties, Thiesing was employed as a pattern maker. Then his father told him that anyone who worked as hard as he did should be working for himself. He has been self-employed ever since as a cabinet maker, floor sander, and house remodeler. When he finished redoing a house, he painted it yellow with green trim, a combination still visible in New Bremen. His main task now is building a new house next door to his own. He began in 1987 and the project goes on and on, because he's afraid he'd be at a loss (or worse) if he finished it. His own house took him only four years to build, from 1976 to 1980. Afterward, in 1981, he got married for the first time. His bride was a widow, Sarah Miller from Wapakoneta.

Just as Thiesing followed his father and grandfather into woodworking, he learned scavenging—reusing materials—from them. What he buys new are concrete, sheetrock, roofing, some windows. Otherwise, his materials are old, garnered mostly from showing up for demolitions. The wood ornamentation in his house's gables was once stair railings in a bank. The driveway is paving bricks that used to be Second Street. The lock tender's house yielded the flagstone; the two bay windows are from Gilbert's funeral home. Asked how he designed his house, Thiesing explains that when using scavenged materials, it's quicker to design around what you have.

Indoors the marble in his entry floor is from the Washington Street bank. He took pocket doors from a

▶ Reuben's house

church and used them to make parquet floors, while his wainscoting was the Missionary Alliance Church floor. The livingroom ceiling beams came from a barn that he took down in 1976; an old house in Chickasaw yielded heating pipes. When the bathroom door opens, it follows the arc he cut out of the adjacent counter and the shelves below: a demonstration of skill for its own sake.

To be ahead in the end, a scavenger has to know materials. Brick, for instance. Builders in old New Bremen used three different kinds: hard outside brick, semi-hard inside ones, and, between the other two, soft brick for insulation. Baked just enough to hold it together, the soft brick conducts heat more slowly than the hard. One time at a demolition Thiesing was going along, picking out all the hard bricks, and he noticed others following him, picking up what they thought were good bricks he'd left behind.

While building his house Thiesing had to learn how to lay bricks, which have to be straight in all dimensions, so he consulted a young man who was the son and grandson of bricklayers. Thiesing can point out his own first brick, set out while his tutor was there. On that wall also he set flagstones canted out from the wall to support a double window. Those were the stones the mason asked him about. Thiesing explained that he'd made sawhorses to hold a form in place.

But if Reuben Thiesing was a novice bricklayer, he is a grand master in wood, even woods that are no longer used. For instance, he knows that elm, now nearly vanished because of Dutch elm disease, made good house siding. So do redwood, poplar, and cedar. White oak is good outside or inside, but not red oak. If used outside the red, hard though it is, will weather so much that in six months you can break it with your finger. Maple is so hard that it rings under a hammer. It was even used for makeshift threshing machine bearings, but they caught fire if not lubricated. The best porch floor is fir, because it won't splinter under bare feet. Beech is good for rolling pins because it has no taste.

Thiesing believes the best wood is quartersawn, which has a grain of close, parallel lines. For quartersawing, the log is first quartered lengthwise, then sliced into boards. Some wood is wasted, so quartersawing is more expensive than sawing a whole log into parallel slices. Ash hardens with time, so it used to be the top choice for flooring; but a product like quartersawn ash for flooring is simply not available today. Thiesing, of course, has an ash floor in his house. It came from the old mill and was tongue-and-grooved by hand.

One person who admires Thiesing's work is Mary Ann Olding, a Cincinnati preservationist who used to live in New Bremen. When she was overseeing restoration of Cincinnati's Memorial Hall, Olding wrote Thiesing that three contractors had told her the floors had to be replaced. She decided she would believe them only if Thiesing, who was in his mid-seventies, concurred, so he went down to Cincinnati. He was dismayed when he first saw the floors. Years of wet galoshes had brought in enough water to ruin some boards. But he agreed to come back and make the necessary repairs. He explained to Olding that he could save the floor because he had his own tools and his own system. But he remembers that really he was reluctant. "I don't like the city. I don't like motels. I don't like charging."

Memorial Hall was built with wainscoting and flooring in quartersawn oak. The wall panels are 18-20 inches wide—that means trees of more than 36 to 40 inches in diameter. For replacement wood of exactly the right color and age, Thiesing decided to scavenge the flooring of another room in Memorial Hall, a small changing room. He devised a special jig to cut floorboard patches that would fit in seamlessly. The whole job took two weeks. He would start at 7 and work until 8 or 9 at night without stopping, Olding says, unless she brought him lunch. He remembers a day when he was matching repairs near the door, in the area that had the most damage. Olding, who'd been watching, left to take a phone call. "When she came back," he says, "she couldn't find the patch."

Sometimes craft is crafty.

Post script: Reuben Thiesing died in August 2000. The unfinished house was sold to his long-time co-worker/disciple, who has been completing it. Thiesing's own house was sold in late 2001; the buyer told the family she wanted to keep the house as it was.

Access: From New Bremen go north on State Route 66 to State Route 219; drive east to New Knoxville. Distance is about seven miles. A shortcut, New Knoxville Road/County 65A, is a right turn off S.R. 66 just north of the New Bremen line.

FIRST GERMAN EVANGELICAL REFORMED CHURCH, NOW FIRST UNITED CHURCH OF CHRIST, 1894, 1913, 1923
Bremen Street/County 65A at St. Marys Street, northwest corner, New Knoxville

German settlers colonized this part of Ohio, and towns were either Protestant, like New Bremen and New Knoxville, or Catholic, like Minster and Fort Loramie to the south. What they were, they still are, by and large. Though New Bremen did build a Catholic church in the years after World War II, New Knoxville is smaller and hasn't yet seen the need. This red brick church is fat because it has had two large additions, the first to the west for Sunday-school classes, the second to the east to expand the sanctuary. It's now a very substantial building, with an immense two-part Gothic window appearing on each of the three sections. As is common in this area, you can find the church just by watching for the 125-foot clock tower, itself fattened by four round corner turrets.

New Hampshire, Auglaize County
(Also in Auglaize County: Wapakoneta.)
New Hampshire, Ohio, sounds more like a list of states than the address of a great barn.

Access: Take U.S. 33 to New Hampshire; then drive east on State Route 385. Barn is on road's north side three miles east of town, is best seen when driving westbound (from State Route 117), and is visible for about a mile. (Though the farm's post office is Lakeview, actual location is closer to New Hampshire.)

MANCHESTER BARN, 1908
Horace Duncan, Knightstown, Indiana, builder
29249 State Route 385, near New Hampshire, NRHP
Private barn; farm is not accessible to visitors

Seen from across the fields, the Manchester Barn is fat, round and improbable. It's the barn whose size (100 feet in diameter), height (80 feet), and flamboyance have made it Ohio's most celebrated. It's been copied in Iowa, featured on PBS television in "Barn Again", reproduced in porcelain miniatures, and pictured on tee shirts. But in the real world, it's a working barn, used for cleaning, bagging, and processing seed. Owner Tim Manchester's family has been farming here since 1858. In 1908 his great-grandfather, Jason Manchester, hired an Indiana builder named Horace Duncan, who arrived with his own crew and recruited more locally, set up a

▶ MANCHESTER BARN

sawmill a mile away in the woods, and then spent most of the summer
building the barn. Before leaving, he put a big semicircular sign over the high
main door, giving the farmer's name, the year, the place, Maple Avenue Farm,
and his own name. This barn was a work worth signing. The shape is hatlike.
The main roof, comparable to the crown, is domical. On top it has an
ornament, a relatively small round, windowed cupola; below it has more roof,
sloping and brimlike. Between the crown and the brim is a hatband—a
narrow strip of wall with oculi, or little round windows. Below the brim is
the barn wall, with two levels of square windows all around; siding is vertical
boards. The barn was built for livestock, with rings of wedge-shaped stalls—
cattle outside, horses inside—and an 18-by-45-foot silo in the middle; but
the farm hasn't had livestock since 1970. Manchester says the building is hard
to take care of; he'd just repaired a section of the roof that blew off, and every
few years it needs a $3-4,000 paint job. On the other hand, it makes a really
distinctive logo for his seed business.

New London, Huron County

(Tour with Milan and other Huron County sites,
Norwalk and Monroeville, listed together; for routing see
Milan.)

¶ What puts New London on the architectural map is not
its buildings but its ties with Philip Johnson, Ohio's most
famous contribution to twentieth-century architecture.
Though recognized less for his Ohio origins than for his
career as a New York architect, critic, and teacher,
Johnson was born in Cleveland in 1906; but the Ohio
place most closely associated with him is New London.
This was the home town of Johnson's father, Homer, a
Cleveland lawyer. It's where Homer Johnson brought his
family every summer, where Philip retreated in the 1930s
when he toyed with right-wing politics, and where his
first building is amouldering in the brush beside a country road. ¶ New London is a village of some 2,600 people
in the southeast corner of Huron County. The Johnsons
arrived when Philip's grandfather married into the
Townsends, who had come to New London from Massachusetts in 1815 and had a farm outside town, where the
Johnsons spent their summers, and also a house in town.
Homer Johnson had strong civic ties to New London,
where people still remember him. "Homer," says Thom
Mezick, owner of the New London *Record*, "had this
town's interest at heart." In 1916, Homer and Andrew
Carnegie gave the town its handsome library. Homer
contacted Carnegie, who agreed to give $10,000; then
Homer acquired the site and surreptitiously donated the
remaining $10,000—surreptitiously because Carnegie
stipulated that the whole community was supposed to
raise matching funds, not a single donor. The library,
designed by Cleveland architects Bohnard & Parsson, is at
67 South Main Street/State Route 60. ¶ Later, Homer
helped persuade the Federal government to build the post
office, which is of interest because of its 1940 New Deal
mural by artist Lloyd Ney. Depicting stories from the
town's past, the mural was the only abstract work of the
thousand done in post offices in the 1930s and early

▶ NEW LONDON LIBRARY

1940s. The Federal bureaucrats tried to block this one, but were overcome by Ney's zealous lobbying and by public sentiment in New London, where the postmaster and 19 petition-signing Rotarians all supported the artist. The Post Office is at 86 East Main Street/State Route 162.

Access: From the Ohio Turnpike exit at Norwalk; drive south on U.S. 250/State Route 13 to State Route 162; drive four miles east to New London.

A Short Tour of New London Buildings Associated with Philip Johnson

1) The 1867 Townsend House in town is now a private home at 135 North Main Street/State Route 60. When Philip Johnson came back to New London in the 1930s, this was where he lived. He also did some remodeling, installing modern floor-to-ceiling-glass walls in the livingroom. The glass walls are still there, between storm windows on the outside and curtains inside. One of these glass walls is visible, just barely, from the side street to the south. It's right behind the porch.

2) The 1845 Greek Revival house that was once the manse of the Townsend Farm is at 4306 Fayette Road. To see, drive north of the village on State Route 60 to Fayette Road, Township 42. Turn left; white house will be on right. House is private, but visible from the road.

3) To see the ruins of Philip Johnson's first building as a graduate architect, a shed, continue west on Fayette to first intersection, Town Line Road, Township 79. Turn south/left. Shed is on the right across from a farmhouse; it's near the road but may be hard to see. It's on private property.

Shed Ado: Philip Johnson and New London—For the moment, a small building in ruins lingers beside a country road near New London. Since the structure was only a tool shed and is no longer needed, its abandonment is hardly remarkable. But this was no ordinary shed. When built in 1944, it was an advanced design, in the International Style, the first work of Philip Johnson after he graduated from architecture school in his late thirties. At the time, Johnson knew as much as anyone in America about the International Style. Even so, "extraordinary tool shed" is an oxymoron.

But this shed really was a good building. It was flat-roofed and rectangular, built of gray cinder blocks with a band of two-foot-high clerestory windows all around, above the block walls and just below the roof. In the middle of the facade a pair of doors was set under four-foot high transom windows. All the glass was ribbed on one side, like a fine corduroy, so that it was translucent but not transparent. Philip Johnson recalls that he himself liked this shed for its symmetry, calmness, and reasonably priced materials. "I was my own client," he adds: an interesting note, for Johnson has often claimed that he is his own best client.

At least until Frank Gehry designed a museum in Bilbao, Spain, for over 20 years no one else approached Philip Johnson as America's best known living architect. It is a truism, often repeated by both Johnson and those writing about him, that he is not the century's greatest architect—not so great as those who originated forms, like Frank Lloyd Wright or Mies van der Rohe or Gehry. But most critics would place Johnson not far behind the titans. He worked with Mies van der Rohe on New York's 1958 Seagram Building; with John Burgee he ushered in Post Modernism with the AT&T Building, done in 1984. And he has designed some buildings widely recognized as masterpieces. One that I've seen is the Museum for Pre-Columbian Art at Dumbarton Oaks in Washington, D.C.—it took my breath away. Another, which I haven't seen, is his home in New Canaan, Connecticut: a complex of nine structures, including his famous residence, the 1949 Glass House.

And what has Philip Johnson done in Ohio? His best known work is a 1983 addition to the Cleveland Play House—an addition that I found a letdown next to the original. He also did a couple of buildings on the Ohio State University campus, red-brick structures of so little distinction that hardly anyone in Columbus even knows Johnson did them. Then too, there's the International Style tool shed in New London. "Didn't I do anything more interesting in Ohio than that?" Johnson wonders. Even to him, it was only a shed, though a satisfying one.

The collapsing shed is located on what was once the Townsend Farm, where the Johnsons spent their summers when Philip was growing up. Though Homer Johnson lived and practiced law in Cleveland, he was originally from New London, where he kept the Townsend Farm's 2,000-acres in production with 14 tenant farmers. As a child and young man, his son Philip spent a lot of time on the farm and was a great summer worker there. So recalls his sister, Jeannette Dempsey of Cleveland.

Homer Johnson died in New London in 1960, and the Townsend farm acreage has been sold off. Starting in 1979 Mary Lou Rapp and her husband owned the main house, plus the ice house and laundry house, both with cupolas, in the yard; the road in front has the remnants of an allée of trees. Philip Johnson visited the old homestead in summer, 1994; he told Rapp he remembered his mother planting the trumpet vine in the front yard and his father meeting with farm workers in the gazebo. In summer the Johnsons kept a pair of black swans on the pond in back.

Homer Johnson provided well for his three children. He gave his son Alcoa stock that he had because of his Oberlin College friendship with Charles Martin Hall, who discovered a lucrative way of processing aluminum. Though the stock was not guaranteed to do well, it did; so Philip Johnson has always had money. As a young man he traveled so much in Europe, and looked at architecture so intently, that in New York early in 1932, when he was only 25, he was co-curator of a Museum of Modern Art exhibit that showed America what the International Style was all about. The show, which focused particularly on European buildings from the 1920s, was received quietly at the time but has reverberated ever since in the annals of American architecture. Stripped down and austere, using a lot of glass, the International Style virtually monopolized office-building design in the 1950s and 1960s.

It was 1940 before Philip Johnson decided to enroll in architecture school at Harvard. He was 34 at the time; as a student he was excused from a class that studied the book he had co-authored on the International Style. In his first year he began building a glass-walled house for himself in Cambridge near the university; in 1942 he moved in. Then early the next year Johnson was drafted into the army; and, given the exigencies of wartime and his class

rank as valedictorian, Harvard gave him his degree that spring. He spent a year and a half as an army private, assigned to humble home-front duties like cleaning latrines until he was discharged for old age at 38. It was while on a leave during his army career that Johnson designed the tool shed; biographer Franz Schulze gives the date as 1944. Since Johnson had done the house in Cambridge, Massachusetts earlier, the shed wasn't his first building; but it *was* his first building as a graduate architect.

▶ UNITED METHODIST CHURCH

Long after it had been abandoned, the shed's roof collapsed, though the walls and an adjacent chimney remained standing. That was still its condition in 1997, when I met Oberlin historian Geoffrey Blodgett (who died in November, 2001) in New London. On that bright spring morning, the village's downtown, a broad street lined with parked pickup trucks and low-rise red-brick buildings, was a busy place.

Architecturally, the high point there is the United Methodist Church, built of brick in two contrasting shades. At the main corner a Neoclassical building, once a bank, had a Pizza House awning sticking out between the two columns; outside one column a large round exhaust fan made a bizarre ornament.

When Jeff Blodgett and I reached the tool shed, we were dismayed to find gable-shaped beams lying on the ground inside. International style tool sheds have to have flat roofs; a gable roof would demote this one from architectural leadership to ordinary farm shed. So later, when I talked to Dorothy and John Thomson, who used to live across the road from the shed, my first question was about the roof, and both were sure it had been flat. So at least the style was secure.

But not the roof itself, whose collapse the Thomsons witnessed. "We were sitting on our porch," Dorothy says, "and we heard the noise—kaboom. We went outside to watch. It didn't go all at once. Mostly it was noisy, the pieces of glass falling and breaking." It was the late 1980s, a mild enough day for the Thomsons to be on the porch.

John Thomson remembered how the shed was built: a flat roof supported by wooden trusses, with clerestory windows the height of the trusses. Later I showed my snapshots to an architect friend, who could discern that the trusses were supported by braced wooden posts set at intervals along the walls. After falling, they might have looked like gables. Besides holding up the roof, the posts would have braced the walls: a clever solution, my friend thought.

Dorothy Thomson said the shed had been an apple storage barn. In fact, about half the people in New London who are aware of the building's existence, say it was used for apples or cider. I consulted an apple grower, and she insisted that apples are always stored in the dark. Johnson's sister, Jeannette Dempsey, resolved this uncertainty. The shed was built in wartime when, she says, "it wasn't legal to build on a whim. So he pretended it was to store apples, because there was an orchard nearby." Johnson himself is quite sure its purpose was as a tool shed and work shop.

In 1934 Johnson left the Museum of Modern Art and moved back to New London; for the next six years it was his home base. He settled in the Townsend House on North Main Street and began dabbling in politics—a pursuit he dropped after enrolling in architecture school in 1940. In 1941 correspondent William Shirer's *Berlin Diary* appeared. In it Shirer called Johnson, whom he'd met in Europe during the 1939 Nazi invasion of Poland, an "American fascist". Ever since, Johnson has been trying to apologize for his 1930s politics; his activities then, he told the *Plain Dealer*'s Steven Litt in summer, 1997, were a "terrible mistake." But while in New London, he was associated with Father Charles Coughlin, a Detroit-based anti-Semitic radio preacher. And when he met Shirer, Johnson was a correspondent for Coughlin's newspaper.

In the mid-1980s, Jeff Blodgett researched Johnson's New London years by working his way through the library's collection of 1930s newspapers, which covered Johnson's gadfly appearances at the town council, his organizing farmers to protest low milk prices, and his role in the New London chapter of Coughlin's National Union for Social

▶ NEOCLASSICAL PIZZA, NEW LONDON

Justice. Johnson's town council protests were muted by his appointment as president of the New London Park Board; he donated a new Chevrolet as a 1937 Labor Day lottery prize. While Blodgett was burrowed in the library, whenever a resident who'd been around in the 1930s came in, the librarians introduced him. That was how he learned about the boozy post-Prohibition party Johnson gave at the high school for young people.

On a balmy day in May, 1996, I heard Philip Johnson speak at the Cleveland Institute of Art's 113th commencement; it's an art school both his parents supported, and his sister still does. An on-stage trio played *Pomp and Circumstance* for the graduates, most of whom had earned bachelor's degrees in the fine arts. Almost 90, the speaker looked like an old man, with an old man's walk and, behind the black-framed glasses he

designed years ago to give himself a trademark, an old man's sere face. Then he gave a wonderful, funny, ten-minute speech, one artist to fellow artists. That fall Johnson fell gravely ill after surgery—so ill that it was almost a surprise when he showed up in Cleveland again the next summer. He came to see *Turning Point,* his sculpture installed on the Case Western Reserve campus late the year before.

As for the shed, the New London Historical Society had an architect from Norwalk look at it. "He said it would cost $20,000 to restore," recalls member Martha Sturges. "We had $50 in the treasury." Sturges has not forgotten the shed—once she called Jeannette Dempsey, then a society member, for more information. "Philip Johnson is well known here," Sturges explains. "Fame doesn't hurt a bit when it comes to remembering somebody."

Norwalk, Huron County

(Tour with Milan, Monroeville, and New London; for routing see Milan.)

¶ Most of the Western Reserve, the Northeast Ohio region that Connecticut owned in the late 1700s, was bought and sold off by a land company. The exception was the westernmost section, today most of Huron and Erie Counties, called the Firelands because it was reserved for people who had had property burned by the British during the Revolutionary War. Not opened for settlement until 1805, the Firelands, says Ohio historian George W. Knepper, "became the most New England of regions" because of its architecture, town names, Calvinist religion, culture, and education. Norwalk was the heart of it all. Today it's a relatively lively county seat with lots of wonderful old houses. ¶ The Firelands Historical Society at 4 Case Street, P.O. Box 572, Norwalk 44857, 419/668-6038, has a free flyer on local buildings. It's available by mail or in person; seasonal hours, closed in winter. The Society sponsors guided tours of West Main Street in May and sometimes also in the summer; and it sells an audio-visual tour tape for $26.50.

Access: U.S. 250/State Route 13 runs north-south through Norwalk and at the south end intersects with U.S. 20/State Route 18. Main Street/State Route 61 intersects U.S. 250 downtown.

BARNARD CORTRITE HOUSE, 1888
131 East Main Street, Norwalk
Private house

The Cortrite House is a favorite of Lakewood Victorian specialist Craig Bobby, who points out that Norwalk's good houses aren't limited to West Main Street. Bobby is partial to Second Empire houses such as this one, a very good example.

NORWALK PUBLIC LIBRARY, 1905
46 West Main Street, Norwalk, NRHP/West Main Street District
Public library, 419/668-6063

This Carnegie library is especially grand. It has columns at the entrances and a high round dome on top, plus a central stained-glass skylight inside.

▶ Norwalk Female Seminary

MOSES KIMBALL HOUSE, 1833
54 West Main Street, Norwalk, NRHP/West Main Street District
Private house

One of the earliest homes in the historic district, the Kimball House became a twentieth-century tenement that was rescued by a prize-winning restoration. It's a red brick Federal style house with stepped gables and a one-story front porch that had to be reconstructed.

NORWALK FEMALE SEMINARY, 1848
Simeon Porter, Hudson
114 West Main Street at Pleasant Street, Norwalk, NRHP/West Main Street District Private house

The Norwalk Female Seminary is a beautiful house. It so delighted architectural historian Eric Johannesen that he pronounced it "the Greek Revival masterpiece of the [West Main Street] district. The monumentality of its facade and correctness of its proportion and detail are rarely equaled in Ohio." And the University of Notre Dame's Thomas Gordon Smith, who was writing about the early nineteenth-century builder's guide author Archer

Benjamin, declared that though the Female Seminary's builder borrowed from Benjamin, overall he "achieved a better solution than Benjamin the architect could have accomplished." ¶ In the late 1980s, Norwalk historian Henry Timman discovered that Simeon Porter was the Seminary's architect. At least in some circles, this came as a surprise, for both house and architect were well known but had never been linked. Timman found the architect because, in search of material for his weekly historical column, he regularly pores over old newspapers. Thus he came across a notice published early in 1847 to announce that the Female Seminary, designed by "Mr. Porter of Hudson," was seeking construction bids. As a source, that's as reliable as it gets. ¶ The son of Lemuel Porter, who did Tallmadge Church, Simeon Porter started in Hudson but later practiced in Cleveland. Traditionally he's been credited with the Western Reserve Academy Chapel, an attribution Hudson preservationist Priscilla Graham challenges; but the Female Seminary can only enhance his reputation. ¶ It's a two-story brick building with a pair of fluted Ionic columns flanking the central door and pilasters at the corners. The girls' school opened in 1850; eight years later a bank panic forced it to close. The building was converted to a residence. ¶ By the early 1990s the house was badly neglected, but in 1995 Richard Parsons and Joseph Casey came in and made the structure sound again. They discovered that originally the second floor was not classrooms but one large room; they will leave it divided into bedrooms. But Parsons and Casey are restoring the east porch and have filled in a wall where windows were added. In the first-floor rooms, they've uncovered Female Seminary blackboards set flush with the wall plaster. One is very low, for the littlest girls.

THADDEUS B. STURGES HOUSE, 1832
99 West Main Street, Norwalk, NRHP/West Main Street District
Private house

When this house was built for Thaddeus B. Sturges, a politician, Norwalk was a place with muddy streets and only 400 people. The house, in a mixture of Federal and Greek Revival styles, has a front porch with four unusual two-story octagonal columns.

Access: U.S. 20/State Route 18 covers the few miles between Norwalk and its neighbor to the west, Monroeville.

JOHN HOSFORD HOUSE, 1856
64 Sandusky Street/U.S. 20, Monroeville, NRHP
Private House

The Hosford House is one of Ohio's best octagons. It's brick, Italian Villa style, with an arcaded porch on three sides. On top is an octagonal cupola whose round-arched windows light a spiral stairway that ascends the full height of the house. Ray Luce, former state historic preservation officer, found that of the 30 octagon houses constructed in nineteenth-century Ohio, 26 survive—the remarkably high rate shows how people have always treasured these curiosities. Other structures, like Circleville's first courthouse and several schools, have also been octagons. Besides the Hosford House, three other eight-sided houses are in this guide. They are in Marshallville and Kinsman in Northeast Ohio, and in Hamilton in Southwest Ohio.

Ottawa, Putnam County

(Also in Putnam County: Glandorf.)

❡ Putnam is a rural county where no town is bigger than Ottawa, the county seat, which has 4,000 people. Ottawa, says Common Pleas Judge Randall Basinger, "is what many people picture as a quaint rural town." In fact the whole of Putnam County seems to have stepped aside from modern stresses. The population, divided between German Catholics and Mennonites, has remained relatively stable through the years. "We don't have crack cocaine on any scale," says the judge. "The divorce rate is low." ❡ One thing the county does have is a courthouse of uncommon elegance. And, as Basinger observes, since the population hasn't outgrown it, the courthouse is much as it was originally.

Access: U.S. 224 arrives from Findlay and I-75 to the east and becomes Main Street in town.

PUTNAM COUNTY COURTHOUSE, 1913

Frank L. Packard with associate architect Ralph Snyder, Columbus
245 East Main Street/U.S. 224, Ottawa, NRHP
Courthouse open weekdays; 419/523-6200

In the Putnam County Courthouse, Common Pleas Judge Randall Basinger has a two-story courtroom with a coffered ceiling; he presides from a high and massive oak bench. Amid the pilasters along the walls, portraits of all his predecessors are watching. This courthouse, Basinger says, was ambitious from the beginning, for voters approved a $200,000 bond for its construction — this at a time when farmland was $20 an acre. As farmland is now around $2,000 an acre, Basinger estimates a comparable building today would cost $20 million. Following the shape of its downtown square, the three-story courthouse is rectangular, 93 feet wide and 127 feet deep. Built of limestone in a Second Renaissance Revival style, it's an island of stone amid the red brick of Main Street. The first two floors have heavy rustication, or deeply grooved stonework, and high round-arched openings; on the top floor pairs of columns alternate with rectangular windows that have balustrades at their bases. Ohio State's Douglas Graf finds the courthouse's top and bottom so dissimilar that they seem like "two buildings imposed on each other, which makes it awfully interesting." Both the balustrades and the pairs of columns work to connect the top and bottom, he says. And the little rectangular friezes above the upper windows echo a frieze that continues all around the building below the cornice; 20 inches deep, it has steer heads and other bas-relief designs. Roselia Verhoff, who worked in the courthouse 13 years, including eight as auditor, also appreciates the building, which has been little altered and remains much as it was originally. "The people point to it with

▶ Putnam County Courthouse

pride," she says. "We were the last part of Ohio to be developed. We don't have recreational areas. But if you were to come here one of the first places I'd ask you to go is the courthouse." Also, she says, the interior is laid out well. The auditor and treasurer work together regularly; so do the auditor, recorder, and engineer; it helps that their offices are on the same floor.

OTTAWA WATERWORKS BUILDING, 1904
1035 East Third Street, one block north of Main Street/U.S. 224,
Ottawa, NRHP
Municipal facility set in a park

A place with one exceptional building usually has others. In Ottawa, this one-story waterworks illustrates that. Its most distinctive feature is the red-tile hip roof, steeply pitched and flared, with a miniature of itself on the small louvered cupola. Walls are red brick with a four-foot base in rough-cut sandstone.

Perrysburg, Wood County
(Toledo [Vol. I] is just to the north.)

Access: For a building so easy to see from the freeway, the Islamic Center is tricky to drive to. Exit from I-75 at U.S. 20. Take 20/Sandusky Street northwest to first left, Boundary Street; turn left and take Boundary about three quarters of a mile to State Route 199/Louisiana Avenue; turn left and drive over I-75; immediately after freeway Scheider Road is on right; turn and drive to building.

▶ ISLAMIC CENTER

ISLAMIC CENTER OF GREATER TOLEDO, 1983

Talat Itil, Toledo
25877 Scheider Road, Perrysburg
Tours available for groups by prearrangement;
419/874-3500

Both fortunately and unfortunately, the best way to see this mosque is from I-75. It's fortunate because the sight of dome and minarets rising from the flat farmland is astounding, and zillions of drivers can share it. Unfortunate, because it's worth your life to linger. It's best visible at the intersection of I-75 and I-475; stopping on the berm is possible only when traffic is light. The nation's largest mosque with traditional architecture, it serves a Toledo-area congregation of 500 families and 23 different nationalities; they chose this rural site to accommodate other facilities, including a school and housing for the elderly. The architect, a Turk who practiced in Toledo, the late Talat Itil, gave his congregation a Turkish-style mosque, characterized by circular minarets and a slightly flattened dome. Middle Eastern countries each have their own style of mosque; if this one were Saudi, for instance, the dome would be higher and the minarets octagonal. Here, the 60-foot dome is set over the mosque's central focus: an octagonal prayer rug for 1,000 people. All Muslims are supposed to pray five times a day; minarets originally provided a high balcony for broadcasting prayer reminders. Though no longer used that way, they are part of the traditional design. Here the minarets are 135-feet tall, accessible by spiral staircases. In late 1996, a heavy gale took the conical top off one; it landed, without injury or damage to anything but itself, in the parking lot, and a replacement was ordered.

Sandusky, Erie County

(Lake Tour includes Sandusky, Marblehead, and Lake Erie islands. From Sandusky take State Route 2 west and north to Marblehead Peninsula, where road intersects with State Route 163, which goes east to Marblehead and west to Port Clinton and ferries.)

❡ Sandusky's diagonal streets often bedevil the tourists who flock to the city's Cedar Point Amusement Park. They might find solace in being confused by the world's only street layout based on the Masonic symbol of an open Bible, a mason's square, and an open compass.

❡ A Mason named Hector Kelbourne did the platting in 1818. The compass legs are the diagonal Huron and Central Avenues; Columbus Avenue is the center of the open book (usually shown today as the letter G for God); the right angle of the mason's square is supposedly formed by East and West Park Streets, though they come together in an angle of less than 90 degrees. As a representation of the Masonic symbol, concedes Sandusky preservationist Ellie Damm, the plan "isn't exactly 'pure'." ❡ John Reps, an authority on American town plans, noted that Sandusky's singular layout gave the city three large triangular parks. But Reps really thought the plan a disappointment because the diagonals terminate "at open spaces rather than at the sites designated for public buildings. Here was lost a splendid opportunity to create a little regional capital with something

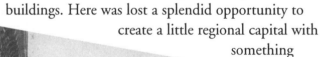

of the elegance of a Williamsburg." Rather than a fine urban plan, the result was merely eccentric. ¶ A brochure, "Sandusky Downtown Architectural Walking Tour" and other guides are available from the Erie County Visitors Bureau at 4422 Milan Road/State Route 250, or from the Old House Guild, at the Eleutheros Cooke House below. See especially Wayne Street's row of stone houses—plus the 1884 brick Queen Anne at 531—and the 1929 State Theatre at Columbus Avenue and Water Street, recently renovated.

Access: Of the two principal Ohio shoreline routes, State Route 2 bypasses Sandusky to the south while U.S. 6 goes through town near the lake. Both are intersected by the north-south State Route 4; take it into town, where it becomes Columbus Avenue and is one block west of Wayne Street. Of course Water Street is near the lake.

ELEUTHEROS COOKE HOUSE, 1844

1415 Columbus Avenue, Sandusky, NRHP
Ohio Historical Society Museum; fee; open daily except Monday; 419/627-0640

At least in Ohio, a Greek Revival house whose wall is topped with castle-like crenellation is an uncommon sight. Add to that an interior that's a 1950s period piece, and you have the Eleutheros Cooke House. Originally built downtown, the house was moved here in 1878, after the death of Eleutheros Cooke and his wife.

ORAN FOLLETT HOUSE, 1837

404 Wayne Street at Adams Street, Sandusky, NRHP
Museum owned by Sandusky Library; closed January-March; open spring and fall weekends and Tuesday through Saturday afternoons from June through August; 419/627-9608

The Oran Follett House is one that, as preservationist Ellie Damm wrote, ranks with Ohio's most outstanding Greek Revival mansions. To earn such status, it has more than one remarkable feature. The most noticeable is the front entry porch with curved stairways on both sides. The first-floor door is unusually high because the raised basement below it was raised more than usual. That was because the limestone bedrock is so close to the surface here. This basement has a bedrock floor. Another unusual feature is the stone, a golden limestone. It was quarried nearby and, Damm says, the gold color was found only near the top of the deposit. The local stone permitted many limestone houses, but the others have the more familiar gray. The Follett House also has a widow's walk, small, decorative frieze windows, and Doric columns on the porch. When in 1989 Ellie Damm published her book, *Treasure by the Bay: The Historic Architecture of Sandusky, Ohio*, she led off with her intention to "redress a long-standing omission. Sandusky ... has been an undiscovered treasure." A native Sanduskian, she herself noticed her city's

▶ ORAN FOLLETT HOUSE

architecture only after she'd seen Williamsburg; but once aware, she became a formidable advocate. She was the one who, in 1979, coordinated 60 volunteers in the first comprehensive architectural inventory of an Ohio city—in one fell swoop, the inventory landed 95 buildings on the National Register. More recently, one of Damm's biggest challenges has been Cedar Point Amusement Park, which hasn't had preservation as a high priority. In spite of Damm's letters in the late 1990s reminding the park of the success of fabulous old hotels elsewhere (San Diego's Hotel Coronado and Mackinaw Island's Grand Hotel), by 2001 Cedar Point had remodeled the Breakers Hotel right out of its National Historic Landmark status.

▶ FOLLETT HOUSE FOUNDATION DETAIL

HUBBARD'S BLOCK, 1854

Sheldon Smith, Sandusky
101 West Water Street, Sandusky, NRHP/Water Street Commercial Buildings
Shops at street level

West Water Street has a fine row of old commercial buildings from the 1830s-1860s; Hubbard's Block is one of the most attractive. Four stories high and built of stone, it has rows of round-arched windows over an arcaded ground floor.

▶ SANDUSKY RAILROAD DEPOT

LAKE SHORE & MICHIGAN SOUTHERN RAILROAD DEPOT, 1891

Shepley Rutan and Coolidge, Boston
North Depot Street at Carr Street, several blocks east of State Route 4 just north of the railroad tracks, Sandusky, NRHP
Amtrak station; depot for bus and emergency medical services

Two Ohio towns, Sandusky and Painesville, have Lake Shore & Michigan Southern railroad stations by Boston architect H.H. Richardson's successor firm, Shepley Rutan and Coolidge. Both depots are Richardsonian Romanesque, stone with high hip roofs with broad flared eaves, but Painesville's (see also) has a round end that gives it an edge. On the other hand, Painesville doesn't have Sandusky's extraordinary freight depot, whose hip roof descends at two angles, first sharply and then less so; the eaves are so broad that the little stone building becomes mushroom-like.

Van Wert, Van Wert County

(Also in Van Wert County: Venedocia.)
❡ Architecturally, Van Wert is a delight and a frustration. Clearly at one time the citizenry embellished the town with exceptional buildings, like the stone Chateauesque house at 308 South Washington, or, on East Main Street, the 1899 stone block that housed a grocery wholesaler, or the hotel across from the courthouse. But today this downtown, which could again be so lustrous visually, is mostly just another disappointment, with facades (if still standing) let go and half slathered in siding. ❡ Elizabeth France Lewis has lived in Van Wert since 1950, when she

arrived with her husband, who ran a nearby limestone quarry. Though she grew up in Perrysburg, she is descended on her mother's side from Welsh immigrants who settled in Allen County, in the Welsh-speaking village of Gomer (see also), where newcomers never had to learn English. Van Wert, Lewis avers, was always both English and Welsh; the only Germans were the Brumbacks, whose name lives on in the library. ¶ Peony Capital of the World before World War II, Van Wert was also the only place on earth where Liederkranz cheese was made from a culture someone had stumbled on. Then in the 1960s the factory burned down and the fire destroyed the culture, which could never be restarted.

Access: Just south of U.S. 30 and U.S. 224, Van Wert straddles U.S. 127, called Washington Street in town. Main Street intersects Washington. Sites are listed west to east.

BRUMBACK LIBRARY, 1901
David L. Stine, Toledo
215 West Main Street, at North Jefferson Street, Van Vert, NRHP
Library open to the public daily except Sunday; 419/238-2168

This was the first county library in the United States—the state of Ohio had to pass a law permitting it. John Sanford Brumback, a banker and dry goods merchant, left money for it in his will. As a widow's only surviving son, he himself had never even been able to attend school regularly; at ten, he was trading horses. He left $50,000 for a library building to be maintained by

▶ BRUMBACK LIBRARY

county-wide property taxes, a novelty at the time. The state legislature acted in 1898, the year after Brumback's death; and in 1899 the cornerstone was laid. Thousands of people attended the ceremony and parade. In January 1898 the *Van Wert Presbyterian* declaimed: "A good free library is worth more to us than half a dozen opera houses." The bequest covered the building, furnishings, and 2,700 new books, supplementing 1,800 from the old library. In the first few years after the dedication on January 1, 1901, at least one library branch was set up in each township; altogether, there were 16, most housed in stores. Today there are five branches. The building has a mix of Romanesque and Gothic features. Monochromatic, it is built of rough-cut gray sandstone. Two towers, one round, the other shorter and square, both crenellated at the top, flank the entry. In 1992 the Reed Memorial Addition at the rear, in matching stone and the same style as the original, greatly expanded library space. All shelves and almost all functions moved into the new building and the people followed, leaving the old building's barrel-vault reading room virtually unused.

CENTRAL FIRE AND CASUALTY COMPANY, NOW PARK PLACE, 1904

120 West Main Street at North Jefferson Street, Van Wert
Private office building; architectural tourists normally may see the third-floor dental office, described below, during business hours

This downtown building has an unusually elegant design. Just as remarkable, it's the exception to the rule in Van Wert and has been restored. Kitty-corner from the library, this four-story brown brick office building has a row of seven three-part Palladian windows on the fourth floor, crowning the Jefferson Street facade. The middle floors have three-window bays on both street facades; windows have terra-cotta trim; the copper cornice has been restored. The building looks so good because a group of investors, one of them a dentist named John Eversman, bought it in 1990 and began a four-story rehab, including enclosing the ground-floor store. By 1997 they finished, and the building was fully rented. On the third floor Dr. Eversman's patients now sit in chairs facing out bay windows, overlooking the park and the library.

▶ PARK PLACE

▶ VAN WERT COURTHOUSE

COLLINS FINE FOODS, 1930
Carl Hoke, Van Wert and Toledo
223 North Washington Street, just north of the tracks, Van Wert
Grocery store and wine shop; 419/238-0079

One story high, just a door and two shop windows wide, this little building
has a wonderful facade. The roof, of rough-cut multi-hued slates, has low
parapets at the gable ends; over the door in the center front, there's a single
dormer.

VAN WERT COUNTY COURTHOUSE, 1876
Thomas J. Tolan and Son, Fort Wayne
121 East Main Street, Van Wert, NRHP
County courthouse

This is one of Ohio's most famous courthouses. It's Second Empire in style,
red brick with limestone and metal trim that never misses a chance to
ornament a corner or window or doorway; Cleveland architect Robert Gaede
compares it to a wedding cake. G.E. Kidder Smith, a New York-based
architect and critic who in 1981 had the temerity to publish *The Architecture
of the United States*, a two-volume work featuring a thousand buildings,

included the Van Wert County Courthouse. He admired its "overall cohesion" and its "firm and colorful presence" on Main Street. He wrote, "The proliferation of white limestone quoins and framings of the openings gives vertical contrast to the white horizontal basement and to the white mid-building banding, with both shining against the red brick." Since he wrote, the basement level has become dark gray. Starting with the cement-block elevator tower right inside the front door, taking up a third of the stairway width, the interior is a disappointment. The good news is that the building is well maintained.

Access: To reach the Marsh Foundation School drive east on Main Street to Wayne Street; turn left/north and cross the tracks; then take the second right onto Lincoln Highway. The Marsh Foundation will be on the left.

MARSH FOUNDATION SCHOOL, C. 1926

Langdon, Hohly and Gram, Toledo
1229 East Lincoln Highway, Van Wert, NRHP
School and residence for children needing homes; visitors may drive around the grounds and may see the Administration Building interior if they first stop at the office; groups may prearrange tours; 419/238-1695

This lovely complex of Jacobean Revival buildings, well laid out and little changed, is an unexpected delight. It looks like a college campus, but in fact, it was built as an orphanage. ¶ It was the legacy of George H. Marsh, who lived in the fancy Italianate house next door. He was a man into many businesses, not all local, for he was a shareholder in 19 banks across the country. By the early 1870s he owned Van Wert's Eagle Stave Factory, which he made the country's biggest in barrel staves. When all the local timber—raw material for staves—had been used, he had a steam locomotive built in Lima, to ship lumber from Paulding County; then he himself went into the railroad equipment business. Besides, people say he was a lucky gambler. ¶ When he died at 86 in 1920, Marsh provided for his daughter and then left the rest of his estate—$5 million—to endow the Marsh Foundation, which was to build and run a home and school with hands-on agricultural and vocational training for orphans, particularly ones from Van Wert and northwest Ohio. Today northwest Ohio has fewer orphans, but the Marsh Foundation accommodates school-age children who will benefit from a secure and structured environment; referrals come from families, courts, and social service agencies. So says James Price, the Marsh Foundation's secretary-treasurer. Now 35 children are enrolled, down from the 75-125 who once lived here. They attend classes and help farm the adjacent 200 acres or tend stock, including cattle, sheep, and horses. The trust still provides 80 percent of the funding. ¶ This institution is unique in Ohio and like few others in the nation, but it was the last wish of Marsh's wife, Hilinda, who died in 1900. Her husband's will specified buildings "as comfortable and home-like as may be made." He didn't say handsome, but the complex's six Jacobean Revival structures stand out architecturally. Five are set in an arc perhaps a hundred yards from the largest, the Administration Building. Four still function as residence halls. All the buildings are different but related in style, two-to-four-story heights, brick and stone trim. The best and easiest to see

▶ MARSH FOUNDATION SCHOOL ADMINISTRATION BUIULDING

are the two to the west. The Administration Building houses some offices, classrooms, a high-ceilinged library, and an auditorium sometimes used for community events. A walk around the first floor shows that alterations have been minimal and the detailing is good, as in the vertical mullions, or dividers, in door windows.

Venedocia, Van Wert County
(Also in Van Wert County: Van Wert Country Churches tour includes Venedocia; for routing see Glandorf.)

Access: From Van Wert, take State Route 116, called Hospital Drive where it intersects U.S. 127 on the south side of town, and drive east to Venedocia. (Country Churches tour approaches from another direction.)

SALEM PRESBYTERIAN CHURCH, 1898
Wing and Mahurin, Fort Wayne
15240 Main Street/State Route 116, Venedocia
To see inside call the church, 419/667-4142

The Welsh who founded Venedocia held their first religious service on the first Sunday after their arrival in 1848. Though for many years they had scarcely any English-speaking neighbors, by 1895 the village had an English church also, Venedocia Presbyterian, which in the 1910s merged with the Welsh congregation as Salem Presbyterian Church. Every year on the Sunday of Labor Day weekend, the church holds a Welsh singing festival called a Gymanfa Ganu, for which hundreds of people assemble to sing hymns in four-part harmony. The tradition may be Welsh, but the hymns are sung in English. All this was a surprise for Rev. Wendy Pratt, a non-Welsh Presbyte-

▶ SALEM PRESBYTERIAN CHURCH

rian minister who arrived in 1996 and by now spells and pronounces Ge-
mahn'-va gah'-nee with perfect ease. Pratt's amazement at Venedocia was all
the greater because she arrived after 11 years in the depressed city environs of
Gary, Indiana. In Venedocia, the membership of her church (230) exceeds
the population of the village (158); attendance on an ordinary Sunday is 100.
If Venedocians aren't aware of their blessings, their pastor says she surely is.
Salem Presbyterian Church is easily the biggest, fanciest building in
Venedocia. It's brown brick with rough-cut gray stone trim. Two towers, (one
tall, one short), a cupola, and a dormer all have pointed and flared roofs. In
1902 the pastor, Rev. Edward Roberts, claimed that Salem Church was "the
prettiest chapel that the Welsh have in America." He added that notables
from abroad averred that even in Wales, there was none prettier. But in
Wales, avers Mary Ann Olding, who went there to look, churches do look
much like this one. Now a Cincinnati-based preservationist, Olding
compared buildings in Ohio's Welsh communities with those in the old
country. This church, she learned, is Welsh in its use of stone trim with
brick, and in the central gable in front.

Wapakoneta, Auglaize County

(Also in Auglaize County: New Hampshire and New Bremen.)

¶ At one time Wapakoneta's Auglaize Street must have been among Ohio's best downtowns. Though now diminished by the likes of sheet siding and some modern buildings of little merit, it still has an unusually good array of late nineteenth- and early twentieth-century Main Street buildings; a few are mentioned here.

¶ Wapakoneta's downtown went on the National Register in 1989, and in 1990-1991 it enjoyed a spurt in facade renovations. But overall the downtown was not helped by a 1991 referendum that rescinded a historic preservation ordinance. At that time the Eagles Club, 2,338 members strong, had razed two historic buildings next to its hall in order to put up a new ballroom. Sarah Norman, now a Cleveland attorney and then a law student with the National Center for Preservation Law in Washington, was called in to help preservation interests in Wapakoneta. She remembers the Eagles as a "very powerful constituency group." They pushed for withdrawal of the ordinance; and they won. ¶ Wapakoneta is not the only Ohio community to vote to cancel a preservation ordinance; Pomeroy did, too, also with ruckus and rancor. About a hundred Ohio communities do have preservation ordinances, which typically call for review before demolitions in a specified area. Contrary to what many people think, a National Register listing by itself does not prohibit a building's razing.

Access: Auglaize Street used to be U.S. 33, which now passes through on the south side of town. From modern 33, take exit marked for County 25A and State Routes 501, 198, and 67. Drive north on Willipie Street, turning left/west at Pearl Street, to see the courthouse and its heating plant, as well as St. Joseph Catholic Church (1911; DeCurtins; a Cross-Tipped Church). Continue north on Willipie, which passes the WAPA Theatre at Number 19 and gives the best approach to Auglaize Street.

▶ DISTELRATH BLOCK

**COURTHOUSE BOILER,
1894**
*Kremer and Hart
Perry and Pearl Streets, northeast
corner, Wapakoneta
Auglaize County Courthouse heating
plant*

The boiler house is a small square
building with a distinctive line. It
has a hip roof topped by a square
ventilation cupola with its own hip
roof, from whose point the stack
rises. Though clearly akin to the larger, more formal courthouse, the boiler is
a tad less refined.

AUGLAIZE NATIONAL BANK, 1911
Andrew DeCurtins, Lima
36 East Auglaize Street, NRHP/Wapakoneta Commercial HD
Private commercial building

In the early twentieth-century, banks thought a Neoclassical facade would
assure customers of safety forevermore. Here Andrew DeCurtins, of the
family that made its name designing Catholic churches, showed that he could
also succeed with classical features on a tiny, two-story building.

HIRSCH BUILDING, NOW Z TUXEDO, 1885
AND DISTELRATH BLOCK, NOW ZOFKIE CLOTHING, 1890
2 and 4 East Auglaize Street, NRHP/Wapakoneta Commercial HD
Private commercial buildings

This pair of three-story buildings looks wonderful at the end of Willipie
Street. Both are crowned with decorative gables that include the names of the
original proprietors, who had reason to be proud. Behind the fancy facades
are two shops offering, most appropriately, fancy clothes.

TAEUSCH BUILDING, NOW ROSER INSURANCE, LATE 1800s
22-24 West Auglaize Street, NRHP/Wapakoneta Commercial HD
Private commercial building

The middle of this building's handsome facade has two showy decorative
panels—the top one a Masonic symbol—made of cast iron. The top has
turrets and a delicate iron railing that looks like lace trim.

**Access: Toward the west end of Auglaize Street's commercial district,
turn left/south on Blackhoof Street.**

HEMMERT CONTRACTOR, NO DATE
6-8 South Blackhoof Street,
NRHP/Wapakoneta Commercial
HD
Private building

This is a wonderful example of a
building that makes up for tiny
size with a cunning facade,
presumably to show off the
skills of contractor Hemmert,
whose name appears in raised
letters. Two windows and a door
wide, frame, it has moldings,
rosettes, and decorations in the
gable.

▶ HEMMERT CONTRACTOR

Waterville, Lucas County

(Maumee Valley tour includes Waterville; for routing, see Maumee.)

¶ John Pray, a native of Rhode Island and a New York State resident, checked out Dayton and Cleveland before settling in Waterville in 1818 and buying acreage all around. At least in one respect, it's lucky he chose Waterville. Had the Columbian House been built in Dayton or Cleveland, today it likely would not be Ohio's least altered early inn. In fact, it likely would not be.

Access: From Maumee U.S. 24 is fastest, but the scenic route is River Road/County 1684, which passes Columbian House.

COLUMBIAN HOUSE, 1828, 1837
John Pray, builder, Waterville
3 North River Road at Farnsworth Road, Waterville, NRHP
Restaurant serving dinner Tuesday through Saturday and Sunday brunch;
419/878-3006

What Waterville needed, decided town founder John Pray, was a stagecoach inn to serve travelers headed toward Detroit or Fort Wayne. So, nine years after he built the saltbox that's now at the back, Pray built the Columbian House. The year was 1837 and the inn became the area showplace,

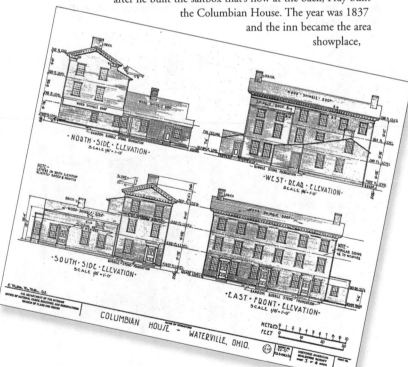

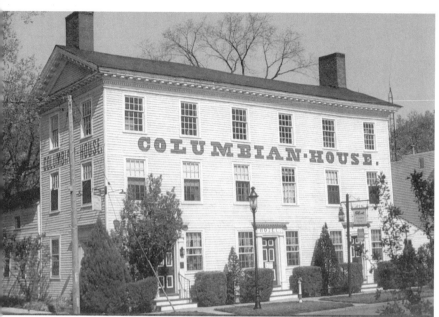

▶ Columbian House

though it lost its edge in the 1840s when the canal went a few blocks west, along the route U.S. 24 takes today. By the late 1920s the building was vacant and derelict, and a Toledo antiques dealer came along and rescued it. Later owners opened a restaurant in the 1940s; and after 15 years of trying, Tom and Peggy Parker succeeded in buying it in 1993. ¶ Hand-hewn beams up to 14 inches thick support the building; most woodwork and doors are black walnut. The style is a mix of Federal and Greek Revival. The first floor, which originally had a tap room and parlor, is now four diningrooms and a kitchen. The second floor is bedrooms, furnished for display; and the third is a ballroom that Tom Parker is restoring. It runs the length and width of the building, 20 by 60 feet, with fireplaces at each end, a cove ceiling, 14 windows, and two-inch white ash floor boards. ¶ The facade's most intriguing feature is the gradual increase, from south to north, in spacing between the six windows. Parker says the increase is two to three inches per window, so that the northernmost windows are 10 to 12 inches farther apart than the southernmost. When the inn was built, it was diagonally across the street from the town square just to the south; from the square the windows looked evenly spaced. Parker suggests the variation was deliberate, to enhance the building's appearance. ¶ Is it possible, that an early nineteenth-century builder in Waterville had the sophistication of the Greeks? Ohio State's Douglas Graf is doubtful, because uneven spacing was so common at the time, even in a building like Mount Vernon. "If you had the sophistication to do that, that's not the building you'd be doing," he says. He adds, cautiously, "I could be wrong."

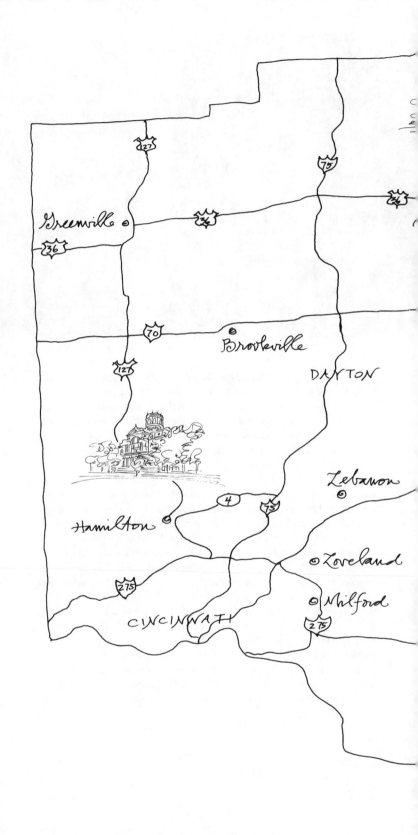

Bellefontaine

68

West
Liberty

Urbana

Springfield 70

Xenia

68

71

Wilmington

41

32

41

West
Union

Southwest Ohio

Ohio State's Douglas Graf really likes Southwest Ohio. Driving through its countryside on a fine June day, he waves his hand toward the horizon. "Isn't it beautiful?" he says. And a few miles farther on, he does the same again. He likes the rolling terrain, the woodlots scattered among fields, the handsome farmsteads. It happens that Southwest Ohio is where Graf, who grew up mostly in Washington, D.C., and who was educated at Princeton and Harvard, first became aware of places and buildings. He spent his first six years in Seven Mile, west of Middletown, and then two weeks every summer at his grandfather's farm near Oxford. For him, this scenery looks just as it should, ideally. ¶ It's a mostly level landscape because glaciers filled in valleys, though in some places they left deposits, such as those around Springfield, that formed new ridges. Forested almost everywhere when settlers arrived, it had areas with enough primeval beauty to inspire landscape painters. For example, Robert Scott Duncanson's painting, *Blue Hole, Little Miami River*, in the Cincinnati Art Museum, depicts an awesome forest, enormous boulders, and a serene pond that's lured three fishermen. ¶ Somehow, this lovely landscape became the setting for most of Ohio's wackiest buildings. Loveland

▶ PEOPLE'S FEDERAL, SIDNEY

Castle, assembled on the banks of the Little Miami from concrete blocks cast in milk cartons, is the prime example, though near West Liberty the two Piatt Castles (one bizarre on the inside; the other, on the outside) follow not far behind. Besides, in and near Bellefontaine there are the Holland Theatre and the Coffeepot, originally a coffee shop built in the shape of a percolator. West Union has the showy Tet Woods Building, and Xenia, the similar Dodds Monuments. ¶ Not all Southwest Ohio architecture is eccentric. The region has two buildings of national significance, Frank Lloyd Wright's Westcott House in Springfield, and Louis Sullivan's Peoples Federal Savings & Loan in Sidney. It has buildings that are extraordinary civic amenities, such as the Plaza Hotel in Piqua, Greenville's Memorial Hall, and Wilmington's Murphy Theatre. And it has towns, like Hamilton, Sidney, and Springfield, with the stuff of good architectural tours.

Bellefontaine, Logan County

(Also in Logan County: West Liberty, to the south on U.S. 68: together, a tour of some eccentric Americana.) ¶ Bellefontaine—"beautiful fountain" in French—does itself proud with a fine big fountain in front of the courthouse, which is a handsome 1871 Second Empire structure by architect Alexander Koehler. The courthouse has a statue of Justice looking spooky (it *is* a white statue) in a third-floor window over the door, but its interior is rather nondescript.

▶ LOGAN COUNTY COURTHOUSE

Access: Bellefontaine, at the junction of U.S. 68 and State Route 47, is just off U.S. 33. The courthouse faces U.S. 68/Main Street; it's flanked on the south by the nation's first concrete street, and on the north by Columbus Avenue, where the Holland Theatre is.

SCHINE'S HOLLAND THEATRE, 1931
Peter M. Hulsken, Lima
127 Columbus Avenue East, Bellefontaine, NRHP
Theater under renovation; preliminary reopening planned for 2002; 937/592-9002

The Holland Theatre, Cleveland architect Bob Gaede promised me, "is small but unique." He probably didn't realize just how unique the Holland is, for it turns out to be the nation's only Dutch-themed theater; architect Peter M. Hulsken was so delighted with it that he patented his design. When I first saw the theater in 1995, I easily spotted its steep Dutch-looking stepped gable in downtown Bellefontaine, but that was just the teaser. Luckily I'd arrived just after the movie theater, as it still was then, opened in the late afternoon; an enthusiastic employee took me to see the main auditorium, where the side walls were lined with Dutch buildings and windmills whose blades really turned. It was an amazing place, though a little truncated; for in the 1970s, the theater had been converted into a five-screen multiplex. In 1999 the then-closed Holland Theatre was rescued. That year some of the theater's fans formed the non-profit Logan County Landmark Preservation to own and manage the Holland, which a benefactor had donated. Plans are to restore the original, single auditorium, with dressing rooms, lighting, and rigging. The atmospheric ceiling—with

▶ SCHINE'S HOLLAND THEATRE

twinkling stars overhead—will also be restored; and of course the windmill motors will again be in good working order. The goal is a county performing arts center. Not only is the Holland America's only Dutch-themed theater, but all the buildings in the auditorium are replicas of actual structures in the Netherlands. Lima architect Hulsken (1881-1949) was Dutch himself, and he includes the 1637 house where he was born. Hulsken had good credentials, for he was trained in Amsterdam and at Paris's École des Beaux Arts; after he came to the U.S. in 1905, he worked in the Detroit office of Albert Kahn. Hulsken's other work included the Mercer County Courthouse in Celina, also in this guide.

Access: The coffeepot is on the east side of U.S. 68 north of Bellefontaine, 3.8 miles north of U.S. 33.

COFFEEPOT, NOW PART OF OHIO STATE EAGLES RECREATION PARK, C. 1936

Charlie Hemphill, builder, Belle Center
5118 U.S. Route 68 North
Former coffee shop, now shed at campground; 937/593-1565

Especially along important roads, a building's shape can act as an enormous sign. Here the adjacent campground hired carpenter Charlie Hemphill to build this coffeepot to house a little coffee shop, serving coffee and doughnuts. Inside it had a round counter and stools; outside, just like a real percolator, it had a glass knob on top. It became such a distinctive landmark

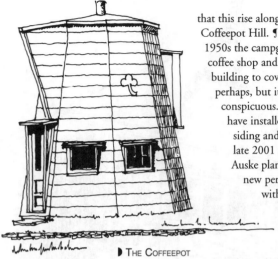

▶ THE COFFEEPOT

that this rise along U.S. 68 became Coffeepot Hill. ¶ By the end of the 1950s the campground closed the coffee shop and moved the building to cover a well. Moved perhaps, but it is still conspicuous. The local Eagles have installed new vinyl siding and windows; and in late 2001 manager Linda Auske planned to put up a new percolator-type knob with a light (the old knob apparently was lost during siding installation) and to restore the pot's handle (which has been lost for a long time.) In Ohio, the coffeepot is a rarity, for the state has few historic examples of a building as sign; this is the only one in this guide. However, there is a modern example in Newark: Longaberger's basket-shaped headquarters. ¶ The coffeepot is an octagonal structure, tapered slightly like a real percolator, 12.5 feet across at the ground, about 15 feet high. One day a former manager noticed a group of people who parked, unloaded computers from their car, and started taking pictures. It seems the coffeepot is their computer company's logo. ¶ The builder, the late Charlie Hemphill, was a farmer as well as carpenter. He also built houses, including, in 1958, a solid one in Westerville for his daughter, Lois Scott. She remembers that he used to joke that the coffeepot was his monument. It's one of them, anyway.

Brookville, Montgomery County

(Other George Franklin Barber houses are in Mansfield, [Northeast], Mount Vernon [Central], and Barnesville [Southeast].)

¶ Because Brookville is relatively small—it had 5,200 people in 2000—it's a perfect place to see the work of George Franklin Barber, a mail-order architect of Victorian houses. Barber's plans enabled people in the hinterlands to have architect-designed houses.

Access: Brookville is west of Dayton and just south of I-70. From the interstate take exit 21 for Brookville; go south on Arlington Road; turn left/east on Wolf Creek Street, which continues to downtown and intersects Market Street.

SAMUEL SPITLER HOUSE, 1894

George Franklin Barber, Knoxville
14 Market Street, Brookville, NRHP
Brookville Historical Society museum open afternoons first Saturday and
Sunday each month; fee; 937/833-3470

Architect George Franklin Barber, who mailed house plans to places all over America, specialized in Queen Annes, and his designs were never dull. He seized every opportunity to add a decorative fillip: a porch, a fancy bracket, a turret, a bay. For example, this frame house, painted in the original cream with dark green trim, has seven porches and a projecting octagonal turret. It has Stick style patterns in the frame siding and shingles as well. The design is also the one that Barber chose for his own house in Knoxville. ¶ Because this is a museum, it's possible to see the interior, which featured Brookville's first indoor bathroom; owner Samuel Spitler was a miller and plumber. Basically this is a seven-room house that looks like 12; perhaps that's one reason Barber was so popular. What most impressed me about the interior was how pleasant the second-floor hall was on a hot summer day. The hall passes all the way through the house, ending at porches whose doors were open, so the inside was full of breezes. ¶ This house was slated to be torn down in 1974. At that time it was located on the lot directly behind where it is now, on the funeral home's parking lot. The Brookville Historical Society raised enough money to move it and then, with the help of Spitler's daughter, who was still alive, restored the interior.

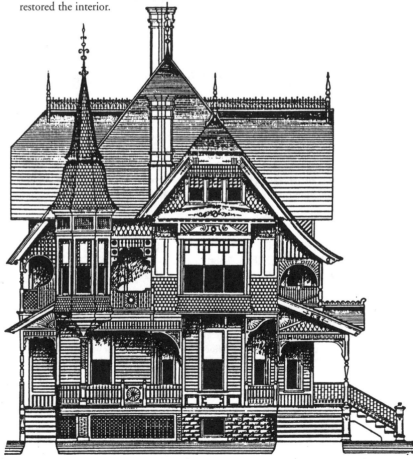

▶ PLAN BOOK VERSION OF SPITLER HOUSE

Greenville, Darke County

(Western County Seats: Tour with Troy, southeast on U.S. 36 and State Route 41, then Piqua and Sidney to the north off I-75. Greenville is also relatively near Cross-Tipped Churches tours; see Carthagena [Northwest].)

¶ Greenville has an unusually busy downtown, but its chief architectural delight is an amenity a block away from Broadway. It's a landscaped one-block park that

▶ GREENVILLE LIBRARY

contains the library, a theater, and a school. It signals a civilized place.

Access: U.S. 127 bypasses Greenville to the east. From it U.S. 36 and State Route 571 go west into downtown; 571 becomes South Broadway, the main drag; the Courthouse, 1874, by Edwin May of Indiana, is on South Broadway at West 4th Street. Turn left/west on 4th, which in a block reaches the three buildings described here.

EIKENBERRY AND CHRISTOPHER MOZART STORES, NOW BIDDLESTONE'S, 1888

126 West 4th Street, Greenville, NRHP/Greenville South Broadway CD Store

Eikenberry and Christian Mozart Stores wanted an elegant modern facade. Here, below an elaborate cornice and a sign with the original store name and date, the second and third floors are almost all windows and window dividers. The first floor has been altered; interior is not of interest.

CARNEGIE LIBRARY, NOW GREENVILLE PUBLIC LIBRARY, 1903

W.S. Kaufmann, Richmond, Indiana
520 Sycamore Street, Greenville, NRHP
Public library; 937/548-3915

In many ways Greenville's Carnegie library was typical of its era—the combination of buff brick, red-tile roof, and formal central section appear again and again in Ohio. This is, at least, a very good example. The entry, with a pair of side windows and an arch above the door, is Palladian. The interior has a fireplace (how gracious libraries were), stained glass, and fine high ceilings revealed when dropped ones were removed in the mid-1990s. Though the collection has grown enormously since the library opened (from 9,000 volumes to 100,000) the building has managed without additions. That's partly because years ago it gained the basement space a museum used to occupy, and partly because more recently, the attic was redone as staff offices.

HENRY ST. CLAIR MEMORIAL HALL, NOW MEMORIAL HALL, 1910

Howard & Morrison, Columbus
215 West 4th Street, Greenville, NRHP
Auditorium, art gallery, school offices and facilities; 937/548-3185

Although other Ohio towns have libraries not vastly different from Greenville's, I know of none that has an institution like Memorial Hall. Henry St. Clair, a wholesale grocer, and his wife donated $135,000 to build it. Lucky Greenville. The building is a handsome brick and stone Neoclassical Revival, set back on a lawn. Inside, besides music rooms for the junior high next door and school board offices, Memorial Hall has a community art gallery and theater. It brings the arts to Greenville. ¶ Over 14 years, from 1985 through 1998, Mary Frances Shultz, a fifth-generation Greenville resident on one side and fourth-generation on the other,

▶ MEMORIAL HALL

spearheaded a Memorial Hall renovation. The school board had been managing the building; but not too surprisingly, it was a low priority for them. Shultz, who scheduled artists for the Darke County Center for the Arts, watched as her venue deteriorated. Then in 1985 she and two friends took action. They had a little party, plied a group of well-heeled people with barbecued chicken and wine, and generated some excitement about restoring Memorial Hall. Over the years, excitement raised the $2 million that the whole project took. It was virtually all private money. ¶ The Restoration Committee did everything, except for the roof and school offices, which the school board took care of. After calling in an architectural consultant, Thomas Dues of Dayton, the Committee divided all the work into one-year stages. The first was the colored glass, which an expert from Philadelphia came to assess. "He almost had a seizure when he saw the windows," Shultz says. He declared that some sections came from Tiffany. Including smaller windows in landing restrooms, he valued Memorial Hall's art glass at $250,000. So the awed Restoration Committee had the windows cleaned, the leading repaired, and protective glass installed on the outside. ¶ Plaster and painting took two years instead of one because of a temporary funding shortfall in the late 1980s. The very last stage, in 1998, was air-conditioning, landscaping, exterior lighting, chandeliers to replace the long-missing originals, and the bronze plaque with donors' names. Besides, the stage floor had to be done again. The first replacement floor, in pine, was too soft and already hacked up, so a more durable oak replaced it. ¶ Not surprisingly, the refurbished auditorium has been a big success. "Acoustics are just fantastic," Shultz says. "A vocalist will stand on stage and whisper first. Then their eyes widen and they look around and they say, 'Oh, I'd like to take this home.' I've heard that time and again."

Hamilton, Butler County

(Tour with Lebanon, accessible by State Routes 4 and then 63.)
¶ Though it's a manufacturing center with a population of over 60,000, Hamilton seems remote from most of the rest of Ohio, partly because it's not on an interstate. Architecturally, it's worth seeking out. ¶ To see more in Hamilton: Rossville, on the west side of the Great Miami River and part of Hamilton, is a distinct architectural entity, with a nineteenth-century Main Street and attractive residential neighborhoods (for one, see "D" Street south of Main.) ¶ The Greater Hamilton Convention and Visitors Bureau distributes an illustrated brochure, "Walking Tours of Historic Hamilton, Ohio". Their address is 1 Riverfront Plaza; 513/844-8080; 800/311-5353. ¶ This tour starts downtown, then goes north to German Village, and finally, goes east on Dayton Street.

Access: To reach Hamilton from I-71, exit at Lebanon; pick up State Route 63 in town and drive west, past I-75, to State Route 4, which goes south into Hamilton. From the south, take 4/Dixie Highway north from I-275. At High Street/State Route 129 turn west to downtown and sites on High Street.

MEMORIAL BUILDING, ALSO CALLED SOLDIERS, SAILORS & PIONEERS MONUMENT, 1902

Frederick Noonan, Hamilton
3 South Monument Avenue at High Street, Hamilton, NRHP/Hamilton
Historic Civic Center HD
Memorial and museum, open Monday through Saturday; 513/867-5823

The Memorial Building is downtown Hamilton's architectural high point. Not only is the building good, but it has a site that makes it a focal point. The main drag, High Street, leads to the Memorial, which then becomes the pivot where the road veers to the right onto the bridge to Rossville. Besides, the building is seen well from the other side of the river. ¶ Fifty feet square and 100 feet high, the Memorial is monumental but contained. It's Neoclassical, two stories plus a basement, clad in sandstone, crowned by a round cupola that's an open colonnade. On top of the cupola, a 17-foot locally cast bronze statue, *Victory*, represents a Civil War soldier with one arm raised in triumph. Both front and rear facades have dominant round-arched central windows with flanking Doric columns. ¶ Inside, the first floor is a single room dominated by a grand stair; over the landing there's a large painted window depicting women making bandages during the Civil War. On the walls, marble tablets list pioneers and Civil War soldiers. Actually, the names of all Butler County veterans from all wars are on the premises, but those from

▶ MEMORIAL BUILDING

the twentieth century are probably on cards. "It's a hundred dollars a name for engraving now," curator Mary Clark Harlan explains. "In 1902 it was three cents a letter." She has no doubt of the Memorial's importance to Hamilton. The city uses it as its logo.

▶ BUTLER COUNTY COURTHOUSE

BUTLER COUNTY COURTHOUSE, 1889
D.W. Gibbs, Toledo
101 High Street at Second, Hamilton, NRHP
Courthouse, 513/424-5351

The D.W. Gibbs courthouse suffered a serious fire in 1912, so the octagonal tower is a replacement from the early 1930s. Prior to building a new Government Service Center (1999) for the courts, Butler County undertook a $2 million exterior renovation of this old courthouse. While it seems sad that the Common Pleas courts prefer a service center to a courthouse, the $2 million investment will keep the building viable at least for Probate and County courts.

SECOND NATIONAL BANK, NOW STAR BANK, 1931
219 High Street, Hamilton,
Bank

Though the 1936 Hamilton Municipal Building, a handsome New Deal structure across the street from the Monument, provides the city a prominent Art Deco building, this bank might easily be missed. It's a four-story Art Deco, with a high arched window over the door.

Access: From High Street turn north on Second Street, pass YMCA, and turn right/east on Dayton Street. Pass YWCA and turn north on Third Street to see Lane-Hooven and library. At next corner, Linden Street, turn left/west one block to Second to see Benninghofen. Then return to Dayton and turn left/east to other sites. Church is one block south on Sixth. To see a fine group of late nineteenth- and early twentieth-century houses, continue east on Dayton Street to State Route 4.

YOUNG MEN'S CHRISTIAN ASSOCIATION, 1914
Frederick G. Mueller, Hamilton; associate architects, Shattuck & Hussey, Chicago
105 North Second Street at Market, Hamilton,
YMCA

This mostly red-brick four-story YMCA has a quirky mix of features, including white terra cotta arches and columns at the doors, terra cotta string courses, and a loggia at the top.

YOUNG WOMEN'S CHRISTIAN ASSOCIATION, 1931
Antenen Engineering
244 Dayton Street at Third Street, Hamilton, NRHP/German Village HD
YWCA

In Hamilton, the YWCA is also way above average architecturally. It has a fine Jacobean Revival building, brick with stone trim. L-shaped, in the crux of the L it has an elaborate stone entry pavilion facing the corner.

▶ LANE-HOOVEN HOUSE

LANE-HOOVEN HOUSE, NOW HAMILTON COMMUNITY FOUNDATION, 1863

James Elrick, Hamilton, builder
319 North Third Street, NRHP
Hamilton Community Foundation
offices; open to the public 9-4
weekdays for self-guided tours;
group tours may be arranged;
513/863-1389

Except when the 1913 flood rose
six feet high on the first floor, this
octagon house has been blessed,
in the preservation sense.
Meticulously restored, it's in daily
use as offices and is readily
accessible to the public. The
house has been altered—in 1895
a bedroom and bath were added
and a parlor enlarged on the north
side; a greenhouse once attached
on the south side has gone—but

▶ LANE-HOOVEN STAIRCASE

such changes seem relatively minor. Probably the house is doing so well because it's a double-header on the popularity scale: at once an octagon and Gothic Revival. Two stories plus a cupola, it has fancy milled woodwork on the gables. Painted brick with stone trim on the outside, inside the house has butternut and ash trim, 14-foot ceilings, and a central staircase that's a lovely spiral. This house also has a wonderful feature I haven't seen anywhere else: bedrooms with Gothic-arched ceilings. The Lane-Hooven House, named for its first owner, Clark Lane, and for the Hooven family, who lived in it 47 years, is in Hamilton's nine-block German Village Historic District.

LANE PUBLIC LIBRARY, 1867
Attributed to William Blackall, Hamilton
300 North Third Street at Buckeye Street, Hamilton, NRHP/German Village HD
Public library; 513/894-7156

Just three years after building his own house, Clark Lane built a free library across the street. For a year he ran the library himself, and then he offered it to the city. After a heated debate, voters passed a referendum assuring the library's ongoing upkeep, and thereby gave Hamilton the first free library west of the Alleghenies. Lane believed that books were "a powerful factor" in the make-up of the best people. Not only did he give Hamilton a library, he also co-founded a machine works and foundry that was, according to historian James Schwartz, the genesis of this city's important metal industries, which included 28 foundries at the turn of the last century. Thus in Hamilton, Clark Lane provided for both mind and body. Architecturally, the original octagonal Romanesque Revival library has acquired many wings and a confusing interior layout. The original section is evident from the street and is still fine inside. Its walls are lined by bookshelves between the tall dark arches of the window and door moldings.

BENNINGHOFEN HOUSE,
NOW BUTLER COUNTY HISTORICAL MUSEUM, 1861
327 North Second Street, Hamilton, NRHP
Museum; fee; 513/893-7111

The Butler County Historical Society runs a museum in this serene brick Italianate house, whose porch has elaborate spindlework. John Benninghofen was a German immigrant and industrialist who bought the house in 1874; his family remained in it until 1949.

BENDER BROTHERS, LATER BECKETT PAPER,
NOW INTERNATIONAL PAPER, 1895
400 Dayton Street at Fifth Street, Hamilton,
Private; offices and warehouse for on-site paper mill

Though "only" an industrial building, this four-story Italianate structure in gray-painted brick has a bracketed cornice and decorative lintels over the windows. Originally a sawmill, it became a paper plant later. Foundries weren't all Hamilton had; it was, and is, a paper manufacturing center.

▶ TRINITY EPISCOPAL

TRINITY EPISCOPAL CHURCH, 1888, 1893

A.C. Nash, Cincinnati
115 North Sixth Street at Butler, one block south of Dayton, Hamilton
Church; 513/896-6755

Hamilton's Trinity Episcopal Church has many distinctive features. For one, Cincinnati architect A.C. Nash liked elongated, pointed tower roofs. Below this one, he set an open belfry with wide pointed-arch openings on all four sides. Another distinctive feature is the stone, so uneven that the surface seems jagged. In the words of church historian Kathleen Neilan Stuckey, it's "blue limestone laid up very rough and showing broken surfaces, with trimmings of Berea sandstone." Then there are the two stepped gables, one at the street end of the building, the other at the side over the vestibule. And finally, this church has an unusually lovely interior: a dark wooden ceiling above, dark pews below, mostly white walls, and stained glass—most prominently, in an altar window from Austria. The church was built in two stages: first the nave, in 1888; then five years later the rest, including the tower and chancel. The style is English Gothic. In suburban Cincinnati, Architect Nash did the extraordinary Wyoming Baptist Church (see also, Vol. I), which has an even steeper tower roof.

Lebanon, Warren County

(Tour with Hamilton, accessible by State Routes 63 and 4.)

¶ Among Ohio's lovely older towns, Lebanon is exceptional, for its downtown, transformed into an antiques center, is thriving. The principal intersection of Broadway and Main Street is a fine hub, with the Golden Lamb Inn, City Hall, and the Carnegie Library on three of its corners. The architectural high point is an ensemble of nineteenth-century houses on the hill along Cincinnati Avenue; all are on the National Register as part of the Floraville Historic District.

Access: Lebanon is just west of I-71. Take State Route 48, which becomes Broadway downtown, or State Route 123, which becomes Main Street. South of Broadway-Main intersection, Cincinnati Avenue/ U.S. 42 is second turn west. Houses are listed here from east to west.

GLENDOWER, 1835

105 Cincinnati Avenue, Lebanon
Glendower State Memorial, house
museum owned by Ohio Historical
Society and run by Warren County
Historical Society; fee; summer hours
only; 513/932-1817

Built by an attorney, John Milton Williams, and named for Welsh hero Owen Glendower, this is a handsome if predictable red-brick Greek Revival house. It has a two-story central section flanked by one-story wings. Like the other houses in this row, it's set back about 200 feet from the road.

THE PILLARS, C. 1847

119 Cincinnati Avenue, Lebanon
Private house

▶ GLENDOWER

The story is that the builder of this Greek Revival house, Robert Boake, took the plans his brother-in-law had used for Glendower next door. He also had the nerve to build a markedly fancier place, with four two-story Ionic columns on the front porch.

THE GOTHIC, C. 1850
207 Cincinnati Avenue, Lebanon
Private house

The unpredictable Gothic takes its name from the gingerbread trim, but the style is Italian Villa. The house is brick and asymmetrical, with a tower. Of the four houses, this is the favorite of Ohio State's Douglas Graf. "Stuff's happening," is how he assesses the facade.

BRYN HRFRYD, C. 1840
227 Cincinnati Avenue, Lebanon
Private house

This is another brick Greek Revival house, with two-story Corinthian columns on the porch. Foliage makes Bryn Hrfryd harder than to see than the other houses here.

Loveland, Hamilton County
(Loveland is a suburb of Cincinnati [Vol. I]. Lebanon, north on U.S. 22 and State Route 48, is near enough for a companion tour.)

Access: From I-71 take exit 19 and drive east about three miles on Fields Ertel Road. Turn right/south on Rich Road; take the second left, Mulberry Road, which leads down to the castle.

CHATEAU LAROCHE, OR LOVELAND CASTLE, 1929-1981
Harry D. Andrews, Loveland
12025 Shore Drive
Castle; tours available; call for hours; 513/683/4686

Loveland Castle is the work of a man eccentric enough to cast 32,000 concrete bricks in cardboard milk cartons, mostly quart-sized, and then build walls of them. Inspired by castles he'd seen in France during World War I, Harry D. Andrews gave his version a French name, Chateau Laroche, or Rock Castle. The rocks came from the bank of the Little Miami River in front of the site; by 1981 Andrews estimated that 56,000 pailfuls of stones had been lugged in by hand. The stones mostly built the outside walls, while the concrete bricks mostly were used inside. ¶ Though Loveland today is largely suburban, when Andrews bought the riverside site in the 1920s, it seemed an appropriately rustic campground for the boys in his Sunday school classes. After these boys vowed to follow the Ten Commandments, Andrews dubbed them Knights of the Golden Trail. When their tents wore out, he suggested that the youths bring him stones for assembling two stone huts, which eventually evolved into the bases of the two towers facing the river. With the boys already knights, it followed that two stone huts would become a castle. ¶ Construction progressed slowly before 1955, but then Andrews retired and had more time to work

▶ LOVELAND CASTLE

on it. He moved into the Dome Room, which had a fireplace and a ceiling dome that experts had told him could not be built. But Andrews was himself an expert, a structural engineer. Resting on bedrock, his castle has round supporting arches in stone, a balcony, a round bay, crenellated parapets. The highest tower, 36 feet tall, has corbelling, or masonry canted outward to support something above. The corbelling was to make the tower harder to climb, for defense was often a design (though presumably not an actual) consideration. Thus the door has 238 pieces of wood, set in three layers with grains running in all directions, and 2530 nails. Andrews was confident it would resist sword or axe. ¶ Toward the end of his life, Andrews said he had done 99 percent of the construction work himself, though he accepted many donations of cement and milk cartons. Since 1929 he'd spent $12,000 on Chateau Laroche, including land, water well, electricity, oil furnace. The 50,531 visitors in 1980 slowed construction, though perhaps turning 90 was also a factor. He died the next year, when his trousers caught fire while he was burning trash, and he refused to have his legs amputated. ¶ By his will the castle went to the Knights of the Golden Trail, who keep it open, maintain and extend it. Tired of carrying stones by the pailful, they did buy a tractor.

Milford, Clermont County

(Companion tour: Cincinnati suburb of Mariemont, Vol. I.)

Access: East of Cincinnati, I-275 exits at State Route 28, which in Milford just to the west is also Main Street; Promont, on south side of road, has a sign.

PROMONT, 1866
906 Main Street/State Route 28, Milford, NRHP
Greater Milford Area Historical Society museum; fee; Friday and Sunday afternoons; 513/248-0324

This Italian Villa once was lord of all it surveyed from its hilltop site. Promont's yard, now much diminished, is still big enough for a good view of the house's east side and its four-story tower which was not only for show. It also housed stairs and, with the windows open in summer, drew warm air up and away. The distinctive tower roof has concave sides rising to a point. On the west facade the Greater Milford Area Historical Society has reconstructed the porch. Alas, it overlooks a Krogers and its shopping center. Built by a man who profited from the Civil War mule trade, Promont

▶ PROMONT, WEST PORCH

later became the home of Governor John M. Pattison. Besides the tower, he could enjoy 16-foot ceilings and 14-and-a-half-foot doors, as well as different ceiling moldings in every room.

Piqua, Miami County

(Tour with Troy to the south and Sidney to the north, both also off I-76.)

¶ Piqua has a municipal historian, whose title is apparently unique in Ohio. As municipal historian, James C. Oda answers local history questions at the library, runs the museum, and wielded a hammer in the museum's 1989 rehab. History doesn't take all his time, though. He's also the library director.

Access: From I-75, U.S. 36 goes west into Piqua, where it becomes
Ash Street and intersects Main Street. "A Walking Tour of the Piqua-
Caldwell Historic District," an illustrated flyer prepared by the Piqua
Historical Society, is available at the Chamber of Commerce, 326 North
Main Street, 937/773-2765.

SCHMIDLAPP FREE SCHOOL LIBRARY, NOW PIQUA HISTORICAL MUSEUM, 1890

J. W. Yost, Columbus
509 North Main Street, Piqua, NRHP/Piqua-Caldwell HD
Historical museum; for hours call Flesh Public Library, 937/773-6753

What we see from the outside is the facade J.W. Yost did in 1890, when the
building was already 55 years old. It was built as a grocery store for the
Schmidlapp family, who lived upstairs. A son, Jacob G., made lots of
money in Cincinnati,
donated this building to
Piqua schools, and hired
Yost to redesign the front
for a library. The result is
a Richardsonian
Romanesque design in
red sandstone; the carving
included faces between
the second-floor
windows. Municipal
historian James C. Oda
says that later in the
1890s, extra space was
added at the back of the
building. During a 1989
renovation, plaster was
stripped from that
addition's ceiling,
revealing a series of
shallow round vaults in
brick—it seems the

▶ Piqua Historical Museum

addition, built to house books, was meant to be fireproof too. Rehabbers
were so impressed that they left the brick exposed.

ROW HOUSES, 1840S

419-427 North Main Street, Piqua, NRHP/Piqua-Caldwell HD
Private shops; some upstairs apartments

This is a row of five diminutive brick buildings from the 1840s-1850s canal
era—the canal ran right behind them. They have commercial space on the
ground floor, pairs of windows on the second. In the small facades, the
windows seem large, as if surprised. James Oda says he and others have
done a lot of work trying to find out exactly when these were built. His
conclusion: "It's a muddle."

PLAZA HOTEL, NOW FORT PIQUA HOTEL, 1892

J.W. Yost, Columbus
116 West High Street at North Main, Piqua, NRHP
Rehab candidate

As Miami County prepared to build a new courthouse in 1884, Piqua claimed the county seat, which Troy refused to relinquish. The "courthouse war" ended with the state legislature opting for Troy. But Piqua still wanted architectural parity. Two local capitalists hired the architect who'd done the courthouse, J.W. Yost of Columbus, to design a grand hotel facing Town Square. In the end, Jim Oda says, the hotel is not so high as the courthouse, but it has more square footage. ¶ It also succeeded as the symbol of Piqua. "Our history revolved around this building," Oda says. Presidents—Teddy Roosevelt, Warren G. Harding, William H. Taft—spoke from the balcony overlooking High Street. An early anti-saloon league meeting was here, as was the first bar after Prohibition. In 1947, at the hotel's corner lunch counter, Negroes demanded to be served and for the first time, were. Socialist rallies met here; when World War II flying ace Don Gentile arrived home after the war, he came here. The Mills Brothers, whose father had a barbershop across the street, sang in front of the hotel. During the Vietnam War, young men who'd been drafted waited here for the bus that took them to Cincinnati. "This isn't just a building," says Oda. "It's the focal point of our heritage." ¶ The style is Richardsonian Romanesque, of rough-cut limestone on the two streetside walls, plain brick in back. Four-and-a-half stories high, the structure has ground-floor shops, round-arched windows and a corner tower with a pyramidal roof. The main entrance on High Street has a porch covering the sidewalk. Carving, with foliation and faces, is exquisite. Contemporary newspapers reported the carver as William (or James) Whyte of Dayton. The faces are so realistic that they were said to be portraits of people on the street. (The same story appeared regarding the Wood County

Courthouse, see also, in Bowling Green, apparently done by the same people.) ¶ The hotel introduced Piqua's first indoor plumbing. But since all the bathrooms originally were in the basement, it's not surprising that in 1914 the building was completely remodeled, bringing plumbing upstairs. The first floor's atrium, under an amber glass vault, is still there. ¶ The hostelry survived, first as Favorite Hotel, then as Fort Piqua, until 1989. Eight years later a local industrialist bought the building and donated it to Piqua Improvement Corporation, which evolved into a city agency. In late 2001 the library was talking about terms for its moving into the hotel, along with the museum. The renovation tab would be a daunting $8 to 9 million. For Jim Oda, this option would put all his roles, as historian, museum and library director, under one roof. ¶ Besides, it would revitalize Piqua's heart.

▶ PIQUA HOTEL, DETAIL

To see more in the Piqua Caldwell (pronounced co-well) Historic District: From the hotel, walk a few blocks west on High to Caldwell Street, then north a block to West Ash, to see the Westminster Presbyterian Church, 1890, also by J.W. Yost. When the stone carver finished the hotel he did some faces on the church. Yost also did the Barber House, an 1894 Queen Anne at 324 West Greene, one more block north. Continue up Caldwell to see Jim Oda's favorite block, after West North Street. He likes the diversity of styles on the west/left side of the street: Second Empire, Italianate, Prairie, Queen Anne. Turn right on Boone; at the next corner you'll come to underwear baron Leo M. Flesh's 1907 Chateauesque style house at 650 North Downing—historically, Piqua was an important underwear manufacturing center, with as many as 12 different companies in the business at different times. Across the street, behind what is now a row of two-story condos, Flesh's underwear competitor, John P. Spiker, built his 1923 house. Though one was a Democrat and one a Republican, though they also owned rival banks, Flesh and Spiker were friends, Oda assures us. As municipal historian, he knows things like that. He works in the Flesh Public Library, 124 West Greene Street, which was built in 1907 as The Piqua Club for men. When the club foundered in the Depression, Leo Flesh bought the Jacobean Revival building and donated it to the library.

Access: Go north on Main Street to river; turn northwest onto State Route 66, which just past corporate limits comes to the cemetery.

FOREST HILL CEMETERY BUILDINGS, 1890S, 1904
8660 N State Route 66, Piqua
Private cemetery; 937/773-2614

The cemetery has a picturesque one-story office building with a little tower; it was built in 1904. Brick with contrasting trim, it has a hip roof that slopes down into broad eaves supported by curving white wooden brackets. Two small white frame buildings north of the entrance are also picturesque. Dating from the 1890s, one is a restroom and the other an employee break room.

▶ KISER HOUSE

St. Paris, Champaign County
(Also in Champaign County: Urbana.)

Access: St. Paris is on U.S. 36 12 miles west of Urbana.

KISER HOUSE, 1913
149 East Main Street/U.S. 36, at Washington, St. Paris
Private apartments

St. Paris, which has been holding at under 2,000 people for over a century, saw its fortunes peak when several companies made carts and carriages here and the village became, fleetingly, the "Pony Wagon Town." Today it must be impossible to drive through without noticing this house—which is probably just what John W. Kiser wanted. A native son, he married the local merchant's daughter, moved to Chicago, and made a pile; his company was the world's largest horseshoe manufacturer. Not about to move back to little St. Paris year round, the Kisers redid her family's place as their summer house and called it Garden Glow. This is the result. ¶ The front part of this house is a Neoclassical flourish of 14 fluted Ionic columns, all two stories high. They enclose an open front porch and, at both sides, second-story porches, now screened. The door is central, with a balcony above; the pediment contains a three-part Palladian window. After all this, the back of the house is relatively quiet. ¶ Having made this triumphal statement in St. Paris, Kiser apparently decided he didn't really need to live there at all. Two years later he bought himself another summer house outside New York City—an acquisition he soon sold because he became ill. He died in Chicago in 1916, at the age of 59.
¶ See also the Mooney House in Woodsfield, Monroe County, in Southeast Ohio. It's a similar, exactly contemporary remodeling that produced another small town's most flamboyant building.

Sidney, Shelby County
(Tour with Piqua and Troy, both to the south and also off I-75.)
¶ On Sidney's Courthouse Square, the intersection of Court Street and Ohio Avenue is one of Ohio's architectural high points, for it has very good buildings on all four corners. One of the four buildings, by the great American architect Louis Henri Sullivan, is so remarkable that it lures architectural tourists from places like Brazil and Germany, Massachusetts and Colorado.

Access: State Route 47, which is Court Street downtown, comes into Sydney's Courthouse Square from I-75 to the west and from Bellefontaine to the east. A flyer on touring downtown is available from the Sidney-Shelby County Chamber of Commerce, 100 South Main Street, Suite 201, Sidney, 45365; 937/492-9122

▶ SHELBY COUNTY COURTHOUSE

SHELBY COUNTY COURTHOUSE, 1881

George H. Maetzel, Columbus
100 East Court Street, Sidney, NRHP/Sidney Courthouse Square HD
Courthouse, 937/498-7230

This Second Empire courthouse is praised often for its site—it's in the
middle of a square that's in the middle of downtown. The building, mostly
limestone and sandstone, has a high central tower, four entrances, four
corner towers. Inside, though dropped ceilings and hanging fluorescent
lights make the courtroom a disappointment, the gleaming woodwork is a
delight. It was stripped of paint by janitor Ron Cavender, who did the job
on his own initiative (and often on his own time) before he retired in 1996.

▶ MONUMENTAL BUILDING

MONUMENTAL BUILDING, 1876

Samuel Lane, Cleveland
133 South Ohio Avenue at Court Street, NRHP/Sidney Courthouse Square HD
County-owned building; Veterans' Service Office on ground floor;
Municipal Court occupies top two floors

Built as a memorial to Civil War dead, the stone-faced Monumental
Building is a tall three stories of Victorian Gothic. It was built for many
purposes: library, municipal and township offices, fire department, and, on
the third floor, opera house. Around the turn of the century the fire marshal
closed the opera house for want of adequate exits. So for almost a century
the auditorium remained, a mothballed curiosity, with its stage framed by
columns, its U-shaped balcony resting on iron posts, and an octagonal
dome in the ceiling overhead. ¶ The Monumental Building was the first of
14 Civil War memorial halls built by Ohio towns. Shortly after the end of
the war, in 1867, Sidney started raising money with a lottery; then when
voters almost unanimously passed a bond issue in the mid-1870s, it had a
full pot. In recent decades the building was almost empty and neglected,

until a $300,000 rescue fixed the roof and other acute problems in 1994. Two years later the Veterans Service Office, which displays the plaques with the names of Shelby County's war dead, moved into the first floor. ¶ Then in early summer, 1999, Rich Wallace, an attorney and a Monumental Building trustee, announced the Municipal Court would take over the rest of the building—as it has, following a $3 million renovation; a courtroom now occupies the opera house. And what does the fire marshal make of this? Tony Zircher of Sidney architects Freytag & Associates said the two staircases make the fire marshal happy. Everyone else is happy with two elevators. ¶ What a great success for Sidney, to find a good use for the Monumental Building, and the money to make it happen.

PEOPLES SAVINGS & LOAN ASSOCIATION, NOW PEOPLES FEDERAL SAVINGS & LOAN, 1917

Louis H. Sullivan, Chicago
101 East Court Street/State Route 47 at Ohio Avenue, Sidney, NHL, NRHP
Bank; tours may be prearranged; 937/492-6129

▶ PEOPLES FEDERAL, DETAIL

The front part of Peoples Federal Savings & Loan, designed by Chicago architect Louis H. Sullivan, houses the bank's two-story lobby; the tail-like single-story back section contains offices. The building is brick, with terra cotta outlining the facade's large blue mosaic arch, the tall rectangular windows on the side, and the cornice. Much of the ornamentation is in the curly-leafed forms so associated with this architect that they are called "Sullivanesque". At the corners of both front and side walls single-pane rectangular windows anchor the composition; a row of them continues, below a terra cotta band and panels, into the low office wing at the back.

▶ PEOPLES FEDERAL

The Best Bank—Toward the end of his career, between 1906 and 1920, Louis Henri Sullivan (1856-1924) of Chicago did eight remarkable banks in small Midwestern towns, including two in Ohio, in Sidney and Newark. One of America's great architects, Sullivan had seen his career peak earlier, during his 12-year partnership with Dankmar Adler, from 1883-1895. While Adler was the engineering expert who smoothed relations with clients, Sullivan was the design genius who first gave aesthetic coherence to tall buildings, who became known as the father both of the skyscraper and of modern architecture.

But working on his own in later years, Sullivan had a tough time. He refused to compromise, he drank, he didn't always have enough work to support himself. Though he had designed over 100 buildings between 1880 and 1895, in his last 30 years he did only 20, including the eight banks. Although these relatively small banks were all in relatively obscure places, he gave them thoughtful attention, treating them as if they were major projects in major cities. The result is that they are among his finest designs, carrying on his own modern, American style. Of the eight, Sidney's was the one that Sullivan himself thought the best.

Like the others, Peoples Saving & Loan came about because of an enlightened individual in the community. In Sidney he was a bank officer named LaFayette M. Sturdevant, who learned of Sullivan while touring Europe in 1914. Back in Ohio, Sturdevant went to Newark to see the architect's bank there, and then he persuaded his fellow trustees to invite Sullivan to Sidney. The architect came, and the bankers told him their requirements.

For two days Sullivan sat on the curb contemplating the site. Then he told the trustees that the design was ready in his head. He did a sketch for them and provided a cost estimate. A director objected that banks should have classical columns in front. Sullivan's answer was to roll up his drawing and prepare to leave, even though he needed the job. Anyone, he declared, could give Peoples Savings columns, but only he could offer this functional modern design. The directors came round, and by May, 1917 the final drawings were in Sidney. Perhaps because he wasn't too busy, Sullivan came back to supervise construction. Robert Bertsch, a bank officer who retired in 1990 and for years afterward gave tours, heard that the architect sat on a keg of nails in the middle of what became the lobby, while the floor around him became littered with his cigarette butts.

The son of an Irish father and a Swiss mother, Louis Sullivan was born and grew up in Massachusetts. He studied architecture for a year at Massachusetts Institute of Technology and later, for another year, at Paris's École des Beaux-Arts; he worked in the Philadelphia office of architect Frank Furness. In the 1870s he settled in Chicago, where he became Adler's partner and where the young Frank Lloyd Wright was to start out working for him. Wright, in what was for him a rare tribute, called Sullivan the "Master".

Peoples Savings was a building with many intentions. The clients wanted—and got—a modern, efficient bank; it functions well. Sullivan wanted it (and all his work) to be essentially American, with plain geometric shapes and naturalistic ornament. He wanted it to be "democratic"—to minimize the gulf between banker and customer. And as Lauren Weingarden, an art historian who studied Sullivan's banks, wrote, he wanted to deify the commonplace. With its central aisle leading up to the vault door, with a crucifix-like design on its upright side windows, the bank has religious overtones. In fact, as Bob Bertsch noted, people often come in expecting a church.

Peoples Savings looks like nothing else in Sidney. At the same time, it related to its neighbors in scale and materials. (The two immediately adjacent structures have been changed.) Most of the buildings on Courthouse Square were red-brick Italianate structures.[*] The two most conspicuous neighbors, the Courthouse and the Monumental Building, used styles and ornament with European origins and thus represented the imported design that Sullivan hoped to leave behind.

Peoples Savings displays an array of colors. According to Weingarden, the exterior brick includes 14 different shades of reds, browns, grays. A two-foot band of marble at the base of the outside walls is dark green. Glass mosaics are blue in the front arch, bright green in the side panel. Terra cotta is a gray-green on the facade, buff on the side, light orange in the cornice band.

Much to the general amazement when the bank first opened, the interior walls are a smooth, dark-brown brick. Floors and counters are marble, and the lobby has a rectangular skylight. The room's focal point is the gleaming metal vault door, round, at once massive and intricate, directly opposite the door at the far end of the lobby. It's the first thing an entering depositor will see. It is meant to reassure him, for both symbolically and actually, it represents security. As the door is kept open during banking hours (a fact Sullivan checked when preparing the design), the vault itself is to the right, off center so the door can be central. To Weingarden, the vault door demonstrates machinery and art as one, while she likens the adjacent vault to an altar.

Peoples Savings has always taken good care of this building; inside and out, it looks much as it did when new. Bob Bertsch listed some changes—for instance, the original furniture was sold; the tellers have carpet underfoot rather than cork; they now face bulletproof glass. Bertsch took especial delight in Sullivan's mechanical ingenuity. For instance, the lobby has two marble benches that are warm in winter, for both contain radiators. Also, the architect ordered tight double glazing for the windows, which made the interior quieter and also enhanced his air cooling system—he cooled by circulating air that fans blew over water in a cistern under the sidewalk.

Bertsch gave an interesting tour. But then, he had great material.

[*] *One that remains is an 1895 building at 129 East Court. Now the Shelby County Annex, it's a commendable example of reuse.*

▶ Spot Restaurant

SPOT RESTAURANT, 1913, 1941

201 South Ohio at Court Street, Sidney, NRHP/Sidney Courthouse Square HD
Restaurant

At the Spot Restaurant we celebrate not the original but the 1941 remodeling, which put on the enameled steel Art Moderne facade. Here the seven-foot wide round neon sign ("The SPOT to Eat") becomes part of the architecture. Besides, the food is good, as the restaurant's popularity shows.

FIRST NATIONAL EXCHANGE BANK,
NOW BEHR DESIGN, 1915

114 East Poplar Street, on the north side of the square, Sidney, NRHP/Sidney
Courthouse Square HD
Private offices

First National Exchange Bank has a Neoclassical Revival facade—the type that at least one director of Peoples Savings expected Louis Sullivan to do. Ohio State's Douglas Graf calls this slender, single-bay facade "stunning"— in just 21 feet it's complete with door, a pair of columns and a pair of pilasters. It's clad in white marble; large and small dentils enclose the pediment. Mike Behr, whose design business occupies the basement, bought the building in 1996. Not long afterward he called in an exterminator who asked him if he knew the building had a third floor. That was how Behr discovered that he'd bought more building than he knew. Though most of the interior has been altered, the third floor retains an original marble fireplace and stained-glass ceiling. Behr hopes to restore it. A few doors west at 128 East Poplar, Harris Jeweler, originally E.E. Kah Jewelry, 1915, is another three-story commercial building—along with First National Exchange Bank it was among four built after a fire the year before. The jeweler's building is a white terra cotta confection topped with a little balustrade.

Springfield, Clark County

(With more sites than any other one place in this volume, Springfield stands alone as a tour.)

¶ "Springfield," says Douglas Graf, "must have been amazing in 1889." Graf, an associate professor of architecture at Ohio State, scouts Ohio for good stuff, and he's gone to Springfield again and again. In April, 1995, as I was just starting my field work for this guide, he showed me Springfield; it was as if he were unwrapping an especially delightful present. This tour is based in good part on his: a present for all of us. ¶ In the late nineteenth and early twentieth centuries, Springfield was a prosperous place, but money does not produce good architecture by itself. What Springfield also had, Graf says, was "a patron class that saw good architecture as part of their civic function." Today's Springfield benefits from their legacy, but it is also a depressed industrial city. Much has been torn down, and new buildings often have not attained the quality of those they replaced (a misfortune not exclusive to Springfield.) ¶ For this guide Springfield is divided into West Side; Downtown and South Fountain Avenue; and East Side, in that order.

West Side

Access: Springfield is just north of 1-70 and accessible from five exits, which from east to west are U.S. 40, State Route 41, State Route 72 (most direct to downtown), U.S. 68, and State Route 4. This tour starts on U.S. 68 on Springfield's west side. Take the U.S. 40/State Route 4 exit from U.S. 68. Turn west on U.S. 40; then, following the sign for Ohio Masonic Home, almost immediately turn south.

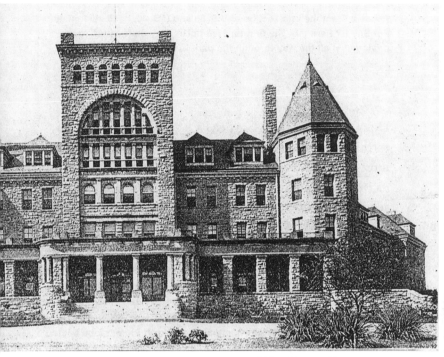

▶ Ohio Masonic Home

OHIO MASONIC HOME, NOW BUSHNELL HALL OF OHIO MASONIC HOME, 1895

John Eisenmann, Cleveland
5 Masonic Drive, Springfield
Bushnell Hall is now administrative offices for retirement community with various on-site facilities; lobby visible by prearrangement; 937/325-1833; 888/ 248-2664

The Ohio Masonic Home is hard to miss because of its great site. It's at the top of a broad hillside sweep of lawn, where the building is silhouetted against the western sky. It's named for Asa Bushnell, a Springfield industrialist and Ohio governor, who helped arrange the Masonic Home's land acquisition here, even though he wasn't himself a Mason at the time. ¶ Built of a rough-cut buff stone, the home has a front porch that looks as though it's intended for rocking chairs. A massive central tower, six stories high, has wings that end in octagonal towers with pointed roofs. The home was built for elderly Masons and their wives; until the mid-1950s children, usually orphans, also lived on this campus. Today the retirement facility is open to non-Masons as well. ¶ Timothy B. Strawn, president of the Ohio Masonic Home Benevolent Endowment Foundation, was able to tell me that the front hall's stained glass window was by Von Gerichten Art Glass of Columbus, but he was unable to find out whether the architect, whose name he had as Brother John Eisenman, was John Eisenmann of Cleveland, famous for engineering the Cleveland Arcade. ¶ But in mid-2000 Craig Bobby of Lakewood, surely the state's leading architect detective, confirmed its architect was *The* Eisenmann. Bobby's source was a 1903 Cleveland newspaper article that specifically credited Eisenmann with Springfield's Ohio Masonic Home.

Access: From the intersection of U.S. 68 and U.S. 40, head east on 40.
For Snyder Park take the first turn left/north. Stay on the park road,
driving east all the way through the park to Plum Street.

Snyder Park

Doug Graf really likes Snyder Park. "Isn't this heaven on earth?," he says. "It looks like England. This must be the most beautiful river in Ohio." It's Bush Creek, wending its way between low, grassy banks. ¶ The Snyder family acquired the site in 1827, and in 1895 two descendants, John and David Snyder, offered 217 acres to the city as a park, on condition that paths be installed. They were, and by 1897 the transfer was complete. The next year David's will assured Snyder Park a $200,000 endowment.

Access: From Snyder Park turn left/north on North Plum; stone posts
of Ferncliff Cemetery entrance appear almost immediately on the left.
Turn into the cemetery and drive up to the Bushnell Mausoleum,
which is at the top of the hill in cemetery Section P.

BUSHNELL MAUSOLEUM
Ferncliff Cemetery, Section P, Springfield

Asa Bushnell, manufacturer and former governor, died early in 1904, in his 70th year. Before he died, says cemetery superintendent Harold Pendleton, the small Greek temple that was to be his tomb was installed at Ferncliff's best site. Built of Vermont marble—even the roof is marble—the structure has front and back porches, Doric columns and entablature. Four columns wide, six deep, it is exquisitely proportioned. A metal screen encloses the central section, where three crypts line each side. "It seems perfect for a tomb—the stasis of death on the interior but on the outside it's dynamic," Graf says. "I'd love to know who designed it. He really knew his history." ¶ Who designed it is a good question indeed, for the Bushnell Mausoleum is arguably the best private example of a temple-tomb in Ohio. The only hint we have is in a typewritten cemetery history, perhaps from 1937, at the Clark County Historical Society. The unnamed author, more interested in the tomb's price than its designer, wrote that the tomb "cost enough, it is rumored, to build a fine house. It was built for Mr. Bushnell by an ex-senator of the United States who was at the head of a marble company and a very good friend of Bushnell's." ¶ In 1996 a great-granddaughter of Asa Bushnell, Frances J. Dunburg, died and left half of her estate for the maintenance of the Bushnell Mausoleum and five family plots elsewhere at Ferncliff. So in spring 1997 the cemetery received a check for almost half a million dollars, with a promise of more to come. Ferncliff poppped the money into its checking account and, contemplating other needs, chafed

▶ Bushnell Mausoleum

that the legacy, which ultimately totaled $890,000, was so restricted. When I heard about it, I began hoping some of the money might go to research the Mausoleum's origins. ¶ Ferncliff's well planned winding roads also attracted Doug Graf's notice. "It's nice how this cemetery is laid out," he said, judging partly on how easy it was to reach Bushnell's Mausoleum at the top of the hill. He added that Ferncliff isn't quite up to Cincinnati's Spring Grove Cemetery (see also). ¶ As it turns out, when Ferncliff was founded in 1863, it hired a designer, John Dick, who came from Cincinnati where he'd been working for Adolph Strauch at Spring Grove. Strauch was the country's leading creator of the lawn-plan cemetery. Twenty-nine years old when he came to Ferncliff, Dick was a native of Scotland, where he started working as a landscape gardener; he came to the United States in 1854. In Springfield Dick laid out Ferncliff and served as landscape gardener and superintendent until he died in 1906. He was buried at Ferncliff.

To see Wittenberg University: Take Ferncliff's north entrance onto West McCreight Avenue and circle around, turning right/south onto Woodlawn Avenue and right/west onto Ward Avenue into campus; drive uphill. A booklet with an architectural walking tour is available at the public relations office, Recitation Hall. Wittenberg's towers are west side landmarks; the old brick building with the round-domed cupola is Myers Hall, 1851. Drive around and back onto Ward; take it to North Fountain; turn south to U.S. 40/North Street, and pick up route below.

Access: From Ferncliff drive south on Plum to U.S. 40/North Street; turn right/west and drive to Western Avenue; turn left/south to High Street; P.P. Mast House is across the street.

▶ P.P. Mast House

P.P. MAST HOUSE, NOW CASTLE KNOLL, K.W. HESS OHIO PYTHIAN HOME, 1882

901 West High Street at Western Avenue, Springfield
Administration building for retirement complex; 937/322-3271

Springfield's great industrialists all live on in the names of their houses. And they did care about those houses. This one sits atop the highest hill in the west-side neighborhood that Phineas P. Mast hoped would attract the rest of Springfield's rich elite. In that ambition he was disappointed, but he surely could have found some consolation in his worldly successes. His companies made farm machinery, gasoline engines, and iron fencing; he founded the Second National Bank of Springfield; he bought a farm magazine and moved it to Springfield, where it became the basis for Crowell Collier, leading magazine publishers through the mid-twentieth century. ¶ Mast's inspiration for his house came from a trip to Italy; he was so impressed by cabinet work and stone masonry there that he brought 29 Italian craftsmen to Springfield to work on his house. It is a tall two-and-a-half story structure clad in rough-cut stone. Though it is clearly a Victorian house, its style—with elements of Italianate, Romanesque, Queen Anne, Renaissance, and so on—resists slotting. The most conspicuous feature is a round tower at one corner of the facade; it's open at the third-floor level, where a ring of slender stone columns support a roof the shape of a Hershey's Kiss. The roof's slates are set in a swirling pattern. ¶ The 29 Italians must have included some fine carvers, for the interior woodwork, in black walnut, cherry, and mahogany, is exceptional. Doug Graf was especially impressed with the Art Nouveau-like stairway, whose bottom railings, solid wood, swirl outward to end on both sides in lion's heads and paws. In his office, Manager Wayne Davis has cabinet glazing in beveled crystal and a built-in roll-top desk, with each drawer distinctly carved. ¶ However impressive this house is to us, Mrs. Mast didn't like it and refused to live here after her husband died in 1898. In 1913 the family sold it to the Knights of Pythias for $15,000, though only 30 years before, it had cost $225,000 to build. The Pythians, whose retirement facility here is open to non-Pythians, added the red-brick building at the back of the house so long ago—1921—that it too is venerable. ¶In 1881-82 Phineas Mast also built the red-brick Italianate house across the street; he lived there while the main house was being finished.

Access: From P.P. Mast House drive east on High Street; turn right/ south at Fountain to see the City Building, now a museum, which is in the first block. From I-70 take State Route 72 north; in downtown turn left/west on Main Street and then turn left/south on Fountain to City Building.

Downtown

"This would be fabulous if they got rid of the parking lots," Doug Graf complains in downtown Springfield. "How many parking lots do you see in Boston?" ¶ In architectural circles, downtown Springfield is known both for what it has and for what it's torn down. Losses, Graf says, include the Arcade that the city acquired to save, at least until the roof leaked. What he calls one of Ohio's best Beaux Arts train stations was torn down for an overpass. The commercial downtown was done in by a mall on the outskirts. "It's not as though that mall is any great treat," Graf observes. Nor has it helped that most post World War II construction has not approached the old in design quality. ¶ Fortunately some local people, including James H. Lagos, who owns the Bushnell Building, have been taking an interest in the really good buildings that remain. And one real prize that has been saved is the old City Building, which Graf calls "unbelievable."

▶ CITY BUILDING

CITY BUILDING, NOW HERITAGE CENTER OF CLARK COUNTY, 1890

Charles A. Cregar, Springfield
117 South Fountain Avenue, Springfield, NRHP
Clark County Historical Society museum and Archives; some county offices;
museum open Tuesday through Saturday; 937/324-0657

More amazing than beautiful, the four-story City Building has, for a
building, serpent-like proportions: it's 50 feet wide and 456 feet deep. The
front and back ends have stone facing and high central towers (the one in
front looms another four stories above the roof, the one in back, three stories)
while the building's long stretch between towers is red brick with stone trim.
Richardsonian Romanesque, the building originally accommodated the city
markets traditionally on this site, as well as city offices. The second floor had
two two-story rooms, one a council chamber, the other an opera house. And
in front of the City Building, a 40-foot Baroque fountain gushed grandly
enough to give Fountain Avenue its name. In disrepair in the 1930s, the
fountain was removed, and has been replaced with one of modest ambition.

¶ In fall, 1998, as the Clark County Historical Society planned to restore the building's exterior and gut the interior for a museum, Society director Floyd Barman walked on the multi-colored tile floors, past food vendors and the shoeshine stand. "This is the museum store," he announced, though at the time only he could see it. Barman explained that the building's 300 windows and 20 doors made it less than ideal for a museum. Light damages exhibits, which are so expensive that they have to last for 20 years. The Historical Society was loath to black out the windows; fortunately they declined to brick them up. So the plan was to build a box set three feet from the windows to enclose displays; and, in the two-year restoration ending early in 2001, that was how it was done. ¶ That's one reason the building looks as good as it does today on the outside. The towers had lost their pyramidal roofs, which have been restored with fiberglass copies covered with slates; they were assembled on the ground and lifted up by cranes. The fiberglass provided a way to restore the City Building's original look without the weight and expense of reconstructing in the original materials. Inside, museum exhibits occupy both the large second-floor rooms and half the downstairs. ¶ A half-cent one-year sales tax generated over $5 million for the project. Altogether, public and private funds for renovation and exhibits totaled $8-9 million, with another $4-5 million for an endowment. If not for the museum project, Barman said, the building would be lost. ¶ The new Springfield City Hall, 1979, by Skidmore, Owings and Merrill, is kitty-corner from the City Building at 76 East High.

Access: The rest of this downtown tour is a loop on foot. From the City Building walk one block north on Fountain to Main; turn right to see Bushnell Building. Then continue on Main to Limestone; turn left/north two blocks to North Street, passing courthouse, post office, newspaper, and church. Then turn around and go south on Limestone to High; turn left/east one block to Spring, where Lagonda Club and Bushnell Library are on corner. Turn around and return to starting point.

BUSHNELL BUILDING, LATER BLOCKS DEPARTMENT STORE, 1893

Shepley Rutan and Coolidge, Boston
14 East Main Street, Springfield, NRHP/Main Street Buildings
Offices, dance and health studios, restaurant

As becomes obvious, Asa Bushnell, who built this handsome office building in 1893, left his name all over Springfield. Bushnell's partners in Warder, Bushnell, and Glessner, a farm machinery manufacturer and forerunner of International Harvester, were Benjamin Warder and John J. Glessner. By 1885 Warder and Glessner had moved to Washington and Chicago, respectively, and both commissioned houses from the great Boston architect H.H. Richardson (1838-1886). Largely because of those houses—especially Glessner's, found in almost every book on American architecture—their names live on, for Richardson was a truly original architect, the creator of Richardsonian Romanesque. After Richardson's relatively early death, Bushnell asked someone else to do his own Springfield house (below), but when he built this office building in 1893, he turned to Richardson's successor firm, Shepley Rutan and Coolidge. A five-story structure in brick

▶ BUSHNELL BUILDING

and stone with terra cotta trim, the Bushnell Building is a stylistic mix, not Richardsonian Romanesque but more Beaux Arts or Renaissance; windows rise in pairs and in threes, with arches toward the top. Originally a bank, shop, and offices, the building was Wrens department store for many years, then Blocks. In 1903 the store gave itself an L shape, adding an entrance around the corner on Fountain Street. The similar facade there is a pallid imitation. In 1994 Springfield attorney James H. Lagos bought the then vacant building and has been restoring it for tenants.

CLARK COUNTY COURTHOUSE, 1924
William K. Schilling, Springfield
101 North Limestone Street, at Columbia Street, Springfield
Courthouse; 937/328-2458

Doug Graf particularly likes this part of downtown because of its impressive cluster of institutional buildings from the 1920s. As for the Clark County Courthouse, he describes it as "amazingly urbane, restrained, sophisticated." It's a domed Neoclassical Revival structure by William K. Shilling, a local architect assigned to rebuild after a 1918 fire.

U.S. POST OFFICE, 1934
William K. Shilling, Springfield
150 North Limestone Street at North Street, Springfield
Post office

This post office, says Doug Graf, who seems to have an eye for Shilling's work, is "fabulous." Art Deco, it has walls faced in a gold Ohio sandstone with gray bands that the metal trim picks up. The building's slightly higher central section has eagles at its corners and

▶ U.S. POST OFFICE

a slight battering, or tapering, in the wall. Interior has been altered.

SPRINGFIELD NEWS-SUN, 1929
Schultze & Weaver, New York
202 North Limestone Street at North Street, Springfield
Newspaper offices

Graf has a still positive but more restrained appraisal of the Italian Renaissance style newspaper building: "completely competent." Just before designing this building, architects Schultze & Weaver had been working on the $40 million Waldorf Astoria Hotel in New York, according to Anita Beaver, *News-Sun* librarian. In 1927 they did a somewhat similar building for the Canton newspaper (see also, Vol. I).

▶ SPRINGFIELD NEWS-SUN

COVENANT PRESBYTERIAN CHURCH, 1927
George E. Savage, Philadelphia
201 North Limestone Street at North Street, Springfield
Church; 937/325-2427

And Covenant Presbyterian Church, Graf says, is "beautiful." It's Gothic Revival, Indiana limestone, with a good interior, including stained glass windows by P.J. Reeves of Philadelphia. On a hot summer afternoon in 1998, the church's well-treed lawn, enclosed by the building on two sides, was the most pleasant place in all downtown.

LAGONDA CLUB, 1895
Frank M. Andrews, Dayton
South Spring and East High Streets, northwest corner, Springfield, NRHP
Vacant building

Springfield, Doug Graf observes, "is now depressed, which tends to maintain stuff." Built of brick, stone, and terra cotta, the lovely Lagonda Club is vacant but still standing. It has lush ornamentation and, at the third floor, a diamond pattern in contrasting brick. Elegant though the building is, it overlooks the multi-lane Spring Street whose priority is moving traffic out of downtown. The Lagonda was an opulent, exclusive club for the rich, over-leisured heirs to the founders of Springfield's manufacturing fortunes. So wrote George H. Berkhofer, then Clark County Historical Society

▶ LAGONDA CLUB

director, in preparing a National Register form in 1974. In spite of its architectural virtues, the Lagonda Club lost members to the Springfield Country Club and closed in 1923. The Chamber of Commerce bought the building and occupied it for 40 years, "constantly nibbling away at the former elegance," Berkhofer noted; the main stairway and musicians' balcony were removed. Berkhofer also mentioned that architect Frank M. Andrews, who had a Dayton office for a few years before moving on to New York, got this job because he was related by marriage to a Springfield man. The marriage broke up in 1909 when Andrews married (though only for a while) actress Pauline Frederick. Today, most of Frank Andrews's major Ohio work is either vacant—the Dayton Arcade (see also, Vol. I) and the Lagonda Club—or, as in the case of National Cash Register's old Dayton factory buildings, gone. Happily, in the last few years a tenant has moved into one, at least: the Gidding-Jenny Building in Cincinnati (see Vol. I).

WARDER PUBLIC LIBRARY, NOW WARDER CENTER 1890

Shepley Rutan and Coolidge, Boston
137 East High Street at South Spring Street, Springfield, NRHP
Now quarters for Clark
County Literacy Coalition;
interior accessible weekdays;
937/323-8617

Apparently library
benefactor Benjamin
Warder was so well pleased
with his H.H. Richardson
house in Washington, that
he turned to the successor
firm of Shepley Rutan and
Coolidge for this building.

▶ WARDER LIBRARY, DETAIL

A one-and-a-half story L-shaped structure with an octagonal tower inside the L's bend, Warder Library is a very good example of Richardsonian Romanesque architecture. The rough-cut sandstone is tan with brown trim

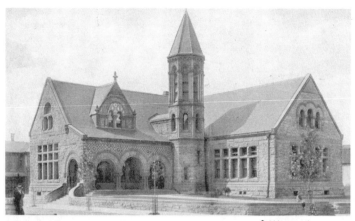

▶ WARDER LIBRARY

around windows and arches, while the arcaded front porch has clusters of short pillars, fine carving, and a red and tan checkerboarding in stone over the arches. The site is the same unhappy corner that the Lagonda Club shares. Interior has been altered somewhat, but has a great fireplace.

Access: From downtown drive south on Fountain Avenue, passing the Bookwalter House, below; at Miller Street drive one block east to Limestone Street.

South Fountain Avenue

For a time Springfield's South Fountain Avenue has been on the verge of a renaissance that's been slow in arriving, so it's not a neighborhood everyone would notice. But it puts Doug Graf in a state of enthusiastic delight; he calls it "world-class" as he drives along, hailing shabby relics by their styles. ¶ "Italian. Eastlake. Prairie. What a classy street. Tight front lawns, huge porches. Look at that spectacular gable, Neoclassical Revival. There's a house I like a lot, with the porte cochere; it's a compacted version of something very grand. Columbus doesn't have all this. That's a third-floor poet's nook. See those amazing little eyebrow windows. In fairly recent memory this would have been a great neighborhood." ¶ When he turns left on Miller Street, he sounds a fanfare—"Dah, dah"—and lo, there sits South High School: bedomed, becolumned, and proud, as a school should be.

▶ Springfield South High School

FRANCIS BOOKWALTER HOUSE, 1876

611 South Fountain Avenue, Springfield, NRHP
Private house

Not all of South Fountain Street is shabby, as the Francis Bookwalter
House, in a symmetrical Second Empire, shows. The wooden walls and
curving trim are painted in contrasting colors, and the roof has at least three
different colors of slate, forming patterns.

SPRINGFIELD HIGH SCHOOL, NOW SPRINGFIELD SOUTH HIGH SCHOOL, 1911

Albert A. Pretzinger, Dayton
700 South Limestone Street at Miller Street, Springfield
High school

South High School has a Beaux Arts facade, a dome, paired columns on the
central section and again on the end pavilions. Often I hear that a building
is based on something else, and then it isn't. But this school does appear to
draw inspiration (though not its dome) from its alleged source, the Library
of Congress in Washington.

East Side

Access: Drive north on Limestone Street to East High Street; turn right/east for all the sites listed below.

JOHN FOOS HOUSE, 1875

810 East High Street, NRHP/East High Street District, Springfield
Private house

John Foos was, as his house shows, a rich man. He made his money in manufacturing—in 1870 he and P.P. Mast formed Mast, Foos & Company to make farm machinery. Foos built his house in limestone on the outside and carved walnut inside, with a servants' wing at the back in red brick and oak, respectively. In recent years, during and after a ten-year restoration that helped make the house as fabulous as it was originally, it served first as offices and then as a combination bed and breakfast and antique shop; in 1993 the front hall—with its long, multi-colored tile floor, high doors and dark woodwork, and chandelier suspended from the 16-foot ceiling—made such a great picture that it appeared on the cover of *Ohio Magazine*. In May 2001 a new owner bought the property with a view to bringing the Foos House back to where it started.

Again, it's a private house.

▶ JOHN FOOS HOUSE

RINEHART-BOWMAN HOUSE, 1873

815 East High Street, Springfield, NRHP/East High Street District
Private offices

This stone Italianate house might look as elegant as it is, if it weren't
competing with John Foos's showstopper across the street. Foos built this
house too, and gave it to a daughter. The name, Rinehart-Bowman, refers
to later owners.

ASA BUSHNELL HOUSE, NOW RICHARDS, RAFF & DUNBAR MEMORIAL HOME, 1888

Robert H. Robertson, New York
838 East High Street at Walnut, Springfield, NRHP/East High Street District
Funeral home; except during funerals, visitors may see interior; 937/325-1564

Next door to the Foos House and on the very same ridge, is Asa Bushnell's
own Richardsonian Romanesque house. In 1851, when he was 16, Bushnell
came to Springfield from his parents' Cincinnati home. He started as a clerk
in a dry goods store and studied bookkeeping to advance himself.
Ultimately he advanced all the way to the presidency of Warder, Bushnell
and Glessner, a huge farm machinery manufacturer whose factories were at
the bottom of the hill behind this house. ¶ Much like Bushnell himself, one
writer observed, his house is massive, solid, and accessible, rather than high
and aloof like Foos's house. After twice turning down a chance to run for
governor because he was busy running the company, Bushnell accepted in
1895 and was elected to two terms, serving from 1896 to 1900. After
proclaiming his inaugural address from his house's porch, he ran a state
administration devoted to promoting business interests. People urged him
to live in Columbus, but he declined, claiming he had a better house in
Springfield. He came home by horse and carriage, changing horses in
Lafayette. ¶ Besides the main house, this property has a large carriage house
and an intriguing caretaker's home—stone below; dark brown shingles
above; a funeral director lives in it—at the back. All three were done by a
New York architect, Robert H. Robertson (1849-1919) who in
the 1880s specialized in Richardsonian
Romanesque. Thus the house has

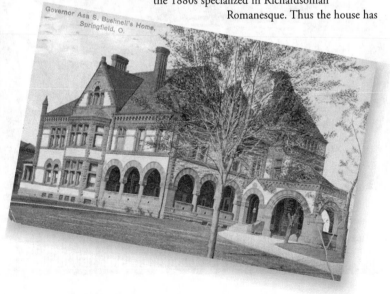

Governor Asa S. Bushnell's Home, Springfield, O.

the style's characteristic round arches, short columns, and rough-cut stone in contrasting colors: buff limestone on walls, brown sandstone in the trim. Exterior walls are 30 inches thick; those on the inside, 18 inches. Both floors and subfloors are an inch thick, for soundproofing; and every room has a fireplace, though the house has always had central heating. The woodwork, in oak, in American, white, and French walnuts, in cherry and Honduras mahogany—a *ceiling* is mahogany—is superb. ¶ In 1939, after the house had been empty for ten years, funeral director Austin Richards bought it and fixed it up upstairs for his home and downstairs for his funeral business. Still a funeral home—the round porch is a viewing room; the third-floor ballroom has a casket display—the house is beautifully kept. In the early 1990s that meant two year-and-a-half-long restoration projects, one exterior, the other interior. President Richard L. Dunbar says just repairing the red tile roof cost $200,000. Lucky house.

▶ Westcott House

WESTCOTT HOUSE, 1909
Frank Lloyd Wright, Chicago
1340 East High Street at South Greenmount Avenue, Springfield, NRHP
Private apartments; house to be restored

The Westcott House is Ohio's only early, Prairie style Frank Lloyd Wright house. Emulating the long horizons of the prairie, these houses were horizontal in line, though slightly elevated for a view. Stretched along its hillside, the Westcott House looks unmistakably Wrightean. It also has the signature pair of planter-urns in front—a Wright trademark. ¶ A long arbor, which was behind a wall along Greenmount Avenue, linked the main house, set toward the front of the lot, to a stable and garage at the back. The main entrance is at the side, a characteristic placement for Wright, Doug Graf says. At about 6 and a half feet, the door is also low, so that entering becomes a sort of genuflecting. Graf admires the complicated Greenmount Avenue facade, which seems active with a mix of deep and narrow overhangs, with horizontal beams that seem to fly, with the jewel-like garage wing at the back. ¶ Burton J. and Orpha Westcott moved from Richmond, Indiana to Springfield in 1903. At that time Westcott was manufacturing seeding machines, but he is remembered for the Westcott Motor Car Company, which produced splendid automobiles from 1916 until the early 1920s. Orpha Westcott was a modern-minded woman who wanted Frank Lloyd Wright to design their house. Stephen Siek, who published a monograph on the Westcott House in 1978, reported that Wright habitually studied his clients, and so the architect came to Springfield and lived with the family for a while. By early 1907 the final design was ready, and construction began that year. The Westcotts and their young son and daughter moved in in 1909, though the house wasn't finished until 1911. ¶ Because Wright was so influential, it is hard to realize now how advanced this house was in 1907. It had a wide, low hip roof and an incredibly wide chimney; outside walls were a gleaming stucco, with stained oak timbering. It had rows of casement windows under the eaves. It had one very large (20 by 60 feet) open living, dining, and reception room. Wooden screens—combination screens, bookcases, seats, and light fixtures, flanked the fireplace. The front of the house had a terraced patio and garden. Wright did visit the site during construction, but when he wasn't there Orpha Westcott and the family doctor kept close tabs on construction. ¶ The Westcott House was converted into apartments in 1944. In recent years owner Sherri Snyder, who remarkably still had the original working drawings for the house, became resigned to being unable to restore it herself. Finally, in September 2000 she sold it for $300,000 to the only buyer she really trusted, the Chicago-based Frank Lloyd Wright Building Conservancy—the Westcott was its first purchase of a Wright building in jeopardy. As a condition of sale ownership has transferred to a local group, the Westcott House Foundation, but the Conservancy has permanent control over the planned $4 million restoration and later upkeep. Architect was to be Lauren Burge of Chambers, Murphy & Burge of Akron. As of late 2001, Matt Cline, site manager and a trustee, said work was expected to start in the coming winter. The hope was to reopen the Westcott House as a house museum by late 2003. The whole transaction looks like a great boon for Ohio architecture. ¶ A complete list of Wright's buildings in the state accompanies the Weltzheimer House in Oberlin, Northeast Ohio.

CITY HOSPITAL,
NOW SPRINGFIELD COMMUNITY HOSPITAL, 1932
Eastman and Budke and Marlay Lethly, Springfield, with consultants Tietig & Lee, Cincinnati
2615 East High Street at Burnett Road, Springfield
Hospital

The Art Deco City Hospital sits on a hill facing a corner; it has a central tower and five-story wings angling forward. Doug Graf's comment: "Isn't that fabulous?"

▶ MIAMI COUNTY COURTHOUSE

Troy, Miami County

(Tour with two towns to the north off I-75, Piqua and
Sidney, and with Greenville, northwest on State Route 41
and U.S. 36).

¶ One day in the mid-1990s, while having breakfast in
Celina, I overheard some telephone line installers talking
about all the work they'd had lately in Troy. Sure enough,
the decade was a boom time for this city, which grew 13
percent, to 21,999 people, and now has its own sprawling
suburbs.

**Access: Troy is just east of I-75. Both State Routes 41 and 55 have
exits into town or reach it from the east.**

▶ MIAMI COUNTY COURTHOUSE

MIAMI COUNTY COURTHOUSE, 1888, 1982, 1998

J. W. Yost, Columbus, 1888; Gaede Serne Zofcin Architects, Cleveland, 1982;
John Ruetschle Associates, Dayton, 1998
215 West Main Street/State Route 41, Troy, NRHP
Courthouse; 937/332-6800

The Miami County Courthouse is a proud building indeed. Built of
sandstone with a limestone base, it has four equally imposing facades, each
with its own stairway leading to its own becolumned porch, and each with
walls intermittently enlivened by pairs of pilasters. About half the building's
160-foot height is above the roofline. Four domes are on low square corner
towers, while the tallest and largest dome is on a high central tower with an
encircling colonnade. All the rooftop constructions are cast iron, which was
both cheaper and lighter than stone and was, after all, good enough for the
dome of the Capitol in Washington. Architect Joseph Warren Yost was a big
name in courthouses in the 1880s. In Ohio he did five altogether, starting
with the one in Cambridge, Guernsey County, in 1883. Of the five the one
in St. Clairsville, Belmont County, 1886, is most similar to Miami
County's, which is the more opulent. This courthouse also has had two
major restorations in recent decades. The first, 1982, was largely interior;
the second, 1998, exterior. The building across the street at the rear was
built as a powerhouse, while a Safety Building, 1974, is next door to the
east.

Leading Courthouse Revolutions—In 1974 Franklin County, having built itself a new high-rise courthouse, tore down the old one: an 1887 Second Empire building designed by Columbus architect George H. Maetzel. Bad as that was for Columbus—that neighborhood has never really come back—at the time it was hardly surprising. The surprise is that since 1974, no Ohio county has torn down its old courthouse.

Miami County was thinking about it in 1975. That year Cleveland architect Robert C. Gaede was called in to take a look at the old courthouse, to see if it was worth saving. "Can you believe that?," Gaede asks, shaking his head as he recalls. "Of course it was worth saving. But it was old, dirty, drafty. The toilets were bad. Stained glass had become opaque with dirt. Walls had been painted landlord green. Wiring, conduits, and telephone lines festooned the walls, went up and over the doors—it was frightening. The light fixtures were hanging fluorescent. The courtroom was cut in half with a drywall partition. Plaster was falling."

Starting the next year, Gaede's firm oversaw a major restoration, mostly interior, of the Miami County Courthouse. The county decided on a step-by-step program with electrical, plumbing, and air updating; staggered over six and a half years, it cost $1.3 million in Federal revenue-sharing funds. At that time the idea of restoration was, Gaede says, still in its infancy. It is hard to remember just how daring, how pioneering it was in 1976 for Miami County to contemplate spending $1.3 million on an old building.

When the job was finished in 1982, Miami County was proud beyond measure; it had recaptured a work of art in its midst. Gaede was delighted. "Isn't it gorgeous?" was his assessment. Now he could spout off on the courthouse's virtues. The floor plan, for instance. When he looks at it he quivers with aesthetic pleasure. "It's a Palladian plan," he says, referring to the sixteenth-century Italian architect who recast classical idioms so well that some of his ideas carry his name to this day. "Palladio," Gaede continues, "laid out some of his great country estates in this manner." Thus the floor plan has a symmetry in its four quarters: a pair of halls cross in the middle; large rooms are in the four corners.

Gaede admires the detailing: "The rotunda features busts of all the ethnic people that made up America, flora and fauna motifs. The high frieze band has birds and other creatures in the leaflet pattern. The people, animals, and flora of Ohio are all captured in plaster. The flooring is of encaustic ceramic tile, which came in single-color hues so the floors were put together in geometric patterns. The Troy courthouse celebrates the versatility of encaustic tiles. And what a magnificent staircase this is. You can't believe that staircase. But in 1975 it was a tossup whether it would be preserved."

Though what Miami County did was unusual at the time, it's since become standard procedure. Admittedly, during the last quarter century some county courts have moved out of the old buildings and into new ones, where ceilings are low and ambiences, banal; but the fact is the old structure still stands and is in use—perhaps, as in Butler County, it's even newly restored. In a trend unprecedented in the history of Ohio, county after county has restored its courthouse; in 1997-98 Bob Gaede was redoing the one in Henry County,

(1882, by Toledo architect D.W. Gibbs), a fine example of Second Empire. But the Henry County job included both inside and outside; the $4 million total was funded by a levy that voters approved by a margin of 52 to 48.

As for Miami County Courthouse, the award-winning 1976-82 job turned out to be just the start; for restoring only the inside was not enough. The main problem outside was the nine cast iron structures—five domes and four pavilions with pediments—on the roof. The problem wasn't that they were old, but that they had never been properly maintained. After years of caulk here and recaulk there, no one could tell where water was coming from—and water was coming. The cast iron was rusting and cracking; pillar bases were so eroded that they were structurally endangered. So in 1994, after two public hearings, the commissioners approved a five-year quarter percent sales tax for the courthouse's exterior restoration. This time the tab was going to be multiples of the first: $5.9 million, including the cast iron restoration, slate roof repairs, new pointing and new windows—wood windows just like the old ones except for the introduction of double glazing.

In tackling the roof domes, the county undertook the largest cast-iron restoration ever done in the United States. Restoring badly damaged cast iron is a tricky business. Only five companies in the world, and two in the United States, do this type of work. The one that did the Miami County Courthouse was Utah-based Cast Iron Management, whose project manager, Steve Brown, and his wife Sarah made Troy their home for two years starting in July 1996; in winter 1997-98 the high dome was still swaddled in plastic.

On the five domes and their bases and the four pavilions, the deteriorated metal had to be taken down by hand, piece by piece, examined, and then repainted or recast. Highly ornamented cast iron structures like these were made of small pieces of cast iron skin—here, there was a total of 14,500 pieces in 1,750 different shapes. Beforehand, Brown expected to recast 25 percent of the pieces, but as it turned out, the rate was closer to 45 percent. That meant 6,500 pieces of domes and pavilions were recast: poured into sand molds prepared with customized patterns.

Newly cast pieces were so rough that they needed grinding and sanding, and then, because most of the casting was in Utah, the pieces traveled to Troy by truck—Sarah Brown kept track of parts and shipments. A truck trip from Utah gave the new pieces time to form a film of rust, so after arrival they had to be sandblasted before being given two coats of paint. Parts that were sound enough not to need recasting were simply sandblasted and painted, and then the domes and pavilions were put back together with silicone in the joints and another two coats of paint.

After that, all that was left, by contract, was providing a maintenance plan for the future. Miami County wanted a printed guide to tell them how often to inspect, how often to repaint, how to prepare for painting, what kind of paint to use.

It's wonderful. This county that led the courthouse-restoration revolution, may lead the next one too—the maintenance revolution.

HAYNER HOUSE, NOW TROY-HAYNER CULTURAL CENTER, 1914

Allyn Company, Cincinnati
301 West Main Street, Troy, NRHP
Community center open to the public; 937/339-0457

Mary Jane Hayner was a tough woman, for even though her husband owned a distillery, she dared to march through the streets on a pro-temperance crusade. The year after he died she ordered plans for this house, completed the next year. Stone on the ground floor, half-timbered on the second, the house has Jacobean Revival elements. It thrives as a community center.

HOBART BROTHERS, NOW MIAMI COUNTY OFFICES, 1943

Freeman A. Pretzinger, Dayton
501 West Main Street, Troy
County office building

A sleek Art Deco office building with round Art Moderne corners is hardly a common sight on Main Street. This one, the former headquarters of Hobart Brothers, manufacturers of electrical and welding equipment, has walls of glazed white tile with contrasting bands of green tile near the roofline. When the owner no longer needed the building and a national drugstore chain proposed razing it, brothers William and Peter Hobart helped the county buy it in summer, 1997; by 2000 it had been renovated and turned into county offices.

Urbana, Champaign County

(Also in Champaign County: St. Paris, west on U.S. 36. Also nearby: Go north on U.S. 68 to West Liberty and Bellefontaine.)

¶ Demonstrating an impressive geographical awareness, early Urbana named its four principal streets for Ohio watersheds. Thus the road to the south was Ohio and the one to the north, Erie; Miami went west and Scioto, east; and they all led to Monument Square, which perhaps missed an opportunity by not having a fountain. Today Miami and Scioto Streets/U.S.36 and State Route 29 still have their original names, but Ohio and Erie are now South and North Main Street. Alas.

Access: Urbana is north of Springfield and south of Bellefontaine on U.S. 68. From I-70, both U.S. 68 and State Route 29 lead to downtown. This tour starts by going from east to west on Scioto and Miami Streets/U.S. 36.

History on Vacation—When John Bry tours the houses of Urbana, he talks as though he's spent all his life soaking up the place. He points out the house that has ceiling frescos in the diningroom. He knows the one with a 12-arm gas chandelier, still lit in the evenings. He points out the Lustron house (in prefabricated enameled steel, at 883 Scioto); the home of a general who was second in command in the Pacific in World War II; the elegant little house that started out as an also elegant privy across the street. He knows Urbana's three historic economic booms: first 1812 (the town was a wartime assembly point for American troops), then the 1850s (railroads), and finally the 1870s-1890s (agriculture and manufacturing).

Bry knows Champaign County too. For instance, East of St. Paris, he turns north from U.S. 36 onto Heck Hill Road to reach Spring Grove Cemetery, where he showed me the only stone arm chair that I've ever seen in a cemetery. It symbolized the empty chair at home, Bry said; or, it provided a seat for someone visiting the grave. It was far from the only such chair John Bry had ever seen, though at the time, he was only 24.

Until Bry arrived in 1989, Urbana pretty much took its buildings for granted. Having just graduated from high school in Auburn, Indiana, he was almost 18 when his parents moved to Urbana. But because of his parents and a grandmother, who all through his childhood took him to see old houses and cemeteries, Bry was already a confirmed old-building buff, who had taught himself American architectural history. When he went to college, he enrolled in one of the few historic preservation programs available then, at Southeast Missouri State University in Cape Girardeau.

That made Bry only a vacation-time resident of Urbana, but he vacationed industriously. He thought the buildings of Urbana were as good as those he'd traveled to see with his parents, so he began studying them. He talked to people, and he did research at the library and the courthouse. Before long, people were telling him he knew more about Urbana than lifetime residents.

Studying wasn't all he did. Bry also founded the Champaign County Preservation Alliance. His mother, Connie Bry, launched the alliance's annual Urbana Historic Home and Garden tour in 1993. (Tours are in June; 800/791-6010.)

And John Bry personally saved an Urbana building that he thinks may be unique in the nation: an octagonal outhouse. This privy was on a farm whose buildings were slated for demolition, so Bry arranged a rescue. He found a forklift to hoist the little building onto a flat-bed trailer and haul it through town to his parents' back yard, where it remains. It's not visible from the road now, because when it was vandals almost immediately tried to set it on fire. Bry describes the 1872 octagonal outhouse as board and batten with slate roof, two windows, plaster walls, and wallpaper. It's a four-holer.

After college Bry took a job as Main Street manager in Flora, Illinois. When I met him in the spring, 1996, I'd never heard of such a job because, Bry explained, Ohio was one of only ten states with no Main Street program. It has established one since, called Downtown Ohio, Inc. Under the aegis of the National Trust, Main Street programs use a multi-pronged approach to revitalize downtowns. The keys include design, which means keeping a community's unique set of historic buildings looking good;

▶ Loudenbach house, Scioto Street

promotion; organization; and economic restructuring, or helping merchants be competitive. Talking about downtown doldrums, Bry said, "I used to blame Wal-Mart, but now I think Wal-Mart isn't responsible. It's people who say, 'Oh I can't compete.' I think downtowns have lost their competitive edge. For example, Wal-Mart stays open until 8, but the stores downtown close at 5."

After leading a successful Main Street program in Flora, Bry was hired away in 1998 by Columbus, Indiana, one of America's most architecturally minded communities, with a series of public buildings designed by nationally prominent architects going back to the 1940s. But having an architectural showcase is not enough to assure the health of downtown, so Columbus called in John Bry.

Then two years later, Urbana started organizing its own Main Street program, consulting Bry as they made plans; ultimately, he was asked if he'd consider working in Urbana. Bry decided he does his best work in smaller towns; he could see Urbana's possibilities; and so, since May 2000, John Bry has been back, heading Ohio's first county-wide Main Street program. He's again president of the Champaign County Preservation Alliance. He bought and started restoring two old buildings, an Italianate house for himself and a three-story downtown hotel that, he says, may be the place where Ivory soap was invented.

And the man who knows Urbana buildings and history best, is finally living there full-time.

H. C. LOUDENBACH HOUSE, 1895

Yost & Packard, Columbus
524 Scioto Street, Urbana, Scioto Street HD
Private house

On a street of good, nineteenth-century houses, this is a showpiece. Partly it's the dark red color—the brick and matching terra cotta trim. It's also the slender corner tower, topped with a witch's hat roof, a steep cone with flared eaves. All four facades have gables with a set of three windows, Palladian with the central one arched; two dormers have the pointed roofs and flared eaves of the tower. The interior is a little more reserved: oak and fruitwood woodwork, pocket doors, tile fireplaces, a staircase with a large stained-glass window. The diningroom has a built-in buffet with a curved arch fronting a recessed mirror. The tower has a tiny room, just over 6 feet across and accessible from a third-floor crawl space. It's turned out to be a perfect clubhouse for the ten-year-old grandson of owner Pearl Sue Moyer, who bought the house in 1995. Yost & Packard also designed the First Presbyterian Church, 1894, 116 West Court Street at Walnut.

▶ Loudenbach House

▶ CHANCE STABLE

CHANCE STABLE, C. 1895
Yost & Packard, Columbus
Rear of 438 Scioto Street, Urbana, Scioto Street HD
Private

The Chance House at 438 Scioto Street is a brick Second Empire built
about 1862. But in the back yard, visible from the sidewalk, this house has
a Shingle style stable that is the very spawn of 524 Scioto, above. At least, it
has similarities, including, besides a fanciful spirit, Palladian windows in the
gables and dormers with flared roofs. The stable's siding is brick and
shingle; a cupola has a bell-shaped roof. Inside, there's a brick floor and four
large stalls with windows—the best horse's stall has a wooden floor. A chute
delivered feed from the loft to ceramic troughs. The groom had a large
upstairs room for living and sleeping; the chimney provided him heat in
winter. Outbuilding origins often are hard to trace, but this one turned up
in *Architectural Realities*, a promotional book issued by the Yost & Packard
firm. A barn for Frank Chance of Urbana appears there, in the "Classified
List of Public and Private Structures." The Allen County hamlet of Gomer
also has a fancy in-town stable, Dr. Jones's Barn (see also, Northwest).

THOMAS GWYNNE HOUSE, 1844
400 Scioto Street, Urbana, Scioto Street HD
Private house

Set back on a large lot, this Gothic Revival house is from Andrew Jackson Downing's *Cottage Residences*, 1842. So is the Upham-Wright House in Newark (see also, Central). John Bry says that one long-time owner of the Gwynne House, a man named Weaver, the richest man in the county, was so enchanted with Gothic Revival motifs that his cemetery mausoleum uses them too.

▶ THOMAS GWYNNE HOUSE

MILLER-MOSGROVE HOUSE, 1842
323 Miami Street, Urbana
Private house

West of Monument Square, this is an unusually good brick house. According to John Bry, it's from an 1835 pattern book, *The Beauties of Architecture* by Minard Lafever (1798-1854), a New York architect whose books helped popularize Greek Revival. Bry calls this house one of the best Greek Revivals he's ever seen in Ohio, and he avers that it's well preserved inside and out. He especially admires a three-story spiral staircase in tiger maple.

Access: To see Urbana University, on Miami Street go several blocks west of Main and turn left/south where a sign points toward Dewey Avenue, which leads to College Way.

BAILEY HALL, 1853
William Russell West, Cincinnati
579 College Way, at the foot of College Way, Urbana, NRHP/Urbana College Historic Buildings
With adjacent Barclay Hall, now Johnny Appleseed Museum; check hours or by appointment; 937/484-1301

Originally the campus's only building, Bailey Hall is in a handsome Italian Villa style. The design was by one of the Statehouse architects, William Russell West, who three years later did the Greek Revival dormitory, Oak Hall. Urbana's prosperous Swedenborgian community, whose Protestant beliefs are akin to Lutheranism, founded Urbana University, which Bry describes as the world's first and only Swedenborgian institution of higher learning. Today the university retains some ties to the church, but is largely independent.

Access: Backtrack on College Way to Reynolds Street and drive a few blocks east to South Main.

SWEDENBORGIAN CHURCH, 1881

Rev. Frank Sewall, Urbana
330 South Main Street at Reynolds, Urbana
Swedenborgian church and wedding chapel; 937/653-6810

Rev. Frank Sewall was wearing many hats when he designed this limestone church for his congregation; he was also president of Urbana University. The story is that this church is a half-scale replica of one Sewall saw in Italy. It's built of limestone from Springfield, has round-arched windows and door, and has a square bell tower that, at 97 feet, 4 inches, is higher than the nave is long. Unlikely as it seems, the bell vanished in the 1950s. Glendale's Church of the New Jerusalem (see also, Vol. I) is also Swedenborgian.

West Liberty, Logan County

(Also in Logan County: Bellefontaine, to the north on

▶ MAC-A-CHEEK CASTLE

U.S. 68; between them, a tour of eccentric Americana. Loveland also has a castle.)

¶ The Piatt brothers, one a Civil War general, the other an iconoclastic newspaper editor, came home to West Liberty to build a pair of houses known ever since as the Piatt Castles. One is fancy on the outside; the other, on the inside.

Access: From U.S. 33 north of Marysville and south of Bellefontaine drive west on State Route 287. Both castles are a little east of West Liberty, Mac-o-Chee on the north side of 287 as it meets State Route 245. To reach Mac-a-Cheek, continue west on 245 for almost a mile; take first turn left/south at Township Road 47.

▶ Mac-o-Chee Castle

DONN PIATT HOUSE, MAC-O-CHEE, NOW MAC-O-CHEE CASTLE, 1881

John L. Smithmeyer, Washington, D.C. and William McCoy Piatt, West Liberty
State Route 245 at County Road 1, West Liberty, NRHP
House museum run with Mac-a-Cheek; fee for each house; open some hours
year-round except January and February; 937/465-2821

"There is a singular strain of contradiction in the Piatt blood," observed Henry Howe, who spent his life reporting on nineteenth-century Ohio. For instance, as Protestants the Piatts fled France to escape Catholic persecution, but in the then predominantly Protestant United States, they became Catholics. Then there was Benjamin Piatt, a Cincinnati judge who in 1826 moved his family to a log cabin and 1,700 acres near West Liberty. After making their own names, two of his children came back and built themselves houses here. Those houses, too, show "a singular strain of contradiction." ¶ Mac-o-Chee was actually the second of the two houses and, today, it has the more conventional interior and more unusual exterior. Flemish-inspired, enclosing the front of an earlier Gothic Revival cottage, the house looks exotic. Donn Piatt, a Washington editor who served at the U.S. legation in Paris, saw in France a castle he wanted to emulate in West Liberty. John Smithmeyer drew preliminary plans for him. Smithmeyer was an ill-fated Washington architect who devoted 15 years to the Library of Congress, then was fired and never paid. Though Smithmeyer did drawings for Piatt, the design was completed by the owner's nephew, William McCoy Piatt (1846-1927). ¶ Mac-o-Chee is best seen approached from the west on State Route 245; it looms in the distance, dominated by steep gables and a four-story tower. The stone trim is rough-cut, contrasting with smooth stone on walls. The interior has good woodwork and paneling, as well as wall and ceiling paintings by Oliver Frey, a Swiss artist who worked in both houses. ¶ While the other house has never left Piatt ownership, this one was sold five years after Donn's death in 1891. Later farm machinery was stored in the hall. When a buyer moved in in the 1940s, she brought her furniture by Palm Beach architect Addison Mizner. Her heirs sold house and furniture to Piatt descendants in 1956; it was opened as a museum in 1958. ¶ Mac-o-Chee is probably this guide's only house that's featured in a poem. James Whitcomb Riley, a friend and frequent guest here, wrote "Donn Piatt of Mac-o-Chee." It reads in part:

> Donn Piatt of Mac-o-chee!
> What a darling destiny
> Has been mine—to meet him there—
> Lolling in an easy chair ...

ABRAM SANDERS PIATT HOUSE, CHATEAU PIATT, NOW MAC-A-CHEEK CASTLE, 1871

10051 Township Road 47, West Liberty, NRHP
House museum run with Mac-o-Chee; fee for each house; open some hours year-round except January and February; 937/465-2821

Compared to Mac-o-Chee, this house's exterior may be more like that of other Victorians, but its interior is, so to speak, off the wall. In fact, along with chairs whose legs are cattle horns, Native American relics, glass doorknobs filled with mercury (they look like silver but never tarnish), this house has a folk paneling the likes of which you won't see anywhere else. It's a series of sharp triangular points as decoration over doors and bookcases in the library and office. They were designed by William McCoy Piatt, son and heir of this house's builder, General Abram Sanders Piatt; William also completed plans for Mac-o-Chee. He had no formal architectural training; his profession was inventing farm machinery. ¶ Some of the original interior woodwork includes wall paneling with a row of slender Gothic arches, in oak. The wood floors have inlaid stars, herringbone patterns, sunbursts. The house's wood all came from the property; similarly the rough-cut limestone was quarried here and installed in two-foot blocks. A four-story tower has a flared roof; mansard roofs with dormers encircle the house. A particularly rough section of the front wall was built that way, part of an enclosed greenhouse, the roughness providing holds for climbing plants. ¶ As early as 1919 the family was living in the servants' quarters and showing the rest of the house to tourists, but it really became an attraction in the 1950s, when Jim and Bill Piatt, great-grandsons of Abram, were living here with Bill's family. Piatts lived in Mac-a-Cheek until the 1980s.

West Union, Adams County

(The Serpent Mound, a world-class construction predating the focus of this book, is also in Adams County. Go north from West Union on State Route 41; turn left/west on State Route 73.)

¶ West Union's most imposing building is the Wilson Children's Home, 1884, designed by J.W. Yost; it's on Wilson Drive just south of State Routes 41/125 on the east side of town. Unfortunately, the Children's Home's central tower has lost its pointed roof above and the wooden porch in front of the entry below. For its most distinctive building, West Union relied on Saripta Woods, a merchant.

▶ TET WOODS BUILDING

Access: State Route 41 goes to West Union. One place to find 41, is from U.S. 50 southwest of Chillicothe.

TET WOODS BUILDING, 1914
Attributed to Tet Woods, West Union, NRHP
307 Main Street/State Routes 41 and 125, near Cherry Street, West Union

When he was passing through West Union, Doug Graf spotted this exotic glass-fronted store; there's just nothing like it anywhere, though Graf likens it to Dodds Monuments, 1905, in downtown Xenia (see also). Both are three-story commercial/apartment buildings with glass and balustraded balconies in front. Graf describes the Tet Woods Building as "naive but inventive." He says it's as if the design were based on verbal models that the builder wasn't quite sure how to realize. ¶ Saripta M. Woods—"Tet" was her nickname—was a businesswoman who started out modestly in West Union, selling hats; by 1900, a county historian described her store as "one of the most fashionable millinery emporiums in Adams County." Fourteen years later, she needed a larger place of business for a full line of dry goods; this building was her solution. Mostly of block, it has glass windows in front on the first and second floors, and a roofed porch with a balustrade on the third floor. That top floor was originally an apartment with lacy wooden partitions shown in Stephen Kelley's book, *Landmarks of West Union.*

❡ It's possible to look in the windows and see what was once the shop. A U-shaped second-floor balcony runs the length of the building, overlooking the main floor; decorative columns provide support. Older residents told Kelley that Tet Woods designed the building herself, incorporating design details she admired. (It may have helped also that her brother-in-law was a builder.) Her own house, similarly quirky but less ambitious, is number 503 on North Street (two blocks north of Main) at the southeast corner of the Boyd Avenue intersection. ❡ The daughter of a physician, Tet Woods was born nearby in Wamsley, and came to town about 1890. So reports West Union genealogist Hazel Roush. When Woods died in 1929, her obituary called her store "one of the most magnificent buildings in this part of the country." It later housed a Singer sewing-machine outlet. A more recent owner dubbed it a Victorian Social Club, where the socializing was illicit and landed the owner in prison. Its reputation thus sullied locally, the Tet Woods Building languishes, unused and declining—in late 2001 many second-floor windows were broken.

Wilmington, Clinton County
(Also nearby: Xenia, north on U.S. 68.)

❡ Twenty and thirty years ago, Wilmington was the sort of Ohio town that attracted a small but noticeable influx of people from other places, even from out-of-state. The place had many advantages. While set amid farm fields, Wilmington wasn't all that far from Cincinnati, Dayton or Columbus. It was a college town, home of Wilmington College. It had a pretty and bustling red-brick downtown stretched along South Street, where the focal point, fittingly, was the stone Neoclassical Clinton County Courthouse (1919, by Weber, Werner & Adkins). And the city had good older residential areas and interesting byways, like the 20-acre arboretum near the hospital. ❡ As in most Ohio towns, toward the end of the twentieth century Wilmington preservationists had good days and bad. On the good side, the splendid Murphy Theatre was rescued from abandonment and refurbished in the late 1980s and early 1990s. The courthouse was restored, all the better to show off its impressive three-story central hall. But at the same time, during just 10 years, nearly a dozen downtown buildings were razed and not re-placed—for a while downtown itself seemed in jeopardy. Then at the turn of the new century, in an about face, a new mayor, David Raizk, came into city hall, and by

▶ MURPHY THEATRE, SAMUEL WALKER NEXT BUILDING AT LEFT

2002 Wilmington was even trying to launch a Main Street Program. ¶ The hope was, not just to keep downtown vital, but also to put some sparkle back into its daily life. The hope is, to keep Wilmington the kind of small town people want to move to. And live in.

Access: From I-71 take State Route 73 east into Wilmington. In town 73 becomes Main Street/U.S. 22 eastbound, and passes the buildings below.

SAMUEL WALKER MEMORIAL BUILDING, 1914, REHAB 1996
64 West Main Street, Wilmington, NRHP/Wilmington Commercial HD
Restaurant, banquet facilities; 937/383-6664

The Samuel Walker Memorial Building is an unusually good downtown commercial building, built with money authorized by the will of one Samuel Walker. What Walker really wanted was a museum and library

funded by rent from a ground-floor commercial tenant. But by the time the will had been contested, with some success, Andrew Carnegie had assured Wilmington a library. Thus it happened that for 72 years, rent collected from the furniture store in the Walker Building went to the Carnegie library. In recent years a developer named Jeff Borton updated the building and put in a restaurant and banquet facilities. Brick with terra cotta tiles, the two-story building's facade has three large arched windows upstairs, and even larger rectangular windows downstairs.

MURPHY THEATRE, 1918
Dittoe Fahnestock Ferber, Cincinnati
50 West Main Street, Wilmington, NRHP/Wilmington Commercial HD
Theater run by community non-profit; performance series; 937/382-3643

The son of an immigrant Irish plasterer who settled in nineteenth-century Wilmington, Charles W. Murphy grew up and moved beyond plastering and beyond his home town to make his fortune in Chicago. He did so well that from 1906-1914 he owned the Chicago Cubs as they won four pennants and two World Series. After he'd sold the Cubs in the mid-1910s, Murphy began to think in terms of what he could do for Wilmington. He decided to build a theater. Not an ordinary theater, but a splendid one.
¶ Construction material came in 175 railroad cars; Italian artisans spent

weeks finishing the interior woodwork, the molded ceiling, and proscenium arch; a decorator came from Chicago. The outside was brick with terra cotta trim, round-arched windows, a bracketed cornice, and the name Murphy painted on the back wall in letters big enough to be seen from the railroad. Saying that it would be his monument, Murphy named the theater for himself. He spent $250,000 on it; in a town of just 5,000 people, it had 1,000 seats. On opening night three performances were sold out, and another 3,000 people were turned away. The manager was Charles Murphy's brother Frank, who'd opened the town's first movie theater in 1907. ¶ The Murphy was an all-purpose theater: vaudeville, drama, high-school graduations, movies. In the 1940s it acquired its Art Moderne marquee. In the early 1980s it closed, and in the late 1980s a community group took over, and volunteers starting painting all the plaster flowers and fillips. The biggest rehab boost came from Columbia Pictures, which was in town filming *Lost in Yonkers* in 1992. In search of perfect period backgrounds, the movie company redid the Murphy's lobby by pulling the carpet off the terrazzo floor, painting, fixing the chandeliers, and redoing the marquee.

Xenia, Greene County

(Also nearby: Wilmington, south on U.S. 68.)
¶ Xenia has a prominent stone courthouse (1900, by Cincinnati's Samuel Hannaford & Sons), a good assortment of old houses (for example, see East Second Street), and, on the south side of town, the lovely hilltop campus of a one-time orphanage. The single most exceptional building is a business downtown.

Access: From I-70, take U.S. 68 south. Dodds Monuments is two blocks west of the courthouse on Main Street/U.S. 35 Business.

DODDS MONUMENTS, 1903, 1906
123 West Main Street/U.S. 35 Business, Xenia
Private commercial building; grave monument showroom open during business hours; 937/372-4408

Originally, this structure was built in St. Louis for the 1904 world's fair. The seven apartments upstairs housed fair workers, while the first floor provided exhibit space. When George Dodds, a granite merchant from Xenia, heard the building was to be demolished after the fair, he bought it to take home and use as his company headquarters. Distance was no problem. Dodds had the building dismantled and its parts catalogued and loaded onto 15 railroad cars. During the next two years the whole thing was reassembled in Xenia. ¶ Not surprisingly, George Dodds was no ordinary stone merchant, for in 1906 his company, founded in 1864, was the world's leading granite retailer. With three quarries in Vermont and branch offices in Chicago, New York, and St. Louis, Dodds provided stone for

▶ Dodds Monuments

architectural landmarks like McKim, Mead & White's Boston Public Library and H.H. Richardson's Allegheny County Courthouse in Pittsburgh. ¶ This history of Dodds Monuments comes from Eric Fogarty, who has owned the company since 1984. When Fogarty came along the quarries and branch offices were long gone, but the gravestone business remained—the preparation and customizing of granite memorials. After the tornado of 1974, Dodds Monuments was Xenia's westernmost building still standing—everything beyond it had been leveled; that's why the town's western edge all looks relatively new. As for Dodds Monuments, it lost only some colored glass and wooden

▶ Dodds DETAIL

balusters. ¶ To say the least, this building is unusual. Most detailing is on the facade, where the first floor has large windows and paired columns; the second and third floors have bay windows on both sides and long balustraded balconies in front of windows in the middle. The 20-foot high showroom is on the west side, at the front. The other side has two stories of offices tucked into the same space, plus an opening that leads back to an air shaft. Most of the siding is limestone; the cornice is metal; stone is polished black granite and red sandstone. ¶ Ohio State's Douglas Graf compares Dodds Monuments to the Tet Woods Building, 1914, in West Union (see also). Both are three-story commercial/apartment buildings with glass and balustrades in front.

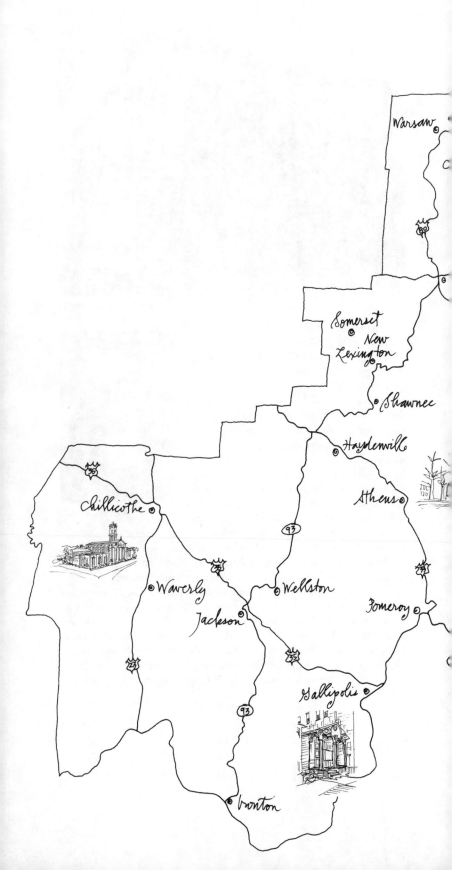

Warsaw

Somerset
New
Lexington

Shawnee

Haydenville

Athens

Chillicothe

93

Waverly

Wellston

Jackson

Pomeroy

23

Gallipolis

93

Ironton

Zoar

77

850

Cadiz

Freeport

Morristown

70

Bethesda

Barnesville

800

Pleasant City

77

Woodsfield

800

Archers Fork

80

Marietta

Southeast Ohio

Southeast Ohio is hill country, where in places relief reaches 600 to 800 feet. It is the only part of Ohio never covered by glaciers, which rearranged the rivers anyway. One result was the Ohio River, which twists along in its canyon, etching state boundaries. Another is that some rivers—including the Licking, the Hocking, and the Scioto—rise in plains and then, in a seemingly contrary way, flow through hills. ¶ To the architectural eye of Ohio State University's Douglas Graf, Southeast Ohio's hills seem "claustrophobic". A church, or even the Meigs County Courthouse, nestled at the foot of a hill is a common sight, while towers that can be seen from a distance, like Pleasant City's St. Michael's Byzantine Catholic Church or the courthouses of Belmont and Perry Counties, become the exception rather than the rule. ¶ Southeast Ohio was the first part of the state to be settled and today, is the least densely populated. It has no cities. Excepting especially the valleys of rivers past and present, it has the state's poorest soil, so farmers moved on, abandoning their holdings, and forests grew back. Now in places Southeast Ohio is as close to wilderness as Ohio gets; sometimes, the lonely landscape on the way to a building—like the house at Archers Fork, or Ourant

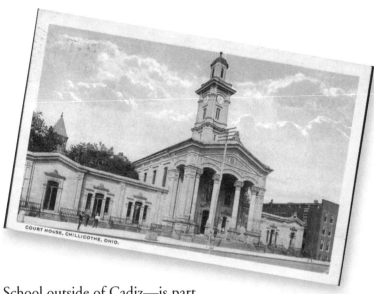

COURT HOUSE, CHILLICOTHE, OHIO.

School outside of Cadiz—is part
of seeing it. And architectural destinations
include towns that almost everyone has left. ¶ Of the ten
counties with highest unemployment rates in late 2001,
six were in Southeast Ohio. Poor though the region is
now, at some time or other in the past every county had
money. Some came from oil, iron, or railroads; more
came from coal—in 200 years Ohio produced 3 billion
tons of coal (mostly high-sulfur)——transmuted into the
still-surviving grand houses of mine owners. And some
money came from high-quality clay, typically found in
underground seams just below coal. Such clay made
decorative tiles for courthouse floors and still yields
elegant red roof tiles made in New Lexington. It permitted Haydenville, founded as a company town for a tile
producer, where some houses still flaunt their decoration
in sewer tiles. ¶ Southeast Ohio also had its full share of
enlightenment. The first settlement, by the Ohio Company at Marietta, provided such a good example of how
to establish a frontier community, that it set a pattern for
development west of the Alleghenies. Athens has the first
college building in the Northwest Territory, Ohio
University's Cutler Hall. And then there are towns, like
McConnelsville, Chillicothe, and Barnesville: places so
interesting that they deserve to be destinations.

▶ WAERNICKE HOUSE

Archers Fork, Washington County
(Also in Washington County: Marietta.)

Access: The easy route is to drive northeast of Marietta on State Route 7, which follows the Ohio River; 20 miles later, at Wade, turn north on County 14; drive 3.8 miles and turn right onto Township 36, which reaches the house in 1.4 miles. The country route is to take jiggly State Route 26 northeast from I-77 just above Marietta; at Dart turn right/south on County 14, which intersects Township 36 1.4 miles from house, as above; turn left.

WAERNICKE HOUSE, 1864
Independence Township Road 36, Archers Fork, NRHP
Private house, clearly visible from road

Part of seeing this house is finding it. The roads are narrow and windy, through lots of scrub forest; taking the long approach via State Route 26 will give you the feeling you've reached the beyond of beyond. Then the road bridges Archers Fork and suddenly a large brick house jumps into view. The sight is astonishing. The second thing I saw was also a surprise. Convinced that I was a thousand miles from anywhere, I was taking some pictures when a car pulled up and a woman, then the house's owner, and her four children tumbled out. She said she was just coming back from taking her son to soccer practice. Archers Fork is not really so far as it seems. The house, built by an immigrant German tobacco grower named Ernst Waernicke, has two-and-a-half stories, gable ends, a sandstone foundation, and size: it's 54 feet wide, 40 feet deep. The front door is partly hidden by a white wooden porch with latticework forming bell-shaped arches between the posts. Inside, the first and second floors both have four very large corner rooms, most with fireplaces. Also on the property, facing the street at the side, is the old Hille Store, c. 1875, a busy place in the tobacco and oil eras.

Athens, Athens County

(Haydenville, a little to the north off U.S. 33, makes a companion tour.)

❡ Before Mary Anne Reeves took a job there in 1984, she had never heard of Athens, Ohio. She herself grew up in Litchfield, Connecticut; and after earning a master's in history and art at Florida State University, she came to Athens as a regional rep for the Ohio Historic Preservation Office. So imagine her surprise, when she learned that the people who settled Athens were from Litchfield County, Connecticut, just as she is. In Athens's State Street cemetery, she recognizes names of families she knew growing up—she's sure they're the same families, because she's researched it. Though her part of Connecticut has become suburban since she moved away, Athens, with its hills and farms, has brought her full circle. It's like the Litchfield County of her childhood. ❡ I met Mary Anne Reeves on my first trip to Athens in pursuit of buildings, in 1994. Though in 2000 the Preservation Office closed its regional branches and she's taken a midweek job in Columbus, she still lives in Athens, and her knowledge of southeast Ohio is profound. She was the first person to tell me about many of the buildings in this guide, like Barnesville's Presbyterian Church, or the Lock Keeper's House in Marietta, or the town of Shawnee in Perry County. But the very first place on her list, the one she talked about the longest, was the Athens Lunatic Asylum, an array of buildings now called The Ridges. Later that day she drove me up the hill so that I could see for myself. She was right. It is an amazing place.

Access: To reach the Ohio University campus, exit from U.S. 33/U.S. 50 at State Route 682 North, on the south side of Athens. At the traffic light turn right/north onto Richland Avenue, and at the second light, turn left onto Court Street. At the second intersection turn right onto Washington Street; in first block you'll come to the Athens City Parking Garage, where you can free yourself of your car. (These complicated directions are those Ohio University gives out. Navigating Athens is not for the fainthearted.) Walk back, or south, one block to College Green at Court and Union Streets. The university's three old buildings are the Green's focal point; Galbreath Chapel is next to them.

▶ CUTLER HALL

COLLEGE EDIFICE, NOW CUTLER HALL, 1818, NHL, NRHP/CAMPUS GREEN HD

Benjamin Corp, Marietta
East Wing, now Wilson Hall, 1837, NRHP/Campus Green HD
West Wing, now McGuffey Hall, 1839, NRHP/Campus Green HD
Ohio University office buildings

It is wonderful to walk across the green toward Ohio University's three old red brick buildings; they make such a lovely ensemble that a university logo features a picture of them. They form a U at the top of the hill, with the oldest and tallest Cutler Hall in the center, flanked at right angles by Wilson and McGuffey. With their stepped gables, Wilson and McGuffey have the looks, but Cutler has the history: it was the first college building in the Northwest Territory. It's had many alterations since, including elevating the roof by three feet in 1883 and lowering the roof by three feet in 1947. Manasseh Cutler was a university co-founder; William Holmes McGuffey, whose reading texts schooled generations of Americans, and Robert Wilson were presidents. Don't bother to go inside these venerables, unless you wonder what a modern office building looks like.

GALBREATH MEMORIAL CHAPEL, 1958

Perry, Shaw, and Hepburn, Boston; and Kehoe and Dean, Boston
Chapel space for university meetings, lectures, weddings; open daily except Saturdays and July; 740/593-2722

Galbreath Chapel is a post-World War II essay in historic allusions—Ohio State's Douglas Graf dubs it "proto Post Modern." The chapel is small, seating only 150, and

▶ CHAPEL INTERIOR

octagonal; the interior, in off-white with brown, has an elegant simplicity, though in winter 1997 it was altered somewhat to accommodate a large organ. Red brick outside, the chapel has a white porch with four Doric columns. Above, a conical spire rises over the cupola, which has an Ionic colonnade encircling windows that provide light for the interior.

Graf says the chapel combines Georgian brick and simplicity with a "French Enlightenment cupola filtered through English lenses to make it palatable to Americans. It's way out of step with the 1950s but it's creative and provocative." He suggests comparing it to another college chapel of the same time: St. Stephen's Episcopal Church, 1953, at Ohio State University in Columbus (see also, Vol. I). This chapel is a memorial to Helen Mauck Galbreath, John Galbreath's first wife, whom he married in 1920 and who died in 1949. He was a poor country boy working his way through Ohio University when he met Helen Mauck, the daughter of a Gallipolis judge; he was a dishwasher at her sorority. According to legend, their first kiss was at the place where the chapel now stands.

▶ GALBREATH CHAPEL

Galbreath went on to become hugely rich through real-estate investments; Columbus-based, he also owned the Pittsburgh Pirates and two Kentucky Derby winners.

POSTON HOUSE, NOW PRESIDENT'S HOUSE, 1899
29 Park Place, Athens, NRHP/Campus Green HD
Ohio University president's house; not open to the public

Down the hill behind Cutler Hall, the college president occupies the manse of a one-time coal baron. The brick has been painted buff; trim is white; a red-tile Ludowici-Celadon roof protects it all. Starting in 1994, the new president's wife, René Glidden, herself stripped white paint from the oak stairway inside.

Access: To drive to the Ridges from the city garage downtown, take Washington Street west one block to Congress; turn left/south and continue south onto Richland Avenue as far as State Route 682. Turn right there; in a quarter mile, turn left and drive uphill to the Ridges.

ATHENS LUNATIC ASYLUM, NOW THE RIDGES, OHIO UNIVERSITY, NRHP

The road winds through the woods and up the hill, and then suddenly at the crest the woods recede and a panorama of immense

▶ ASYLUM ADMINISTRATION BUILDING

brick buildings appears. It is a sight unique in Ohio: the state's only surviving nineteenth-century hospital complex. Originally run as a self-sufficient farm, it represents an era when all state institutions were so grandiose. ¶ For about 75 years the asylum was Athens' most important institution, for until after World War II, Ohio University was just a small school. Patients always outnumbered students, hospital staff outnumbered faculty, and the superintendent was much better known locally than the university president. But like all mental hospitals, by the 1980s the one in Athens had shrunk, while the university had grown. As a symbol of the transfer of power, the university and the hospital made a swap early in the 1990s. The hospital got land in town for a new facility, and the university got The Ridges. ¶ The Ridges has different types of buildings from different eras—they reflect changing theories on how to care for the mentally ill—so the sprawling asylum also provides architectural variety. It began with the whole asylum under one expansive roof, that of the vast central Administration Building, with its setback residential wings. Dining-hall and other additions multiplied later at the rear; even farther back farm and service buildings went up. At the turn of the century the cottage plan introduced separate buildings for smaller groups of patients; five of those here were designed by Columbus architect Frank L. Packard. ¶ What the university got at The Ridges were two dozen or so buildings and 600,000 square feet of space, mostly in reasonable condition; one third are now again in use. One cottage has become a research center, and two others will house the library of George Voinovich, alumnus, U.S. senator and former governor; the auditorium is a dance facility; the medical hospital, a business incubator; and planner John Kotowski has his office in a one-time geriatrics building. He insists the university expects to use still more of the space. And as of early 2000, all they'd torn down was a hog house. ¶ What the university didn't get was the landscaping that traditionally surrounded state institutions. Here the gardens, laid out in the 1870s, included 72 different trees and shrubs; the four man-made lakes had three man-made islands. They were all lost when a 1968 flood control project changed the course of the Hocking River. ¶ Although Ohio University owned The Ridges when I first met preservationist Mary Anne Reeves in 1994, she was worried about its future; today, she is much more hopeful. She was pleased that the Voinovich papers would be housed at The Ridges. She'd been impressed when 50 people turned out for a talk she gave on asylum history. And an even bigger crowd filled the Auditorium when an architect from Albany, New York spoke on rehabbing more of the Administration Building. John G. Waite proposed, for one, reopening a second- and third-floor auditorium. He also suggested tearing out added ducts and relying instead on the ventilation channels originally built into the walls.

ATHENS LUNATIC ASYLUM ADMINISTRATION BUILDING, NOW LIN HALL, 1874

Levi T. Scofield, Cleveland; 1990s rehab by Glaser Associates, Cincinnati
Kennedy Museum of American Art, gallery; weekday hours; 740/593-1304

When you look at this Administration Building, you can easily believe that it took six years to build. It was 853 feet long, over 60 feet deep, and used 18.5 million bricks, all made on site, and then put together to reemerge in High Victorian Gothic. Besides bricks the building has structural steel, which was

advanced for the time. And of course it has wood in, say, the heavy brackets in the eaves, which alternate with frieze windows that can barely be seen from the ground. The building's taller middle section has its towers intact, plus an elaborate iron porch added in the 1890s. Today the Kennedy Museum of American Art occupies the renovated ground floor of the central

▶ LIN HALL, INTERIOR

section. Fortunately, the museum also did some restoration, so the hall, with its tile-and-marble floor and high round-arch doorways, looks very good indeed. It's possible to drive around this building, to see the additions at the back (a couple are octagonal) and adjacent cottages.

AUDITORIUM, 1901
E.O. Fallis, Toledo
The Ridges, Athens

The auditorium is the first building a visitor sees at the top of the hill, and a handsome Neoclassical structure it is. Red brick with white trim, it has columns on the front and a round green dome on top. E.O. Fallis was one of Toledo's best architects in his day. How fortunate for The Ridges, that state contracts attracted such talents.

Access: From the Ridges return to Richland Avenue and turn right/ south; drive to U.S. 33/Pomeroy Road and turn left; drive uphill to Longview Heights Road and turn left; at three-way stop stay left; at Y junction stay right on Longview Heights. Fellowship, on left and not visible from road, has sign marking driveway.

UNITARIAN FELLOWSHIP, 1971
John Spofforth, brick sculptor, Athens
184 Longview Heights Road, Athens
Unitarian fellowship hall; 740/592-2083

At first glance, the Unitarian Fellowship is a commonplace contemporary building, a 30- by 60-foot rectangle, two-and-a-half stories, with a gable roof. But a closer look reveals that it is not commonplace at all, for the walls, especially the long side wall facing the parking lot, are works of art in brick. Fellowship members built this structure themselves to economize; it just happened that one of them was John Spofforth, who is the country's only combination artist-construction bricklayer. ¶ "A few of us artist types had romantic ideas," recalls Bob Borchard, who was one of the builders and is now a retired Ohio University faculty artist. "But the economics types gave us a square box. Then we got John Spofforth in." The economics types planned a low-cost block building with metal sheathing. Artist/mason Spofforth built the rectangular block building, but he went on to sheathe it artistically, in brick laid in wavy patterns that were to become his signature. ¶ Borchard and another artist, a university colleague named Cliff McCarthy, made other contributions. McCarthy did a wall painting inside and wooden balconies outside, while Borchard covered the two front doors in metal. He applied the metal—discarded newspaper aluminum offset plates on the inside and salvage copper outside—to wooden forms and then hammered it all together with 28,762 brass-coated nails. Borchard and McCarthy also made the two dozen irregularly placed stained glass windows. Small round tunnels through the block and brick wall, with abstract patterns in colored glass at the outer end, the windows are similar in concept to ones Swiss architect LeCorbusier used in Europe. Here the tunnels are 16- to 18-inch long ceramic sewer pipe sections painted white inside. The colored glass, which was set in a plastic resin, was cull from a West Virginia glass plant. At night, when the building is lighted inside, the windows become blobs of color floating in the darkness.

▶ UNITARIAN FELLOWSHIP

Bricklayer Artist—The Brick Institute of America lists 22 brick sculptors, says John Spofforth, who is one of them. The other 21 all carve soft green brick before it's fired; usually then a mason constructs their design. But so far as Spofforth knows, he is the only one who at once builds and sculpts with bricks. He invented what he does, but he didn't come upon it precipitously, for at the time he was 40 years old. Though for 17 years he'd thought of himself as an artist, at 40 he was at a crossroads. He could become a photographer—he'd already worked as one; he'd studied photography—or he could try something completely new, with bricks. The Unitarian Fellowship gave him just the opportunity he needed, to become America's only bricklayer artist.

Now, a quarter century later, Spofforth has done about 75 brick sculptures, half near Athens and the others scattered around the eastern United States. The Unitarian Fellowship remains his largest work, though in 1976 he also did a house on the main street of The Plains, a village near Athens. One thing about the kind of brick sculpture Spofforth does, is that a viewer who's not already there has to travel to see it. It's always installed on site, and it's always permanent, at least potentially. Another thing is that brick sculpting is not a profession casually acquired. Not only did Spofforth spend seven years studying fine arts, he spent 11 working as a mason and bricklayer; he started as an apprentice right out of high school. By the time he worked on the Fellowship, he was a highly skilled craftsman. That was essential. Understanding the medium's potential put him in control.

Doing the Fellowship was a course of artistic discovery. He put up the block building the first year, 1969. The next year he laid the brick for the first floor on the ends of the building, the front and the back, and on the far side. That year, he was only moderately adventurous. He jutted out some bricks to play with shadows; he started building bulges and rounding corners. But in 1971 he had the breakthrough, the insights that brought him closer to his own artistic vision. The moment is in the soaring wave of bricks above the front doors. Then he conceived the idea of a "continuous line" that would obliterate the rectangle. So at the second-floor level and on all the parking-lot wall, the brick patterns became fluid and organic. They realized possibilities that no one else had ever imagined for brick.

Spofforth is particular about his materials—only sand-mold bricks will do. Wherever he is going to work, he first has to find a nearby brick plant that makes them, as not every one does. They are described as "handmade," which means they're shaped in wooden forms filled and leveled by hand. The forms are dusted with sand beforehand, to give the finished bricks a sandy surface texture. But for Spofforth the sand-mold brick's most important feature is that it is solid and uncored, so he can cut it to fit in a design. In the Unitarian Fellowship he used 35,000 bricks made in Galena. They are multi-colored: red, tan, brown, and purple. The mortar is red, applied in joints of a consistent width, a sign of good brickwork. He tooled a line into the mortar. That, Spofforth says, draws the eye to the mortar as well as to the brick.

People who worked on the Unitarian Fellowship still remember a hapless building inspector who showed up during construction. First he saw all the holes in the long wall—holes prepared for round colored-glass windows. "My God, it's terrible," the inspector said. "The vandalism you've had already." Once those had been explained, and the inspector was satisfied that the holes didn't undermine structural integrity, he went around to the back wall and saw the chimney Spofforth had built; again he was calling "My God." The chimney's in a mode the artist descriptively dubs "molten-wax." Spofforth assured the inspector the chimney wasn't collapsing. He explained how the chimney was supported, and the inspector went away reassured. Spofforth had enough experience that, he says, "I knew what I could and could not do." He supported his work with metal rods, wire mesh, and cantilevering.

Such devices enabled him to do the long parking-lot wall, the building's best. Here the patterns seem to move; lines of brick flow in and out, up and down, forming bulges, waves, arcs. And they eschew sharp corners. When viewed from the driveway, the corner between the front wall and the long wall is meant to seem to disappear. "It looks like one flat surface rather than one with a corner sticking at you," Spofforth says. "The corner flattens out." This stolid material was coming alive, creating illusions. Spofforth was elated.

Besides, as well laid brick, it will last.

▶ BRADFIELD BUILDING

Barnesville, Belmont County

(Also in area: Woodsfield south on State
Route 800, Bethesda east on State Route 149,
Morristown north of Bethesda on County
Road 26.)

¶ Barnesville has several uncommon features: a busy
downtown; Olney Friends School, which is a small
Quaker boarding high school; a Quaker meetinghouse;
and, amid a good collection of Victorian houses, two
buildings that are shoo-ins for a state-wide architectural
guide. ¶ At 1,309 feet above sea level, Barnesville is the
highest incorporated town in Ohio; it used to brag about
being the "high" in the middle of Ohio. This fact comes
from Bruce Yarnall, who spent five years there as preservation officer and then another two as editor of the
Barnesville *Enterprise*. Population, now about 4,200,
peaked with the 5,002 people counted in 1940. Then
when the town fathers found out that a municipality of
over 5,000 had to become a city with a paid fire department, they deannexed two houses and four residents.

**Access: From I-70 take State Route 800 south to Barnesville, in which
that highway is called Chestnut Street. Call Belmont County Tourism
for brochures, 740/695-4359.**

GEORGE E. HUNT HOUSE, C. 1895

George Franklin Barber, Knoxville
402 North Chestnut Street, opposite Cherry Street, Barnesville,
NRHP/Barnesville HD
Private house

Victorian house expert Craig Bobby of Lakewood lists Barnesville's George E.
Hunt House as one of his Ohio favorites by mail-order architect George
Franklin Barber, who was based in Tennessee.

FIRST PRESBYTERIAN CHURCH, 1903

Frank L. Packard, Columbus
124 North Chestnut Street, NRHP/Barnesville HD
Presbyterian church; open during office hours weekday mornings, or by
appointment; group tours may be arranged for a small fee, 740/425-3144

This church is so wonderful, so exuberant, that the first time I saw it, it took
my breath away. Imagine how my delight grew when I learned that Ohio has
four similar churches and a fifth that is somewhat similar. All were built of
the same splendid and distinctive red sandstone from a Mansfield quarry. In
it red predominates, but other colors—browns, greens, tans, grays, golds,
pinks—appear as well, turning Ohio State's Doug Graf into an enthusiastic
admirer. "There aren't many buildings," he says, "where you can stand a foot

from the wall and just be
enchanted." That's partly
because, though from a
distance the stone looks red,
the polychromy emerges as
you go closer. So does
weather modeling of the
relatively soft stone. "It keeps
on carving itself," says Graf.
Ohio's four similar churches
were all completed between
1900 and 1903, when this
Arts and Crafts design was
clearly the concept of the
hour; it's distinctive with
flared eaves, exaggerated
buttresses, and Gothic arches
combined with a pagoda-
roofed tower. Though the
four churches look like
siblings they were designed
by three different architects.

▶ FIRST PRESBYTERIAN CHURCH

Perhaps it's not surprising that Columbus's Frank L. Packard, who at his
death in 1923 was credited with an astounding 3,400 buildings, was involved
with two, this one in Barnesville and another in Upper Sandusky. Inside this
sanctuary is on an octagonal Akron Plan; woodwork is oak; windows are of
Belgian stained glass. The two other red-stone Arts and Crafts churches in
this guide are in Napoleon (Northwest) and Dayton (Vol. I).

BRADFIELD BUILDING, NOW WESBANCO, 1891

101 East Main Street at Chestnut Street, Barnesville, NRHP/Barnesville HD
Bank

This three-story Richardsonian Romanesque building is downtown
Barnesville's largest, fanciest commercial and office block. Originally it
housed the First National Bank of Barnesville in the corner rooms, and the
Bradfield family's dry goods store on the eastern side. In the 1930s the store
became a five-and-dime that survived until 1992, when WesBanco bought
the bank and the building. Fortunately WesBanco restored the facade—upper

windows had been
boarded up; and the
stone was so dark that
no one realized it was
a rose sandstone.
Rough-cut and carved,
the stone is used here
with red brick. The
roof line has a fine
parapet, turrets, and a
gable above the
original store.
WesBanco redid the
dime-store windows
with a modern facing
in red brick and glass.
This wonderful
building is a happy
surprise, but so is the
fact that a Bradfield
was associated with
the bank from 1865,
when John Bradfield
founded it, until
1996, when C.J. (Joe)
Bradfield retired. Joe,
John's great-grandson,
was the fourth family
member to serve as
president of the bank,
though, as he points

▶ BRADFIELD BUILDING

out, not all the presidents were Bradfields. Joe's son is a banker too, but in
North Carolina. How did Barnesville prosper? It was a stop on the B & O
line from Pittsburgh to Columbus (the Prairie style depot has been
refurbished for reuse); it had a strong merchant class; it had factories that
made mining cars, paper, shoes, glass, and clothing. And of course, it had the
First National Bank of Barnesville. After World War II the economy relied on
coal mining, which has virtually ceased since 1981.

To see more in Barnesville: The 1878 Stillwater Meetinghouse, a
Quaker building still in use, is on Sandy Ridge Road off State Route
147 just east of town (740/425-2776).

The Avenue, Epworth Park, Bethesda, O.
Pub. by Harrison's

Bethesda

(Also in area: Barnesville.)

¶ Bethesda is a very small town, but it definitely has a downtown, which is on Main Street, a quarter mile south of Epworth Park.

Access: From Barnesville take State Route 147/East Main Street east to Bethesda; in town, turn right/south on County 26/Main Street.

EPWORTH PARK, C. 1875-1925

Main Street, Bethesda

Privately owned summer campground; open April-November; tour on foot after parking near entrance, or in lot behind adjacent Methodist Church, or in downtown Bethesda; festival weekend in July; for information call United Methodist Church office in St. Clairsville, 740/695-0155

Of Ohio's three surviving summertime chautauqua communities, the largest and best known is Ottawa County's Lakeside (see also), where nineteenth- and early twentieth-century cottages, a hotel and auditorium are still in use. A second, near Lancaster, has a still-standing but unused hotel; its cottages have been greatly altered. Epworth Park is the third. All three have lovely natural sites; Epworth Park's is hilly, wooded terrain with a pond; with the 59 small frame cottages, it is a charming place. Typical camp meeting cottages, these are gable-front frame structures with first- and second-floor porches in front. Though some have decorative carving in the gables, and some have an arched fanlight over the second-floor porch door, the architectural impact comes from the ensemble—the rows of porch-on-porch houses in the lovely, woodsy setting. ¶ Epworth Park began in 1870 as a church camp with tents; by 1879, 40 permanent cottages had been built; the number peaked at 95 in 1924. Right next door to the Methodist Church—chautauquas were predominantly Methodist—Epworth Park had a wooden auditorium and a hotel. In 1961 the auditorium was replaced by a steel shed; in 1965 the hotel

▶ Epworth Park

was razed; by the 1970s it was almost a ghost town. ¶ Recently a July festival has drawn as many as 2,000 people, and the owners association has actively encouraged rehabbers. Bruce Yarnall was one. Before he left Belmont County for Columbus in 1996, Yarnall was co-owner of a cottage he bought for $450 in 1990. The low price was conditional on his making repairs, which escalated to $16,000—oak supports had rotted, so the cottage's rear sagged 28 inches below the front. Ultimately repaired and painted, it looked bright as a fine morning. It has a corner bay just big enough for the windows on its three sides. ¶ For Yarnall, the cottage was just one of seven properties he acquired to save. Three were in his home town, Somerton, which is also where Yarnall got his start in history. Between the ages of 13 and 31, he wrote the 645-page *Somerton Area Heritage: The History of Somerset and Wayne Townships, Belmont County, Ohio, Including the Villages of Boston, New Castle, Somerton and Temperanceville*. If you wonder how two remote and hilly townships that never had a combined population as high as 2,000, accumulated 645 pages of history, the book is available at the OHS library.

▶ OURANT SCHOOL

Cadiz, Harrison County

(This tour includes two rural places, a school and a barn. This guide has three old rural schools—all very different—in this region; others are in Southington and Peninsula, both listed with Northeast Ohio.)

¶ At its highest point, Cadiz has the Harrison County Courthouse, 1895, a fine stone building by Yost & Packard, well maintained. When I first saw it in the 1980s, the courthouse had an adjacent cottage built of coal and used as a tourist information office. Of course, a house of coal was a celebratory thing; it honored the source of the county's wealth, the mineral that helped populate the place. ¶ But in 1995, in conjunction with a courthouse renovation, the house of coal was taken down and fell apart in the process. Why take down a unique building that was so special, so true to the place? Partly, it seems, it may have been a misguided take on historic restoration, for it wasn't part of the original courthouse. But, given the virtual demise of the Ohio coal industry, perhaps the coal house's collapse was also a truth.

¶ Harrison County has two exceptional rural buildings that provide a back-of-beyond tour: the one-room Ourant School in Freeport Township west of Cadiz and a polygonal barn near Freeport in the county's southwest corner.

Access: Cadiz is at the junction of U.S. 22 and 250 and State Route 9. Ourant School is west of Cadiz off County 2/Deersville Ridge Road. From the west side of Cadiz, County 2 is accessible at U.S. 250/U.S. 22 intersection; drive west; Ourant Road is fifth left; school will be on right.

OURANT SCHOOL, 1873

Ourant Road, Nottingham Township, near Cadiz, NRHP
Former one-room school now maintained by alumni

Ourant School is in a place so rural, so isolated, that being there reveals what a small country school was all about. It's an old, one-room school, white frame with a red metal roof and a bell cupola athwart the gable. Though the school closed in 1941, the building still exists because alumni and then their children have been meeting for reunions since 1945. In the early 1990s they undertook restorations—including securing the building on its foundation, replacing the roof, and fixing the bell—that came to over $23,300. The inside was fixed up too. If you look in the windows you'll see the desks, blackboard, and new tin ceiling. One reunion not long ago brought back Golda Rose McMullen, who lives in Tuscarawas County. In 1927, when she was 20, McMullen had her first teaching job at Ourant School. She stayed for a few years, time enough to teach all eight grades, though never all eight at once. Like the students, she had to walk to school, but her walk, three miles each way, was longer than theirs. When she returned, McMullen was surprised to see the school much as it was in her day—the coal shed and even the two privies, one for boys and one for girls, are still there.

Access: To reach Stewart Barn from Ourant School, return north to County 2 and turn left/west; drive to Deersville. From there take County 21/Mallarnee Road left/south to start of State Route 799; continue south on 799 to State Route 800 and Freeport. On south side of town, take a sharp right turn onto County 27/Skull Fork Road; barn is within half a mile, on left. (State Route 800 continues south to I-70, and past I-70 to Barnesville, also in this guide.)

STEWART BARN, 1924

Skull Fork Road, County 27, Freeport
Private barn

This is Ohio's only 16-sided barn; Muskingum College's Lorle Porter wrote that it is the only one in Ohio, and one of only four in North America. It's frame (boards are horizontal), painted red, and topped by a 16-sided cupola with vents in each side.

Chillicothe, Ross County

(Circleville, north on U.S. 23, makes a good companion tour. So does Waverly, listed here as an addendum to Chillicothe).

¶ Ohio's first capital, Chillicothe remains one of the state's best towns for historic architecture. That makes the endless, particularly dull sprawl that oozes out around it especially disappointing.

¶ Within the space of a few downtown blocks, Chillicothe's Paint Street has exceptional stuff: the courthouse, an ensemble of large, red-brick commercial blocks, and a number of excellent old houses. Besides, because it leads to Paint Creek, the street has a great name. It's a legacy from the Shawnees whose word for *paint* was *yoctangee*.

Access: From U.S. 23 exit at Chillicothe Main Street and drive west to Paint Street and downtown.

ROSS COUNTY COURTHOUSE, 1858
E. Collins and Charles Autenrieth, Philadelphia
2 North Paint Street at West Main Street, Chillicothe
Courthouse; 740/773-2330

The Ross County Courthouse has an "exotic quality," says Cleveland architect Robert C. Gaede. "There's nothing else like it in the state." It's an elegant Italianate, all stone in front and brick with stone trim in back. The main building, two stories high with a tower above and a porch with

▶ ROSS COUNTY COURTHOUSE

Corinthian columns in front, has one-story wings on both sides. Each wing has three doors to offices whose original occupants we know because their titles, such as Auditor or Treasurer, appear in raised stone letters over the doors. No other Ohio courthouse has anything like these wings, which originally were just one room deep. Additions have accrued behind—and above: an early one, in the 1860s, was the cupola for a bell on the clock tower. The Courthouse's interior may not be quite so spectacular as the

exterior, but the courtroom is so good that some people have deemed it Ohio's best. I first saw it in the late 1980s. While I was admiring the dark woodwork, coffered ceiling and bronze chandelier, Judge J. Donald Ratcliff (who has since died) came walking through. After two terms on the Common Pleas bench, Ratcliff had retired in 1981, but he was still practicing law. He stopped to point out that the white bas relief portrait over the bench was Tiffin, the first governor, and the bench itself was rebuilt of chestnut in 1901. He said that in the early 1900s huge crowds routinely turned out for

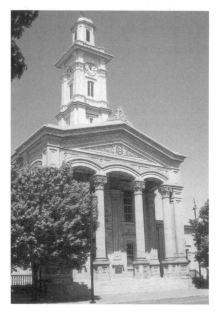

trials, while an audience of five or six is now typical. In the 1920s when he was a boy, he would come after school and during vacations and sit in the front row, listening. He learned to recognize the sheriff and all the policemen.

Paint Street's Red-Brick Commercial Blocks

In the two long blocks running from Second Street to Fourth, Chillicothe has an astonishing ensemble of five large, three-to-four-story commercial buildings, dating from 1875 to 1896, all in red brick, all with ornamental towers or dormers: the Grandes Dames of Paint Street. In their size and architectural detailing, they demonstrate how important and how prosperous Chillicothe was in the late nineteenth century. And in late 1998, virtually all

▶ NIPGEN BLOCK

their first-floor commercial spaces were occupied. Perhaps this ensemble helped bring about the city and county Law Enforcement Center (1988, URS Dalton, Columbus) at North Paint and Second streets, built to be compatible—it's two stories, red brick with contrasting trim and a three-story corner tower.

NIPGEN BLOCK, C. 1875

59 North Paint at East Second, Chillicothe, northeast corner, NRHP/Chillicothe Business District
Commercial building: ground-floor shops; upstairs apartments

According to Patricia Medert of the Ross County Historical Society library, the Italianate Nipgen Block is really two buildings. The section to the north was the I.O.O.F., the International Organization of Odd Fellows, a fraternal group. Dormers, including three under high, tapered roofs, ornament the top of the building; windows have stone trim. Ground floor has high-ceilinged store spaces with expansive glass fronts between iron pillars.

VALLEY HOUSE, THEN WARNER HOTEL, NOW O'DELL BLOCK, 1854, RENOVATED 1886

29 North Paint Street, between East Second and East Main Streets, Chillicothe, NRHP/Chillicothe Business District
Commercial building: ground-floor shops; upstairs apartments

This three-and-a-half story hotel has the look it acquired when Jacob Warner updated it in the 1880s, to make it fit for the likes of William McKinley, William Howard Taft, and Theodore Roosevelt. This site has always had a hotel or tavern; it still has a restaurant.

CARLISLE CORNER, 1885
1-3 South Paint Street at East Main, southeast corner, NRHP/ Chillicothe Business District Commercial building: ground-floor shops; upstairs offices and apartment

▶ O'DELL BLOCK

Located diagonally across from the courthouse, the Carlisle Corner lives up to its prominent site with a mansard roof, dormers, and a round corner tower rising three stories above the cornice. Notice also the round-arched brick entry facing Main Street.

FOULKE BLOCK, 1896

Arthur Shaner
14 South Paint Street, south of West Main, Chillicothe,
NRHP/Chillicothe Business District
Commercial building: ground-floor shops; upstairs offices and apartments

The Foulke Block is handsome, well kept, fully occupied or nearly so, and big—owner Robert B. Althoff thinks that at 50,000 square feet, it's the region's biggest commercial block. It's also well maintained, because in 1978 Althoff was one of a group of tenants who, he says, "bought it out of a sense of desperation." The manager, a bank trust department, had let the building go—the new owners spent ten times their purchase price fixing it up. Now, says Althoff, "It's in exquisite shape. We're very proud." ¶ To survive, all these brick blocks need a strong downtown. Lately Althoff has been despairing because the county commissioners decided to consolidate jobs from scattered downtown locations in a former Hart's store on the outskirts.

The Foulke Block – Chillicothe

▶ FOULKE BLOCK

"It's a blow psychologically," he says. "If they'd made that investment downtown it could have made a real difference." Sole owner of the Foulke Block since 1998, Althoff sees the building as his commitment to downtown. "I look on this as a stewardship," he muses. "Maybe the next generation will figure it out." The Foulke Block, at least, will survive for the next generation.

❡ Four stories high, the building has elegant iron balconies and a Richardsonian Romanesque stone door. Windows, stone-trimmed, are in trios; the end wall has bay windows; the cornice is ornate. When Althoff became an owner in 1978, upper floors were residential, the second floor had a traditional "attorneys' row", and a department store occupied most of the basement and first floor, and part of the upper floors too. ❡ The department store and residents soon left, and now the upper floors are mostly offices, except for a corporate apartment and the fourth- and fifth-floor penthouse where Althoff himself lives. That some days he works in the Merrill Lynch office on the first floor, means he has a choice of elevator or stairs for commuting. That on the other days he commutes to a suburban Columbus Merrill Lynch office shows that towns, even relatively prosperous ones like Chillicothe, are not in the best of times.

SCHILDER BLOCK, 1890
49 South Paint Street at East Fourth Street, northeast corner, Chillicothe
Commercial building: ground-floor shops; upstairs office and apartment

Three-and-a-half stories high, the Italianate Schilder Block has prominent white attic dormers. At one time it housed a theater.

South Paint Street's Houses

South Paint Street luxuriates in fine old houses. It also has the former Post Office, Neoclassical Revival, at Fifth Street, now a school. Ohio State's Douglas Graf admired even the auto brake and tire shop at Fifth Street—though it disrupts the residential continuity, he liked the architecture. Just off Paint Street on West Fifth Street, the Ross County Historical Society has two 1838 houses: a museum at number 45 and the David McCandless McKell Library next door at number 41.

▶ BARTLETT HOUSE, SIDE

ST. MARY'S CONVENT, 1816
61 South Paint Street, Chillicothe
St. Mary's Church chapel, offices, meeting and
Sunday school rooms

Such a nicely balanced facade: it gave St. Mary's Convent serenity without dullness. It's Federal style, two stories, with a recessed central section: door and a pair of columns below, porch and iron railing above.

MOSES R. BARTLETT HOUSE, 1848
Attributed to Nathan B. Kelly, Columbus
134 South Paint Street, NRHP/Chillicothe's Old Residential District
Private house

What a beautiful house this is. It's Greek Revival, a story-and-a-half, painted brick. The facade, which has two tall windows and a door, also has a porch with four slender Corinthian columns. The decorative carving seen on the porch is restrained and very lovely. Moses R. Bartlett, originally from upstate New York, came to Chillicothe while still in his teens, in 1835, and then prospered enough in grain and pork packing to build this house just 13 years later. The owner today is an attorney, Deborah Douglas Barrington. Though her office is now across the street, it used to be in a red brick wing added at the back before she bought the house in 1982. The interior has a central hall with two large rooms on both sides and at the end, a stairway curling upward. Because of the similar columns, people—including Talbot Hamlin—have assumed that this house and the handsome one next door, the Noah Wilson House, c. 1845, at 122 South Paint, were both done by the same architect. In his seminal 1944 book on Greek Revival architecture, Hamlin attributed the houses "to a Cincinnati architect, Kelly." In fact, Nathan B. Kelly practiced architecture not in Cincinnati but in Columbus at least from 1835 to 1865. Though best known for working on the Statehouse in the late 1850s, in 1845-47 Kelly also designed the Pickaway County Courthouse—a Greek Revival courthouse with Ionic columns—which brought him closer to Chillicothe at the time of these houses.

To see more near downtown Chillicothe—Second Street: Walk two blocks west on Second Street, from Paint to High. After the parking lots and the Elks Club (an old building), you'll come to two tiny and now derelict Greek Revival houses, two windows and a door wide, at 64 and 68. (Another across the street has been renovated and is in use.) At number 69, look for Poland House, c. 1850—Gothic trim drips from its gables; and at number 79 the narrow brick house, c. 1860, has a second-floor bay window and a flamboyant pointed dormer roof on the third floor. (The last two are part of NRHP/ Chillicothe Business District.) On the south side again, an impressive row of five two-story buildings, one a double, leads up to the corner at numbers 84-98; upstairs they all have windowed bays. Across the street from them is the relocated white Art Deco hamburger restaurant with a stepped tower, Carl's Town House, moved from South Paint in 2001 when the church wanted the site for its parking lot. The next block has good houses, including some Victorians, like that at 187 West Second.

Chillicothe: Beyond Downtown

Access: To reach the Pump House from downtown drive one block east (toward U.S. 23) on Main to Mulberry; turn left/north and drive into Yoctangee Park; follow signs; Pump House will be on the right.

PUMP HOUSE, NOW PUMP HOUSE CENTER FOR THE ARTS, 1882

Enderlin Circle, Yoctangee Park, Chillicothe
Gallery and shop; 740/772-5783

Originally a water pumping station, this red brick building was twice scheduled for demolition before it was converted into a gallery in 1991. In the nineteenth century, a water plant could have round-arched windows, a three-story tower, stone trim. How nice that a gallery can in the twentieth.

Access: To reach hilltop residential neighborhoods, from downtown drive west on Main Street; when U.S. 50 veers to the right, turn left onto Carlisle Place and drive uphill. At top of the hill take first right onto Highland, which ends at Mountain House.

▶ PUMP HOUSE CENTER

MOUNTAIN HOUSE, 1853

8 Highland Avenue, Chillicothe, NRHP
Private house

Marie Janssen and her son Oscar Janssen came to Chillicothe from Germany.
In 1853, after planting vineyards and building this Gothic Revival version of
a castle overlooking the Rhine, they opened it as Mountain House, a beer
garden and winery. All went well until the mid-1870s, when a blight killed
off area vineyards. Arts and Crafts artisan Dard Hunter, an authority on
hand-made paper who published hand-crafted books, bought the house in
1919; it's now the home of artist Dard Hunter III, who's continuing his
grandfather's work.

**Access: To reach Adena, from downtown take Main Street west to
State Route 104/High Street (immediately before turn for hill above);
turn right/north and follow 104 just past U.S. 35 intersection; take
signed turn left onto Pleasant Valley and then Adena roads. Alternatively, from U.S. 23 take U.S. 35 west to State Route 104 exit; turn north
and take signed turn as above.**

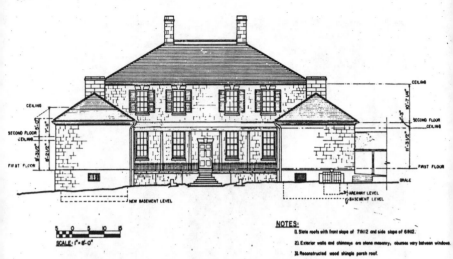

NORTH ELEVATION

NOTES:

1) Slate roofs with front slope of 7IN12 and side slope of 6IN12.
2) Exterior walls and chimneys are stone masonry, courses vary between windows.
3) Reconstructed wood shingle porch roof.
4) Stone steps and dry-laid stone garden wall.
5) Iron garden fence.

SCALE: 1" = 8'-0"

THOMAS WORTHINGTON HOUSE, NOW ADENA STATE MEMORIAL, 1807

Benjamin Latrobe, Washington, D.C.
848 Adena Road, Chillicothe, NRHP
Ohio Historical Society house museum; 800/319-7248; 740/772-1500. House closed in June 2001 for construction of visitor center and renovation, including reinterpretation of interior; call to check date of reopening and hours

Before he became Ohio's sixth governor in 1814, Thomas Worthington built himself a U-shaped house with a two-story central section and one-and-a-half-story wings in the front. One of the wings was, and is, an office; the other, a kitchen. A one-story porch with slender columns runs across the center. The house was built of dressed sandstone; the roof was, and is again, wood shingles painted red. Materials came from the yard—admittedly, a 5,000-acre yard; stone was quarried on site; the black walnut, ash, and oak all grew here. Adena is the oldest building in this guide. In anticipation of the Ohio Bicentennial in 2003, the OHS is building a new visitor center and restoring the house and grounds.

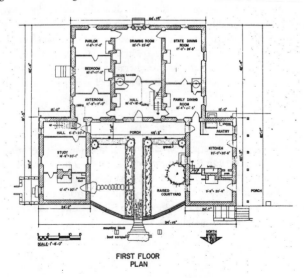

FIRST FLOOR PLAN

The Farm—Though we often think of pioneers as impoverished immigrants, many of Ohio's early settlers were ambitious, well-heeled Americans. One such was Thomas Worthington, who moved his family from Virginia to Ohio in 1798. Four years later, modeling himself on Virginia gentry, he began building a stone house that he called a plantation. Most surprisingly, at a time when architects were rare, he asked one, Benjamin Latrobe, to design his house.

Though Latrobe never visited the site, he was definitely Worthington's architect. Having grown up in England, Latrobe (1764-1820) came to America in 1795. In 1798, with the design of the Bank of Pennsylvania in Philadelphia, he gave America its first national architectural style, Greek Revival. Latrobe is best known for his work on the Capitol in Washington, which he rebuilt after the British destroyed it in the War of 1812.

But at least to Mary Anne Brown, Latrobe is best known for Thomas Worthington's house, Adena. Brown started as a summer tour guide at Adena in 1959, when she was still in high school, and has never really left; since 1976 she has been site manager. Her 40 years or so at Adena have long since surpassed the time Worthington himself spent here, for he died at 53, only 20 years after his house was finished in 1807.

For Worthington, endowed with an inheritance, Ohio seemed a land of opportunity, and so it proved. His Ohio holdings ultimately increased to 25,000 acres, one fifth at Adena. He also became a political leader, an early advocate for statehood, and in 1802 he personally took the state constitution to Washington for congressional approval. He would also become one of Ohio's first U.S. senators and a two-term governor.

Through Mary Anne Brown's years at Adena, she studied the house and its origins; in 1981 she did a master's thesis on it. In the 1960s and on her own initiative, she traveled around just to meet Worthington descendants. In Texas she found some who'd never heard of Thomas Worthington. She found others on both coasts; and she went to a Worthington family reunion in Doylestown, Pennsylvania. She knows of two Worthingtons in Ohio today, both transferred here by employers.

Thomas Worthington's house is ambitious, formal, and dignified. He eschewed ornamentation, like cornices and chandeliers, but to him simple did not mean humble. He wanted a Virginia-style house. Mary Anne Brown made five trips to Charles Town, now in West Virginia, which was laid out by George Washington's brother Charles and which is near where Worthington grew up. To Worthington, a Charles Town house called Harewood represented how the gentry lived; and Brown sees much of Harewood in Adena. Worthington's wife, the former Eleanor Swearingen, also had her input in planning the house. She was no shrinking violet, but a woman strong enough to run the estate's stills, mills, and farms when her husband was away.

Adena was also Latrobe's. The proof is in three letters, now held in Maryland at the Baltimore Historical Society, from Latrobe to Worthington.

▶ Adena

In these letters Latrobe is apt to start out like a typical correspondent, excusing his delay in writing, even while he was working on the plans. He mentioned Mrs. Worthington's suggestions, discussed how thick the doors should be, which direction the house should face, and which way to lay floorboards. In this north-facing house, floorboards run north to south in the projecting wings and main-house central area, east to west in the sides. The floors, avers Brown, have never sagged or squeaked.

When Brown did her thesis, she was never able to determine how Worthington happened to choose Latrobe. It's possible he met the architect through Thomas Jefferson in Washington in 1802. Or, he might have approached Latrobe independently. In any case, the floor plan has features characteristic of Latrobe's work. One is the first floor's circular traffic pattern. Another is allocating distinct areas for various purposes, such as formal entertaining or family dining. That's especially clear on the second floor, where the children have one side of the house and guests the other; and the twain scarcely meet, probably a good idea. The house, Brown concludes, is "thoughtfully laid out."

Adena stayed in the family until 1896, when the widow of Thomas Worthington's eldest son died. In 1903 George Hunter Smith bought the house as a summer residence and promptly installed bathrooms, central heating, and electricity. His family gave the house to the State of Ohio in 1946, and the Ohio Historical Society began taking out bathrooms, to restore it to Worthington's era. Partly restore it. The heating system stayed in, and so did electrical outlets, if only for vacuuming.

The OHS restoration could hope to be relatively authentic because, though the Worthingtons didn't save furniture, they always saved papers, including estimates, bills, diaries, and pictures. Among these papers was a complete description of the house in 1821. It was prepared by a Philadelphia insurance agent, who spent two weeks at Adena. He documented not furnishings, but the dimensions of rooms, whether they were painted or papered or had unusual architectural features, such as the bookcases in Worthington's office. The insurance company, Brown says, is still in business. She visited them too. They have a copy of the Worthington inventory in their archives.

Because of saved bills, the names of the stone masons, brothers John and Presley Morris, are also known; but whether or not their crews were local craftsmen or some of the freed slaves Worthington brought from Virginia, is not known. Similarly, the names of the carpenters, George McCormick and Conrad Christman, are known; McCormick stayed on to make furniture.

Adena, carefully recreated, opened as a museum in 1953. But no one calls it a plantation. That name, says Brown, was used only briefly. Adena was in Ohio, so it became a farm.

To see more near Chillicothe—Waverly, Pike County

South of Chillicothe on U.S. 23, Waverly, the seat of Pike County, is an old town with charm. But for me the highlight there is a section of country road. It's State Route 335, heading east at the north edge of Waverly. The road passes along a bluff above the Scioto Valley, through rich agricultural land. For a couple miles or so, this road is completely rural and unspoiled—a rare sight nowadays. It is ornamented with half a dozen proud red-brick nineteenth-century manses, flaunting the wealth that the land yielded; they were splendid to see, at least in winter, when most could be seen. Then when I was back there in spring, 1999, a crew was preparing a foundation for a new, non-farm house. For the first time in decades, this place was changing.

Gallipolis, Gallia County

(To see more in the area, Pomeroy is upriver, State Route 7, or Jackson is up the road, U.S. 35).

❡ Just as at Marietta the Ohio Company provided the very model of how best to establish a frontier settlement, so at Gallipolis, the Scioto Company demonstrated the opposite. In France it recruited people eager to escape the Revolution; but when they arrived in America, it turned out the Scioto Company didn't own the land. To cap it all, the agent absconded with everyone's money. The prospective settlers, today called the French 500, persisted and ultimately

▶ RIVERBY ARTS CENTER

triumphed, though what you'll find in modern Gallipolis is not a French town, but a venerable American one.

❡ The central square, between First and Second Avenues at State Street and called Public Square, is lovely for itself, for the buildings around three sides, and for the view of the Ohio River on the fourth. Besides those mentioned below, the Henking House at 24 State Street, c. 1890, is a fine Queen Anne. And First Avenue is good for houses as far east as Riverby, an arts center at number 530.

▶ OHIO VALLEY BANK BUILDING

Access: From U.S. 35 take State Route 160 to Second Avenue/State Route 7; turn right to State Street, where the Ohio Valley Bank Building is at the corner facing the park. At the next corner, Court Street, turn left to First Avenue; turn left/east; the deVacht house is just past State Street on the river side of the street. Continue east on First to Locust, where Lawyer's Row is in the block on the left. This tour is an easy walk, which you can extend with a map and guide to all Gallipolis's historic buildings, available at the Gallia County Convention and Visitors Bureau, 61 Court at Third Street, weekdays and summer Saturdays; 800/765-6482.

OHIO VALLEY BANK BUILDING, 1896
Yost & Packard, Columbus
366 Second Avenue, NRHP/Gallipolis Public Square and Garden Lots HD
Private apartments and ground-floor shop

In the Ohio Valley Bank, Yost & Packard gave Gallipolis a downtown building of exceptional quality. Brick and stone, it's an elegant three-and-a-half story structure with an extraordinary Chateauesque roof; even the dormers have three-part Palladian windows. When I saw the building again in spring, 1999 the roof, formerly the color of terra cotta flower pots, had been painted a bright lipstick red. I was hoping that what I saw was a primer, but a couple years later that was proving just wishful thinking. Window glass also was painted red.

JOSEPH DEVACHT HOUSE, 1811
413-417 First Avenue, NRHP/Gallipolis Public Square and Garden Lots HD
Private house

A frame row house is unusual anywhere, especially in Ohio, where this one may be unique. This two-story Federal row house was originally four stores, with the shopkeepers' residences upstairs. Today, it houses two families and no stores. Former tourism director Kim Sheets Schuette said the arched passageway through the building is called a Dog Trot—she doesn't know why. (Ohio State's Douglas Graf says it's a Southern rural house type.) Builder Joseph deVacht was one of the French 500, the original 1790 settlers.

LAWYER'S ROW, 1875
21-25 Locust Street, Gallipolis
Private offices

These three frame-and-brick shotgun houses (one story, one room wide, at least two rooms deep) are the survivors of the original Lawyer's Row across the street from the courthouse; in mid-1997 only one was a law office. Number 25, the closest to Second Avenue, has Carpenter Gothic carving on the front porch.

▶ LAWYER'S ROW

Haydenville, Hocking County

(Athens, south on U.S. 33, makes a companion tour. For a thematic tour, see Shawnee, a coal-mining town developed at the same time as Haydenville. Shawnee is ten miles northeast; take State Route 595; in New Straitsville jog left to State Route 93 north. Though distinctive, both these towns are hanging on by a thread.)

¶ Haydenville was a tile manufacturer's company town, where the local products—brick, hollow tile, glazed tile block, and fancy tile and brick—built local buildings. Though many examples are gone and the place is poor, some structures—particularly the Methodist Church—remain to delight us.

Access: From U.S. 33 southbound south of Logan, exit at State Route 595 but turn the other direction, south onto County Road 25/ Haydenville Road, which after two miles through town rejoins U.S. 33 to the south.

HAYDENVILLE METHODIST CHURCH, NOW HAYDENVILLE UNITED METHODIST CHURCH, 1893

Jack Heath, builder, Chicago
16798 Haydenville Road, Haydenville, NRHP/Haydenville Historic Town Church

On one of my early visits to Haydenville, I met Jim Grover, who was digging up weeds from between bricks in the Methodist Church's sidewalk. He showed me the sanctuary, whose recent restoration had helped push Sunday attendance up from two or three to 20 or 30. The outside of the church has eight different kinds of bricks and blocks, including ones that are textured, dimpled, patterned with stripes or circles, or in varied colors. Concludes Jim Grover, "They must have been putting it up there for a showpiece." They succeeded. To build the church, a contractor named Jack Heath brought a crew in from Chicago; his men hand-chiseled many of the bricks. Peter Hayden's family gave the church a stained-glass window in his memory. Always a devout Methodist and a benevolent town proprietor, he died at 81 in 1888, before the church was built.

Advertisement: The Houses of Haydenville—Columbus businessman Peter Hayden named his company town, which served his iron furnace in the 1850s, for himself. When iron declined, clay and coal deposits led to a new industry, whose factory went up on the furnace's abandoned sandstone foundation. Haydenville Mining and Manufacturing produced a line of brick and ceramic tiles that it celebrated here at home, for from 1870 to 1919 the workers' houses were built and embellished with the local product. Waterproof, fireproof, and relatively maintenance-free, Haydenville itself became the company's best commercial.

Some later houses built of wood were "not nearly as nicely made," says Nyla Vollmer, president of the Haydenville Preservation Committee. The community is a poor one, but what bothers Vollmer is not caring, as evidenced by trash in the wrong place. "These," she'll say, gesturing toward an unkempt property, "are some of the less proud."

The tile and brick plants were torn down in 1961, and in 1964 a Pennsylvania realtor bought the town and began gradually selling it off.

As a company town, Haydenville is distinctive in having varied housing. These are representative types on Haydenville Road, going south from the church. Haydenville Historic Town is on the National Register of Historic Places.

1) The carry-out store, just below the church on the left, is in one of the three remaining doubles.

2) Next, on the right side, is a row of ten tidy saltboxes, with front porches and contrasting tiles at the corners and as trim around windows.

3) On the left, three one-and-a-half-story houses from the 1870s are some of the most interesting in town; they have ostentatious tile displays, including pieces of hollow sewer tile embedded in the brick work.

4) On the left after Wandling Road there's a group of five two-story brick houses; some have wooden decoration in the gables.

5) Turn left at Frog Hollow Road.

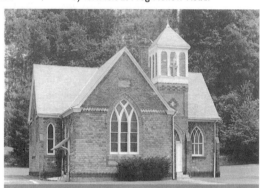

▶ METHODIST CHURCH

On the left, is Nyla and Ken Vollmer's white two-story house, once occupied by company superintendents. The story is that the house was Columbus-built where it was dismantled for shipment to Haydenville. There it was reassembled—all this to please the whim of a manager's wife who didn't appreciate the local stuff. What she got is a board siding, beveled so that it looks like stone.

6) South on Haydenville Road another half mile is the last surviving example of Haydenville's round houses. National Fireproofing, which in 1907 bought the company, built this house in 1919 of a dark red silo tile. Originally one of perhaps ten, it had one room up and one room down. Here the rooms have since been divided, but the house, Vollmer says, "still has a path." Which naive city dwellers (like me) may translate as meaning, no indoor plumbing.

Ironton, Lawrence County

(State Route 93, Ohio's clay and coal route, links Jackson
and Ironton.)

❡ Founded only in 1849, Ironton is a place where the
best old houses trace their origins to particular iron
furnaces. The city was the hub of the Hanging Rock iron
region, which extended into Ohio's Jackson, Scioto, and
Vinton Counties and across the Ohio River. Production
petered out by World War I because all the forests had
been cut and no more wood was handy for the charcoal
used in making iron.

**Access: U.S. 52 follows the river south to the edge of Ironton; exit at
State Route 93, which, as Park Avenue, heads west for downtown. It
intersects Fifth Street (one-way southbound) and Sixth (one-way
northbound). A flyer, "Historic Ironton: A Brief Tour" is available from
the Greater Lawrence County Area Convention & Visitors Bureau, P.O.
Box 488, South Point, Ohio 45680; 740/532-9991.**

BIDE A WEE, 1905

504 South Fifth Street at Adams Street, Ironton, NRHP/Rankin HD
Private house

Bide A Wee is a picturesque house built of rough-cut stone, with curved
wooden brackets in the eaves and a dominant front porch. It was constructed
by James Bird, an ironmaster from England. But the most celebrated owner
was the world's
only woman
ironmaster,
Nannie Kelly
Wright, who
lived here from
1920-1930.
She named it
Bide a Wee.
Pictures of the
interior as it
was in her day
are on display
in the Nannie
Kelly Wright
room at the

▶ BIDE A WEE

museum, in the Colonel George N. Gray House, listed here after this house.
Used at times as a single-family home and at other times as apartments, the
house has a central hall big enough for entertaining or, the owner says, for
the children and their bicycles on rainy days.

Iron Matron—A 1920s photograph taken in Bide a Wee shows Nannie Kelly Wright standing tall, her mouth set, her eyes looking directly into the lens. "No-nonsense" is the description for her, but no-nonsense with feminine frills. Her earrings droop, her rope pearls encircle her neck four times and descend onto her bosom, bands of diamonds glitter at her wrist. Her dress has a flower pattern in brocade perhaps, or lace. This is the woman who was the world's only female ironmaster. Judging by this portrait, that makes perfect sense.

The daughter of a properous river captain, she married Lindsey Kelly, an Ohio state senator from Ironton who was in the iron business; in 1885 the Kellys purchased Center Furnace.

But Nannie was not a woman to disappear into domestic life. Instead, she was keeping her eye on the skittish iron markets, and in 1896, anticipating stronger demand, she started buying up land at Center Furnace; perhaps her father, still alive at the time, helped with financing. She spruced up the furnace equipment and company houses; she hired workers. She revitalized the church and school at Superior, the nearby town.

Historian Virginia Bryant says Kelly dressed for hard work at the furnace in a rough calico dress, or perhaps even pants; she sometimes slept in charcoal bins. She commuted regularly between her houses at Superior and Ironton, sometimes on horseback, but usually in a coach pulled by Kentucky horses and driven by a liveried coachman. "She carried a curling iron in the carriage," Bryant wrote. "One night between the furnace and Ironton, a would-be robber stopped the wagon. He looked in and said, 'My God, it's Nannie Kelly,' and with that he caught a curling iron in the face."

When the Spanish American War broke out, Center Furnace was one of the few iron producers ready to go. Before the end of the year, Nannie Kelly could afford her first world cruise. By the turn of the century, she was said to be the second richest woman in the world.

Nannie Kelly did know how to spend money. In 1904 she went to London to be presented to King Edward VII. Altogether she was to make 14 trips to Europe and three world tours, in 1898, 1906, and 1913. She could also make short trips in style. About 1906 she decided to move a house she owned to another lot a block away. On the day of the move, as the house crept up the street, Nannie Kelly and her friends were in the livingroom playing cards.

Of her houses, Kelly is associated most with Bide A Wee—she's the one who had the name carved over the door. In Paris she hired an artist to come to Bide A Wee to paint four wall murals, and she furnished the house with trophies from her travels, including art and antiques.

Nannie never recovered from the stock market crash of 1929, though she wasn't completely wiped out. She had so many fine things that, after she lost Bide A Wee to the bank in 1930, she could assure herself some income by gradually selling off her treasures. Usually she had enough money to live in hotels in Huntington and in Ironton, though at one point she and her art collection descended on a cousin who lived with her husband and daughter in a two-bedroom apartment, and then stayed eight months. Kelly died in Ironton in 1946, four days after her 90th birthday. She was buried in the dress she wore when presented to King Edward VII.

COLONEL GEORGE N. GRAY HOUSE, NOW THE LAWRENCE COUNTY MUSEUM, 1870

506 South Sixth Street, Ironton, NRHP/Rankin HD
Museum open for tours Friday-Sunday afternoons; donation;
closed January-March; 740/532-1222

This house takes the name of the man who bought it in 1878 and added the tower, making it a proper Italian Villa style manse. A Civil War veteran, Gray managed the Hecla and Vesuvius iron furnaces. His descendants lived in the house until 1977. One museum room is devoted to ironmaster Nannie Kelly Wright. Photographs are on display, and also her silver letter opener, lace hankies, and recipe book.

Jackson, Jackson County

(Also in Jackson County: Wellston.)
¶ In 1971 Barbara Summers, a burned-out theatrical stage manager in Manhattan, abandoned the city and moved—where else?—to Jackson County. She's been active there as director of the Southern Hills Arts Council, which gradually has been refurbishing downtown Jackson's 1930 Art Deco Markay Theatre. Now the lobby is an art gallery, and the former store space, a classroom. Summers has been eager to start on the auditorium renovation. After that, she expects to be back in the theatrical business, this time as a producer. "Life," she says, "is hysterical the way it comes round."

Access: From U.S. 35 exit at East Broadway and drive west to downtown Jackson. At Main Street, turn left for Knights of Pythias Lodge Hall. To see the Livesay-White House continue on Broadway for several blocks to South Street; house is just to the left on the south side of South.

KNIGHTS OF PYTHIAS LODGE HALL, 1870; THIRD FLOOR, 1890; FACADE, 1896

276 1/2 Main Street, Jackson
Private lodge hall; ground-floor store

The Knights of Pythias Lodge Hall has a highly ornamented metal facade, painted blue and topped by an octagonal tower. To an outsider the detailing looks as though it might contain fraternal symbols, but it doesn't, according to lodge member Gerald Rhea. What is significant is the color; blue is a Pythian color. ¶ When I met Rhea and two of his fraternal cohorts, I told them I was especially pleased to shake their hands, because, while I'd been admiring Pythian buildings all over Ohio (Akron, Toledo, Springfield), actual Pythians seemed relatively rare. Here in Jackson Rhea was one of 15 50-year members in his lodge; but membership totaled a respectable 140 and the age range, starting at 18, was promising. ¶ At that time the building was shrouded in scaffolding for window and tower repairs, brick work, and repainting. Though the lodge has a maintenance fund, Pythian Robert Williams said they'd never have been able to manage without a

▶ Knights of Phythias Lodge

revitalization grant for half the costs. Jackson had received a $400,000 Community Development Block Grant—matching Federal funds for downtown facades and code work. "It's a by-God difficult thing to get," said arts activist Barbara Summers. Including the Knights of Pythias, 16 owners were fixing their properties. ¶ This building was constructed in 1870 as a two-story commercial property; the third floor, the Pythians, and the High Victorian cast-iron and sheet-metal cladding all arrived in the 1890s. The third-floor meeting room, 42-by-64 feet, has stained-glass windows and a beautiful maple floor.

LIVESAY-WHITE HOUSE, C. 1845; PORCH, 1878

63 East South Street, Jackson
Private apartments and
doctor's office

This house has a porch with six Doric columns and two pilasters, all festooned with carved Eastlake ornamentation that appears also in the gable braces. According to legend, the designer was copying a pattern— or perhaps, a mix of patterns—he'd seen in New Orleans. A doctor

▶ Livesay-White House

bought the house in the 1980s and made extensive additions at the rear; now it contains the doctor-owner's office and apartment, a dental office, and a rental apartment. Some of this information came from the late Marjorie Sellers, who kept all Jackson's old houses under her wing.

Marietta, Washington County

(Also in Washington County: Archers Fork.)
¶ The founding of Marietta, the first European settlement in Ohio, was as non-speculative as any colonization enterprise in North America. So declared John W. Reps, an authority on historic town planning in America. ¶ The Ohio Company, a group of New England Revolutionary War veterans, founded Marietta. The company's activities became so closely linked with United States expansion beyond the Appalachians that Reps believed neither would have succeeded without the other: "The speedy settlement of the west with the orderly formation of territorial and then state governments was due in considerable measure to the Ohio Company and its leaders." As Marietta went, so went the nation. ¶ Though today the city's older sections are pleasant and attractive, Marietta is rich in good buildings, but not in extraordinary ones. What it does have, at the confluence of the Muskingum and Ohio Rivers, is an extraordinary site. ¶ To see more in Marietta—*A Window to Marietta* is a soft-cover book for sale at Marietta museums and at the Washington County Historical Society Library, 417 Second Street, basement, weekdays, 740/373-1788.

Access: I-77 goes south to Marietta, passing very near Pleasant City (see also) on the way. From I-77 drive into downtown on State Route 7/ Pike Street, from which Becker Lumber is visible just before Green Street intersection. To see Lock Keeper's House turn left on Green to Front Street; turn right; house is on left in a couple blocks, between Butler and Putnam Streets. To reach college, take Putnam away from river to Fifth Street.

Second Arrivals

Marietta started with an unusually enlightened plat, which both set aside public lands and respected Hopewell mounds. To the city's credit, both survive at least in part today. ¶ Done in 1788 by the first settlers, the plat was oriented to the Muskingum River, whose banks were reserved as public land—some of that riverfront is still

parkland. Streets were
laid in a grid paralleling the river. Most of the preexisting
Indian earthworks, which were long-abandoned Hopewell
mounds, remain today because the original plat preserved
them in public squares. The mounds were assigned Latin
names. One was the Sacra Via, or Sacred Way, apparently
built as a broad processional path from the river uphill to
a large rectangular mound, Quadranaou. ¶ Originally
Sacra Via must have been a spectacular sight, with its two
parallel embankments, 231 feet apart, 360 feet long, and
up to 17 feet high. The first generation of settlers left
these embankments intact, says Marietta resident Marilyn
Ortt; so did the second generation. But then the third
generation saw economic opportunity; they decided to
use the clay—it went into bricks for the 1857 Unitarian
Universalist Church downtown at 232 Third Street.
Today, a pair of streets named Sacra Via marks the site.
They enclose a broad parkway extending from the river
uphill to Third Street/State Route 60. Across Third just to
the northeast is the Quadranaou mound, popularly called
Turtle, in a park. ¶ Another mound, called Conus, is in
the middle of Mound Cemetery, where many of the
pioneers are buried. Thirty feet high, conical in shape and
ringed by an embankment and moat, Conus has benches
on its summit, which is accessible by a stone stairway

▶ Lock Keeper's House

installed in 1837 because climbers were wrecking the mound. The cemetery fronts Fifth Street at the top of Scammel Street. ¶ Though Quadranaou and Conus are essentially intact, in 1913 the Public Library was built on top of the last large mound, Capitolium, at Fifth and Washington Streets. According to Wesley Clarke, a Marietta-based Ohio Department of Transportation planner/archaeologist, a 1990 addition to the library permitted the only scientific evaluation ever done on a Marietta mound. It fixed the date at A.D. 200. ¶ All the mounds and buildings mentioned here (except the Betsey Mills Club and the separately listed Becker Lumber) are on the National Register, Marietta Historic District.

BECKER LUMBER AND MANUFACTURING COMPANY, NOW MARIETTA MILLS, 1901, 1997

736 Greene Street/State Route 26 just east of junction with Pike Street/State Route 7, Marietta, NRHP
Former mill, now apartments

Best seen from State Route 7, this former lumber and planing mill is a massive four-story brick structure with stepped gables and fourth-floor dormers. Developer Arthur Howard Winer converted it into apartments in 1996-97. All those dormers on the roof, he says, turned into "rather sweet apartments with great vistas."

THE LOCK KEEPER'S HOUSE, 1899
243 Front Street, Marietta
Vacant; awaiting reuse

This guide has several romantic Dutch-looking buildings. This one was a
Lock Keeper's House that has long outlasted the lock and dam once here on
the Muskingum. It is, Marilyn Ortt says, a favorite of people in Marietta,
which probably accounts for its long survival even while empty. When new, it
had tile ornamentation in both of its stepped gables, front and back, as well
as a band of tile around its brick walls between the first and second floors.
Though the tiles are now gone from the street-side gable, they remain on the
river side and provide a good reason to walk around the building. In summer
2001 the city, which owns the Lock Keeper's House, stabilized the structure
prior to a pending restoration, perhaps as a museum. Other Dutch moments
in Ohio include the Holland Theatre in Bellefontaine (Northwest) and
Dayton's Arcade (Vol. 1).

MARIETTA COLLEGE CHAPEL BUILDING,
NOW ERWIN HALL, 1850
Rufus Erastus Harte, Marietta
Fifth Street pedestrian mall through campus from Putnam Street, Marietta
College classrooms and offices

It's not uncommon to hear of an Ohio building modeled on something in
New England or Europe, but it is definitely uncommon to hear of one
modeled on another in Ohio.
Apparently Erwin Hall was.
Rufus Harte, a lawyer who
drew the plans for Erwin Hall,
studied at Hudson's Western
Reserve College, whose Chapel
(see also) is similar to the
Marietta building. Both are
three-story red brick Greek
Revival structures with pilasters
on the facade and multi-stage
white towers. Cleveland
architectural historian Eric
Johannesen, who discovered
this likely antecedence, noted
that there are some differences.
For instance, the Marietta frieze
is brick, while Hudson's is
wood. And unlike Hudson's
Chapel, Erwin has an intact
row of the tops of six immured
chimneys on each side. Except
for those, the prototype has the
edge, especially if considering
interiors. Erwin Hall really
faces downhill, across the green

▶ ERWIN HALL

toward Fourth Street. The back door, which now functions as the main entry,
was added in a 1970-71 renovation that removed everything old from the
interior. Among the losses was a Gothic Revival ceiling on the third floor, a

▶ THE CASTLE

relic of two literary society rooms that were lavishly decorated and furnished some time after 1850 and abandoned in 1912. Kenyon College in Gambier has restored two such rooms in Ascension Hall, (see also).

Access: The streets on the other side of Putnam contain many picturesque houses and Mound Cemetery, described above. Four of those houses, listed here in order for touring on foot, are of particular interest.

MILLS HOUSE, NOW THE MARIETTA COLLEGE PRESIDENT'S HOUSE, C. 1822

301 Fifth Street at Putnam Street, Marietta
College president's house, not accessible to the public

Federal style, brick, with a becolumned porch, the house has a terraced side yard. Colonel John Mills bought the house in 1836 and it remained in his family for a century; it's been the college president's house since 1937. What a beautiful perk.

THE HOUSE OF SEVEN PORCHES, 1835

331 Fifth Street, Marietta
Private house

The style is Greek Revival, while the porches are Southern. Thus the House of Seven Porches reflects both New Hampshire and South Carolina, previous homes of Diarca Howe Allen, the professor who built it. Four porches are in the front; three more extend across the back, which faces downhill. (At least in winter, they can be seen from the alley below.)

THE CASTLE, 1855
John M. Slocomb, Marietta
418 Fourth Street, between Scammel and Wooster Streets, Marietta
House museum open year round some days every week; 740/373-4180

This brick Gothic Revival house looms so imposingly on its hillside that its nickname—The Castle—seems entirely appropriate. It has an octagonal tower outside, and interesting woodwork inside.

THE BETSEY MILLS CLUB, 1927
Donald P. Hart, New York
300 Fourth Street at Putnam, Marietta
Community center and restaurant; interior accessible to the public; 740/373-4981

What a handsome Georgian Revival complex this is. William Mills, who lived up the hill in what is now the President's House, built it in memory of his wife, Betsey Gates Mills, who in 1898 began teaching a group of girls who later became a club. Though initially its gym, diningroom, and other facilities were for girls and women, it's now open also to men. The 1927 construction project incorporated two older frame houses facing Fourth Street, one of which Betsey Mills was born in.

Harmar

On the west bank of the Muskingum, Fort Harmar was already in place when the first settlers arrived in 1788—indeed, it was an incentive in picking the site. Harmar later became a separate municipality that merged with Marietta in 1890. Buildings mentioned here are all on the National Register, Harmar Historic District. ¶ The Washington County Historical Society has taken title to The Anchorage/Putnam Villa, an Italian Villa with a good interior at 403 Harmar Street, at the foot of Putnam Avenue, and is restoring it. I hope that some day they may be able to remove the facade's ghastly brick elevator shaft, added by a former occupant, a nursing home. ¶ Like The Castle, The Anchorage was designed by John M. Slocomb (1811-1882), who came to Marietta in 1832. ¶ Two Harmar houses have glorious sites.

Access: To reach the Levi Barber House, from Marietta cross to Harmar on the Putnam Street bridge; then take an immediate sharp left onto Fort Street; continue past the low railroad overpass to the end of the street.

LEVI BARBER HOUSE, 1829
Joseph Barker, Marietta
407 Fort Street, Marietta, NRHP/Harmar HD
Private house

From its riverside perch, the Levi Barber House looks out over the confluence of the Muskingum and Ohio Rivers: a wonderful view of water, water almost forever. The view's price has been floods; in 1913 the water rose 27 inches above the second floor. The Federal style house is one of two remaining local buildings by master builder Joseph Barker, discussed after this in Marietta North. Levi Barber, born in Vermont, came to Marietta in 1799. A surveyor, he did Woodsfield's unusually nice plat. His house has always remained in his family.

Access: On the Harmar side of the Putnam Street Bridge, turn right onto Gilman Avenue; at State Route 7 South/Fort Harmar Drive turn left and drive up the hill. Turn right on State Route 676/Lancaster Street and continue up the hill; when Lancaster turns right continue straight onto Alta Street; turn left on High Street; the John Kaiser House will be on your right at Bellevue.

JOHN KAISER HOUSE, 1902
George Theodore Hovey, Marietta
300 Bellevue, Marietta, NRHP
Private house

Up on Harmar's hillside is this good Queen Anne, which architectural historian Nancy Hoy says was, like all local Queen Annes, built with oil money. As signs and street names indicate (the house faces Bellevue between Vista Street and Lookout Point) the view is superb.

Marietta North

Access: Take State Route 60/Third Street north from Putnam Street; road passes Sacra Via, on left. To see Colonel Barker House, continue north on 60. Just north of Marietta in Devola, turn left/west on Masonic Park Road/County 341. In one mile, after Putnam School, 341 turns right/north. Continue on it almost another mile, just past a sign for Halcyon Drive, to a white house on the left.

COLONEL JOSEPH BARKER HOUSE, 1811
Joseph Barker, Marietta
Masonic Park Road, near Marietta, NRHP
Private house

This house is within a quarter mile of the Muskingum River, because in 1811, that was the only route to town. Carpenter builder Joseph Barker, designer of the region's most famous early house, the Blennerhassett

▶ COLONEL JOSEPH BARKER HOUSE

Mansion, planned his own house with two rooms down, two up, a center hall, and probably a lean-to kitchen at the back. It seems small today, at least for a family with ten children. ¶ But it is not a modest house. It has elegant details, like the blind elliptical arches for the three second-story windows, and an entry door with sidelights and a fanlight above. An addition at the back dates from the mid-nineteenth century. ¶ Born in New Hampshire, educated at Exeter Academy, and trained in carpentry by his father, Barker (1765-1843) arrived in Marietta in 1789. At first he soldiered, farmed, and built boats; later he was elected a state legislator, a county commissioner, and a common pleas judge—he served in a courthouse he designed. That courthouse is gone, as are Blennerhassett, the elegant Hildreth House downtown, and the Exchange Hotel in Harmar. Historian Nancy Hoy, who has researched all Marietta's historic architects, says only three of Barker's buildings remain here: his own house, the Levi Barber House in Harmar, and his son's house, on State Route 7 at Willow Island Lock east of Marietta. ¶ Blennerhassett Mansion was built on the Ohio River island plantation of a rich Irish republican, Harman Blennerhassett, and his wife Margaret. Ultimately Aaron Burr persuaded Blennerhassett (who, according to a contemporary, Samuel Hildreth, always was a little gullible) to join a potentially treasonous scheme to establish a new republic in the Southwest. The scheme failed; both men lost their honor and their fortunes; Blennerhassett Island passed to a creditor, and in 1811 the mansion burned down. But for the first six years of the nineteenth century, before the family fled, Blennerhassett plantation was the stuff of legend. ¶ "Mr. Blennerhassett," wrote Hildreth in 1852, "may be considered as the greatest benefactor that had ever settled west of the mountains." In setting up his island estate, Blennerhassett poured $40,000 into the local economy. Some went to Joseph Barker, who built the house—frame rather than stone because Blennerhassett feared earthquakes—in 1799-1800. The two-story central section was an impressive 52-by-30 feet. Porticos extended on both sides, curving to form half of an ellipsis and ending in single-story 25-by-20-foot offices, one for servants, the other for the master's library. In 1985 a replica was built on the island, which is a West Virginia state park.

▶ MORGAN COUNTY COURTHOUSE

McConnelsville, Morgan County

(For touring, McConnelsville is on State Route 60 between Zanesville and Marietta, and not all that close to
either. However, it's an excellent destination.)

¶ According to Councilman Galen Finley, visitors to
McConnelsville always love the place, though "with our
highway system, you almost can't get here from there."
But three of the roads that do reach McConnelsville, State
Routes 60, 78, and 376, are scenic highways. The village
itself is also good to look at—it built well and then kept
itself. The keeping is ongoing. Take for example the 1873

brick Italianate house at 288 East Main. In the mid-1990s the owners, Mona and Darrell Newton turned down a real-estate broker who offered to buy their house for an unnamed client—a fast-food operation, Mona concluded, when the agent promised the Newtons they could keep the bricks. ¶ Then there was a former judge who left Morgan County $1.7 million to buy or build something and put his name on it; he had done well with his investments and was grateful to the county for electing him. Happily the commissioners chose not to build but to buy and reuse a red-brick commercial building on Main Street downtown, a former furniture store. Under renovation for use as county offices, it should reopen in August 2002 as the Carlos M. Riecker Building. ¶ McConnelsville's square is an unusual shape, a slightly skewed diamond, with buildings facing the angled sides and streets, including State Route 60/Main Street, entering at the corners and then navigating a roundabout. Morgan County was coal mining country; in the mid-1990s three employers, including a mine, closed, leaving some empty stores on Main Street and, in the late 1990s and early 2000s, the state's highest unemployment rate. ¶ To see more old houses, look at North Kennebec; the streets south of East Main Street; and the green at East Main and Tenth Street/State Route 376. One of McConnelsville's houses has a well known restaurant: Howard House, 507 East Main Street; 740/962-5861.

Access: From Zanesville and I-70 to the north or Marietta to the south, take State Route 60 to McConnelsville, where the highway is called Main Street. Kennebec intersects at the square.

MORGAN COUNTY COURTHOUSE, 1858, 1886, 1960
William P. Johnson
East Main Street at North Kennebec Avenue, northeast side of square,
McConnelsville, NRHP/McConnelsville HD
Public courthouse; open weekdays

The Morgan County Courthouse started as a mostly Greek Revival building fronted by a porch with four two-story columns. Almost 30 years later, in 1886, the Second Empire clock tower was added; and in 1960 the building was extended at the back. Ohio State's Douglas Graf observes that, seen from the side, the row of chimney tops at the roof edge echoes the columns.

▶ McConnelsville Opera House

THE OPERA HOUSE, 1892
H.C. Lindsay, Zanesville
West Main at North Kennebec Avenue, McConnelsville, northwest side of square,
NRHP/McConnelsville HD
Community auditorium in building with shops and village offices and council
chamber; current movies shown Friday through Monday; tours by
prearrangement; 740/962-3030

McConnelsville's square is all the more impressive for its buildings, including
both the white-painted courthouse on one side, and the substantial red-brick
Opera House on another. Built by the village with offices and shops flanking
the theater entrance, the Opera House opened in May 1892 with *The
Mikado* and Morgan County's first electric lights. Through the decades it
offered vaudeville, silent and then sound-track movies; but then in the 1960s
owner Galen Finley had to save the Opera House more than once. ¶ Finley
bought the theater business in 1962, when he was 23, and then held onto it

for 30 years. He says he saved it with prayer and politics—as well as help
from the community; for instance, when the state fire marshal threatened to
close the Opera House in the mid-1960s, the United Mineworkers
contributed new fire extinguishers, exit doors, and lights. In 1967, when
village officials began talking about converting the Opera House auditorium
into offices or, better yet, tearing it down, Finley ran for mayor with a one-
issue save-the-Opera-House campaign. He won two-to-one and served two
years, long enough to snuff out threats to theater. ¶ In 1992 a non-profit
corporation took over the Opera House theater's lease and ownership, and
toward the end of the decade Mona Newton was booking the weekend
movies and keeping accounts. Income, she said, was covering expenses, but
grant money helped with repainting, new candy counter, and replacement
seat cushions. ¶ The Richardsonian Romanesque Opera House is three stories
high with a four-and-a-half story central tower. Just indoors, the lobby, barely
big enough for the concession stand, leads to an auditorium that is very nice
indeed. It seats 570, including 200 in the balcony. It functions well, with
good sight lines from every seat and excellent acoustics. (Some modern
theaters fail to do so well.) ¶ As for Galen Finley, who's been an ordained
minister since the 1970s, he left the Opera House to have more time for
ministering and perhaps even to have his own chapel. Of course he found
and restored the perfect chapel, an 1852 Greek Revival building not far from
the Opera House on North Kennebec Avenue; it was a church originally, and
now it is again.

SERRELL RICHARDSON HOUSE, 1838
214 East Main Street at South Eighth, McConnelsville,
NRHP/McConnelsville HD
Private house

I.T. Frary, who surveyed the state's historic dwellings in his 1936 book, *Early
Homes of Ohio*, called this the Old Stone House. When it was built
McConnelsville had
virtually no roads, and stone
from a quarry upriver came
down the Muskingum River
by barge. The house's
dressed sandstone blocks
show their tooling even now.
The center of the facade has
an entry door and, above it,
a three-part Palladian
window of impressive
elegance. The limestone
lintels and sills have
carvings, including oval
sunbursts, still visible in
spite of weathering. Serrell
Richardson was an
Englishman who never lived
in the house. It became a
tavern, with the bar in the
basement and sleeping
rooms upstairs.

▶ SERRELL RICHARDSON HOUSE

Morristown, Belmont County

(Also in Belmont County: Barnesville.)

¶ Morristown is one of Ohio's old National Road towns, built in the early nineteenth century along the state's first interstate highway. Here, just a little north of I-70 but seeming completely remote, two-story brick buildings line the sidewalks. Morristown is a tranquil time warp.

Access: At I-70 exit 208, take State Route 149 north to U.S. 40; turn left/west and drive into Morristown. Almost immediately, take a right fork onto the Old National Road, which is Main Street in town. Historic district includes Main, Church, which parallels it to the north, and West Cross, Middle Cross, and East Cross Streets.

SWANEY HOUSE, 1846
311 Main Street, Morristown, NRHP/Morristown HD
House owned by Belmont Technical College for restoration and use as teaching lab in hands-on preservation program

One reason that Morristown is still mostly intact, is that in 1975 Margaret Dankworth thought she'd like to own an orchard. She found one in Morristown, though it came with an old Greek Revival house. An architect convinced her she should restore the house, and she did. For a while, she even ran an antiques shop there. But then when the Ohio Historic Preservation Office declared Morristown the state's best preserved National Road town, Dankworth became really involved with the buildings of Morristown. She researched the 60 original houses that the Preservation Office identified; and in early 1980, the Morristown Historic District landed on the National Register. ¶ Margaret Dankworth, now retired, a St. Clairsville resident, was a park executive and director of the National Zoo Association in Wheeling. While that was what she did during business hours, the rest of the time she was rescuing Morristown. Through the years, she bought eight houses to be sure they'd be saved. She restored five, sold two to others who restored them, and gave one to nearby Belmont Technical College, which in 1989 was setting up a program to teach hands-on preservation crafts; this house, still under restoration, became their lab. Today Dankworth owns just one house. Simon Herbert, one of the teachers in Belmont's program, is her tenant. ¶ Of the 60 houses originally counted, 45 remain today—in spite of Margaret Dankworth's efforts, that's a 25 percent loss rate in about 20 years. But she's still keeping an eye on Morristown. Since 1999 she's been worried about the town's most conspicuous building. She said, "We have a call to save the Black Horse Inn. It's one of the few taverns still standing on the National Road." The owners are two men who rent meeting rooms and provide catering, but their business hasn't succeeded; and in late 2001, the inn was going into its third year on the market. ¶ "We just need money," Dankworth mused. "Of course everybody does." Even more than money, what we really need is more Margaret Dankworths.

Fixing Classes: Belmont Tech—On a rainy January afternoon, the students' cars are parked along Main Street in Morristown. Their license plates show that most have come from somewhere else—from New York, Wisconsin, Pennsylvania, Florida, and Connecticut. They've come all this way so that today, inside an old brick house and under primitive conditions, they can learn something about fixing old buildings.

With their coats on, they're standing in a dank, completely bare room that once was a parlor, and learning how to determine original paint colors. The professor, Simon Herbert, demonstrates two techniques for collecting samples. First he cuts a bull's-eye chip with a razor—a chip cut like a saucer, to expose all the paint layers; later, it can be analyzed under a microscope. Secondly, he sands a small circular area on the wall, working most intensely in the middle and less toward the edges, so that concentric rings of colors emerge, the oldest at the center. Then Herbert divides his class into two-person teams and assigns each pair a different part of the house— stair risers, a ceiling, a door frame, a baseboard—on which to practice paint sampling.

This is the 1846 Swaney House, a two-story brick on the Old National Road. When in 1989 Belmont Technical College founded its program to teach people how to fix and restore old buildings, Margaret Dankworth, a Morristown preservationist, donated this house to the school. That it was such a wreck, Herbert says, made it a perfect lab for training students in hands-on preservation. It had a leaking roof, bricks had fallen out of the walls, floor beams were rotten. One wall was bowed—it had been constructed with undersized studs—and another had to be jacked up. Says Herbert happily, "If I could have made a list of all the things I wanted in a student lab, I couldn't have done better."

Very slowly, at the rate of 12 hours' class time a week, the Swaney House has been coming back to usefulness. Students have rebuilt the foundation, repaired the roof, and fixed the brick walls. They took off a poorly built addition at the back. On this January day, the west parlor has no flooring, for the rotten beams underneath needed repair and replacement. Except for the roof— contractors had to be called in for that, Herbert says, "because we couldn't leave it open indefinitely"— students have been doing all the work; when they finish, the house will be sold and another acquired. Neighbors who will tolerate a semi-permanent construction site are essential for all this, though in the end, they'll have a restoration masterpiece in their midst. Anyway, Simon Herbert is one of the neighbors. He lives across the street.

St. Clairsville's Belmont Technical College has Ohio's only hands-on preservation program; it's the country's only such program leading to an associate's degree. It takes its slogan from the nineteenth-century English art critic, John Ruskin. "The greatest glory of a building," Ruskin wrote, "is not its stones, nor its gold. Its greatest glory is in its Age." But in this country today, says David Mertz, old buildings are lost for want of people who know how to restore them at a reasonable cost. That's a shortage Belmont Tech wants to help correct.

In 1989 Mertz became the first professor in the historic preservation program; Herbert, who arrived four years later, was the second. The two of them are the only full-time faculty, though part-timers teach some courses. Mertz, an architect who grew up helping his father build houses, is a solid 6-foot Pennsylvanian who knows, say, how to assess different types of mortar joints. Herbert is an Englishman, improbably from the Channel Island of Jersey, who trained in Britain as an industrial engineer and found his vocation—working on old buildings—in North America. After four years' restoration work on a Hudson River Valley mansion, he earned a master's in preservation from the University of Pennsylvania.

Belmont Tech's program is nationally known. Ads in national magazines, *Old House Journal* and *Preservation*, attract about half the students. Mertz has been active with the National Council for Preservation Education and its chairman from 1998 to 2000. And students regularly take part in brief off-campus showcase restoration projects. They've worked on concrete at Falling Water and windows at West Point. They helped redo the slate of the roof of a National Park Service house in Milford, Pennsylvania. They've also worked on local projects, like repairing the cupola and the slate on the old one-room Great Western School near St. Clairsville. What they don't do is repair privately-owned houses.

Located in a building on Ohio University's campus near St. Clairsville and about six miles from Morristown, the preservation program has particular needs. Its storerooms have boxes of dowels, fireplace mantles, and a collection of window sash weights; its library has books not only on repair and maintenance of houses, but also on table-saw techniques. Painting and wallpaper students have a lab with individual closet-sized nooks where at the start of the quarter they remove paint and paper the last person installed. Then Herbert knocks a few holes in the drywall, which they repair, and finally they paint and hang paper.

Preservation students have field trips too—to architecturally noted places like Charleston, Chicago, and Washington, D.C. Mertz's favorite is Washington because of the National Building Museum's construction exhibits.

Almost all training in building crafts or architecture focuses on new construction, Mertz says. New construction today uses standardized, modular units, so repairs are done by tearing out and replacing. Historic buildings not only were less standardized, but also construction techniques were completely different. For example, says Mertz, studs in old buildings often aren't level, because leveling the wall was the plasterer's job; but drywall looks terrible on studs that aren't level. Or, 160-year old windows don't have to be thrown out; they can be rebuilt to make them weatherproof again.

Of the 80 to 100 preservation students enrolled in a year at Belmont Tech, half are local—from Belmont, Harrison, and Monroe counties, or nearby West Virginia communities. Local students tend to be younger, but they're more likely to stay in the area with local contractors.

Students who come from Wisconsin or Florida are a relatively mature bunch, who tend to be highly focused. Up to a half have bachelor's degrees; some have master's. A few have bought local houses for themselves, restored them, and then stayed in the area. Many are in second careers. Mertz tells a story about a local woman who was working in a factory and studying preservation part-time for five years—for a full-time student, the course usually takes only a year or two. She ended up as a technician at Thomas Jefferson's house, Monticello—in preservation, a plum of a job. Another of Mertz's career-change stories is about a nationally renowned plaster expert, whom his students intern with in Baltimore. That man studied architecture, toured Europe, took odd jobs like catching snakes in Africa, and finally "dived head over heels into plaster." There he remained.

▶ SWANEY HOUSE

Belmont Tech's program began because of the enthusiasm of two administrators, including former President Steve Meradian, and the benevolent interest of Bob Ney, then a state senator, who helped persuade the General Assembly to provide $150,000 in launch money—the first year, equipment alone came to $90,000. About 20 colleges have called to ask about setting up their own hands-on programs, but only one, in eastern Pennsylvania, has succeeded in doing so. About a dozen non-profit schools offer hands-on training that leads to certificates.

Learning the crafts of preservation means studying topics like crack analysis and parquet floors; it means learning how to replicate decorative plaster by making molds; it means roofing labs. Today's class is in wood science and carpentry, a field in which some of the students have no background. "For those who've never done it," says teacher Simon Herbert, "it's a big step to come out at the end with a bracket."

At the moment he's showing a dozen students in safety glasses how to make a dovetail joint, a cabinetry technique in which flared teeth on two pieces of wood interlock tightly and precisely to make a secure joint. Herbert measures his wood from the center, which gives him seven-eighths of an inch extra. That becomes waste, which he marks with a pencil on both sides of the board. "Mark your scrap," he tells the intent class, explaining that otherwise, it's easy to cut the wrong place. "Believe me," he assures them, "even the old timers do this."

After securing his board in a vise, he starts his saw cut with a chisel point. He introduces a broad-bladed dovetail saw and starts using it, jokily apologizing for not having a speeded-up video. "There's no way you can do this sitting on a stool," he says. "You need to get down and look with your eye at these lines." He complains of the wood's hardness. "This is maple. Not a friendly wood." A student asks, "Is that more true than oak?" "It is," comes the reply. Now Herbert pulls out a thin-bladed coping saw, whose blade can be adjusted to cut on the push or, as the Japanese do, on the pull. A dovetail joint, he declares, trying to be encouraging, is "a piece of cake."

If you remember to mark your scrap.

▶ PERRY COUNTY COURTHOUSE

New Lexington, Perry County

(Also in Perry County: The Round Barn Tour, which
starts in Somerset, passes through New Lexington.
Shawnee is south on State Route 93.)

**Access: State Route 13 intersects I-70 east of Buckeye Lake, and goes
south to New Lexington, where it becomes Main Street and meets up
with State Route 93.**

PERRY COUNTY COURTHOUSE, 1886

Joseph W. Yost, Columbus
105 North Main at Brown Street, New Lexington, NRHP
County courthouse; 740/342-2045

The Perry County Courthouse, turrets and all, soloed on the full-color cover
of Clair Stebbins' 1980 book, *Ohio's Court Houses*. The color brought out
architect Joseph Yost's take on Richardsonian Romanesque, with the brown
walls and buff trim, a switch on the more usual light walls and dark trim.
Two stories over a raised basement (gray stone), the building has a splendid
40-foot clock tower, high enough to be seen in the neighboring countryside.
The interior has lots of massive round arches, tile floors, and an iron newel
post that's about 8 feet high. Regina Coffman, a janitor, told me that kids
used to go up in the tower. Finally one youth went up at night and pretended
to be a ghost. He scared enough people that the tower has been locked ever
since.

Ludowici Overhead: New Lexington's Ludowici-Celadon—
When Jerry Smith came back to Ohio, he began seeing Ludowici roofs everywhere. Heightened awareness came with his new job, for after 30 years in the glass business, the last 14 in California, he'd returned to make roof tiles at New Lexington's Ludowici-Celadon. Even the familiar roofs he'd known as a child in Wilmington, he now recognized as Ludowici roofs. There the rural Quaker church he'd attended had a Ludowici roof. So did the Catholic church, a house he'd always admired on Main Street, and the Wilmington Public Library. How did he know they were Ludowici roofs? He spotted their high-bump terminals—that is, a raised round bump at points where the top ridge and a side ridge meet. No other company ever made those signature bumps. Once a person spots them, they jump off roofs everywhere.

At least that's been my experience. I'm walking around Bexley, where I live, studying roofs, and finding some high-bump terminals. I've also been looking for tile roofs without high-bump terminals (which not even all Ludowici roofs have). What I've learned is that more roofs than I had ever imagined are designed to deceive; and they succeed with me. They mimic a more expensive material, or a desirable material that doesn't normally last. Roofs that I used to think were wooden shakes, are likely as not tiles. A roof that looks like slate might be slate, but it also might be tile or asbestos or concrete or a slate composite. Smith, an architect who graduated from Ohio State University, says the ideal American roof is bark, because colonists used bark, which was available, light and water resistant. So Ludowici makes one tile named Colonial and another named Americana, both with bark-like undulations on the surface.

The roof-tile plant, east of New Lexington on Tile Plant Road, is not terribly conspicuous, yet Ludowici-Celadon is the only roof-tile maker east of the Mississippi. Clay products are one of Ohio's traditional industries, aligned along the clay belt, a 10- to 20-mile swath running roughly on a diagonal from Ironton to Canton and then swinging east to East Liverpool. Though clay is commonly part of dirt (it's what makes dirt stick to your feet), the clay in this region had both quality and abundance enough to spawn a major industry in kiln-fired products.

Found under coal formations, this clay was excellent for pottery, sewer pipes, bricks, roof tiles, and heat-resistant flue and oven liners; at one time every cafeteria in America was using Ohio dishes. In 1909, clay lured Ludowici-Celadon to New Lexington from Alfred, New York, where all the company's wooden buildings had just burned down. It was a young company, formed only three years earlier when the Ludowicis, immigrant German tile makers descended from Italian potters named Ludovisi, bought Alfred's Celadon Terra Cotta Company.

Jerry Smith has learned that clay can be more temperamental than glass. The components Ludowici uses are shale, which looks like dirt but turns red when fired, and fire clay, which looks like dirt but turns a pale buff when fired. Before mining, a shale sample has to be fired to check the color. After mining, the materials have to "sour". The shale and fire clay are dumped behind the plant, mixed together and left to sit 6 to 12 months for souring. At first this seemed like a waste of time to Smith; he thought a shorter time might be enough. It wasn't. Now a slow-souring convert, he explains that the process is really moisture evening out to the molecular level, making the material consistent.

Ludowici makes a roof tile that lasts in cold-weather climates because its surface is vitreous, or glass-like, from firing at 2000 degrees F., a higher temperature than is used for brick. It's moisture-resistant also because it's very dense, made from fine particles that processing compacts. Firing is done in modern tunnel kilns installed in 1992, when the company abandoned its beehive ovens. Shaped like large igloos, beehives took a week to load, a week to heat up, a week to cool, and a week to unload. Fast firing takes 30 hours, including everything. It is ten times more efficient than beehives.

Thirty percent of Ludowici's output is unglazed red roof tiles. All the rest are glazed with a ceramic that provides color and/or finish, matte or glossy. Smith says Ludowici will match any color. A lady in Montana sent five rocks whose colors she wanted her roof to match. They were peach, brown, two grays, and green. Shingles may be glazed so they look old, as in "aged cedar" or "aged copper"; they may be bright blue or green. They may also be the color of slate, for while tiles cost $200 for a 10-by-10-foot square, slate costs $300. Besides, says Smith, they last 75 to 100 years and then, with the roofing felt underlay replaced, can be reused, with any needed new tiles mixed in.

Red tile roofs often have Spanish tiles, more or less S-shaped in cross section and laid to overlap. Mission-style tiles are pans and covers, C-shaped in cross section and also laid overlapping, pans underneath. Some tiles are just flat shingles, while others are hinged—ridged or indented along the edges so they fit together. Surfaces may be crude, sandy, or smooth; they may have fine or large parallel ridges. The top of the line is a style with "chipped irregular butts."

For one of its buildings Yale University ordered tiles with chipped butts and sides. That meant that before the tiles were glazed and fired, workers in New Lexington nicked them with chipping hammers. Close up one of these hand-chipped tiles looks like a weird mistake, but Smith insists that from the ground, the finished roof looks wonderful.

Since Smith started at Ludowici, the most exotic job has been the roof of the 33-story New York Life Building in Manhattan. It has a steep, ten-story roof, all done in tiles glazed with $200,000 worth of real gold. This was a replacement roof, but the original glaze had been lead-based, so it couldn't be used today. It took Ludowici six months to work out a modern glaze with the right gloss and the same expansion rate as the tile body. They also had to develop a gold-colored underlay glaze, to disguise spots where the real gold glaze wears away.

For glazing, Ludowici sent its finished yellow tiles over to St. Clairsville China Company. There women who usually decorate china applied the real gold glaze with full brushes and one-way strokes. Then, because the gold glaze required a relatively low 1,480 degrees for firing, the china company did that too. The finished product, flat interlocking shingles in real gold, were worth $56 each, compared to $3 for ordinary tiles. Not surprisingly, when the gold roof was installed at Madison and 27th, the story made the papers. This was a roof that was what it seemed. On it, all that glitters *is* gold.

Buildings in this guide with Ludowici roofs include the President's House in Athens, the Dayton Art Museum (Vol. I), and the Bushnell House in Springfield.

▶ St. Michael's

Pleasant City, Guernsey County
(If driving south to Marietta [see also] on I-77, Pleasant
City is a short detour.)

**Access: From I-77 south of Cambridge, exit at State Route 313; drive
west to County 52, which leads south onto Pleasant City's Main Street,
which in turn intersects Church Street.**

ST. MICHAEL'S GREEK CATHOLIC CHURCH,
NOW ST. MICHAEL'S BYZANTINE CATHOLIC CHURCH, 1916
300 Church Street, Pleasant City
*Church; by prearrangement, the pastor, the Rev. Seraphim Chewning, will show
the church to visitors; 740/685-3292*

St. Michael's Byzantine Catholic Church, built of red brick by immigrant
East European coal miners, is set on a hilltop. It looms over Pleasant City,
which stretches along Main Street below. Together, the Byzantine-style
church and the old mining town combine symbiotically in a whole. Perhaps

because the coal ran out in the 1930s, the village, its population down to 400, has changed little. St. Michael's three-stage domed tower dominates the skyline as always, except that in recent decades it's been visible from I-77. ¶ If the church's outside is unchanged, the interior has reflected the parishioners' struggle with their origin as East rather than West Europeans. In the 1950s, wanting to be less different from Roman Catholics, the parish painted out wall and ceiling decorations, including the names of original donors, and removed the doors from the icon screen. Three decades later they changed their minds and, though the overpainting remains, they had new doors made for the screen, which is the church's jewel. ¶ Traditionally, the screen divides the altar from the people—the holy from the secular; only a bishop or priest can pass through the central door; only deacons and servers through the two side doors. Built of carved wood painted white with gilding, ornamented with icons, this screen was built by an itinerant craftsman who worked in the area from 1918-20. The icon at the bottom right represents this church's patron, St. Michael; the one at the left is St. Nicholas, patron of the Byzantine Catholic church in America. ¶ Outside, behind the church, Bernard Turanchik, unofficial church historian and retired postmaster of Pleasant City, swivels around, pointing out where the mines were, all of them within two miles: Walhonding to the south; Buffalo, northeast; Derwent, north; Banner, northwest; and Moss, west. Below, at Main and Church Streets, he notices the Methodist Church, which looks large and prosperous. It has benefited from legacies, Turanchik says. He has started urging his fellow parishioners to consider bequests for St. Michael's, which is down from 400 families to 100.

Pomeroy, Meigs County

(Gallipolis is downriver—State Route 7—and Athens, north on U.S. 33.)

¶ Hemmed in by hills, Pomeroy grew long and skinny along the Ohio River; central downtown is just two streets deep—Main and Second Streets; Court Street connects them. One upshot is that Pomeroy claims to be the nation's only village with no four-way intersections.

Access: U.S. 33 goes to Pomeroy, where it becomes Main Street.

MEIGS COUNTY COURTHOUSE, 1848
Second Street, Pomeroy, NRHP/Pomeroy HD
Courthouse open weekdays

Almost like courtiers, the two- and three-story commercial buildings of Court Street line the way to the Meigs County Courthouse, at whose back a hill rises. Among Ohio courthouses today, this one is distinctive, for behind its two front columns, it has paired, curved stairways on a recessed central porch. The stairs lead to a balcony that looks back down Court Street, over Main Street, and across the river to the hills of West Virginia. Clair Stebbins,

▶ MEIGS COUNTY COURTHOUSE

who visited and described all Ohio's courthouses, wrote that for $15 Meigs County bought the plans from Scioto County, which had already used them. The plans covered what are now the top two floors of the building's middle section. Later the porch was added, the ground floor was excavated and built, and the wings were built. The interior has been altered.

Shawnee, Perry County

(Haydenville, a company town developed at the same time as Shawnee, is about ten miles southwest by way of State Route 93 to New Straitsville, and then State Route 595. Both towns are endowed with distinctive buildings and a tiny corps of activists; both hang on by a thread. For other Perry County sites, see New Lexington and Somerset.)

¶ Set amid bounteous deep coal seams, Shawnee celebrated itself in buildings. Two-story frame structures lined Main Street, and upstairs each one had a roofed porch. Prospering merchants built them in the 1870s and 1880s. The sidewalks below were uncluttered because typically the porches were supported not with posts, but by cantilevering—horizontal beams anchored in the house frame. Support brackets, in plain wood or curved iron, helped too; and some porches were ornamented with spindles, balustrades, fancy trim. Though such

▶ Sʜᴀᴡɴᴇᴇ

buildings are often seen in old coal towns, today in Ohio it's rare to see more than a few in one place. That Shawnee is the exception, with one jaunty porch after another, makes it remarkable. ¶ Even in 1976, when the town was listed on the National Register of Historic Places, the nominators wrote that the old buildings were intact, and virtually none had been demolished. That is no longer true. But Shawnee's population peaked at about 4,000 in 1907, and by now only 700 remain—not enough to maintain the buildings. Main Street now has only 17 houses with second-story porches; of those three are brick, only three have upstairs residents, and in late 2001 at least two appeared derelict.

Access: Shawnee is just off State Route 93 between New Lexington to the north and Logan to the south.

HANNAH BROS. AND ADJACENT BUILDINGS, 1870S-1880S
114 East Main Street, Shawnee
Private commercial buildings

Bob Hannah sits at his desk in his store, his computer at his elbow, a display of work gloves over his head, pipe fittings and paint color chips across the aisle. He runs a furniture and appliance store, but, as he explains, "You look for the needs." So for local customers he carries hardware and paint and even appliances, while furniture buyers are more likely to drive in from out of town. If it weren't for the Hannahs, Shawnee might have so few second-floor porches that it couldn't be included in an architectural guide. Gradually, over a 20-year period starting with Bob's grandfather in 1927, the Hannahs bought buildings on Main Street. Counting the main store as two (it has two store fronts), the company owns nine, including six with porches. Of those eight are in use as warehouses or showrooms. Shawnee's most characteristic houses are frame, like Hannah's store. Today the best, most intact row is the one including his store on the south side of East Main Street. Bob Hannah also knows a lot about the difficulties in maintaining these buildings. "The

biggest problem," he says, "is the sandstone foundations. They absorb moisture from the ground and it rots the wood."

COMMUNITY EXCHANGE GIFT SHOP, 1902
117 West Main Street, Shawnee
Store

As a self-described "young, idealistic long-hair," John Winnenberg came to Shawnee during summers in the late 1970s, when he was a student at Bowling Green State University, to work with the Neighborhood Youth Corps. Now he's been involved here for over 20 years, writing grant proposals, serving as "promotional historian" and, with his family, running the Community Exchange Gift Shop. The building is a two-story brick with an upstairs porch in front. Winnenberg, who's from

▶ SHAWNEE

Corning seven miles away, says that the frame buildings on Main Street's west end were destroyed by long-ago fires. The early twentieth-century replacements were built of brick from Iron Clay Brick Company ("just over this hill") and remain solid. Latest on Winnenberg's agenda is a sewer system for Shawnee, which may not sound showy but could well help rescue the town.

WEST MAIN STREET, SHAWNEE, NORTH SIDE

It's a little surprising that Shawnee has *two* opera houses, but that's what accounts for the pair of three-story masonry structures on the north side of West Main Street. The gray one at the corner of North Second Street, built in 1881 as a union hall, is a Hannah Bros. property. The three-story orange brick was built for a fraternal group, the Improved Order of Red Men, in 1909. In 1977 John Winnenberg was one of a group who bought this building for $500, fixed the roof and, through the years, made other repairs as funding permitted. Only in the 1990s could the owners fix the premises for two tenants: the library, which moved in in 1993, and an apartment occupant. Winnenberg supposes he could be more of an activist organizer than he is, but coal towns were labor towns where, as he puts it, "Leaders aren't trusted."

SECOND STREET HILL
The Second Street hill rises up from Main Street to the old Shawnee High School, 1915, at the top. Centered on the street, the site is an elegant one. The high school was consolidated elsewhere in 1963; the elementary and junior high remained in the building until closed in 1993. Though a recreation group has been using the gym, by late 2001 the building had deteriorated and was slated for demolition.

Somerset, Perry County

(Also in Perry County: New Lexington and Shawnee.)
¶ Somerset is an attractive old town that has been buoyed but not spoiled, by a small ex-urban influx from Columbus. Thus on Public Square, where in the center General Phil Sheridan (freshly restored) perches on an ever-rearing steed, the wall of nineteenth- and early twenti-

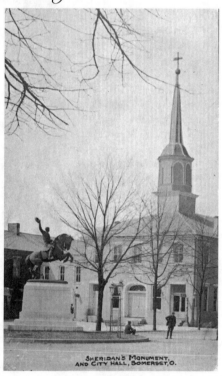

SHERIDAN'S MONUMENT, AND CITY HALL, SOMERSET, O.

▶ OLD PERRY COUNTY COURTHOUSE

eth-century buildings is unbroken and ground-floor spaces are fully occupied. Somerset has an unusual early courthouse, and is the focus also for a tour of three round barns.

Access: Somerset is at the junction of U.S. 22/Main Street and State Route 13/Columbus Street, which intersects I-70 to the north. Public Square is at the junction of the two highways.

OLD PERRY COUNTY COURTHOUSE, NOW SOMERSET VILLAGE OFFICES, 1828

James Hampton
100 West Public Square, Somerset, NRHP/Somerset HD
Village offices and a barber shop; 740/743-2963

Somerset is Ohio's best example of a nineteenth-century county seat, though that's true only because it lost the seat to New Lexington in 1857. So while most county seats tore themselves down and rebuilt, again and again, to keep up with other county seats, Somerset stepped out of the race and kept itself intact. ¶ The Old Perry County Courthouse is one of the state's most remarkable buildings, because it is the only really good example of what all county courthouses and even the state capitol used to look like—in 1840 Ohio had at least 32 important buildings of this type. The prototypical version was a square, symmetrical two-story brick building with a hip roof rising to a cupola, but the Somerset structure long ago lost its squareness with a rear expansion to accommodate a jail. Whatever it has lost in symmetry it more than makes up for with its cupola, whose central octagonal section has eight round-arched windows; it's topped with a rounded roof *and* a spire. The recessed front door has sidelights and, above, an elliptical fanlight with a pattern in leaded glass. ¶ When I first started looking at this old courthouse in the mid-1980s, it was shabby and down-at-heel, but by the mid-1990s it started losing its neglected look. First the village contracted for steeple repairs. Then the Lions Club donated new windows, and everyone who works for the village—clerk, council, mayor, street superintendent—hit the ladders and painted the trim. "That's how we get things done," explains village clerk Beverly Henery. Finally, in 2001, the roof was replaced and the steeple recovered with slate and topped with a ball coated in gold leaf. Money came from the state. (It helps that House Speaker Larry Householder is from Perry County.) All the building improvements left Henery in awe. "It just looks *so* nice," she said. ¶ What remains after all the refurbishing is the legend over the front door: "Let Justice be done if the heavens should fall." After I'd seen that the first time, village staffer Mamie Carter looked up from her deskful of water and sewer accounts and apologized: "Evidently our motto is a misquote."

SHERIDAN HOMESTEAD, 1859

417 South Columbus Street, Somerset, NRHP/Somerset HD
Private house

The story is that General Sheridan built this house for his parents. It's a fine frame Gothic Revival cottage with vertical board-and-batten siding. It has some modern additions.

PERRY COUNTY ROUND BARN TOUR—Wanda Wilson, who cuts my hair, is a Perry County native who told me about the round barns; a distant relative of hers, Evi "Bider" Melick, built at least two of them. I found those two, and then when Perry County's Tourism Center published a "Traveler's Guide" in 1996, I found a third. A fourth round barn is not visible from the road. I heard that it has horizontal siding, an exception to the rule in barns, especially round ones. Then I heard that that it's fallen down. No more copies of "Traveler's Guide" are available. The commissioners had to close the development and tourism office to

▶ New Reading Round Barn

fund 911 emergency service. No doubt, round barns are popular favorites. When Robert Meutzel, owner of the New Reading Barn, put on a new roof in 1995, Deb Hutmire wrote a story that the Perry County *Tribune* featured on its front page. "The early round barns stood on show place farms," she wrote. "These were the farms of wealthy property owners who could afford to indulge in their dreams in an expensive architectural experiment."

Access: This tour is a loop, mostly on state highways, beginning and ending near Somerset. (The route also passes through Somerset and New Lexington.) The first barn is three miles northwest of Somerset's outskirts off State Route 13. In a place where 13 runs due east-west, Reading Township Road 36 is a turn to the south; the barn is one mile down on the left/east side.

---

1) **The New Reading Round Barn** was built in 1917 by Evi Melick and then rebuilt after a 1932 fire by farmer Lawrence "Barney" Gilmore. It's a white barn in fine condition, for owner Robert Meutzel replaced the roof in 1995. The roof is hemispherical and topped with a windowed cupola. Inside a central silo, 35 feet high and 12 feet wide, helps support the roof. In its day this barn accommodated not only horses and cows, but also a pig pen and, later, children roller skating on the concrete floor.

Access: Take State Route 13 into Somerset and, after a jog to the right/ west on U.S. 22 in town, pick up State Route 668 south to Junction City. There turn left/east on State Route 37. About a mile out of town, the first turn on the left is Householder Road, Jackson Township 94-A. Visible also from 37 to the east, the barn is on the west side of House-holder, from which it's best seen a little to the north.

2) **Junction City Round Barn** dates from 1909, making it the oldest of these three. Carpenter Henry McGreevy of New Lexington built it for farmer Mott Thomas. The barn's round red roof is not hemispherical but slopes down at two broad angles. The cupola has a conical roof, also red; the barn is white.

Access: From Junction City go east on State Route 37; in New Lexing-ton turn north on State Route 345, which in a corner of Muskingum County intersects U.S. 22. Turn left/west onto 22. Immediately after the State Route 204 intersection, turn right onto Madison Township Road 95. Barn is in .7 mile.

3) Built in 1927 by Evi Melick for his own farm, the **Sego Barn** is the largest of these three. Like the New Reading Barn, it has a hemispherical roof and a cupola with a curved roof. In the late 1990s, it looked a little neglected.

Warsaw, Coshocton County

(Zanesville, south on State Route 60, makes a companion tour; if driving via Coshocton, take State Route 16 from Coshocton to 60.)

Access: Warsaw straddles U.S. 36 and State Route 60, which meet in west Warsaw and run eastward together for a few miles. The camp ground is east of town.

TABERNACLE, C. 1925

▶ WARSAW TABERNACLE

Riley Brillhart, Warsaw
818 East Main Street/U.S. 36 and State Route 60, Warsaw
Tabernacle at Church of God in Southeast Ohio's Warsaw Camp Ground; annual nine-day meeting begins first Friday after July 4; 740/824-4051

The Church of God Tabernacle is a big, eight-sided frame summer meetinghouse, with prop-up sides. At first glance, it looks a little like the Goodyear Airdock in Akron, though not nearly so huge. Nor is its roof really round, though its hip roof *looks* somewhat rounded. Just below the eaves every section of the building has a pair of relatively small square windows, and just below the windows are the hinges for propping up the sides. Built of vertical wooden siding, these segments normally function as walls; but on a hot day, they can be opened all around, except at the highway end where the platform is. ¶ These prop-up sides used to be fairly common for summer tabernacles, but now are rare. One day shortly before a meeting, I saw them all open. The ceiling inside was like a barn's, all wooden rafters and braces. Rows and rows of empty wooden theater seats faced the platform, its lectern, and the "Expect a Miracle" sign. The whole place seemed at one with the summer day. ¶ I heard from Kristine Gross that the best time to see the Tabernacle really is at night, during the week-long July camp meeting, when the doors are up, the inside is lit, and people are all around. Warsaw's *Historical Collections* gives the 1925 date for the Tabernacle's construction. Before the Church of God purchased it in 1941, it was used by other denominations. ¶ When church members noticed cracked and sagging ceiling beams before the 1999 meeting, they called in a structural engineer who advised not using the building. Two contractors gave restoration estimates of $100,000 and $150,000, but board member Philip Day says they decided against the work because the Tabernacle wasn't quite big enough—it seats 440 and always had an overflow crowd on the lawn. For the next three years meetings used a tent with drop sides. Day summed up in late 2001: "Nothing's been decided." Which at least beats some possibilities.

To see more in Coshocton County—From Warsaw, Coshocton, the county seat, is just down U.S. 36. Its recreated canal town, Historic Roscoe Village, is well known; but the downtown is especially worth seeing. From U.S. 36 take downtown exits and drive south on State Route 16, then east on State Route 541, which passes the 1875 Courthouse. From the Courthouse go south on Third Street to see the lovely Greek Revival Johnson-Humrickhouse House, 1834, now Pomerene Center for the Arts. Return north to Chestnut Street and east to Sixth, to see the extraordinary row of attached houses at 128-148 North Sixth. The six brick American Foursquare town houses have their own separate porches in front, as well as second-floor sleeping porches in back; they have red tile roofs, paired roof brackets, copper gutters.

Wellston, Jackson County
(Also in Jackson County: Jackson.)

Access: From State Route 32 exit at State Route 327 and drive north into Wellston, where 327 and State Route 93 run together. Alternatively, from Jackson take State Route 93 north.

T.J. MORGAN HOUSE, NOW WELLSTON CITY BUILDING, 1905, REHAB AFTER FIRE, 1985
Wilbur T. Mills, Columbus
203 East Broadway at the corner of Pennsylvania Avenue/State Route 93, Wellston, NRHP
City Building and police station

The sight of the "Police" sign with an arrow pointing at a fancy porte cochere, should delight any preservationist. Unfortunately, a 1982 fire gutted the building's interior, but the city didn't give up its showy premises and opted to rehab, even though few tokens of the old elegance survived. Even without the Police sign, Wellston's Italian Renaissance Revival City Building would be hard to miss. Set on a rise at the main intersection, it was built by Wellston Coal and Iron Company founder, T.J. Morgan. What makes it especially noticeable is the combination of red brick

▶ WELLSTON CITY BUILDING

walls and contrasting stone around the windows and in quoins at the corners. In the mid-1950s Morgan's daughter sold the house to the city for $6,000—a bargain; it cost $125,000 to build.

▶ WILLIAM MOONEY HOUSE

Woodsfield, Monroe County

(Tour with Barnesville, the next county seat north on State Route 800.)

❡ Woodsfield is small (436 people in 1990) and poor, but once upon a time, it too prospered, especially between 1890 and 1910, when oil was flowing. ❡ Laid out in 1812, Woodsfield has a fine central square formed by widening Main Street at its Court Street intersection. The square, which has landscaped medians, has an intact wall of buildings around it. They include an Art Deco theater (now a store, though it still has the "Monroe" marquee); a four-story office block, 1903, originally the Monroe Bank; and a grand oil-boom Neoclassical courthouse by Cincinnati's Samuel Hannaford & Sons. But Woodsfield's showstopper is the Mooney House.

Access: From I-70 State Route 800 runs south to the Ohio River, passing through Barnesville first and then, 19 miles later, Woodsfield, where it intersects State Routes 78 and 26.

WILLIAM C. MOONEY HOUSE, 1913
122 North Paul Street, Woodfield, NRHP
Private house

Approach from the north on State Route 800, which as it enters town winds past the cemetery and toward golden arches displayed on a high pole. At a stop light the state highway turns right onto Main Street, but the seeker of the Mooney House goes straight. The house is visible a block away, at the end of the street. Framed by tree branches, it sits proud and unmistakable behind its enormous porch fronted by tall white columns. ¶ Not surprisingly, William C. Mooney, who added the porch in 1913, was a titan in Woodsfield. His father, Colonel Samuel L. Mooney (the rank came from being Colonel of Engineers on Governor William McKinley's staff) built the railroad and owned oil drilling and coal companies as well as the bank. To these enterprises the son added business directorships in Columbus and a term in Congress. The younger Mooney died in 1918, just two years after his father. ¶ The house became grand and Neoclassical when it was remodeled in 1913. Though records were lost in a

courthouse fire, it seems probable that that remodeling was the second major overhaul of a mid-nineteenth century frame house, which earlier had become Queen Anne. After an interval of neglect, the house was bought in 1980 and then kept up by Robert Morris, who lives there, and his parents, Van and Marilyn Morris, who live in Hannibal. The interior has many good features, including oak, cherry, and walnut woodwork, original light fixtures, tile hearths. ¶ Compare the Kiser House in St. Paris, Champaign County, an exactly contemporary Neoclassical remodeling that produced another small town's most conspicuous building.

Zanesville, Muskingum County
(Tour with Warsaw; for routing, see Warsaw.)
¶ When I first saw the Muskingum County Courthouse's main courtroom in the 1980s, it was surely among Ohio's most spectacular for sheer size—it flaunted Zanesville's ambition in 1877. Since then (again mirroring ambition?) that courtroom has been cut in two. On the outside the courthouse still cuts an imposing figure downtown, where Main Street's building stock has a lot of potential.

Access: Zanesville straddles I-70, with older sections south of the interstate. Exit at Fifth Street or Seventh Street and drive south to Main Street/U.S. 40; then turn left/east to St. Nicholas.

▶ St. Nicholas

ST. NICHOLAS CHURCH, 1899
William H. Dunn, Cleveland
925 East Main Street, Zanesville, NRHP
Sanctuary accessible during daylight hours from door on Sillman Street; or, check at rectory behind church; 740/453-0597

A hill rises at the east end of downtown Zanesville's Main Street; and on that hillside is St. Nicholas Church, large and exotic with its three domes on octagonal towers. It is an enticing sight, and it rewards the curious tourist with an unlocked door and in the lobby a cleaning lady who extols the beauty of the building. She does not exaggerate. Zanesville's English- and German-speaking Catholics went their separate ways in 1842; this was the second church the Germans built. The first was higher on the hill, approached by dozens of steps; so this one, with the front door in a raised basement at sidewalk level, was more accessible. It was begun after the grading and paving of Main Street, and at a time when the church had a popular pastor, the Rev. A.L. Leininger, who could take charge. He chose the materials and oversaw contracts. Romanesque Revival in style, St. Nicholas abounds in round-arched windows. Two domed bell towers flank the door, while the large central dome rises 72 feet above the sanctuary's raked floor. The building, 80 by 118 feet, is brick with terra cotta trim; the roof is red slate. Stained glass was by Cincinnati's Frank Shilffarth, chosen over four European firms. The mosaic in the arch over the main door shows Columbus's landing in the new world. Athens preservationist Mary Anne Reeves describes it as "a work of art, made of local Zanesville tile when that industry was in its prime."

To see more in Zanesville—The Putnam Historic District is just to the south; take Sixth Street and cross the Muskingum. Continue south to Jefferson Street and turn right. United Putnam Presbyterian Church, 1835, is straight ahead on Woodlawn Avenue. Its first pastor was William Beecher, Harriet Beecher Stowe's brother. The Muskingum County Convention and Visitors Bureau's "Visitors Guide" includes a Putnam walking tour; 800/743-2303 or 740/453-5004. The Pioneer and Historical Society has regular weekday afternoon hours in Putnam at 115 Jefferson Street; 740/454-9500.

Access: To reach the Headley Inn drive west from downtown on Main Street/U.S. 40. Headley Inn is on the north side of U.S. 40 two-and-a-half miles after crossing I-70.

HEADLEY INN, 1833, 1835
Uzal Headley, builder
5345 West Pike/U.S. 40, near Zanesville, NRHP
Private house; groups may see interior by prearrangement; 740/452-2431

In the 1830s, when the National Road arrived here, the Headley Inn and the even earlier Smith House, 1830, just next door to the east, were built as inns. Though the Smith House's interior has been modernized, the Headley Inn is much as it always was. ¶ The builder was Uzal Headley, who came here from New Jersey in his mid-teens, in 1809. In 1823 he married and spent ten years living in a log cabin before he built the western section of the Headley Inn, the part with a porch in front. This was to be his family's house, but at first it served as an inn for road-building supervisors. It had three bedrooms upstairs and, downstairs, a kitchen with an oversized fireplace where sharpening knives left a dip in the sandstone. (The dip, wrote I.T. Frary, "was mute witness to the tough beefsteak that was served to hungry boarders."") In 1834 Headley got his tavern license, and the next year he built the east part of the Headley Inn, which served National Road travelers until railroads drew away traffic. The inn had three rooms upstairs; a barroom and lounge downstairs. When Headley left in 1863, he sold this building to the farmer next door, Alexander Smith. ¶ The Smiths used the Headley Inn for storing wool, so it stayed unaltered. When automobiles revived National Road traffic in 1922, two of Alexander Smith's granddaughters, Mrs. Harry Ackerman and Mrs. E.B. Howard, converted the old inn into a restaurant open in the summer. As governors and celebrities arrived—celebrities like novelist Louis Bromfield and columnist Earl Wilson—the Headley Inn became well known. In 1961 the restaurant closed, and the building was vacant until 1989. ¶ One day Bernadine and Stephen Brown, native Columbusites who were living in Pittsburgh, took U.S. 40 and came upon the Headley Inn and its

"For Sale" sign. Steve Brown, a consulting engineer who can work almost anywhere, looked in the windows and was ready to buy on the spot. Later he and his wife installed the log cabin at the back to live in while bringing the Headley Inn into the twentieth century (for instance, they added central heating) and constructing a modern addition behind the inn. ¶ Besides its hand-dressed sandstone, original windows and fireplaces, the

▶ HEADLEY INN

house still has stenciled decoration painted on stair risers and baseboards. The painter was Amos M. Edgerley, Uzal Headley's brother-in-law. ¶ Another National Road inn in this guide is the Red Brick Tavern in Lafayette, north of London.

Zoar, Tuscarawas County

(Closest companion tour is Stark County to the north; see Alliance and Massillon in Northeast Ohio and Canton in Volume I).

¶ The Society of Separatists of Zoar was a German religious sect that, to escape persecution at home, sailed to America early in 1817, and by the end of that year had settled on 5,500 acres of Tuscarawas County, Ohio. They organized a formal communal society that thrived by producing everything from apples to pig iron; by 1852 their combined worldly goods were worth $1 million. But the next year their leader, Joseph Bäumler, died, and without him the community declined until formally dissolved in 1898. Today's Zoar is a lovely, tree-shaded village dominated by a multi-building Ohio Historical Society site devoted to its industrious founders. ¶ Though basically a religious leader, Bäumler himself designed the 18-room Number One House, 1835-45, at Main Street and Third, a minimally changed OHS museum, and the attractive red-brick meeting house, 1853, at Main and Fifth, now a United Church of Christ.

Access: From I-77 north of New Philadelphia and south of Canton, take exit 93 and drive southeast on State Route 212, which passes Zoar Hotel (and Bäumler's two buildings mentioned above).

ZOAR HOTEL, 1833, 1850s, 1870S, 1950s
Main Street at Second Street, Zoar, NRHP/Zoar HD
Former hotel to be reconstructed as OHS visitor center; exterior work started in 2001; completion date uncertain; Zoar Village site open summer and spring and fall weekends; 330/874-3011; 800/874-4336

When the Ohio-Erie canal route traversed seven miles of their property, the Zoar community took on the digging job, which, in 1828, earned them enough to pay off the debt on their 5,000 acres. Then canal boats arrived with passengers who had to spend the night on land, so the ever resourceful

▶ ZOAR HOTEL

Zoarites built a hotel. The design, says OHS site manager Kathleen
Fernandez, was basically like that of their houses, though bigger. But only the
hotel was crowned at the fourth-floor level with an octagonal tower topped in
turn by an octagonal cupola, windowed all around. It was high enough to see
the canal and anticipate the arrival of boats bearing customers. As the hotel
prospered, additions accumulated at the back in the 1850s, 1870s, and
1950s. Ironically, by bringing in outsiders who seemed to be having more fun
than the members of the austere, hard-working farm community, the hotel
probably hastened the society's dissolution in 1898. It outlasted both the
canal and the Zoar community, for summer visitors came through the 1920s.
From the 1940s into the 1970s the building was a boarding house and office
building, with a ground-floor restaurant renowned for chicken dinners. That
operation went bankrupt in the early 1980s, and in 1984 the structure was

sold to a man who removed everything added since 1833 and then, giving up on the $5 million needed to restore it into a hotel, sold it to the Ohio Historical Society. When Kathy Fernandez showed it to me in summer 1998, the interior was a bleak scene of wall studs, lath and, incongruously, original paneled wainscoting. Some third-floor rooms were intact, and so were the high octagons reached by a spiral staircase.

▶ ZOAR HOTEL

Photography and illustration

While every effort has been made to trace the copyright holders of photographs and illustrations reproduced in this book, the publishers will be pleased to rectify any inadvertent omissions or inaccuracies in the next printing.

South Main Street, Celina, page ixx, drawing by Frank Elmer

Bibliography

For many buildings in this volume, I consulted the National Register files in the Ohio Historic Preservation Office, Ohio Historical Society, Columbus.

GENERAL

William Howard Adams, *Jefferson's Monticello*. Abbeville Press, New York, 1983.

Elizabeth P. Allyn and Elisabeth H. Tuttle, comp., *A Guide to Historic Houses in Ohio Open to the Public*. National Society of the Colonial Dames of America in the State of Ohio, [Cincinnati], 1984.

Asher Benjamin, *Practice of Architecture, The Builder's Guide: Two Pattern Books of American Classical Architecture*. Introduction by Thomas Gordon Smith. Da Capo Press, New York, 1994.

John J.-G. Blumenson, *Identifying American Architecture: A Pictorial Guide to Styles and Terms, 1600-1945,* rev. ed., American Association for State and Local History, Nashville, 1981.

Mary Ann [Olding] Brown, "Architecture of Cultural Settlements in Western Ohio". Unpublished typescript loaned by the author. 1984.

Margaret Manor Butler, *A Pictorial History of the Western Reserve 1796 to 1860*. World Publishing, Cleveland, 1963.

Richard N. Campen, *Architecture of the Western Reserve, 1800-1900*. The Press of Case Western Reserve University, Cleveland, 1971.

Richard N. Campen, *Ohio, An Architectural Portrait*. West Summit Press, Chagrin Falls, Ohio, 1973.

Edna Maria Clark, *Ohio Art and Artists*. 1932 book republished by Gale Research Company, Detroit, 1975.

Lee Comer and Ted Ligibel, *Lights Along the River: Landmark Architecture of the Maumee River Valley*. Landmarks Committee of the Maumee Valley Historical Society, Maumee, 1983.

John Fleischman, "City Grit". *Ohio Magazine*, January 1992, p. 18ff.

John Fleischman, "Forgotten but Not Gone". *Ohio Magazine*, August, 1995, p. 20ff.

Richard V. Francaviglia, "Main Street: The Origins". *Timeline*, December 1988-January 1989, pp. 29-39.

Richard V. Francaviglia, "Main Street: The Twentieth Century". *Timeline*, February-March 1989, pp. 28-43.

I.T. Frary, *Early Homes of Ohio*. Dover Publications, New York, 1970. This is a reprint of the original 1936 edition.

Stephen C. Gordon, *How to Complete the Ohio Historic Inventory*. Ohio Historical Society, Columbus, 1992.

Talbot Hamlin, *Greek Revival Architecture in America: Being an Account of Important Trends in American Architecture and American Life Prior to the War Between the States*. Oxford University Press, New York, 1947.

Mary Sayre Haverstock, Jeannette Mahoney Vance, and Brian L. Meggitt, comps., *Artists in Ohio, 1787-1900: A Biographical Dictionary*. Kent State University Press, Kent, 2000.

Marcy Hawley and Damaine Vonada, eds., *Particular Places: A Traveler's Guide to Inner Ohio*, Vol. I. Orange Frazer Press, Wilmington, Ohio, 1990.

Henry Howe, *Historical Collections of Ohio*. Henry Howe & Son,

Columbus, 1891.

Eric Johannesen, *Ohio College Architecture Before 1870*. Ohio Historical Society, [Columbus], 1969.

Ray Jones, *Great Lakes Lighthouses, Ontario to Superior*. Globe Pequot Press, Old Saybrook, Connecticut, 1994.

Roger G. Kennedy, *Greek Revival America*. Stewart Tabori & Chang, New York, 1989.

Walter C. Kidney, *Historic Buildings of Ohio*. Ober Park Associates, Pittsburgh, 1972.

George W. Knepper, *Ohio and Its People*. Kent State University Press, Kent, Ohio, 1989.

Michael B. Lafferty, ed., *Ohio's Natural Heritage*. The Ohio Academy of Sciences, Columbus, 1979.

William L. Lebovich, *America's City Halls*. Preservation Press, Washington, 1984.

Richard Longstreth, *The Buildings of Main Street: A Guide to American Commercial Architecture*. Preservation Press, Washington, 1987.

W. Ray Luce, "Squaring the Circle: Octagonal Architecture". *Timeline*, December 1989-January 1990, pp. 3-15.

Virginia and Lee McAlester, *A Field Guide to American Houses*. Alfred A. Knopf, New York, 1984.

Diane Maddex, ed., *Master Builders: A Guide to Famous American Architects*. Preservation Press, Washington, 1985.

Hugh Morrison, *Louis Sullivan: Prophet of Modern Architecture*. W.W. Norton & Company, Norton Library, New York, 1962.

David Naylor, *Great American Movie Theaters*. Preservation Press, National Trust for Historic Preservation, Washington, 1987.

David Naylor, *American Picture Palaces*. Van Nostrand Reinhold Company, New York, 1981.

Allen G. Nobel and Hubert G.H. Wilhelm, eds., *Barns of the Midwest*. Ohio University Press, Athens, 1995.

Elizabeth Pomada and Michael Larsen, *America's Painted Ladies: The Ultimate Celebration of Our Victorians*. Dutton Studio Books, New York, 1992.

Laurie Penrose, *A Traveler's Guide to 100 Eastern Great Lakes Lighthouses*. Friede Publications, Davison, Michigan, 1994.

John C. Poppeliers, S. Allen Chambers, Jr., and Nancy B. Schwartz, *What Style Is It?: A Guide to American Architecture*. National Trust for Historic Preservation in the United States, John Wiley & Sons, New York, 1983.

Lorle Porter, *Discovering Ohio's Hill Country*. Locust Grove Press, [Ohio], 1993.

John W. Reps, *The Making of Urban America: A History of City Planning in the United States*. Princeton University Press, Princeton, New Jersey, 1965.

Leland M. Roth, *A Concise History of American Architecture*. Harper & Row, New York, 1979.

Scott and Antoinette J. Lee, *Buildings of the District of Columbia* in the Society of Architectural Historians series, Buildings of the United States. Oxford University Press, New York, 1993.

Vincent Scully, *American Architecture and Urbanism*. Frederick A. Praeger, New York, 1969.

David A. Simmons, "Carnegie Libraries in Ohio". Ohio Historical Society *Echoes*, Vol. 20, No. 4, April 1981, pp. 5-6.

G.E. Kidder Smith, *The Architecture of the United States*, Vol. 2, *The South and Midwest*. Anchor Press/Doubleday, Garden City, New York, 1981.

G.E. Kidder Smith, *A Pictorial History of Architecture in America*, Vol. II. American Heritage Publishing, New York, 1976.

Jennifer Stoffel and John Fleischman, "Frank Lloyd Wright Built Here". *Ohio Magazine*, October 1990, pp. 39 ff.

William Allin Storrer, *The Frank Lloyd Wright Companion*. University of Chicago Press, Chicago, 1993.

William H. Tishler, ed., *American Landscape Architecture: Designers and Places*. Preservation Press, Washington, 1989.

Robert Venturi, *Complexity and Contradiction in Architecture*. The Museum of Modern Art Papers on Architecture, Second edition. Princeton University Press, Princeton, 1977, reprinted 1992.

Damaine Vonada and Marcy Hawley, eds., *Particular Places: A Traveler's Guide to Inner Ohio*, Vol. II. Orange Frazer Press, Wilmington, 1993.

Lauren S. Weingarden, *Louis H. Sullivan: The Banks*. MIT Press, Cambridge, Massachusetts, 1987.

Marcus Whiffen, *American Architecture Since 1780: A Guide to the Styles*, revised edition. MIT Press, Cambridge, Massachusetts, 1992.

Katharine F. Willi, ed., *A Guide to Historic Houses in Ohio Open to the Public*, prepared by the National Society of the Colonial Dames of America in the State of Ohio. Second edition. Odyssey Press Inc., Westerville, 1996.

Henry F. Withey and Elsie Rathburn Withey, *Biographical Dictionary of American Architects (Deceased)*. Hennessey & Ingalls, Los Angeles, 1970.

TITLES BY PLACE NAME

ATWATER

John J. Horton, *The Jonathan Hale Farm: A Chronicle of the Cuyahoga Valley*. Western Reserve Historical Society, Cleveland, 1961.

BARBERTON

W. A. Johnston and O.E. Olin, *Barberton and Kenmore, Ohio: The Golden Years*. Barberton Historical Society, Barberton, Ohio, 1976.

William Franklin Fleming, *America's Match King: Ohio Columbus Barber 1841-1920*. Barberton Historical Society, Barberton, Ohio, 1981.

Ohio C. Barber, *Anna Dean Farm, Barberton, Ohio: The Story of an American Farm*. Reprinted by the Barberton Historical Society, 1975.

BOWLING GREEN

History of Wood County Ohio; Its Past and Present. J.H. Beers & Co., Chicago, 1897.

Paul Willis Jones, "Courthouse Construction Capers", ms. of unpublished speech, N.D.

Paul Willis Jones, "Wood County Courthouse: Historical Highlights 1894-1994". Wood County Courthouse Centennial Commission, [Bowling Green], 1994.

Craig Wismer, "The Home: History of the Wood County Infirmary", rev. by Marcus Chibucos. Wood County Historical Society, Bowling Green, 1994.

CARTHAGENA AND MARIA STEIN

Mary Ann [Olding] Brown and Mary Niekamp, "Land of the Cross-Tipped Churches". Ohio Historical Society *Echoes*, Vol. 18, No. 12, December, 1979, pp. 4-5.

Sherman Goldenberg, "Land of the Cross-Tipped Churches". Fort Wayne *Journal-Gazette*, N.D.

Maria Stein Center, Sisters of the Precious Blood, *A Guide to the Shrine and Retreat House, Maria Stein, Ohio.* Revised edition, 1989.

Shannon McFarlin, "The DeCurtins Family", Part One. [Celina] *Daily Standard*, November 10, 1977.

Shannon McFarlin, "Preservation—Is It Advisable?", Part Two. [Celina] *Daily Standard*, N.D.

[Sister Octavia], *Not with Silver or Gold: A History of the Sisters of the Congregation of the Precious Blood, Salem Heights, Dayton, Ohio.* Sisters of the Precious Blood, Dayton, 1945.

CELINA

Joyce L. Alig, *Celina, Ohio Sesquicentennial 1835-1984.* Mercer County Historical Society, Celina, 1984.

Joyce L. Alig, ed., *Mercer County, Ohio History 1978.* Mercer County Historical Society, Celina, 1980.

CHILLICOTHE

Jocelyn Gough, *Chillicothe: First Capital Guidebook.* Chillicothe, Ohio, 1980.

History of Franklin and Pickaway Counties, Ohio. Williams Bros., [Cleveland], 1880.

Specifications for a New Court House and Public Offices in Chillicothe, Ross County, Ohio. Metropolis Office, Chillicothe, 1854.

Writers' Program (Ohio), Work Projects Administration, *Chillicothe, Ohio's First Capital.* [Chillicothe Civic Association, Chillicothe, 1941.]

CIRCLEVILLE

W.W. Higgins, "The Boggs House: Local Example of the 'Globe Light Cottage'". *Pickaway Quarterly*, Winter 1997, pp. 10–11.

[W.W. Higgins,] "Circleville City Hall, a Masterpiece", unpublished speech, 1991.

Mary R. Tolbert, "Historic Mount Oval". *Pickaway Quarterly*, Spring 1967, pp. 5-11.

Darlene Weaver, "Boiler House housed attendant". Circleville *Herald*, November 7, 1998, p. 1.

EAST LIVERPOOL

"Carnegie Writes of Boyhood Days", *Toledo Blade*, January 4, 1906.

Chleo Deshler Goodman, "History of Carnegie Public Library of East Liverpool, Ohio", unpublished, May, 1962.

GALION

William Montgomery Brown, *My Heresy: The Autobiography of an Idea.* Reprinted by order of the Crawford County Probate Court, Galion, 1981.

GAMBIER

J.D. Forbes, *Victorian Architect: The Life and Work of William Tinsley.* Indiana University Press, Bloomington, 1953.

"William Tinsley", in *The Biographical Encyclopaedia of Ohio of the Nineteenth Century.* Galaxy Publishing Company, Cincinnati and Philadelphia, 1876.

Richard G. Salomon, "The Old Halls of Kenyon College". *American Antiques Journal*, September, 1946, pp. 6-8.

Richard G. Salomon, "Philander Chase, Norman Nash, and Charles Bulfinch: A Study of the Origins of Old Kenyon". *Historical Magazine of the Episcopal Church*, Vol. XV, 1944, pp. 209-231.

George Franklin Smythe, *Kenyon College: Its First Century.* Yale University

Press for Kenyon College, New Haven, 1924.

Thomas Boardman Greenslade, *Kenyon College: Its Third Half Century*. Kenyon College, Gambier, 1975.

GRANVILLE

Horace King, *Granville: Massachusetts to Ohio*. Granville Sentinel Publishing, Granville, 1989.

Minnie Hite Moody, *Inns and Personalities of Granville and Other Pieces*. Granville Historical Society, 1966.

Jane Ware, "Granville Eyes Its Future". *Columbus Monthly*, June, 1995, pp. 108-116.

HAMILTON

Esther R. Benzing, *Historical Gleanings: Butler County, Ohio*. Printed by D. Russell Lee Vocational School, Butler County, 1976.

James Schwartz, *Hamilton, Ohio: Its Architecture and History*. Hamilton City Planning Department, [Hamilton], 1986.

James E. Schwartz, "Lane Public Library: Commemorating the Years 1866-1997". A booklet published by Lane Public Library, Hamilton, [1997].

Kathleen Neilen Stuckey, "The History of the Episcopal Church in Hamilton, Ohio from 1823 to 1923". Booklet, Hamilton, 1961.

HANOVERTON

Marjorie E. Fair, *In the Ohio Country*. Unitas, Hanoverton, Ohio, 1976.

Wessie Voglesong-Woods, *History of Hanover, Columbiana County, Ohio: 1804-1908*. Review Publishing Co., Alliance, 1908.

HAYDENVILLE

David H. Mould, "The Company Town That Outlived the Company: Haydenville, Ohio". *Journal of Cultural Geography*, Spring/summer 1985, pp. 71-86.

IRONTON

Virginia S. Bryant, *Nannie Kelly Wright*. Lawrence County Historical Society, Ironton, 1989.

KIRTLAND

Roger D. Launius, *An Illustrated History of the Kirtland Temple*. Herald Publishing House, Independence, Missouri, 1986.

LEBANON

Hazel Spencer Phillips, *Traditional Architecture: Warren County Ohio*. [Lebanon, Ohio, 1973.]

LIMA

Harrison Shutt, "Kewpee Hamburgers' History". *The Allen County Reporter*, Allen County Historical Society, Vol. XXXXIX, No. 1, 1993, pp.15-39.

MARIETTA

American Association of University Women, *A Window to Marietta*. Richardson Printing Company, Marietta, 1986.

American Association of University Women, *A Window to Marietta*, Second Edition. Richardson Printing Company, Marietta, 1996.

S.P. Hildreth, *Biographical and Historical Memoirs of the Early Pioneer Settlers of Ohio*. H.W. Derby & Co., Cincinnati, 1852.

S.P. Hildreth, *Pioneer History: Being an Account of the First Examinations of the Ohio Valley and the Early Settlement of the Northwest Territory*. H.W. Derby & Co., Cincinnati, 1848; reprinted Arno Press Inc., New York, 1971.

MARION

Phillip G. Payne, "The Harding Memorial". *Timeline*, September-October

388

1998, pp. 18-29.

MARSHALLVILLE

Historic Heritage of Wayne County, Ohio, comp. by Landmark Committee of the Wayne County Historical Society. Wayne County Historical Society, Wooster, 1976.

MASSILLON

Mary Blanch Oberlin, *100 Years at Five Oaks*. Northwest Printing, Massillon, [c. 1995].

NEWARK

Andrew Jackson Downing, *Victorian Cottage Residences*. Dover Publications, New York, 1981.

Peter Korda and Nick Constantine, "The First Basket Building in the World". *Structure*, Spring, 1998, pp. 15-17.

Marguerite J. McCollum, "Oakwood, Beloved Newark Estate of the Penney Family". Columbus *Dispatch*, April 2, 1939.

Rob McManamy, "No Picnic Getting a Handle on It". *ENR*, November 24, 1997.

Carl Quintanilla, "A Seven Story Basket Goes Up in the Fields of Ohio". *Wall Street Journal*, October 15, 1997, p. B1.

Daniel D. Reiff, "Identifying Mail-Order Catalog Houses". *Old House Journal*, September-October 1995, pp. 30-37.

NEW LEXINGTON

Susan Tunick, Sandra Scofield and Terry Palmiter, "Tile Roofs of Alfred: A Clay Tradition in Alfred, New York". Friends of Terra Cotta Press, New York, 1993.

Jane Ware, "Feats of Clay". *Ohio Magazine*, September, 1992, pp. 42 ff.

NEW LONDON

Geoffrey Blodgett, "Philip Johnson's Great Depression". *Timeline*, June-July 1987, pp. 2-17.

"Johnson Museum Proposed". New London *Record*, April 18, 1985.

Steven Litt, "Estate Captures Aura of Philip Johnson". Cleveland *Plain Dealer*, September 14, 1997.

Steven Litt, "More Than a Home". Cleveland *Plain Dealer*, August 31, 1997.

Julie A. Livingston, "The Development of the New London School District Public Library". An unpublished master's thesis for Kent State University School of Library Science, April 1988.

Karal Ann Marling, *Wall-to-Wall America: A Cultural History of Post Office Murals in the Great Depression*. University of Minnesota Press, Minneapolis, 1982.

Franz Schulze, *Philip Johnson: Life and Work*. Alfred A. Knopf, New York, 1994.

NILES

Joseph G. Butler, Jr., *History of Youngstown and the Mahoning Valley, Ohio*. American Historical Society, Chicago, 1921.

Leland M. Roth, *The Architecture of McKim, Mead and White 1870-1920: A Building List*. Garland Publishing, Inc., New York, 1978.

Leland M. Roth, *McKim, Mead & White, Architects*. Harper & Row, New York, 1983.

OBERLIN

Geoffrey Blodgett, *Oberlin Architecture, College and Town: A Guide to Its Social History*. Oberlin College, Oberlin, 1990.

Geoffrey Blodgett, "Oberlin College Architecture: A Short History". Pamphlet issued by Oberlin College, Oberlin, N.D.

Geoffrey Blodgett, "President King & Cass Gilbert: The grand collaboration". *Oberlin Alumni Magazine*, Winter 1983, pp. 15-19.

Athena Tacha, with Fay Beilis and Amy Brown, "Frank Lloyd Wright at Oberlin: The Story of the Weltzheimer/Johnson House." *Allen Memorial Art Museum Bulletin*, Vol. XLIX, No. 1, 1995.

PAINESVILLE

Perry E. Borchers, "Impressions of an Architect". *Cleveland Architecture 1796-1958*, prepared by the Cleveland Chapter of American Institute of Architects. Reinhold Publishing Corporation, New York, [1958].

Margaret Geissman Gross, *Dancing on the Table: A History of Lake Erie College*. Celo Valley Books, Burnsville, North Carolina, 1993.

Larry Hawkins, "The House That 'Couldn't' Be Saved". *Cleveland Plain Dealer Pictorial Magazine*, April 6, 1952.

Elizabeth G. Hitchcock, *Jonathan Goldsmith: Pioneer Master Builder of the Western Reserve*. The Western Reserve Historical Society, Cleveland, 1980.

PERRY

John Fleischman, "Rich Perry". *Ohio Magazine*, May, 1994, p. 29.

Steven Litt, "Richly Serving Pupils". Cleveland *Plain Dealer*, October 8, 1995, Section K, pp. 1, 4.

Nicolai Ouroussoff, "All in One". *Architectural Record*, July 1995, pp. 76-85.

Ralph Johnson of Perkins & Will: Buildings and Projects. Rizzoli International Publications, New York, 1995.

PUT-IN-BAY AND MIDDLE BASS ISLAND

Charles E. Frohman, *Put-in-Bay: Its History*. Ohio Historical Society, Columbus, 1971.

Ted Ligibel and Richard Wright, *Island Heritage: A Guided Tour to Lake Erie's Bass Islands*. Ohio State University Press, Columbus, 1987.

SANDUSKY

Ellie Damm, *Treasure by the Bay: The Historic Architecture of Sandusky, Ohio*. A Western Reserve Historical Society Publication. Bucknell University Press, Lewisburg, Pennsylvania, 1989.

SIDNEY

Dan Becker, "Their Buildings Now: Sidney Courthouse Square National Register Historic District". A booklet published by River Corridor Project, Sidney, Ohio, 1981.

Richard Wallace, "From a Monumental Past to a Future with Promise". Posted on the Shelby County Historical Society web site, June, 1996.

SOUTHINGTON

Newton Chalker, Memoir, unpublished, 1873.

Agnes Marshall and Lillian Kimmel, "History of Southington, Bicentennial Issue", N.D.

SPRINGFIELD

George H. Berkhofer, *An Architectural Guide to the Houses of Springfield and Clark County, Ohio*. Clark County Historical Society, Springfield, 1976.

A Celebration of a Happy Reflection: The Centennial of the Ohio Masonic Home 1892-1992, Ohio Masonic Home, Springfield, 1992.

Jim Hays, "Divine Wright". Springfield *News-Sun*, January 4, 1998, p. 1B.

"Historical Bushnell home observing its 100th year". Springfield *News-Sun*, August 29, 1988.

William A. Kinnison, *Springfield & Clark County*. Windsor Publications, Northridge, California, 1985.

Montgomery Schuyler, "The Works of R.H. Robertson". *Architectural Record*, October-November-December, 1896, pp. 184-219.

Stephen Siek, "Frank Lloyd Wright's Westcott House in Springfield". *Ohio History*, Summer 1978, pp. 276-293.

Mary Jane Taylor, "A Walking Tour of Wittenberg Architecture", a booklet published by Thomas Library, Wittenberg University, Springfield, Ohio, 1988.

TALLMADGE

John R. Strassburger and David R. Anderson, "Frontier Elegance and Democratic Plainness: Two Churches as Historic Documents". *Smithsonian Studies in American Art*, winter 1990, pp.29-43.

VAN WERT

Saida Brumback Antrim and Ernest Irving Antrim, *The County Library: The Pioneer County Library (The Brumback Library of Van Wert County, Ohio) and the County Library Movement in the United States*. The Pioneer Press, Van Wert, 1914.

Thaddeus S. Gilliland, ed., *History of Van Wert County, Ohio and Representative Citizens*. Richmond & Arnold, Chicago, 1906; reprinted by Windmill Publications, Mt. Vernon, Indiana, 1991.

Floyd C. O'Daffer, *History of Van Wert County*. Fairway Press, Lima, 1990.

WARREN

Alexander T. Bobersky, "The Forgotten Gilded Age Townscape of Warren, Ohio". *Western Reserve Studies Symposium*, 1993.

Alexander T. Bobersky, "Let's Re-Invent Our Community: Civic Action and Leadership". Warren Community Development, unpublished, 1994.

Harriet Taylor Upton, *A Twentieth Century History of Trumbull County, Ohio*, Vols. I and II. Lewis Publishing Company, Chicago, 1909.

WEST UNION

Stephen Kelley, *Landmarks of West Union, Ohio*. Kelley Publications, Seaman, Ohio, 1980.

WILMINGTON

John Baskin, "Murphy's Monuments". *Ohio Magazine*, December, 1988, pp. 30, 79.

John Baskin, "Showboats". *Ohio Magazine*, December, 1988, pp. 30, 79.

WOODSFIELD

Theresa A. Maienknecht and Stanley B. Maienknecht, *Monroe County, Ohio: A History*. Monroe County Historical Society. Windmill Publications, Mt. Vernon, Indiana and Whipporwill Publications, Evansville, Indiana, 1989.

WOOSTER

"Alumni Renovation Kauke Will Include Center Arch" [*sic*], in the [Wooster] *Daily Record*, November 14, 1959.

"Kauke Renewal Starts After Tests on June 6", in the [Wooster] *Daily Record*, May 29, 1961.

Lucy Lilian Notestein, *Wooster of the Middle West*. Kent State University Press, [Kent, Ohio], 1971.

ZOAR

Charles Ballinger, "Zoar", in *Harvest*. J.M. Smucker Company, Orrville, Ohio, [1984].

Sue Gorisek, "From A to Zoar". *Ohio Magazine*, August, 1989.

"OHS Acquires Historic Zoar Hotel". Ohio Historical Society *Echoes*, October, 1996.

Index

Identification of architectural styles and elements

1. End chimney
2. Eave
3. Lintel window head
4. 9 over 6 sash
5. Sidelight
6. Elliptical arch
7. Pedimented gable
8. Tympanum
9. Raking cornice
10. Entablature
11. Metopes
12. Triglyph
13. Doric order column
14. Capital
15. Base
16. Multiple-arched storefront
17. Brackets
18. Hood mold
19. Plate glass
20. Tower

21. Lunettes
22. Stone banding
23. String course
24. Buttress
25. Gothic arched openings
26. Gabled entry
27. Conical turret
28. Decorative brickwork
29. Semicircular arch

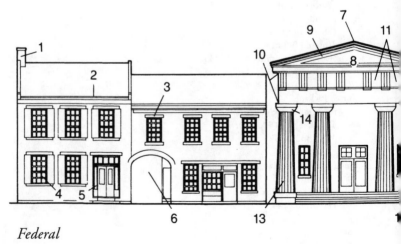

Federal

Greek Revival

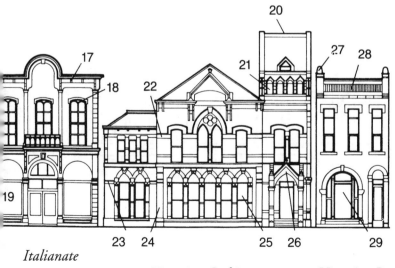

Italianate

Victorian Gothic

Victorian Romanesque

30. Central pavilion
31. Mansard roof
32. Dormer
33. Quoins
34. Turret
35. Finial
36. Bay window
37. Transom window
38. Belt course
39. Pediment
40. Console
41. Pilaster
42. Cornice
43. Modillion
44. Dentil
45. Mansonry round arch
46. Projecting eave
47. Window enframement
48. Chicago window
49. Spandrel
50. Pier
51. Parapet
52. Roman arch
53. Keystone
54. Ionic order column

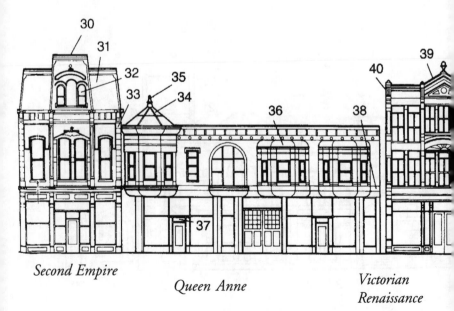

Second Empire

Queen Anne

Victorian
Renaissance

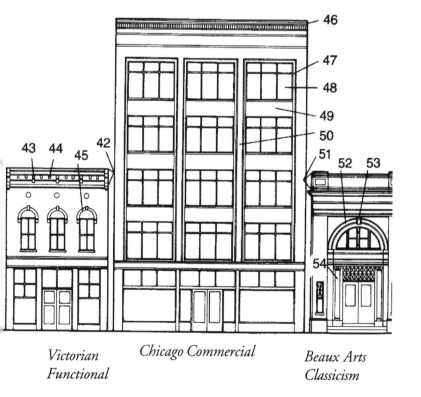

Victorian Functional

Chicago Commercial

Beaux Arts Classicism